MIRROR OF BUDDHISM

(Based on Pāli Sources.)

"Sabbe saṅkhārā aniccā" ti
yadā paññāya passati
atha nibbindati dukkhe
esa maggo visuddhiyā.

—Dhammapada:277.

Other Books by SOBTI

Nibbāna in Early Buddhism (1985)

Studies in Buddhism and Sikhism (1986)

Studies in Panjabi Fiction (1987)

Nirvāṇa in Tibetan Buddhism (1988)

Prajñāpāramitā in Tibetan Buddhism (1988)

The Sikh Psyche : A Study of Fictional Writings of Bhai Vir Singh (1990)

Vipassanā : The Buddhist Way (1992)

Theravāda Buddhism (1993)

My Buddhist Writings (1994)

The Sikh Gurūs (1996)

MIRROR OF BUDDHISM

(Based on Pāli Sources)

Edited by

HARCHARAN SINGH SOBTI

M.A. (Panjabi); M.A.(Philosophy);

LL.B.;Ph.D. (Buddhist Studies)

EASTERN BOOK LINKERS

DELHI : : INDIA

Published by:
EASTERN BOOK LINKERS
5825, New Chandrawal, Jawahar Nagar
Delhi-110007
Phone : 2520287

First Published: 1997

Price: EASTERN BOOK LINKERS EBL Rs. 600-

ISBN : 81-86339-41-8

Lasertype setted by:
UNIQUE PRINT MEDIA
PH.: 7252362

For

Micky Mini and Mānu

my grandchildren

CONTENTS

Editor's Preface

My teaching subject is, of course, Panjabi language and literature. But, some of my pupils, colleagues, friends and relatives, sometimes some of them casually and sometimes some of them seriously, prefer listening to my talks on Buddhism. Almost all of them have inherited religious traditons rooted in theism which advocates an idea of God as Person. So, they have number of prejudices against Buddhism and are heavily loaded with misconceptions regarding the Buddha and Buddhism. I recall one such misconception regarding the portrait of the Buddha.

One day, one of my relatives, an elderly person, came to my house. He was terribly annoyed when he saw the portrait of the Buddha in my drawing room and instantly advised me to immediately remove it, because, *dukkha* and the Buddha go hand in hand. Naturally, I could not stand what he had said, but, the very idea of the Buddha helped me to remain sober and to maintain serenity. Any how, I asked the person whether or not what he had said was the result of his own experience? Very innocently he remarked that 'No! I had only heard like that'.

The Buddha in one of his discoures, *Kesaputta Sutta* included in *Aṅguttara Nikāya*(A.ii.190); has expressed his views in respect of reading, listening and believing. The Buddha was of the view that any idea is not true because one has read it in some scriptures. It is not true either that someone has heard it like that. Neither it is true because it has been believed to be true. The Buddha did not spare even himself and stated that it is not true because he has said it. The Buddha, in fact, wanted that a person should learn to listen to his/her own experiences instead of listening to the scriptures and others. What matters is one's own experience. The Buddha *discovered* the Nibbānic state through this single device of Experience.

Siddhartha, in Hermann Hesse's (1877-1962) *Siddhartha*(1922), in his very first meeting with the Buddha raised the question of one's own experience, Siddhartha addressed the Buddha, thus:

"You have done so by your own seeking, in your own way, through thought, through meditation, through knowledge, through enlightenment. You have learned nothing through teachings, and so I think, O Illustrious One, that nobody finds salvation through teachings. To nobody, O Illustrious One, can you communicate in words and teachings, what happened to you in the hour of your enlightenment......."

-Macmillan India, 1954, p.28.

Siddhartha, elaborating his view-point further states, that:

"That is what I thought and realized when I heard your teachings. That is why I am going on my way-not to seek another and better doctrine, for I know that there is none, but to leave all doctrines and all teachers and to reach my goal alone-or die."

-Idem

Mirror of Buddhism, which is collection of research papers, and (translations) derived mainly from Pāli sources aims at, besides providing informations, to help those *also* who wish to arrive at the stage achieved by Siddhartha and going further neither following the foot-prints of Siddhartha nor that of Siddhartha Gotama, but choose to follow their own.

Buddha Purnimā **HARCHARAN SINGH SOBTI**

3rd May, 1996

D13A/30 Model Town,

Delhi–110009 (India).

Editor's Note

Whenever I feel like reading on any aspect of Buddhism I plan a project that keeps me absorbed in my search for Truth *discovered (and not revealed)* by Gotama Buddha. This time also I wanted to study some aspects of Buddhism which were absolutely new for me. In this process of learning I had discovered some very scholarly and useful research papers on some aspects of Buddhism written by Buddhist scholars of repute. Inspired by the Buddhist dictum *bhavatu sabba maṅgalaṁ,* I decided to edit a collection of papers under the title *Mirror of Buddhism* and shared my desire with my publisher Mr. Sham Malhotra, who approved of the project in hand and I am obliged for his kind gesture.

This collection also contains my own papers. I do not claim to be a scholar of Buddhism, but, my growing interest in Buddhist Studies can hardly be denied by any one familiar with the subject .

I am greatly beholden to other contributors.

Besides exercising choice of papers I have added to it the Preface, Note, Bibliography and Index and have provided diacritical marks where missing

-HSS

ABBREVIATIONS

A.	Aṅguttara Nikāya.
A.S.	Aṭṭhasālini.
Ā.G.	Ādi Granth (Holy Book of the Sikhs).
Bp.	Keith, Buddhist Philosophy.
D.	Dīgha Nikāya.
D.S.	Dhammasṅgani.
Dhp.	Dhammapada.
ERE.	Encylopaedia of Religion and Ethics
It.	Itivuttaka.
JAOS	Journal of Asiatic Oriental Society.
Jā.	Jātakaṭṭhakathā.
K.	Khuddaka Nikāya
LB.	Beal, Life of Buddha
M.	Majjhima Nikāya.
M. Pūraṇi	Manoratha pūraṇi.
Mp.	Milindapañho.
Mv.	Mahāvagga.
P. Dipaṇi.	Paramatthadipanī.
P. Jotikā	Paramattha Jotikā.
P.T.S.	Pali Text Society
S.	Saṁyutta Nikāya.
S.B.B.	Sacred Books of the Buddhist.
S.B.E.	Sacred Books of the East.
S.B.J.	Sacred Books of the Jainas
Sum. Vil.	Sumaṅgala Vilāsinī.
Sn.	Sutta Nipāta.
Ta.	Theragāthā.

Ti.	Therīgāthā.
U.	Udāna.
Vin.	Vinaya Piṭaka.
Vm.	Visuddhi maggo.
ZDMG	Zeitsch rift, Deutsch Morgelle nden Casellsefeft

Note : Quotations wherever referred to or given are from P.T.S. Romanized editions. Where numerals e.g. M.i. 80 separated by a dot is given, the first refers to the volume and the second to the page excepting e.g. U. 80 etc. where numerals refer to page, whereas, in the case of Dhp., Jā, Sn, Ta and Ti the reference is to the number of *Gāthā* or *kathā*.

Namo Tassa Bhagavato Arahato Sammā Sambuddhassa

CHAPTER 1

THE LIFE OF THE BUDDHA

—Henry C. Warren

i. The Buddha : Introductory

In reading the Pāli Scriptures one is impressed with the strong personal influence exercised by the Buddha over the hearts of his followers. He was regarded, not as a mere formulator of dry metaphysical propositions, but as a very wise and compassionate friend of his fellow-men. He was full of tact, and all his ways were ways of peace. To allay discord he would tell a little story or fable with a moral, and his epithet for one of whom he disapproved was merely "vain man." Anger, in fact, had no place in his character, and the reader of this book will find that it had equally none in his religio-philosophic system.

The term "Buddha" means "Enlightened One," and signifies that the person to whom it is applied has solved the riddle of existence, and discovered the doctrine for the cessation of misery. It was by his attainment of this supreme "Enlightenment" or Wisdom that Gotama became a Buddha. During the thirty-five years of his life previous to that event, and during all previous existences from the time he set out towards the Buddhaship, he was a Bodhisatta,---a term which I have freely translated "Future Buddha," but which is more literally rendered "He whose essence is Wisdom."

The Buddha's given name would appear to have been Siddhattha; but as the word means "Successful in his Objects,"it looks as though it might be a simple epithet. The Buddha belonged to the Sakya clan. The word "Sakya" means "Powerful;" and the families that bore the name had a reputation for pride and haughtiness. They were of the warrior caste, but cultivated the peaceful arts of agriculture. By his contemporaries The Buddha is usually called Gotama, or, as the word is sometimes Anglicized, the Gotamid. It is not quite clear why he and others of his clan should bear the name of Gotama in addition to that of Sakya. It may be they claimed descent from the ancient sage Gautama (Sanskrit "Gautama" becomes "Gotama" in Pāli), to whom are attributed some of the hymns of the Rig-Veda; or it may be, as Burnouf has suggested, "because Gautama was the sacerdotal family name of the military race of Sakyas, who, being of the warrior caste, had no ancestor or tutelar saint like the Brāhmaṇas, but might, as the Hindu law permits, have taken the name of the sage to whose family belonged their spiritual guide."

The Buddha was a Hindu, born not far from the Ganges, and during his long ministry wandered about from place to place in the section of country about Benares, very much as did Christ in Judea and Galilee. And just as Christ once left his native country and went to Egypt, so The Buddha is said by native authorities to have paid a couple of visits to Ceylon; but the statement is, I fear, somewhat mythical.

The date of Gotama Buddha is considered to be the sixth century before Christ. It would appear that he lived to his eightieth year,and the time of his death is given by scholars as about 480 B.C.

The first eight sections of the present chapter are from the general introduction to the Jātaka ("Book of Birth-Stories"). These Birth-Stories, five hundred and fifty in number, are so called because they are tales of the anterior existences of Gotama Buddha, while he was as yet but a Future Buddha. The Jātaka is an extensive work; five volumes have already been edited by Professor V.Fausboll, of Copenhagen, and more is yet to come. It consists of the Birth-Stories themselves, with a commentary and a long introduction. Examples of these Birth-Stories will be given further on; here we have only to do with the Introduction, the author of which and of the commentary is unknown.

After a few preliminary remarks concerning the inception and plan of his work, the author begins by quoting entire the Story of Sumedha as contained in the metrical work called the Buddha-Vaṁsa ("History of the Buddhas"). He does not quote it all consecutively, but a few stanzas at a time as authority for his prose statements. In this prose is also some matter of a commentary nature, apparently later glosses and not a part of the original text. In my first translation I give the Story of Sumedha as quoted in this Introduction to the Jātaka, but I give it consecutively and omit the prose, except that of some of the more interesting and explanatory passages, of the glosses especially, I have made foot-notes.

After the Story of Sumedha our author gives formal descriptions of each of the twenty-four Buddhas that preceded Gotama. These descriptions, however, are tedious, and are not here translated. They mainly concern themselves with such details as the height of each Buddha, his length of life, how many conversions he made, the names of his father, mother, chief disciples, etc. But from the point where my third section begins to the end of the ninth I follow the native text without making any omissions. I have divided one continuous text into seven parts, and then given these divisions titles of my own devising.

The reader is thus brought up to the ministry of the Buddha. This ministry lasted some forty-five years, and an account of part of it is given by the author of the Introduction. It is, however, only a part that he gives, just enough to conduct his reader up to the time when The Buddha was presented with Jetavana monastery, the importance of which event to our author will be readily perceived when it is remembered that this was the monastery in which The Buddha is represented as having related the greater part of Birth-Stories. As our author fails to give us a complete life of The Buddha, and as I know of none in Pāli literature, none is attempted in this book. But in order that the reader may have at an early stage an idea of what the matters were wherein the Buddha considered himself "enlightened," one passage is translated from the Mahā-Vagga. It appeared desirable to give the reader a general idea of what the Buddhists consider to be the salient features of their system of religion.

ii. THE STORY OF SUMEDHA.[1]

Translated from the Introduction to the Jātaka (i.3[1]).

12. A hundred thousand cycles vast
And four immensities ago,
There was a town named Amara,
A place of beauty and delights.
It had the noises ten complete[2]
And food and drink abundantly.

13. The noise of elephant and horse,
Of conch-shell, drum, and chariot,
And invitations to partake---
"Eat ye, and drink!"---resounded loud.

14. A town complete in all its parts,
Where every industry was found,
And eke the seven precious gems,[3]
And foreigners from many lands.
A prosperous city of the gods,
Full of good works and holy men.

15. Within this town of Amara
Sumedha lived, of *Brāhmaṇa* caste,
Who many tens of millions had,
And grain and treasure in full store.

16. A student he, and wise in spells,
A master of the Vedās three.
He fortunes told, tradition knew,
And every duty of his caste.

17. In secret then I sat me down,
And thus to ponder I began:
"What misery to be born again!
And have the flesh dissolve at death!

18. "Subject to birth, old age, disease,
Extinction will I seek to find,
Where no decay is ever known,
Nor death, but all security.

19. "What if I now should rid me of
This body foul, this charnel-house,
And go my way without a care,
Or least regret for things behind!

20. "There is, there must be, an escape!
Impossible there should not be!
I'll make the search and find the way,
Which from existence shall release!

21. "Even as, although there misery is,
Yet happiness is also found;
So, though indeed existence is,
A non-existence should be sought.

22. "Even as, although there may be heat,
Yet grateful cold is also found;
So, though the threefold fire[4] exists,
Likewise *Nirvāṇa* should be sought.

23. "Even as; although there evil is,
That which is good is also found;
So, though 't is true that birth exists,
That which is not birth should be sought.

24. "Even as a man befouled with dung,
Seeing a brimming lake at hand,
And nathless bathing not therein,
Were senseless should he chide the lake;

25. "So, when *Nirvāṇa's* lake exists
To wash away corruption's stain,

Should I not seek to bathe threrein,
I might not then *Nirvāṇa* chide.

26. "Even as a man hemmed in by foes,
Seeing a certain safe escape,
And nathless seeking not to flee,
Might not the blameless pathway chide;

27. "So, when my passions hem me in,
And yet a way to bliss exists,
Should I not seek to follow it,
That way of bliss I might not chide.

28. "Even as a man who, sore diseased,
When a physician may be had,
Should fail to send to have him come,
Might the physician then not chide;

29. "So, when diseased with passion, sore
Oppressed, I seek the master not
Whose ghostly counsel me might cure,
The blame should not on him be laid.

30. "Even as a man might rid him of
A horrid corpse bound to his neck,
And then upon his way proceed,
Joyous, and free, and unconstrained;

31. "So must I likewise rid me of
This body foul, this charnel-house,
And go my way without a care,
Or least regret for things behind.

32. "As men and women rid them or
Their dung upon the refuse heap,
And go their ways without a care,
Or least regret for what they leave;

33. "So will I likewise rid me of
This body foul, this charnel-house,
And go my way as if I had
Cast out my filth into the draught.

34. "Even as the owners leave and quit
A worn-out, shattered, leaky ship,
And go their ways without a care
Or least regret for what they leave;

35. "So will I likewise rid me of
This nine-holed,[5] ever-trickling frame,
And go my way, as owners do,
Who ship disrupted leave behind.

36. "Even as a man who treasure bears,
And finds him in a robber-gang,
Will quickly flee and rid him of
The robbers, lest they steal his gold;

37. "So, to a mighty robber might
Be likened well this body's frame.
I'll cast it off and go my way,
Lest of my welfare I be robbed."

38. Thus thinking, I on rich and poor
All that I had in alms bestowed;
Hundreds of millions spent I then,
And made to *Himavant*[6] my way.

39. Not far away from *Himavant*,
There was a hill named *Dhammaka*,
And here I made and patterned well
A hermitage and hut of leaves.

40. A walking-place I then laid out,
Exempted from the five defects,[7]

And having all the virtues eight;[8]
And there I gained the Six High Powers.

41. Then ceased I cloaks of cloth to wear,
For cloaks possess the nine defects,[9]
And girded on a barken dress,
Which is with virtues twelve endued.[10]

42. My hut of leaves I then forsook,
So crowded with the eight defects,[11]
And at the foot of trees I lived,
For such abodes have virtues ten.[12]

43. No sown and cultivated grain
Allowed I then to be my food;
But all the many benefits
Of wild-fruit fare I made my own.

44. And strenuous effort made I there,
The while I sat, or stood, or walked;
And ere seven days had passed away,
I had attained the Powers High.

45. When I had thus success attained,
And made me master of the Law,
A Conqueror, Lord of All the World,
Was born, by name Dīpaṁkara.

46. What time he was conceived, was born,
What time he Buddhaship attained,
When first he preached,-the Signs[13] appeared.
I saw them not, deep sunk in trance.

47. Then, in the distant border-land,
Invited they this Being Great,
And every one, with joyful heart,
The pathway for his coming cleared.

48. Now so it happened at this time,
That I my hermitage had left,
And, barken garments rustling loud,
Was passing o'er them through the air.

49. Then saw I every one alert,
Well-pleased, delighted overjoyed;
And, coming downward, from the sky,
The multitude I straightway asked:

50. "Well-pleased, delighted overjoyed,
And all alert is every one;
For whom is being cleared the way,
The path, the track to travel on?"

51. When thus I asked, response was made.
"A mighty Buddha has appeared,
A Conqueror, Lord of all the World,
Whose name is called Dīpaṁkara.
For him is being cleared the way,
The path, the track to travel on."

52. This word, "The Buddha," when I heard,
Joy sprang up straightway in my heart;
"A Buddha! Buddha!" cried I then,
And published my heart's content.

53. And standing there I pondered deep,
By joyous agitation seized:
"Here will I now some good seed sow,
Nor let this fitting season slip."

54. "For a Buddha do ye clear the road?
Then, pray, grant also me a place!
I, too, will help to clear the way,
The path, the track to travel on."

55. And so they granted also me
A portion of the path to clear,
And I can clear, while still my heart
Said"Buddha! Buddha!" o'er and o'er.

56. But ere my part was yet complete,
Dīpaṁkara, the Mighty Sage,
The Conqueror, came that way along,
Thronged by four hundred thousand saints,
Without depravity or spot,
And having each the Six High Powers.

57. The people then their greetings gave,
And many kettle-drums were beat,
And men and gods, in joyous mood,
Loud shouted their applauding cries.

58. Then men and gods together met,
And saw each other face to face;
And all with joined hands upraised
Followed The Buddha and his train.

59. The gods, with instruments divine,
The men, with those of human make,
Triumphant music played, the while
They followed in The Buddha's train.

60. Celestial beings from on high
Threw broadcast over all the earth
The Erytnrina flowers of heaven,
The lotus and the coral-flower.

61. And men abiding on the ground
On every side flung up in air
Champakas, salalas, nīpas,
Nāgas, punnāgas, ketakas.

62. Then loosened I my matted hair,
And, spreading out upon the mud
My dress of bark and cloak of skin,
I laid me down upon my face.

63. "Let now on me The Buddha tread,
With the disciples of his train;
Can I but keep him from the mire,
To me great merit shall accrue."

64. While thus I lay upon the ground,[14]
Arose within me many thoughts:
"To-day, if such were my desire,
I my corruptions might consume.

65. "But why thus in an unknown guise
Should I the Doctrine's fruit secure?
Omniscience first will I achieve,
And be a Buddha in the world.

66. "Or why should I, a valorous man,
The ocean seek to cross alone?
Omniscience first will I achieve,
And men and gods convey across.

67. "Since now I make this earnest wish,
In presence of this Best of Men,
Omniscience sometime I'll achieve,
And multitudes convey across.

68. "I'll rebirth's circling stream arrest,
Destroy existence's three modes;
I'll climb the sides of Doctrine's ship,
And men and gods convey across.

69. "A human being,[15] male of sex,
Who saintship gains, a Teacher meets,

As hermit lives, and virtue loves,
Nor lacks resolve, nor fiery zeal,
Can by these eight conditions joined,
Make his most earnest wish succeed."

70. Dīpaṁkara, Who Knew All Worlds,
Recipient of Offerings,
Came to a halt my pillow near,
And thus addressed the multitudes:

71. "Behold ye now this monk austere,
His matted locks, his penance fierce!
Lo! he, unnumbered cycles hence,
A Buddha in the world shall be.

72. "From the fair town called Kapila
His Great Retirement shall be made.
Then, when his Struggle fierce is o'er,
His stern austerities performed,-

73. "He shall in quiet sit him down
Beneath the Ajapāla-tree;
There pottage made of rice receive,
And seek the stream *Nerañjarā*.

74. "This pottage shall The Conqueror eat,
Beside the stream *Nerañjarā*,
And thence by road triumphal go
To where the Tree of Wisdom stands.

75. "Then shall the Peerless, Glorious One
Walk to the right, round Wisdom's Throne,
And there The Buddhaship achieve,
While sitting at the fig-tree's root.

76. "The mother that shall bring him forth,
Shall Māyā called be by name;

Suddhodana his father's name;
His own name shall be Gotama.

77. "Kolita, Upatissa[16] too-
These shall his Chief Disciples be;
Both undepraved, both passion-free,
And tranquil and serene of mind.

78. "Ānanda shall be servitor
And on The Couqueror attend;
Khemā and Uppaḷavaṇṇā
Shall female Chief Disciples be,

79. "Both undepraved, both passion-free,
And tranquil and serene of mind.
The Bo-tree of this Blessed one
Shall be the tree Assattha[17] called."

80. Thus spake Th'Unequalled, Mighty Sage;
And all, when they had heard his speech,
Both men and gods rejoiced, and said:
"Behold a Buddha-scion here!"

81. Now shouts were heard on every side,
The people clapped their arms and laughed.
Ten thousand worlds of men and gods
Paid me their homage then and said:

82. "If of our Lord Dīpaṁkara
The Doctrine now we fail to grasp,
We yet shall stand in time to come
Before this other face to face.

83. "Even as, when men a river cross,
And miss th' opposing landing-place,
A lower landing-place they find,
And there the river-bank ascend;

84. "Even so, we all, if we let slip
The present Conqueror that we have,
Yet still shall stand in time to come
Before this other, face to face."

85. Dīpaṁkara, Who All Worlds Knew,
Recipient of Offerings,
My future having prophesied,
His right foot raised and went his way.

86. And all who were this Conqueror's sons,
Walked to the right around me then;
And serpents, Men, and demigods,
Saluting me, departed thence.

87. Now when The Leader of the World
Had passed from sight with all his train,
My mind with rapturous transport filled,
I raised me up from where I lay.

88. Then overjoyed with joy was I,
Delighted with a keen delight;
And thus with pleasure saturate
I sat me down with legs across.

89. And while across-legged there I sat,
I thus reflected to my self:
"Behold! in trance am I adept,
And all the Powers High are mine.

90. "Nowhere throughout a thousand worlds
Are any seers to equal me;
Unequaled in the magic gifts
Have I this height of bliss attained."

91. Now while I sat with legs across,
The dwellers of ten thousand worlds

Rolled forth a glad and mighty shout:[18]
"Surely a Buddha thou shalt be!

92. "The presages that erst were seen,
When Future Buddhas sat cross-legged,
These presages are seen to-day—
Surely a Buddha thou shalt be!

93. "All cold is everywhere dispelled,
And mitigated is the heat;
These presages are seen to-day—
Surely a Buddha thou shalt be!

94. "The system of ten thousand worlds
Is hushed to quiet and to peace;
These presages are seen to-day-
Surely a Buddha thou shalt be!

95. "The mighty winds then cease to blow,
Nor do the rivers onward glide;
These presages are seen to-day-
Surely a Buddha thou shalt be!

96. "All plants, be they of land or stream,
Do straightway put their blossoms forth;
Even so to-day they all have bloomed-
Surely a Buddha thou shalt be!

97. "And every tree, and every vine,
Is straightway laden down with fruit;
Even so to-day they're laden down-
Surely a Buddha thou shalt be!

98. "In sky and earth doth straightway then
Full many a radiant gem appear;
Even so to-day they shine afar—
Surely a Buddha thou shalt be!

99. "Then straightway music's heard to play
'Mongst men on earth and gods in heaven;
So all to-day in music join-
Surely a Buddha thou shalt be!

100. "There falleth straightway down from heaven
A rain of many-colored flowers;
Even so to-day these flowers are seen-
Surely a Buddha thou shalt be!

101. "The mighty ocean heaves and roars,
And all the worlds ten thousand quake;
Even so is now this tumult heard---
Surely a Buddha thou shalt be!

102. "Straightway throughout the whole of hell
The fires ten thousand all die out;
Even so to-day have all expired---
Surely a Buddha thou shalt be!

103. "Unclouded then the sun shines forth,
And all the stars appear to view;
Even so to-day do they appear---
Surely a Buddha thou shalt be!

104. "Staightway, although no rain hath fallen,
Burst springs of water from the earth;
Even so to-day they gush in streams---
Surely a Buddha thou shalt be!

105. "And bright then shine the starry hosts
And constellations in the sky;
The moon in Libra now doth stand---
Surely a Buddha thou shalt be!

106. "All beasts that lurk in holes and clefts,
Then get them forth from out their lairs;

Even so to day they've left their dens---
Surely a Buddha thou shalt be!

107. "Straightway content is all the world,
And no unhappiness is known;
Even so to-day are all content—
Surely a Buddha thou shalt be!

108. "Then every sickness vanishes,
And hunger likewise disappears;
These presages are seen to-day---
Surely a Buddha thou shalt be!

109. "Then lust doth dwindle and grow weak,
And hate, infatuation too;
Even so to-day they disappear---
Surely a Buddha thou shalt be!

110. "Then fear and danger are unknown;
All we are freed from them to-day;
And by this token we perceive---
'Surely a Buddha thou shalt be!'

111. "No dust upwhirleth towards the sky;
Even so to-day this thing is seen;
And by this token we perceive---
'Surely a Buddha thou shalt be!'

112. "All noisome odors drift away,
And heavenly fragrance fills the air;
Even so the winds now sweetness waft---
Surely a Buddha thou shalt be!

113. "Then all the gods appear to view,
Save those that hold the formless realm;
Even so to-day these all are seen---
Surely a Buddha thou shalt be!

114. "Then clearly seen are all the hells,
However many be their tale;
Even so to-day may all be seen---
Surely a Buddha thou shalt be!

115. "Through walls, and doors, and mountain-rocks,
One finds an easy passage then;
Even so to-day they yield like air---
Surely a Buddha thou shalt be!

116 "Existence then forbears its round
Of death and rebirth for a time;
Even so to-day this thing is seen---
Surely a Buddha thou shalt be!

117. "Do thou a strenuous effort make!
Do not turn back! Go on! Advance;
Most certainly we know this thing:
'Surely a Buddha thou shalt be!'"

118. When I had heard The Buddha's speech,
And what the worlds ten thousand said,
Well-pleased, delighted, overjoyed,
I thus reflected to myself:

119. "The Buddhas never liars are;
A Conqueror's word ne'er yet was vain;
Nothing but truth The Buddhas speak---
Surely a Buddha I shall be!

120. "As clods thrown upward in the air
Fall surely back upon the earth,
So what the glorious Buddhas speak
Is sure and steadfast to the end.
Nothing but truth The Buddhas speak--
Surely a Buddha I shall be![19]

121. "As also for each living thing
The approach of death is ever sure,
So what the glorious Buddhas speak
Is sure and steadfast to the end.
Nothing but truth The Buddhas speak---
Surely a Buddha I shall be!

122. "As at the waning of the night
The rising of the sun is sure,
So what the glorious Buddhas speak
Is sure and steadfast to the end.
Nothing but truth, *etc*

123. "As, when he issues from his den,
The roaring of the lion's sure,
So what the glorious Buddhas speak
Is sure and steadfast to the end.
Nothing but truth,*etc*.

124. "As when a female has conceived,
Her bringing forth of young is sure,
So what the glorious Buddhas speak
Is sure and steadfast to the end.
Nothing but truth The Buddhas speak---
Surely a Buddha I shall be!

125. "Come now! I'll search that I may find
Conditions which a Buddha make---
Above, below, to all ten[20] points,
Where'er conditions hold their sway."

126. And then I searched, and saw the First
Perfection, which consists in Alms,
That highroad great whereon of old
The former seers had ever walked.

127. "Come now! This one as first adopt,
And practice it determinedly;
Acquire perfection in thine Alms,
If thou to Wisdom wouldst attain.

128. "As when a jar is brimming full,
And some one overturneth it,
The jar its water all gives forth,
And nothing for itself keeps back;

129. "So, when a suppliant thou dost see,
Of mean, or high, or middling rank,
Give all in Alms, in nothing stint,
E'en as the overturned jar.

130. "But now there must be more than these
Conditions which a Buddha make:
Still others will I seek to find
That shall in Buddhaship mature."

131. Perfection Second then I sought,
And lo! the Precepts came to view,
Which mighty seers of former times
Had practised and had follow'd.

132. "Come now! as second this adopt,
And practise it determinedly;
The Precepts to perfection keep,
If thou to Wisdom wouldst attain.

133. "As when a Yak cow's flowing tail
Is firmly caught by bush or thorn,
She thereupon awaits her death,
But will not tear and mar her tail;[21]

134. "So likewise thou in stages four,
Observe and keep the Precepts whole,

On all occasions guard them well,
As ever Yak cow does her tail.

135. "But now there must be more than these
Conditions which a Buddha make;
Still others will I seek to find
That shall in Buddhaship mature."

136. And then Perfection Third I sought,
Which is Renunciation called.
Which mighty seers of former times
Had practised and had follow'd.

137. "Come now! this one as third adopt,
And practise it determinedly;
Renounce, and in perfection grow,
If thou to Wisdom wouldst attain.

138. "Even as a man who long has dwelt
In prison, suffering miserably,
No liking for the place conceives,
But only longeth for release;

139. "So likewise thou must every mode
Of being as a prison view---
Renunciation be thy aim;
Thus from existence free thyself.

140. "But now there must be more than these
Conditions which a Buddha make;
Still others will I seek to find
That shall in Buddhaship mature."

141. And then I sought and found the Fourth
Perfection, which is Wisdom called,
Which mighty seers of former times
Had practised and had follow'd.

142. "Come now! this one as fourth adopt,
And practise it determinedly;
Wisdom to its perfection bring,
If thou to Wisdom wouldst attain.

143. "Just as a priest, when on his rounds,
Nor low, nor high, nor middling folk
Doth shun, but begs of every one,
And so his daily food receives;

144. "So to the learned ay resort,
And seek thy Wisdom to increase;
And when this Fourth Perfection's gained,
A Buddha's Wisdom shall be thine.

145. "But now there must be more than these
Conditions which a Buddha make;
Still others will I seek to find
That shall in Buddhaship mature."

146. And then I sought and found the Fifth
Perfection, which is Courage called,
Which mighty seers of former times
Had practised and had follow'd.

147. "Come now! this one as fifth adopt,
And practise it determinedly;
In Courage perfect strive to be,
If thou to Wisdom wouldst attain.

148. "Just as the lion, king of beasts,
In crouching, walking, standing still,
With courage ever is instinct,
And watchful always, and alert;

149. "So thou in each repeated birth,
Courageous energy display;

And when this Fifth Perfection's gained,
A Buddha's Wisdom shall be thine.

150. "But now there must be more than these
Conditions which a Buddha make;
Still others will I seek to find
That shall in Buddhaship mature."

151. And then I sought and found the Sixth
Perfection, which is Patience called,
Which mighty seers of former times
Had practised and had follow'd.

152. "Come now! this one as sixth adopt,
And practise it determinedly;
And if thou keep an even mood,
A Buddha's Wisdom shall be thine.

153. "Just as the earth, whate'er is thrown
Upon her, whether sweet or foul,
All things endures, and never shows
Repugnance, nor complacency;

154. "E'en so, or honor thou, or scorn,
Of men, with patient mood must bear;
And when this Sixth Perfection's gained,
A Buddha's Wisdom shall be thine.

155. "But now there must be more than these
Conditions which a Buddha make;
Still others will I seek to find
That shall in Buddhaship mature."

156. And then I sought and found the Seventh
Perfection, which is that of Truth,
Which mighty seers of former times
Had practised and had follow'd.

157. "Come now! this one as seventh adopt,
And practise it determinedly;
If thou art ne'er of double speech,
A Buddha's Wisdom shall be thine.

158. "Just as the morning star on high
Its balanced course doth ever keep,
And through all seasons, times, and years,
Doth never from its pathway swerve;

159. "So likewise thou in all thy speech
Swerve never from the path of truth;
And when this Seventh Perfection's gained,
A Buddha's Wisdom shall be thine.

160. "But now there must be more than these
Conditions which a Buddha make;
Still others will I seek to find
That shall in Buddhaship mature."

161. And then I sought and found the Eighth
Perfection, Resolution called,
Which mighty seers of former times
Had practised and had follow'd.

162. "Come now! this one as eighth adopt,
And practise it determinedly;
And when thou art immovable,
A Buddha's Wisdom shall be thine.

163. "Just as a rocky mountain-peak,
Unmoved stands, firm-established,
Unshaken by th boisterous gales,
And always in its place abides;

164. "So likewise thou must ever be
In Resolution firm intrenched;

And when this Eighth Perfection's gained,
A Buddha's Wisdom shall be thine.

165. "But now there must be more than these
Conditions which a Buddha make;
Still others will I seek to find
That shall in Buddhaship mature."

166. And then I sought and found the Ninth
Perfection, which is called Good-will;
Which mighty seers of former times
Had practised and had follow'd.

167. "Come now! this one as ninth adopt,
And practise it determinedly;
Unequalled be in thy Good-will,
If thou to Wisdom wouldst attain.

168. "As water cleanseth all alike,
The righteous and the wicked,too,
From dust and dirt of every kind,
And with refreshing coolness fills;

169. "So likewise thou both friend and foe,
Alike with thy Good-will refresh,
And when this Ninth Perfection's gained,
A Buddha's Wisdom shall be thine.

170. "But now there must be more than these
Conditions which a Buddha make;
Still others will I seek to find
That shall in Buddhaship mature."

171. And then I sought and found the Tenth
Perfection, called Indifference;
Which mighty seers of former times
Had practised and had follow'd.

172. "Come now! this one as tenth adopt,
And practise it determinedly;
And when thou art of equal poise,
A Buddha's Wisdom shall be thine.

173. "Just as the earth, whate'er is thrown
Upon her, whether sweet or foul,
Indifferent is to all alike,
Nor hatred shows, nor amity;

174. "So likewise thou in good or ill,
Must even-balanced ever be;
And when this Tenth Perfection's gained,
A Buddha's Wisdom shall be thine.

175. "But earth no more conditions hath
That in The Buddhaship mature;
Beyond these are there none to seek;
So practise these determinedly."

176. Now pondering these conditions ten,
Their nature, essence, character,---
Such fiery vigor had they all,
That all the worlds ten thousand quaked.

177. Then shook and creaked the wide, wide earth,
As doth the sugar-mill at work;
Then quaked the ground, as doth the wheel
Of oil-mills when they're made to turn.

178. Th'entire assemblage that was there,
And followed in the Buddha's train,
Trembled and shook in great alarm,
And fell astonied to the ground.

179. And many thousand waterpots,
And many hundred earthen jars,

Were one upon another dashed,
And crushed and pounded into dust.

180. Excited, trembling, terrified,
Confused, and sore oppressed in mind,
The multitudes together came,
And to Dīpaṁkara approached.

181. "Oh, tell us what these signs portend.
Will good or ill betide the world?
Lo! terror seizes hold on all.
Dispel our fears, All-Seeing One!"

182. The Great Sage, then, Dīpaṁkara,
Allayed and pacified their fears:---
"Be comforted; and fear ye not
For that the world doth quake and shake.

183. "Of whom to-day I made proclaim---
'A glorious Buddha shall he be;---
He now conditions pondereth,
Which former Conquerors fulfilled.

184. "'T is while on these he is intent,
As basis for The Buddhaship,
The ground in worlds ten thousand shakes,
In all the realms of gods and men."

185. When thus they'd heard The Buddha speak,
Their anxious minds received relief;
And all then drawing near to me,
Again they did me reverence.

186. Thus on the road to Buddhaship,
And firm determined in my mind,
I raised me up from off my seat,
And reverenced Dīpaṁkara.

187. Then as I raised me from my seat,
Both gods and men in unison
Sweet flowers of heaven and flowers of earth
Profusely sprinkled on my head.

188. And gods and men in unison
Their great delight proclaimed aloud:---
"A mighty prayer thou now hast made;
Succeed according to thy wish!

189. "From all misfortunes be thou free,
Let every sickness disappear!
Mayst thou no hindrance ever know,
And highest Wisdom soon achieve!

190. "As, when the time of spring has come,
The trees put forth their buds and flowers,
Likewise dost thou, O Hero Great,
With knowledge of a Buddha bloom.

191."As all they who have Buddhas been,
The Ten Perfections have fulfilled,
Likewise do thou, O Hero Great,
The Ten Perfections strive to gain.

192. "As all they who have Buddhas been,
On Wisdom's Throne their insight gained,
Likewise do thou, O Hero Great,
On Conqueror's Throne thy insight gain.

193. "As all they who have Buddhas been,
Have made the Doctrine's Wheel to roll,
Likewise do thou, O Hero Great,
Make Doctrine's Wheel to roll once more.

194. "As on the mid-day of the month
The moon in full perfection shines,

Likewise do thou, with perfect mind,
Shine brightly in ten thousand worlds.

195. "As when the sun, by Rāhu freed,
Shines forth exceeding bright and clear.
So thou, when freed from ties of earth,
Shine forth in bright magnificence.

196. "Just as the rivers of all lands
Into the ocean find their way,
May gods and men from every world
Approach and find their way to thee."

197. Thus praised they me with glad acclaim;
And I, beginning to fulfil
The ten conditions of my quest,
Re-entered then into the wood.

END OF THE STORY OF SUMEDHA

iii. A LIST OF FORMER BUDDHAS.

Translated from the Introduction to the Jātaka(i.43[28]).

Now in the same world-cycle that saw Dīpaṁkara, The One Possessing the Ten Forces, there were also three other Buddhas; but as none of them prophesied concerning the future Buddha, I have not mentioned them. In the Commentary, however, all the Buddhas are mentioned from the beginning of that world-cycle on, as follows:---

247. "Taṇhaṁkara, Medhaṁkara,
And also Saraṇaṁkara.
Dīpaṁkara, the Buddha great,
Koṇḍañña, of all men the chief,

248. "Mañgala, and Sumana too,
Revata, Sobhita, the sage,
Anomadassi, Paduma,
Nārada, Padumuttara,

249. "Sumedha, and Sujāta too,
Piyadassi, the glorious one,
Atthadassi, Dhammadassi;
Siddhattha, guide of every man,

250. "Tissa, Phussa, the Buddha great,
Vipassi, Sikhi, Vessabhū,
Kakusandha, Koṇāgamana,
Kassapa also, guide for men,--

251. "All these aforetime Buddhas were,
Tranquil, from every passion free.
And like the sun, the many-rayed,
They chased away the darkness dense,
And having flamed like tongues of fire,
Became extinct with all their train."

Our Future Buddha, in his passage through four immensities and a hundred thousand world-cycles to the present time, has made his wish under twenty-four of these Buddhas, beginning with Dīpaṁkara. But since Kassapa, The Blessed One, there has been no Supreme Buddha excepting our present one. Accordingly, our Future Buddha has received recognition at the hands of twenty-four Buddhas, beginning with Dīpaṁkara.

iv. THE CHARACTERISTICS OF A FUTURE BUDDHA.

Translated from the Introduction to the Jātaka (i.44[20])

"A human being, male of sex,
Who saintship gains, a Teacher meets,
As hermit lives, and virtue loves,
Nor lacks resolve, nor fiery zeal,
Can by these eight conditions joined,
Make his most earnest wish succeed."

These eight conditions were all united in him when he made his earnest wish at the feet of Dīpaṁkara, saying,--

"Come now! I'll search that I may find
Conditions which a Buddha make."

Thereupon, putting forth a strenuous effort,--as it is said,--

"And then I searched, and found the First
Perfection, which consists in alms,"--

he discovered, not only the perfection which is called alms, but also all the others that go to make a Buddha. And in fulfilling them he reached his Vessantara existence[22]. In so doing, all the blessings to Future Buddhas who make the earnest wish were attained by him:---

252. "Such men in every virtue trained,
And destined for the Buddhaship,
In all their weary rounds of birth,
Though cycle-millions come and go,

253. "Are never born inside of hell,
Nor in the intermundane voids.
They never share the Manes' thirst,[23]
Their hunger or ferocity,
And though sometimes of low estate,
Are never of the insect class.

254. "When they appear among mankind,
'T is not as blind from birth they come,
Deafness they never have to bear,
Nor dumbness have they to endure.

255. "They're never of the female sex,
Nor as hermaphrodites appear,
As eunuchs are they never classed,
Those destined for the Buddhaship.

256. "From all the five great crimes exempt,
And pure in all their walks in life,
They follow not vain heresy,
For well they know how karma works.

257. "Though in the heavens they may be born.
Yet ne'er 'mongst those perception-reft;
Nor are they destined to rebirth
'Mongst dwellers in the Pure Abodes.[24]

258. "These pleasure-abnegating men
Live unattached in every birth,
And ever toil to help the world,
While all perfections they fulfil."

Now in accomplishing these Ten Perfections there was no limit to the number of existences in which he fulfilled the perfection of almsgiving; as when he was born as the Brāhmaṇa Akitti, the Brāhmaṇa Saṁkha, king Dhanañjaya, Mahā-Sudassana, Mahā-Govinda, king Nimi, prince Canda, Visayha the treasurer, king Sivi, and king Vessantara. But the acme was reached when as the Wise Hare[25]. he said,---

259. "There came a beggar, asked for food;
Myself I gave that he might eat.
In alms there's none can equal me;
In alms have I perfection reached."

Thus, in this offering up of his own life, he acquired the perfection of almsgiving in its highest degree.

Likewise there was no limit to the number of existences in which he fulfilled the precepts; as when he was born as the elephant-king Sīlava, the snake-king Campeyya, the snake-king Bhūridatta, the elephant-king Chaddanta, and prince Alīnasattu, son of king Jayaddisa. But the acme was reached when, as related in the Saṁkhapāla Birth-Story, he said,--

260. "They pierced me through with pointed stakes,
They hacked me with their hunting-knives;

Yet gainst these Bhojans raged I not,
but kept the precepts perfectly."

Thus, in giving up his own life, he acquired perfection in the keeping of the precepts.

Likewise there was no limit to the number of existences in which he fulfilled the perfection of abnegation by abandoning his throne; as when he was born as prince Somanassa, prince Hatthipāla, and the pandit Ayoghara. But the acme was reached when, as related in the Lesser Sutasoma Birth Story, he said,---

261. "A kingdom dropped into my hands;
Like spittle vile I let it fall,
Nor for it felt the smallest wish,
And thus renunciation gained."

Thus, free from attachment, he renounced a kingdom and retired from the world, and by so doing acquired the perfection of abnegation in its highest degree.

Likewise there was no limit to the number of existences in which he fulfilled the perfection of knowledge; as when he was born as the pandit Vidhūra, the pandit Mahā-Govinda, the pandit Kuddāla, the pandit Araka, the wandering ascetic Bodhi, and the pandit Mahosadha. But the acme was reached when, as the pandit Senaka of the Sattubhatta Birth-Story, he said,--

262. "With wisdom sifted I the case,
And freed the *Brāhmaṇa* from his woe;
In wisdom none can equal me:
In wisdom I've perfection reached,"

and displayed to all present the serpent which lay concealed in the bag, and in so doing acquired the perfection of wisdom in its highest degree.

Likewise there was no limit to the number of existences in which he fulfilled the perfection of courage. But the acme was reached when, as related in the Greater Janaka Birth-Story, he said,---

263. "Far out of sight of land were we,

The crew were all as dead of fright;
Yet still unruffled was my mind:
In courage I've perfection reached."

Thus it was in crossing the ocean he acquired the perfection of courage in its highest degree.

Likewise in th Khantivāda Birth-Story, where he said,--

264. "Like one insensible I lay,
While with his hatchet keen he hacked,
Nor raged I gainṣt Benares' king:
In patience I've perfection reached,"

in enduring great fuffering, while appearing to be unconscious, he acquired the perfection of patience in its highest degree.

Likewise in the Greater Sutasoma Birth-Story, where he said,--

265. "I kept the promise I had made,
And gave my life in sacrifice,
A hundred warriors set I free:
In truth have I perfection reached,"

in keeping his word at the sacrifice of his life, he acquired the perfection of truth in its highest degree.

Likewise in the Mūgapakkha Birth-Story, where he said,--

266. "'T is not that I my parents hate,
'Tis not that glory I detest,
But since omniscience I held dear,
Therefore I kept my firm resolve,"

in resolving on a course of conduct that cost him his life, he acquired the perfection of resolution in its highest degree.

Likewise in the Ekarāja Birth-Story, where he said,--

267. "No fear has any one of me,
Nor have I fear of any one,

In my good-will to all I trust,

And love to dwell in lonely woods,"

in the exercise of feelings of good-will, and in taking no thought for his life, he acquired the perfection of good-will in its highest degree.

Likewise in the Lomahaṁsa Birth-Story, where he said,--

268. I laid me down among the dead,
A pillow of their bones I made;
While from the villages around,
Some came to mock, and some to praise,"

while village children flocked about him, and some spat and others showered fragrant garlands upon him, he was indifferent alike to pleasure and pain, and acquired the perfection of indifference in its highest degree.

The above is an abridgment, but the full account is given in the *Cariyā-Piṭaka*.

Having thus fulfilled all the perfections, he said, in his existence as Vessantara,--

269. "This earth, unconscious though she be,
And ignorant of joy or grief,
E'en she then felt alms' mighty power,
And shook and quaked full seven times."

And having thus caused the earth to quake by his mighty deeds of merit, at the end of that existence he died, and was reborn in the Tusita heaven.

Accordingly the period from the time when he fell at the feet of Dīpaṁkara to his birth in the city of the Tusita gods constitutes the Distant Epoch.

v. THE BIRTH OF THE BUDDHA.

Translated from the Introduction to the Jātaka(i.47[21])

Now while the Future Buddha was still dwelling in the city of the Tusita gods, the "Buddha-Uproar," as it is called, took place. For there are three uproars which take place in the world,--the Cyclic-Uproar, the Buddha-Uproar and the Universal-Monarch-Uproar. They occur as follows:--

When it is known that after the lapse of a hundred thousand years the cycle is to be renewed, the gods called *Loka-byūhas,* inhabitants of a heaven of sensual pleasure, wander about through the world, with hair let down and flying in the wind, weeping and wiping away their tears with their hands, and with their clothes red and in great disorder. And thus they make announcement:--

"Sirs, after the lapse of a hundred thousand years, the cycle is to be renewed; this world will be destroyed; also the mighty ocean will dry up; and this broad earth, and Sineru, the monarch of the mountains, will be burnt up and destroyed,--up to the *Brahmā* heavens will the destruction of the world extend. Therefore, sirs, cultivate friendliness; cultivate compassion, joy, and indifference; wait on your mothers; wait on your fathers; and honor your elders among your kinsfolk."

This is called the Cyclic-Uproar.

Again, when it is known that after a lapse of a thousand years an omniscient Buddha is to arise in the world, the guardian angels of the world wander about, proclaiming:

"Sirs, after the lapse of a thousand years a Buddha will arise in the world."

This is called the Buddha-Uproar.

And lastly, when they realize that after the lapse of a hundred years a Universal Monarch is to arise, the terrestrial deities wander about, proclaiming:—

"Sirs, after the lapse of a hundred years a Universal Monarch is to arise in the world."

This is called the Universal-Monarch-Uproar. And these three are mighty uproars.

When of these three Uproars they hear the sound of the Buddha- Uproar, the gods of all ten thousand worlds come together into one place, and having ascertained what particular being is to be The Buddha, they approach him, and beseech him to become one. But it is not till after omens have appeared that they beseech him.

At that time, therefore, having all come together in one world, with the Cātum-Mahārājas, and with the *Sakka,* the Suyāma, the Santusita, the Paranimmita-Vasavatti, and the

Mahā-Brahmā of each several world, they approached the Future Buddha in the Tusita heaven, and besought him, saying,---

"Sir, it was not to acquire the glory of a *Sakka*, or of a *Māra*, or of a *Brahmā*, or of a Universal Monarch, that you fulfilled the Ten Perfections; but it was to gain omniscience in order to save the world, that you fulfilled them. Sir, the time and fit season for your Buddaship has now arrived."

But the Great Being, before assenting to their wish, made what is called the five great observations. He observed, namely, the time, the continent, the country, the family, and the mother and her span of life.

In the first of these observations he asked himself whether it was the right time or no. Now it is not the right time when the length of men's lives is more than a hundred thousand years. And why is it not the right time? Because mortals then forget about birth, old age, and death. And if The Buddhas, who always include in their teachings the Three Characteristics, were to attempt at such a time to discourse concerning transitoriness, misery, and the lack of substantive reality, men would not think it worth while listening to them, nor would they give them credence. Thus there would be no conversions made; and if there were no conversions, the dispensation would not conduce to salvation. This, therefore is not the right time.

Also it is not the right time when men's lives ar less than a hundred years. And why is it not the right time? Because mortals are then exceedingly corrupt; and an exhortation given to the exceedingly corrupt makes no impression, but, like a mark drawn with a stick on the surface of the water, it immediately disappears. This, therefore, also is not the right time.

But when the length of men's lives is between a hundred years and a hundred thousand years, then is it the right time. Now at that time men's lives were a hundred years; accordingly the Great Being observed that it was the right time for his birth.

Next he made the observation concerning the continent. Looking over the four continents with their attendant isles, he reflected: "In three of the continents the Buddhas are never born; only in the continent of India are they born." Thus he decided on the continent.

Next he made the observation concerning the place. "The continent of India is large," thought he, "being ten thousand leagues around. In which of its countries are The Buddhas born?" Thus he decided on the Middle Country.

The Middle Country is the coutry defined in the *Vinaya* as follows:--

"It lies in the middle, on this side of the town Kajañgala on the east, beyond which is Mahā-Sāls, and beyond that the border districts. It lies in the middle, on this side of the river Salalavatī on the southeast, beyond which are the border districts. It lies in the middle, on this side of the town Setakaṇṇika on the south, beyond which are the border districts. It lies in the middle, on this side of the Brāhmaṇical town Thūṇa on the west, beyond which are the border districts. It lies in the middle, on this side of the hill Usīraddhaja on the north, beyond which are the border districts."

It is three hundred leagues in length, two hundred and fifty in breadth, and nine hundred in circumference. In this country are born The Buddhas, the Private Buddhas, the Chief Disciples, the Eighty Great Disciples, the Universal Monarch, and other eminent ones, magnates of the warrior caste, of the Brāhmaṇa caste, and the wealthy householders. "and in it is this city called Kapilavatthu," thought he, and concluded that there he ought to be born.

Then he made the observation concerning the family. "The Buddhas," thought he, "are never born into a family of the peasant caste, or of the servile caste; but into one of the warrior caste, or of the Brāhmaṇa caste, whichever at the time is the higher in public estimation. The warrior caste is now the higher in public estimation. I will be born into a warrior family, and king Suddhodana shall be my father." Thus he decided on the family.

Then he made the observation concerning the mother. "The mother of a Buddha," thought he, "is never a wanton, nor a drunkard, but is one who has fulfilled the perfections through a hundred thousand cycles, and has kept the five precepts unbroken from the day of her birth. Now this queen Mahā-Māyā is such a one: and she shall be my mother."---

"But what shall be her span of life[26]?" continued he. And he perceived that it was to be ten months and seven days.

Having thus made the five great observations, he kindly made the gods the required promise, saying,--

"Sirs, you are right. The time has come for my Buddhaship."

Then, surrounded by the gods of the Tusita heaven, and dismissing all the other gods, he entered the Nandana Grove of the Tusita capital,--for in each of the heavens there is a Nandana Grove. And here the gods said,"Attain in your next existence your high destiny," and kept reminding him that he had already paved the way to it by his accumulated merit. Now it was while he was thus dwelling, surrounded by these deities, and continually reminded of his accumulated merit, that he died, and was conceived in the womb of queen Mahā-Māyā. And in order that this matter may be fully understood, I will give the whole account in due order.

It is related that at that time the Midsummer Festival had been proclaimed in th city of Kapilavatthu, and the multitude were enjoying the feast. And queen Mahā-Māyā, abstaining from strong drink, and brilliant with garlands and perfumes, took part in the festivities for the six days provious to the day of full moon. And when it came to be the day of full moon, she rose early, bathed in perfumed water, and dispensed four hundred thousand pieces of money in great largess. And decked in full gala attire, she ate of the choicest food; after which she took the eight vows, and entered her elegantly furnished chamber of State. And lying down on the royal couch, she fell asleep and dreamed the following dream:--

The four guardian angles came and lifted her up, together with her couch, and took her away to the Himalaya Mauntains. There, in the Manosilā table-land, which is sixty leagues in extent, they laid her under a prodigious sal-tree, seven leagues in height, and took up their positions respectfully at one side. Then came the wives of these guardian angels, and conducted her to Anotatta Lake, and bathed her, to remove every human stain. And after clothing her with divine garments, they anointed her with perfumes and decked her with divine flowers. Not far off was Silver Hill, and in it a golden mansion. There they spread a divine couch with its head towards the east, and laid her down upon it. Now the Future Buddha had become a superb white elephant, and was wandering about at no great distance, on Gold Hill. Descending thence, he ascended Silver Hill, and approaching from the north, he plucked a white lotus with his silvery trunk, and trumpeting loudly, went into the golden mansion. And three times he walked round his mother's couch, with his right side towards it, and striking her on her right side, he seemed to enter her womb. Thus the conception took place in the Midsummer Festival.

On the next day the queen awoke, and told the dream to the king. And the king caused sixty-four eminent Brāhmaṇas to be summoned, and spread costly seats for them on ground festively prepared with green leaves, Dalbergia flowers, and so forth. The Brāhmaṇas being seated, he filled gold and silver dishes with the best of milk-porridge compounded with ghee, honey, and treacle; and covering these dishes with others, made likewise of gold and silver, he gave the Brāhmaṇas to eat. And not only with food, but with other gifts, such as new garments, tawny cows, and so forth, he satisfied them completely. And when their every desire had been satisfied, he told them the dream and asked them what would come of it.

"Be not anxious, great king!" said the Brāhmaṇas; "a child has planted itself in the womb of your queen, and it is a male child and not a female. You will have a son. And he, if he continue to live the household life, will become a Universal Monarch; but if he leave the household life, and retire from the world, he will become a Buddha, and roll back the clouds of sin and folly of this world."

Now the instant the Future Buddha was conceived in the womb of his mother, all the ten thousand worlds suddenly quaked, quivered, and shook. And the Thirty-two Prognostics appeared, as follows: an immeasurable light spread through ten thousand worlds; the blind recovered their sight, as if from desire to see this his glory; the deaf received their hearing; the dumb talked; the hunchbacked became straight.

of body; the lame recovered the power to walk; all those in bonds were freed from their bonds and chains; the fires went out in all the hells; the hunger and thirst of the Manes was stilled; wild animals lost their timidity; diseases ceased among men; all mortals became mild- spoken; horses neighed and elephants trumpeted in a manner sweet to the ear; all musical instruments gave forth their notes without being played upon; bracelets and other ornaments jingled; in all quarters of the heavens the weather became fair; a mild, cool breeze began to blow, very refreshing to men; rain fell out of season; water burst forth from the earth and flowed in streams; the birds ceased flying through the air; the rivers checked their flowing; in the mighty ocean the water became sweet; the ground became everywhere covered with lotuses of the five different colors; all flowers bloomed, both those on land and those that grow in the water; trunk-lotuses bloomed on the trunks of trees, branch-lotuses on the branches, and vine-lotuses on the vines; on the ground, stalk-lotuses, as they are called, burst through the overlying rocks and came up by sevens; in the sky were produced others, called hanging-lotuses; a shower of flowers fell all about; celestial music was heard to play in the sky; and the whole ten thousand worlds became one mass of garlands of the utmost possible magnficence, with waving chowries, and saturated with the incense-like fragrance of flowers, and resembled a bouquet of flowers sent whirling through the air, or a closely woven wreath, or a superbly decorated altar of flowers.

From the time the Future Buddha was thus conceived, four angels with swords in their hands kept guard, to ward off all harm from both the Future Buddha and the Future Buddha's mother. No lustful thought sprang up in the mind of the Future Buddha's mother; having reached the pinnacle of good fortune and of glory, she felt comfortable and well, and experienced no exhaustion of body. And within her womb she could distinguish the Future Buddha, like a white thread passed through a transparent jewel. And whereas a womb that has been occupied by a Future Buddha is like the shrine of a temple, and can never be occupied or used again, therfore it was that the mother of the Future Buddha died when he was seven days old, and was reborn in the Tusita heaven.

Now other women sometimes fall short of and sometimes run over the term of ten lunar months, and then bring forth either sitting or lying down; but not so the mother of a Future Buddha. She carries the Future Buddha in her womb for just ten months, and then brings forth while standing up. This is a characteristic of the mother of a Future Buddha. So also queen Mahā- Māyā carried the Future Buddha in her womb, as it were oil in a vessel, for ten months; and being then far gone with child, she grew desirous of going home to her relatives, and said to king Suddhodana,--

"Sir, I should like to visit my kinsfolk in their city Devadaha."

"So be it," said the king; and from Kapilavatthu to the city of Devadaha he had the road made even, and garnished it with plantain-trees set in pots, and with banners, and streamers; and, seating the queen in a golden palanquin borne by a thousand of his courtiers, he sent her away in great pomp. Now between the two cities, and belonging to the inhabitants of both, there was a pleasure-grove of sal-trees, called Lumbini Grove. And at this particular time this grove was one mass of flowers from the ground to the topmost branches, while amongst the branches and flowers hummed swarms of bees of the five different colors, and flocks of various kinds of birds flew about warbling sweetly. Throughout the whole of Lumbini Grove the scene resembled the Cittalatā Grove in Indra's paradise, or the magnifcently decorated banqueting pavilion of some potent king.

When the queen beheld it she became desirous of disporting herself therein, and the courtiers therefore took her into it. And going to the foot of the monarch sal-tree of the grove, she wished to take hold of one of its branches. And the sal-tree branch, like the tip of a well-steamed reed, bent itself down within reach of the queen's hand. Then she reached out her hand, and seized hold of the branch, and immediately her pains came upon her. Thereupon the people hung a curtain about her, and retired. So her delivery took place while she was standing up, and keeping fast hold of the sal-tree branch.

At that very moment came four pure-minded *Mahā-Brahmā* angels bearing a golden net; and, receiving the Future

Buddha in this golden net, they placed him before his mother and said,--

"Rejoice, O queen! A mighty son has been born to you."

Now other mortals on issuing from the maternal womb are smeared with disagreeable, impure matter; but not so the Future Buddha. He issued from his moher's womb like a preacher descending from his preaching-seat, or a man coming down a stair, stretching out both hands and both feet, unsmeared by any impurity from his mother's womb, and flashing pure and spotless, like a jewel thrown upon a vesture of Benares cloth. Notwithstanding this, for the sake of honoring the Future Buddha and his mother, there came two streams of water from the sky, and refreshed the Future Buddha and his mother.

Then the *Brahmā* angels, after receiving him on their golden net, delivered him to the four guardian angels, who received him from their hands on a rug which was made of the skins of black antelopes, and was soft to the touch, being such as is used on State occasions; and the guardian angels delivered him to men who received him on a coil of fine cloth; and the men let him out of their hands on the ground, where he stood and faced the east. There, before him, lay many thousands of worlds, like a great open court; and in them, gods and men, making offerings to him of perfumes, garlands, and so on, were saying,---

"Great Being! There is none your equal, much less your superior."

When he had in this manner surveyed the four cardinal points, and the four intermediate ones, and the zenith, and the nadir, in short, all the ten directions in order, and had nowhere discovered his equal, he exclaimed, "This is the best direction," and strode forward seven paces, followed by *Mahā-Brahmā* holding over him the white umbrella, Suyāma bearing the fan, and other divinities having the other symbols of royalty in their hands. Then, at the seventh stride, he halted, and with a noble voice, he shouted the shout of victory, beginning,--

"The chief am I in all the world."

Now in three of his existences did the Future Buddha utter words immediately on issuing from his mother's womb:namely, in his existence as Mahosadha; in his existence as Vessantara; and in this existence.

As respects his existence as Mahosadha, it is related that just as he was issuing from his mother's womb, Sakka, the king of the gods, came and placed in his hand some choice sandal-wood, and departed. And he closed his fist upon it, and issued forth.

"My child," said his mother, "What is it you bring with you in your hand?"

"Medicine, mother," said he.

Accordingly, as he was born with medicine in his hand, they gave him the name of Osadha-Dāraka [Medicine-Child]. Then they took the medicine, and placed it in an earthenware jar; and it was a sovereign remedy to heal all the blind, the deaf, and other afflicted persons who came to it. So the saying sprang up, "This is a great medicine, this is a great medicine!" And thus he received the name of Mahosadha [Great Medicine-man].

Again, in the Vessantara existence, as he was issuing from his mother's womb, he stretched out his right hand, and said,--

"Pray, mother, is there anything in the house? I want to give alms."

Then, after he had completely issued forth, his mother said,--

"It's a wealthy family, my son, into which you are born;" and putting his hand in her own, she had them place in his a purse containing a thousand pieces of money.

Lastly, in this birth he shouted the shout of victory above- mentioned.

Thus in three of his existences did the Future Buddha utter words immediately on issuing from his mother's womb. And just as at the moment of his conception, so also at the moment of his birth appeared the Thirty-two Prognostics.

Now at the very time that our Future Buddha was born in Lumbini Grove there also came into existence the mother of Rāhula, and Channa the courtier, Kāludāyi the courtier,

Kanthaka the king of horses, the Great Bo-tree, and the four urns full of treasure. Of these last, one was a quarter of a league in extent, another a half-league, the third three quarters of a league, and the fourth a league. These seven[27] are called the Connate Ones.

Then the inhabitants of both cities took the Future Buddha, and carried him to Kapilavatthu.

vi. THE YOUNG GOTAMID PRINCE

Translated from the Introduction to the Jātaka(i.54[11])

On this same day the happy and delighted hosts of the Heaven of the Thirty-three held a celebration, waving their cloaks and giving other signs of joy, because to king Suddhodana in Kapilavatthu had been born a son who should sit at the foot of the Bo-tree, and become a Buddha.

Now it came to pass at that time that an ascetic named Kāladevala, who was an intimate friend of king Suddhodana, and practised in the eight stages of meditation, went, after his daily meal, to the Heaven of the Thirty-three to take his noon- day rest. And as he was sitting there resting, he noticed these gods, and said,--

"Why do you frolic so joyously? Let me too know the reason."

"Sir," replied the gods,"it is because a son has been born to king Suddhodana, who shall sit at the foot of the Bo-tree, and become a Buddha, and cause the Wheel of the Doctrine to roll; in him we shall be permitted to behold the infinite and masterful ease of a Buddha, and shall hear the Doctrine."

On hearing this, the ascetic descended from the world of the gods in haste, and entered the dwelling of the king; and having seated himself on the seat assigned to him, he said,--

"Great king, I hear that a son has been born to you. I would see him."

Then the king had the prince magnificently dressed, and brought in, and carried up to do reverence to the ascetic. But the feet of the Future Buddha turned and planted themselves in the matted locks of the ascetic. For in that birth there was no one worthy of the Future Buddha's reverence; and if these ignorant people had succeeded in causing the Future Buddha to bow, the head of the ascetic would have split in seven pieces.

"It is not meet that I compass my own death," thought the ascetic, and rose from his seat, and with joined hands did reverence to the Future Buddha. And when the king had seen this wonder, he also did reverence to his son.

Now the ascetic could look backward into the past for forty world-cycles, and forward into future for forty world-cycles,--in all, eighty world-cycles. And, noting on the person of the Future Buddha all the lucky marks and characteristics, he began to reflect and consider whether or not they prophesied his Buddhaship. And perceiving that undoubtedly he would become a Buddha, he thought to himself," What a marvellous personage he is!" and smiled.

Next he considered in his mind whether he would live to see him attain the Buddhaship; and he perceived that he was not to have that opportunity. For he would die before that time, and be reborn in the formless mode of existence, where it would be out of the power of even a hundred or a thousand Buddhas to come and enlighten him. And he thought,"It will not be mine to behold this so marvellous a personage when he has become a Buddha. My loss, alas, will be great," and wept.

The people noticed his behavior, and said to him,--

"Our good father smiled but a moment ago, and now has begun to weep. Reverend sir, is any misfortune to happen to our young master?"

"No misfortune is to happen to him. He will become a Buddha without any manner of doubt."

"Then why did you weep?" "I wept at the thought of my own great loss; for, alas, I am not to have an oppoutunity of seeing this marvellous person after he has become a Buddha."

Next he considered in his mind whether or not any of his relatives were to have the opportunity; and he saw that his sister's child Nālaka was to have it. And he went to his sister's house, and inquired,--

"Where is your son Nālaka?"

"Good father, he is in the house."

"Call him hither."

"My child," said he to the lad when he had come,"a son has been born in the family of Suddhodana the king, who is the coming Buddha. Thirty-five years from now he will become a Buddha, and you will have an opportunity of seeing him. Retire from the world this very day."

And the child did so, although he belonged to a family possessing eight hundred and seventy millions of treasure; for he thought, "My uncle would not lay such a command upon me for any trifling reason." Sending to the bazaar, he procured some yellow garments, and an earthenware bowl, and cut off his hair and his beard, and put on the yellow garments. And stretching out his joined hands in the direction of the Future Buddha, he said,"I retire from the world to follow earth's greatest being." Then he prostrated himself,so that he touched the ground with the fivefold contact. Having thus done reverence, he placed the bowl in his scrip, slung the latter over his shoulder, and going to the Himalaya Mountains, he there performed the duties of a monk.

And after the Great Being had achieved the absolute and supreme wisdom, Nālaka came to him, and had him prescribe the Nālaka course of conduct[28]. Then, returning to the Himalaya Mountains, he attained to saintship, and adopted that excellent course. And keeping alive for seven months more, and being at the time near a certain Gold Hill, he passed out of existence by that final extinction in which none of the elements of being remain.

Now on the fifth day they bathed the Future Buddha's head, saying, "We will perform the rite of choosing a name for him." And they prepared the royal palace by anointing it with four kinds of perfumes, and by scattering Dalbergia blossoms and other flowers, five sorts in all. And making some porridge of whole rice-grains boiled in milk, they invited one hundred and eight Brāhmāṇas, men who had mastered the three Vedas. And having seated these Brāhmāṇas in the royal palace, and fed them with delicate food, and showed them every attention, they asked them to observe the marks and characteristics of the Future Buddha's person, and to prophesy his fortune.

Among the hundred and eight,--

270. "Rāma, Dhaja, Lakkhaṇa, also Manti,
Koṇḍañña,Bhoja, Suyāma,Sudatta,
These Brāhmaṇas eight were there with senses six subdued;
They from the magic books disclosed his fortune."

These eight Brāhmaṇas were the fortune-tellers, being the same[29] who had interpreted the dream of the night of the conception. Seven of these raised two fingers each, and gave a double interpretation, saying, "If a man possessing such marks and characteristics continue in the household life, he becomes a Universal Monarch; if he retire from the world, he becomes a Buddha." And then they set forth all the glory of a Universal Monarch.

But the youngest of them all, a youth whose clan-name was Koṇḍañña, after examining the splendid set of marks and characteristics on the person of the Future Buddha, raised only one finger, and gave but a single interpretation, saying, "There is here naught to make him stay in the household life. He will most undoubtedly become a Buddha, and remove the veil of ignorance and folly from the world." For this Koṇḍañña was one who had made an earnest wish under former Buddhas, and was now in his last existence. Therefore it was that he outstripped the other seven in knowledge, and saw but one future; in as much as a person possessed of such marks and characteristics would never stay in the household life, but would undoubtedly become a Buddha. So he raised only one finger, and gave that interpretation.

Then the seven Brāhmaṇas went home and said to their sons,"Children, we are old, but whether we ourselves are alive or not when the son of Suddhodana the king shall attain omniscience, you, at least, should then retire from the world under his dispensation."

And after these seven persons had lived out their term of life they passed away according to their deeds; but Koṇḍañña, being younger, was still alive and hale. And when the Great Being, after making the great retirement in pursuit of wisdom, had arrived at Uruvelā in his progress from place to place, he thought: "How pleasant indeed is this spot! How suitable for the struggles of a young man desirous of struggling!" and took up his abode there. Koṇḍañña heard the news that the Great Being had retired from the world, and drawing near to the sons of those seven Brāhmaṇas, he spoke to them as follows:--

"I hear that prince Siddhattha has retired from the world. Now he will unquestionably become a Buddha, and if your fathe.s were alive they would follow after him this very day. If you also would like to retire from the world, come with me. I men to follow after that man in his retirement from the world."

But they could not all agree; and three of them did not retire from the world. But the remaining four did so, and made the Brāhmaṇa Koṇḍañña their chief. and these five persons became known as the "Band of Five Elders."

Then said the king,"What shall my son see to make him retire from the world?"

"The four signs."

"What four?"

"A decrepit old man, a diseased man, a dead man, and a monk."

"From this time forth," said the king, let no such persons be allowed to come near my son. It will never do for my son to become a Buddha. What I would wish to see in my son exercising sovereign rule and authority over the four great continents and the two thousand attendant isles, and walking through the heavens surrounded by a retinue thirtysix leagues in circumference."And when he had so spoken he placed guards for a distance of a quarter of a league in each of the four directions, in order that none of these four kinds of men might come within sight of his son.

On this same day, also, eighty thousand clansmen assembled together in the festival-hall, and each dedicated a son, saying,- "Whether the young prince become a Buddha or a king, we will each one give a son: so that if he become a Buddha, he shall be followed and surrounded by monks of the warrior caste; and if he become a king, by nobles of the warrior caste."

And the king procured nurses for the Future Buddha--women of fine figure, and free from all blemish. And so the Future Buddha began to grow, surrounded by an immense retinue, and in great splendor.

Now on a certain day the king celebrated the Sowing Festival, as it was called. On that day they used to decorate the whole city, so that it looked like a palace of the gods; and all the slaves and other servants would put on new tunics; and, perfumed and garlanded, they would assemble together at the king's palace, where a thousand plows were yoked for the royal plowing.

On this occasion there were one hundred and eight plows, all save one ornamented with silver, as were also the reins for the oxen and the cross-bars of the plows. But the plow that was held by the king was ornamented with red gold, as also the horns, the reins, and the goads for the oxen. And the king issued forth with a large retinue, taking his son along with him. And in the field where the plowing was to be done was a solitary rose-apple tree of thick foliage and dense shade. Underneath this tree the king had a couch placed for the young prince, and spread over his head a canopy that was studded with gold stars; and he surrounded him with a screen, and appointed those that should watch by him; and then, decked with all his ornaments and surrounded by his courtiers, he proceeded to the place where they were to plow. On arriving there, the king took the gold plow, and the courtiers took the silver plows,—one hundred and eight save one, and the farmers the other plows; and then all plowed forward and back. The king went from the hither side to the further side, and from the farther side back again; and the pomp and magnificence of the festival was at its climax.

Now the nurses who were sitting about the Future Buddha came out from behind the screen to behold the royal magnificence. And the Future Buddha, looking hither and thither and seeing no one, arose in haste and sat him down cross-leged, and mastering his inspirations and his expirations, entered on the first trance. The nurses delayed a little, being detained by the abundance of good things to eat. And the shadows of the other trees passed over to the east, but the shadow of the rose-apple tree remained steadily circular. Suddenly the nurses remembered that they had left their young master alone; and raising the screen, they entered and saw the Future Buddha sitting cross-legged on the couch, and also noticed the miracle of the shadow. Then they went and announced to the king,--

"Sire, thus and so is the prince sitting; and the shadows of the other trees have passed over to the east, but the shadow of the rose-apple tree remains steadily circular."

And the king came in haste, and seeing the miracle, he did obeisance to his son, saying, "This, dear child, is my second obeisance."

And thus, in due course, the Future Buddha attained to the age of sixteen years. And the king built three palaces for the Future Buddha, suited to the three seasons,--one of nine stories, another of seven stories, and another of five stories. And he provided him with forty thousand dancing girls. And the Future Buddha, with his gayly dressed dancers, was like a god surrounded by hosts of houris; and attended by musical instruments that sounded of themselves, and in the enjoyment of great magnificence, he lived, as the seasons changed, in each of these three palaces. And the mother of Rāhula was his principal queen.

Now while he was thus enjoying great splendor, one day there arose the following discussion among his relatives:--

"Siddhattha is wholly given over to pleasure, and is not training himself in any manly art. What could he do if war were to occur?"

The king sent for the Future Buddha, and said,—

"My child, your relatives are saying that you are not training yourself, but are wholly given over to pleasure. Now what do you think we had best do?"

"Sire, I do not need to train myself. Let the crier go about the city beating the drum, to announce that I will show my proficiency. On the seventh day from now I will show my proficiency to my relatives."

The king did so. And the Future Buddha assembled together bowmen that could shoot like lightning and at a hair's breadth; and in the midst of the populace, and before his kinsfolk, he exhibited a twelvefold skill, such as none of the other bowmen could equal. All of which is to be understood after the manner related in the Sarabhaṅga Birth-Story. So the assembly of his kinsfolk doubted him no longer.

vii. THE GREAT RETIREMENT.

Translated from the Introduction to the Jātaka(i.58[81]).

Now on a certain day the Future Buddha wished to go to the park, and told his charioteer to make ready the chariot. Accordingly the man brought out a sumptuous and elegant chariot, and adorning it richly, he harnessed to it four state-horses of the Sindhava breed, as white as the petals of the white lotus, and announced to the Future Buddha that every thing was ready. And the Future Buddha mounted the chariot, which was like to a palace of the gods, and proceeded towards the park.

"The time for the enlightenment of prince Siddhattha draweth nigh," thought the gods; "we must show him a sign:" and they changed one of their number into a decrepit old man, broken- toothed, gray-haired, crooked and bent of body, leaning on a staff, and trembling, and showed him to the Future Buddha, but so that only he and the charioteer saw him.

Then said the Future Buddha to the charioteer, in the manner related in the Mahāpadāna,---

"Friend, pray, who is this man? Even his hair is not like that of other men." And when he heard the answer, he said, "Shame on birth, since to every one that is born old age must come." And agitated in heart, he thereupon returned and ascended his palace.

"Why has my son returned so quickly?" asked the king.

"Sire, he has seen an old man," was the reply; "and because he has seen an old man, he is about to retire from the world."

"Do you want to kill me, that you say such things? Quickly get ready some plays to be performed before my son. If we can but get him to enjoying pleasure, he will cease to think of retiring from the world." Then the king extended the guard to half a league in each direction.

Again, on a certain day, as the Future Buddha was going to the park, he saw a diseased man whom the gods had fashioned; and having again made inquiry, he returned, agitated in heart, and ascended his palace.

And the king made the same inquiry and gave the same orders as before; and again extending the guard, placed them for three quarters of a league around.

And again on a certain day, as the Future Buddha was going to the park, he saw a dead man whom the gods had fashioned; and having again made inquiry, he returned, agitated in heart, and ascended his palace.

And the king made the same inquiry and gave the same orders as before; and again extending the guard, placed them for a league around.

And again on a certain day, as the Future Buddha was going to the park, he saw a monk, carefully and decently clad, whom the gods had fashioned; and he asked his charioteer,"Pray, who is this man?"

Now although there was no Buddha in the world, and the charioteer had no knowledge of either monks or their good qualities, yet by the power of the gods he was inspired to say,"Sire, this is one who has retired from the world;" and he thereupon proceeded to sound the praises of retirement from the world. The thought of retiring from the world was a pleasing one to the Future Buddha, and this day he went on until he came to the park. The repeaters of the Dīgha,[30] however, say that he went to the park after having seen all the Four Signs on one and the same day.

When he had disported himself there throughout the day, and had bathed in the royal pleasure-tank, he went at sunset and sat down on the royal resting-stone with the intention of adorning himself. Then gathered around him his attendants with diverse- colored cloths, many kinds and styles of ornaments, and with garlands, perfumes, and ointments. At that instant the throne on which Sakka was sitting grew hot. And Sakka, considering who it could be that was desirous of dislodging him, perceived that it was the time of the adornment of a Future Buddha. And addressing Vissakamma, he said,--

"My good Vissakamma, to-night, in the middle watch, prince Siddhattha will go forth on the Great Retirement, and this is his last adorning of himself. Go to the park, and adorn that eminent man with celestial ornaments."

"Very well," said Vissakamma, in assent; and came on the instant, by his superhuman power, into the presence of the Future Buddha. And assuming the guise of a barber, he took from the real barber the turban-cloth, and began to wind it round the Future Buddha's head; but as soon as the Future Buddha felt the touch of his hand, he knew that it was no man, but a god.

Now once round his head took up a thousand cloths, and the fold was like tho a circlet of precious stones; the second time round took another thousand cloths, and so on, until ten times round had taken up ten thousand cloths. Now let no one think, "How was it possible to use so many cloths on one small head?" for the very largest of them all had only the size of a sāma-creeper blossom, and the others that of *kutumbaka* flowers. Thus the Future Buddha's head resembled a *kuyyaka* blossom twisted about with lotus filaments.

And having adorned himself with great richness,--while adepts in different kinds of tabors and tom-toms were showing their skill, and Brāhmaṇs with cries of victory and shouts of praise saluted him,--he mounted his sruperbly decorated chariot.

At this juncture, Suddhodana the king, having heard that the mother of Rāhula had brought forth a son, sent a messenger, saying, "Announce the glad news to my son."

On hearing the message, the Future Buddha said,"An impediment [rāhula] has been born; a fetter has been born."

"What did my son say?" questioned the king; and when he had heard the answer, he said,"My grandson's name shall be prince Rāhula from this very day."

But the Future Buddha in his splendid chariot entered the city with a pomp and magnificence of glory that enraptured all minds. At the same moment Kisā Gotamī, a virgin of the warrior caste, ascended to the roof of her palace, and beheld the beauty and majesty of the Future Buddha, as he circumambulated the city; and in her pleasure and satisfaction at the sight, she burst forth into this song of joy:--

271. "Full happy now that mother is,
Full happy now that father is,
Full happy now that woman is,
Who owns this lord so glorious!"

On hearing this, the Future Buddha thought, "In beholding a handsome figure the heart of a mother attains nirvāṇa, the heart of a father attains *Nirvāṇa*, the heart of a wife attains *Nirvāṇa*. This is what the says. But wherein does *Nirvāṇa* consist?" And to him, whose mind was already averse to passion, the answer came: "When the fire of lust is extinct, that is *Nirvāṇa*; when pride, false belief, and all other passions and torments are extinct, that is *Nirvāṇa*. She has taught me a good lesson. Certainly, *Nirvāṇa* is what I am looking for. It behooves me this very day to quit the household life, and to retire from the world in quest of *Nirvāṇa*.[31] I will send this lady a teacher's fee." And loosening from his neck a pearl necklace worth a hundred thousand pieces of money, he sent it to Kisâ Gotamī. And great was her satisfaction at this, for she thought, "Prince Siddhattha has fallen in love with me, and has sent me a present."

And the Future Buddha entered his palace in great splendor, and lay on his couch of state. And staightway richly dressed women, skilled in all manner of dance and song, and beautiful as celestial nymphs, gathered about him with all kinds of musical instruments, and with dance, song, and music they endeavored to please him. But the Future Buddha's aversion to passion did not allow him to take pleasure in the spectacle, and he fell into a brief slumber. And the women, exclaiming, "He for whose sake we should perform has fallen asleep. Of what use is it to weary ourselves any longer?" threw their various instruments on the ground, and lay down. And the lamps fed with sweet-smelling oil continued to burn. And the Future Buddha awoke, and seating himself cross-legged on his couch, perceived these women lying asleep, with their musical instruments scattered about them on the floor,--some with their bodies wet with trickling phlegm and spittle; some grinding their teeth, and muttering and talking in their sleep; some with their mouths open; and some with their dress fallen apart so as plainly to disclose their loathsome nakedness. This great alteration in their appearance still further increased his aversion for sensual pleasures. To him that magnificent apartment, as splendid as the palace of *Sakka*, began to seem like a cemetery filled with dead bodies impaled and left to rot; and the three modes of existence appeared like houses all ablaze. And breathing forth the solemn utterance, "How oppressive and stifling is it all!" his mind turned ardently to retiring from the world. "It behooves me to go forth on the Great Retirement this very day," said he; and he arose from his couch, and coming near the door, called out,--

"Who's there?"

"Master, it is I, Channa," replied the courtier who had been sleeping with his head on the threshold.[32]

"I wish to go forth on the Great Tetirement to-day. Saddle a horse for me."

"Yes, sire." And taking saddle and bridle with him, the courtier started for the stable. There, by the light of lamps fed with sweet-smelling oils, he perceived the mighty steed Kanthaka in his pleasant quarters, under a canopy of cloth beautified with a pattern of jasmine flowers. "This is the one for me to saddle to- day," thought he; and he saddled Kanthaka.

"He is drawing the girth very tight," thought Kanthaka, whilst he was being saddled; " it is not at all as on other days, when I am saddled for rides in the park and the like. It must be that to-day my master wishes to issue forth on the Great Retirement." And in his delight he neighed a loud neigh. And that neigh would have spread through the whole town, had not the gods stopped the sound, and suffered no one to hear it.

Now the Future Buddha, after he had sent Channa on his errand, thought to himself, "I will take just one look at my son;" and, rising from the couch on which he was sitting, he went to the suite of apartments occupied by the mother of Rāhula, and opened the door of her chamber. Within the chamber was burning a lamp fed with sweet smelling oil, and the mother of Rāhula lay sleeping on a couch strewn deep with jasmine and other flowers, her hand resting on the head of her son. When the Future Buddha reached the threshold, he paused, and gazed at the two from where he stood.

"If I were to raise my wife's hand from off the child's head, and take him up, she would awake, and thus prevent my deprture. I will first become a Buddha, and then come back and see my son." So saying, he descended from the palace.

Now that which is said in the Jātaka Commentary,"At that time Rāhula was seven days old," is not found in the other commentaries. Therefore the account above given is to be accepted.

When the Future Buddha had thus descended from the palace, he came near to his horse, and said,--

"My dear Kanthaka, save me now this one night; and then, when thanks to you I have become a Buddha, I will save the world of gods and men." And thereupon he vaulted upon Kanthada's back.

Now Kanthaka was eighteen cubits long from his neck to his tail, and of corresponding height; he was strong and swift, and white all over like a polished conch-shell. If he neighed or stamped, the sound was so loud as to spread through the whole city; therefore the gods exerted their power, and muffled the sound of his neighing, so that no one heard it; and at every step he took they placed the palms of their hands under his feet.

The Future Buddha rode on the mighty back of the mighty steed, made Channa hold on by the tail, and so arrived at midnight at the great gate of the city.

Now the king, in order that the Future Buddha should not at any time go out of the city without his knowledge had caused each of the two leaves of the gate to be made so heavy as to need a thousand men to move it. But the Future Buddha had a vigor and a strength that was equal, when reckoned in elephant- power, to the strength of ten thousand million elephants, and, reckoned in man-power, to the strength of a hundred thousand million men.

"If," thought he, "the gate does not open, I will straightway grip tight hold of Kanthaka with my thighs, and seated as I am on Kanthaka's back, and with Channa holding on by the tail, I will leap up and carry them both with me over the wall, although its height be eighteen cubits."

"If," thought Channa, "the gate is not opened, I will place my master on my shoulder, and tucking Kanthaka under my arm by passing my right hand round him and under his belly, I will leap up and carry them both with me over the wall."

"If," thought Kanthaka, " the gate is not opened, with my master seated as he is on my back, and with Channa holding on by my tail, I will leap up and carry them both with me over th wall."

Now if the gate had not opened, verily one or another of these three persons would have accomplished that whereof he thought; but the divinity that inhabited the gate opened it for them. At this moment came Māra,[33].with the intention of persuading the Future Buddha to turn back; and standing in the air, he said,--

"Sir, go not forth! For on the seventh day from now the wheel of empire will appear to you, and you shall rule over the four great continents and their two thousand attendant isles. Sir, turn back!"

"Who are you?"

"I am Vasavatti."

"Māra, I knew that the wheel of empire was on the point of appearing to me; but I do not wish for sovereignty. I am about to cause the ten thousand worlds to thunder with my becoming a Buddha."

"I shall catch you," thought Māra, "the very first time you have a lustful, malicious, or unkind thought." And, like an ever-present shadow, he followed after, ever on the watch for some slip.

Thus the Future Buddha, casting away with indifference a universal sovereignty already in his grasp,--spewing it out as if it were but phlegm,--departed from the city in great splendor on the full-moon day of the month Āsālhī[34] when the moon was in Libra. And when he had gone out from the city, he became desirous of looking back at it; but no sooner had the thought arisen in his mind, than the broad earth, seeming to fear lest the Great Being might neglect to perform the act of looking back, split and turned round like a potter's wheel.[35] When the Future Buddha had stood a while facing the city and gazing upon it, and had indicated in that place the spot for the "Shrine of the Turning Back of Kanthaka," he turned Kanthaka in the direction in which he meant to go, and proceeded on his way in great honor and exceeding glory.

For they say the deities bore sixty thousand torches in front of him, and sixty thousand behind him, and sixty thousand on the right hand, and sixty thousand on the left hand. Other deities, standing on the rim of the world, bore torches past all numbering; and still other deities, as well as serpents and birds, accompanied him, and did him homage with heavenly perfumes, garlands, sandal-wood powder, and incense. And the sky was as full of coral flowers as it is of pouring water at the height of the rainy season. Celestial choruses were heard; and on every side bands of music played, some of eight instruments, and some of sixty,--sixty-eight hundred thousand instruments in all. It was as when the storm-clouds thunder on the sea, or when the ocean roars against the *Yugandhara* rocks.

Advancing in this glory, the Future Buddha in one night passed through three kingdoms, and at the end of thirty leagues he came to the river named *Anomā*.

But was this as far as the horse could go? Certainly not. For he was able to travel round the world from end to end, as it were round the rim of a wheel lying on its hub, and yet get back before breakfast and eat the food prepared for him. But on this occasion the fragrant garlands and other offerings which the gods and the serpents and the birds threw down upon him from the sky buried him up to his haunches; and as he was obliged to drag his body and cut his way through the tangled mass, he was greatly delayed. Hence it was that he went only thirty leagues.

And the Future Buddha, stopping on the river-bank, said to Channa,--

"What is the name of this river?"

"Sire, its name is *Anomā* [Illustrious]."

"And my retirement from the world shall also be called *Anomā*," replied the Future Buddha. Saying this, he gave the signal to his horse with his heel; and the horse sprang over the river, which had a breadth of eight usabhas,[36] and landed on the opposite bank. And the Future Buddha, dismounting and standing on the sandy beach that stretched away like a sheet of silver, said to Channa,--

"My good Channa, take these ornaments and Kanthaka and go home. I am about to retire from the world."

"Sire, I also will retire from the world."

Three times the Future Buddha refused him, saying," It is not for you to retire from the world. Go now!" and made him take the ornaments and Kanthaka.

Next he thought, "These locks of mine are not suited to a monk: but there is no one fit to cut the hair of a Future Buddha. Therefore I will cut them off myself with my sword." And grasping a simitar with his right hand, he seized his top-knot with his left hand, and cut it off, together with the diadem. His hair thus became two finger-breadths in length, and curling to the right, lay close to his head. As long as he lived it remained of that length, and the beard was propotionate. And never again did he have to cut either hair or beard.

Then the Future Buddha seized hold of his top-knot and diadem, and threw them into the air, saying,---

"If I am to become a Buddha, let them stay in the sky; but if not, let them fall to the ground."

The top-knot and jewelled turban mounted for a distance of a league into the air, and there came to a stop. And Sakka, the king of the gods, perceiving them with his divine eye, received them in an appropriate jewelled casket, and established it in the Heaven of the Thirty-three as the "Shrine of the Diadem."

272. "His hair he cut, so sweet with many pleasant scents,

This Chief of Men, and high impelled it towards the sky;

And there god Vāsava, the god with thousand eyes,
In golden casket caught it, bowing low his head."

Again the Future Buddha thought, "These garments of mine, made of Benares cloth, are not suited to a monk."

Now the *Mahā-Brahmā* god, Ghaṭikāra, who had been a friend of his in the time of the Buddha Kassapa, and whose affection for him had not grown old in the long interval since that Buddha, thought to himself,---

"To-day my friend has gone forth on the Great Retirement. I will bring him the requisites of a monk."

273. "Robes, three in all, the bowl for alms,
The razor, needle, and the belt,
And water-strainer,---just these eight
Are needed by th' ecstatic monk."

Taking the above eight requistes of a monk, he gave them to him.

When the Future Buddha had put on his most excellent vesture, the symbol of saintship and of retirement from the world, he dismissed Channa, saying,---

"Channa, go tell my father and my mother from me that I am well."

And Channa did obeisance to the Future Buddha; and keeping his right side towards him he departed.

But Kanthaka, who had stood listening to the Future Buddha while he was conferring with Channa, was unable to bear his grief at the thought, "I shall never see my master any more." And as he passed out of sight, his heart burst, and he died, and was reborn in the Heaven of the Thirtythree as the god Kanthaka.

At first the grief of Channa had been but single; but now he was oppressed with a second sorrow in the death of Kanthaka, and came weeping and wailing to the city.

viii. THE GREAT STRUGGLE.

Translated from the Introduction to the Jātaka (i.65[29])

Now the Future Buddha, having thus retired from the world,--in that place there was mango-grove named Anupiya, and here he first spent a week in the joy of having retired from the world,-in one day went on foot to Rājagaha, a distance of thirty leagues, and entering the city, he begged for food from house to house without passing any by. By the beauty of the Future Buddha, the whole city was thrown into a commotion, like that into which Rājagaha was thrown by the entrance of Dhanapālaka, or like that into which the heavenly city was thrown by the entrance of the chief of the Titans.

Then ran the king's men to the palace, and made announcement,--

"Sire, there is a being of such and such appearance going about the city begging for food. Whether he be a god, or a man, or a serpent, or a bird, we do not know."

Then the king, standing on the roof of his palace, and thence beholding the Great Being, became amazed and astonished, and commanded his men,--

"Look ye now! Go and investigate this! If this person be not a man, he will vanish from sight as soon as he leaves the city; if, namely, he be a god, he will depart by way of the air; if a serpent, he will sink into the ground. But if he be a human being, he will eat the food he has obtained in alms."

Now the Great Being, after collecting a number of scraps, sufficient, as he judged, for his sustenance, left the city by the same gate he had entered, and sitting down with his face to the east, in the shade of Paṇḍava rock; he attempted to eat his meal. But his stomach turned, and he felt as if his inwards were on the point of coming out by his mouth. Tereupon, in the midst of his distress at that repulsive food,--for in that existence he had never before so much as seen such fare,--he began to admonish himself, saying,"Siddhattha, althogh you were born into a family having plenty to eat and drink, into a station in life where you lived on fragrant third season's rice[37] with various sauces of the finest flavors, yet when you saw monk clad in garments taken from the rubbish heap, you exclaimed, 'Oh, when shall I be like him, and eat food which I have begged? Will that time ever come?' And then you retired from the world. And now that you have your wish, and have renounced all, what pray, is this you are doing?" When he had thus admonished himself, his disgust subsided, and he ate his meal.

Then the king's men went and announced to the king what they had seen. And the king, on hearing the report of the messengers, issued hastily from the city, and approaching the Future Buddha, and being pleased with his deportment, he tendered him all his kingly glory.

"Great king," replied the Future Buddha, "I do not seek for the gratification of my senses or my passions, but have retired from the world for the sake of the supreme and absolute enlightenment."

"Verily," said the king, when his repeated offers had all been refused, "you are sure to become a Buddha; but when that happens, your first journey must be to my kingdom."

The above is an abridgment, but the full account, begining with the lines,--

"I sing the man of insight keen,

And his retirement from the world,"

can be found by referring to the "Discourses on Retirement from the World," and its commentary.

Then the Future Buddha, having made the king the required promise, proceeded on his way; and coming to Ālāra Kālāma and Uddaka, the disciple of Rāma, he acquired from them the eight stages of meditation. But becoming convinced that they did not lead to enlightenment, he ceased to practise them. And being desirous of making the Great Struggle, so as to show the world of gods and men his fortitude and heroism, he went to Uruvelā, and saying, "Truly, delighful is this spot," he there took up his abode, and began the Great Struggle.

And those five persons, Koṇḍañña and the others, who since their retiremint from the world, were wandering about for alms through villages, market-towns, and royal cities, here met with the Future Buddha. And during the six years of the Great Struggle, they swept his cell, and did all manner of service for him, and kept constantly at his beck and call,

all the time saying, " Now he will become a Buddha, now he will become a Buddha."

And the Future Buddha, thinking,"I will carry austerity to the uttermost," tried various plans, such as living on one sesamum seed or on one grain of rice a day, and even ceased taking nourishment altogether, and moreover rebuffed the gods when they came and attempted to infuse nourishment through the pores of his skin. By this lack of nourishment his body became emaciated to the last degree, and lost its golden color, and became black, and his thirty-two physical characteristics as a great being became obscured. Now, one day, as he was deep in a trance of suppressed breathing, he was attacked by violent pains, and fell senseless to the ground, at one end of his walking-place.

And certain of the deities said, "The monk Gotama is dead;" but others said, "This is a practice of the saints." Then those who thought he was dead went to king Suddhodana, and announced to him that his son was dead.

"Did he die after becoming a Buddha, or before?" asked the king.

"He was unable to become a Buddha, but in making the Struggle, he fell to the ground and died."

When the king heard this, he refused to credit it, saying, "I do not believe it. Death cannot come to my son before he attains to enlightenment."

But why would not the king believe it? Because of the miracles he had seen,-- the first when the ascetic Kāladevala had been compelled to do homage to the Future Buddha, and the other which happened to the rose-apple tree.

But the Future Buddha recovering his consciousness, and standing up, the deities went a second time to the king, and told him that his son was well again.

Said the king, "I knew that my son could not have died."

Now the six years which the Great Being thus spent in austerities were like time spent in endeavoring to tie the air into knots. And coming to the decision, "These austerities are not the way to enlightenment,"he went begging through villages and market- towns for ordinary material food, and lived upon it. And his thirty-two physical characteristics as a great being again appeared, and the color of his body became like unto gold.

Then the band of five priests thought, "It is now six years that this man has been performing austerities without being able to attain to omniscience. And how much less can he be expected to do so in future, now that he has again taken to ordinary material food begged from town to town! He has become luxurious, and given up the Struggle. For us to look for any benefit to come from that quarter would be as reasonable as if a man were to imagine he could bathe his head in a dew-drop. We will have nothing more to do with him." With that they took their bowls and robes, and left the Great Being, and going eighteen leagues off, entered Isipatana.

ix. THE ATTAINMENT OF BUDDHASHIP.

Translated from the Introduction to the Jātaka (i.68[5])

Now at that time there lived in Uruvelā a girl named Sujātā, who had been born in the family of the householder Senāni, in General's Town. On reaching maturity she made a prayer to a certain banyan-tree, saying, "If I get a husband of equal rank with myself, and my first-born is a son, I will make a yearly offering to you of the value of a hundred thousand pieces of money." And her prayer had been successful.

And wishing to make her offering on the day of full moon of the month Visākhā, full six years after the Great Being commenced his austerities, she first pastured a thousand cows in Laṭṭhimadhu Wood and fed their milk to five hundred cows, and the milk of these five hundred cows to two hundred and fifty, and so on down to feeding the milk of sixteen cows to eight. This "working the milk in and in," as it is called, was done to increase the thickness and the sweetness and the strength-giving properties of the milk. And when it came to be the full-moon day of Visākhā, she resolved to make her offering, and rose up early in the morning, just when night was breaking into day, and gave orders to milk the eight cows. The calves had not come at the teats of the cows; yet as soon as new pails were put under the udders, the milk flowed in streams of its own accord. When she saw this miracle, Sujātā took the milk with her own hands and placed it in a new vessel, and herself made a fire and began to cook it. While the milk-rice was cooking, immense bubbles arose, and turning to the right, went round together; but not a single drop ran over the edge, and not a particle of smoke went up from the fireplace. On this occasion the four guardian angels were present, and stood guard over the fireplace; *Mahā-Brahmā* bore aloft the canopy of state, and *Sakka* raked the fire-brands together and made the fire blaze up brightly. And just as a man crushes honey out of a honey-comb that has formed around a stick, so the deities by their superhuman power collected an amount of vital sap sufficient for the sustenance of the gods and men of all the four great continents and their two thousand attendant isles, and infused it into the milk-rice. At other times, to be sure, the deities infuse this sap into each mouthful; but on the day of the attainment of the Buddhaship, and on the day of decease, they place it in the kettle itself.

When Sujātā had seen so many miracles appear to her in one day, she said to her slave-girl Puṇṇā,--

"Puṇṇā, dear girl, the deity is very graciously disposed to us to-day. I have never before seen so many marvellous things happen in so short a time. Run quickly, and get everything ready at the holy place."

"Yes, my lady," replied the slave-girl, and ran in great haste to the foot of the tree.

Now that night the Future Buddha had five great dreams, and on considering their meaning reached the conclusion, "Without doubt I shall become a Buddha this very day."

And when night was over, and he had cared for his person, he came early in the morning to that tree, to await the hour to go begging. And when he sat down he illumined the whole tree with his radiance.

Then came Puṇṇā, and saw the Future Buddha sitting at the foot of the tree, contemplating the eastern quarter of the world. And when she beheld the radiance from his body lighting up the whole tree with a golden color, she became greatly excited, saying to herself, "Our deity, methinks, has come down from the tree to-day and has seated himself ready to receive our offering in person." And she ran in great haste, and told Sujātā of the matter.

When Sujātā heard this news, she was overjoyed; and saying,"From this day forth be to me in the room of an eldest daughter," she decked Puṇṇā with all the ornaments appropriate to that position. And since a Future Buddha on the day he attains the Buddhaship must needs receive a golden dish worth a hundred thousand pieces of money, therefore the idea occurred to her of putting the milk-rice in a golden dish. And bringing out a golden dish that was worth a hundred thousand, she took up the cooking-vessel and began to pour out the milk- rice. All the milk-rice rolled off like water from a lotus-leaf, and exactly filled the dish. Then, covering the dish with another, which was also made of gold, and wrapping it in a cloth, she adorned herself in all her ornaments, and with the dish on her head proceeded in state to the foot of the banyan-tree. As soon as she caught sight of the Future Buddha she was exceedingly overjoyed, supposing him to be the tree-god; and as she advanced she kept constantly bowing. And taking the pot from her head, she uncovered it, and with some flower-scented water in a golden vase, drew near and took up a position close to the Future Buddha. The earthenware bowl which the Future Buddha had kept so long, and which had been given him by Ghaṭīkāra, the *Mahā-Brahmā* god, at that instant disappeared; and the Future Buddha, stretching out his right hand in an attempt to find his bowl, grasped the vase of water. Next Sujātā placed the dish of milk-rice in the hand of the Great Being. Then the Great Being looked at Sujātā; and she perceived that he was a holy man, and did obeisance, and said,--

"Lord, accept my donation, and go whithersoever it seemeth to you good." And adding, "May your wishes prosper like mine own," she departed, caring no more for her golden dish worth a hundred thousand pieces of money than if it had been a dead leaf.

The Future Buddha rose from his seat and walked round the tree with his right side towards it; and taking the dish, he proceeded to the banks of the *Nerañjarā* and descended into its waters, just as many thousands of Future Buddhas before him had descended on the day of their complete enlightenment.--The spot where he bathed is now a place of pilgrimage named Suppatiṭṭhita, and here he deposited the dish on the bank before descending into the water.--After bathing he dressed himself in that garb of saintship which had been the dress of many hundreds of thousands of Future Buddhas before him; and sitting down with his face to the east, he made the whole of the thick, sweet milk-rice into forty-nine pellets of the size of the fruit of the single-seeded palmyra-tree, and ate it. And he took no further nourishment until the end of the seven weeks, or forty-nine days, which he spent on the throne of wisdom after he had become a Buddha. During all that time he had no other nourishment; he neither bathed, nor rinsed his mouth, nor did he ease himself; but was wholly taken up by the delights of the Trances, of the Paths, and of the Fruits.

Now when he had consumed the milk-rice, he took the golden dish; and saying, " If I am to succeed in becoming a Buddha to-day, let this dish go up-stream; but if not, let it go down-stream," he threw it into the water. And it swam, cleaving the stream, until it came to the middle of the river and then, like a fleet horse, it ran up-stream for a distance of eighty cubits, keeping all the while in the middle of the stream. Then it dived into a whirlpool and went to the palace of the black snake-king, and hit, "click! click!" against the dishes that had been used by the last three Buddhas, and took its place at the end of the row. When the black snake-king heard the noise, he exclaimed,--

"But yesterday a Buddha lived,

And now another has been born."

and so on, through several hundred laudatory verses. As a matter of only yesterday and to-day did the times of the snake-king's appearance above ground seem to him; and his body at such times towered up into the sky to a height of one and three quarters leagues.

Then the Future Buddha took his noonday rest on the banks of the river, in a grove of sal-trees in full bloom. And at nightfall, at the time the flowers droop on their stalks, he rose up, like a lion when he bestirs himself, and went towards the Bo-tree, along a road which the gods had decked, and which was eight *usabhas* wide.

The snakes, the fairies, the birds, and other classes of beings did him homage with celestial perfumes, flowers, and other offerings, and celestial choruses poured forth heavenly music; so that the ten thousand worlds were filled with these perfumes, garlands, and shouts of acclaim.

Just then there came from the opposite direction a grass-cutter named Sotthiya, and he was carrying grass. And when he saw the Great Being, that he was a holy man, he gave him eight handfuls of grass. The Future Buddha took the grass, and ascending the throne of wisdom, stood on the southern side and faced the north. Instantly the southern half of the world sank, until it seemed to touch the Avīci hell, while the northern half rose to the highest of the heavens.

"Methinks," said the Future Buddha, "this also cannnot be the place for the attainment of the supreme wisdom;" and walking round the tree with his right side towards it, he came to the western side and faced the east.Then the western half of the world sank, until it seemed to touch the Avāci hell, while the eastern half rose to the highest of the heavens. Wherever, indeed, he stood, the broad earth rose and fell, as though it had been a huge cart-wheel lying on its hub, and some one were treading on the rim.

"Methinks," said the Future Buddha, "this also cannot be the place for the attainment of supreme wisdom;" and walking round the tree with his right side towards it, he came to the northern side and faced the south. Then the northern half of the world sank, until it seemed to touch the Avīci hell, while the southern half rose to the highest of the heavens.

"Methinks," said the Future Buddha,"this also cannot be the place for the attainment of supreme wisdom;" and walking round the tree with his right side towards it, he came to the eastern side and faced the west. Now it is on the eastern side of their Bo-trees that all The Buddhas have sat cross-legged, and that side neither trembles nor quakes.

Then the Great Being, saying to himself, "This is the immovable spot on which all The Buddhas have planted themselves! This is the place for destroying passion's net!"

took hold of his handful of grass by one end, and shook it out there. And straightway the blades of grass formed themselves into a seat fourteen cubits long, of such symmetry of shape as not even the most skilful painter or carver could design.

Then the Future Buddha turned his back to the trunk of the Bo- tree and faced the east. And making the mighty resolution, "Let my skin, and sinews, and bones become dry,and welcome! and let all the flesh and blood in my body dry up! but never from this seat will I stir, until I have attained the supreme and absolute wisdom!" he sat himself down cross-legged in an unconquerable position, from which not even the descent of a hundred thunder-bolts at once could have dislodged him.

At this point the god *Māra*, exclaiming, "Prince Siddhattha is desirous of passing beyond my control, but I will never allow it!" went and announced the news to his army, and sounding the *Māra* war-cry, drew out for battle. Now *Māra's* army extended in front of him for twelve leagues, and to the right and to the left for twelve leagues, and in the rear as far as to the confines of the world, and it was nine leagues high. And when it shouted, it made an earthquake like roaring and rumbling over a space of a thousand leagues. And the god *Māra*, mounting his elephant, which was a hundred and fifty leagues high, and had the name "Girded-with-mountains,"caused a thousand arms to appear on his body, and with these he grasped a variety of weapons. Also in the remainder of that army, no two persons carried the same weapon; and diverse also in their appearances and countenances, the host swept on like a flood to overwhelm the Great Being.

Now deities throughout the ten thousand worlds were busy singing the praises of the Great Being. *Sakka*, the king of the gods, was blowing the conch-shell Vijayuttara. (This conch, they say, was a hundred and twenty cubits long, and when once it had been filled with wind, it would sound for four months before it stopped.) The great black snake-king sang more than a hundred laudatory verses. And *Mahā-Brahmā* stood holding aloft the white umbrella. But as *Māra's* army gradually drew near to the throne of wisdom, not one of these gods was able to stand his ground, but each fled straight before him. The black snake-king dived into the ground, and coming to the snake-abode, Mañjerika, which was five hundred leagues in extent, he covered his face with both hands and lay down. *Sakka* slung his conch-shell Vijayuttara over his back, and took up his position on the rim of the world. *Mahā-Brahmā* left the white umbrella at the end of the world, and fled to his Brahmā-abode. Not a single deity was able to stand his ground, and the Great Being was left sitting alone.

Then said *Māra to* his followers,--

"My friends, Siddhattha, the son of Suddhodana, is far greater than any other man, and we shall never be able to fight him in front. We will attack him from behind."

All the gods had now disappeared, and the Great Being looked around on three sides, and said to himself, "There is no one here." Then looking to the north, he perceived *Māra's* army coming on like a flood, and said,--

"Here is this multitude exerting all their strength and power against me alone. My mother and father are not here, nor my brother, nor any other relative. But I have these Ten Perfections, like old retainers long cherishd at my board. It therefore behooves me to make the Ten Perfections my shield and my sword, and tc strike a blow with them that shall destroy this strong array." And he remained sitting, and reflected on the Ten Perfections.

Thereupon the god *Māra* caused a whirlwind, thinking, "By this will I drive away Siddhattha." Straightway the east wind and all the other different winds began to blow; but although these winds could have torn their way through mountain-peaks half a league, or two leagues, or three leagues high, or have uprooted forest-shrubs and trees, or have reduced to powder and scattered in all directions, villages and towns, yet when they reached the Future Buddha, such was the energy of the Great Being's merit, they lost all power and were not able to cause so much as a fluttering of the edge of his priestly robe.

Then he caused a great rain-storm, saying, "With water will I overwhelm and drown him." And through his mighty power, clouds of a hundred strata, and clouds of a thousand strata arose, and also the other different kinds. And these rained down, until the earth became gullied by the torrents of water which fell, and until the floods had risen over the tops of every forest-tree. But on coming to the Great Being, this mighty inundation was not able to wet his priestly robes as much as a dew-drop would have done.

Then he caused a shower of rocks, in which immense mountain-peaks flew smoking and flaming through the sky. But on reaching the Future Buddha they became celestial bouquets of flowers.

Then he caused a shower of weapons, in which single-edged, and double-edged swords, spears, and arrows flew smoking and flaming through the sky. But on reaching the Future Buddha they became celestial flowers.

Then he caused a shower of live coals, in which live coals as red as *kiṁsuka* flowers flew through the sky. But they scattered themselves at the Future Budha's feet as a shower of celestial flowers.

Then he caused a shower of hot ashes, in which ashes that glowed like fire flew through the sky. But they fell at the Future Buddha's feet as sandal-wood powder.

Then he caused a shower of sand, in which very fine sand flew smoking and flaming through the sky. But it fell at the Future Buddha's feet as celestial flowers.

Then he caused a shower of mud, in which mud flew smoking and flaming through the sky. But it fell at the Future Buddha's feet as celestial ointment.

Then he caused a darkness, thinking, "By this will I frighten Siddhattha, and drive him away." and the darkness became fourfold, and very dense. But on reaching the Future Buddha it disappeared like darkness before the light of the sun.

Māra, being thus unable with these nine storms of wind, rain, rocks, weapons, live coals, hot ashes, sand, mud, and darkness, to drive away the Future Buddha, gave command to his followers, "Look ye now! Why stand ye still? Seize, kill, drive away this prince!" And, arming himself with a discus, and seated upon the shoulders of the elephant

"Girded-with-mountains," he drew near the Future Buddha, and said,--

"Siddhattha, arise from this seat! It does not belong to you, but to me."

When the Great Being heard this he said,--

"*Māra*, you have not fulfilled the Ten Perfections in any of their three grades; nor have you made the five great donations;[38] nor have you striven for knowledge, nor for the welfare of the world, nor for enlightenment. This seat does not belong to you, but to me."

Unable to restrain his fury, the enraged *Māra* now hurled his discus. But the Great Being reflected on the Ten Perfections, and discus changed into a canopy of flowers, and remained suspended over his head. Yet they say that this keen-edged discus, when at other times Māra hurled it in anger, would cut through solid stone pillars as if they had been the tips of bamboo shoots. But on this occasion it became a canopy of flowers. Then the followers of Māra began hurling immense mountain-crags, saying, "This will make him get up from his seat and flee." But the Great Being kept his thoughts on the Ten Perfections, and the crags also became wreaths of flowers, and then fell to the ground.

Now the gods meanwhile were standing on the rim of the world, and craning their necks to look, saying,--

"Ah, woe the day! The handsome form of prince Siddhattha will surely be destroyed! What will he do to save himself?"

Then the Great Being, after his assertion that the seat which Future Buddhas had always used on the day of their complete enlightenment belonged to him, continued, and said,--

"*Māra*, who is witness to your having given donations?" Said *Māra*, "All these, as many as you see here, are my witnesses;" and he stretched out his hand in the direction of his army. And instantly from *Māra's* army came a roar, "I am his witness! I am his witness!" which was like to the roar of an earthquake.

Then said *Māra to* the Great Being,--

"Siddhattha, who is witness to your having given donations?"

"Your witnesses," replied the Great Being, "are animate beings, and I have no animate witnesses present. However, not to mention the donations which I gave in other existences, the Great seven- hundred-fold donation which I gave in my Vessantara existence shall now be testified to by the solid earth, inanimate though she be." And drawing forth his right hand from beneath his priestly robe, he stretched it out towards the mighty earth, and said, "Are you witness, or are you not, to my having given a great seven-hundred-fold donation in my Vessantara existence?"

And the mighty earth thundered, "I bear you witness!" with a hundred, a thousand, a hundred thousand roars, as if to overwhelm the army of *Māra*.

Now while the Great Being was thus calling to mind the donation he gave in his Vessantara existence, and saying to himself, "Siddhattha, that was a great and excellent donation which you gave," the hundred-and-fifty-league-high elephant "Girded-with- mountains" fell upon his knees before the Great Being. And the followers of *Māra* fled away in all directions. No two went the same way, but leaving their head-ornaments and their cloaks behind, they fled straight before them.

Then the hosts of the gods, when they saw the army of *Māra* flee, cried out, "*Māra is* defeated! Prince Siddhattha has conquered! Let us go celebrate the victory!" And the snakes egging on the snakes, the birds the birds, the deities the deities, and the *Brahmā*-angels the *Brahmā*-angels, they came with perfumes, garlands, and other offerings in their hands to the Great Being on the throne of wisdom. And as they came,--

274. "The victory now hath this illustrious Buddha won!
The Wicked One, the Slayer, hath defeated been!"
Thus round the throne of wisdom shouted joyously
The bands of snakes their songs of victory for the Sage;

275. "The Victory now hath this illustrious Buddha won!
The Wicked one, the Slayer, hath defeated been!"
Thus round the throne of wisdom shouted joyously
The flocks of birds their songs of victory for the Sage;

276. "The victory now hath this illustrious Buddha won!
The Wicked One, the Slayer, hath defected been!"
Thus round the throne of wisdom shouted joyously
The bands of gods their songs of victory for the Sage;

277. "The victory now hath this illustrious Buddha won!
The Wicked One, the Slayer, hath defected been!"
Thus round the throne of wisdom shouted joyously
The Brahmā-angels songs of victory for the Saint.

And the remaining deities, also, throughout the ten thousand worlds, made offerings of garlands, perfumes, and ointments, and in many a hymn extolled him.

It was before the sun had set that the Great Being thus vanquished the army of *Māra*. And then, while the Bo-tree in homage rained red, coral-like sprigs upon his priestly robes, he acquired in the first watch of the night the knowledge of previous existences; in the middle watch of the night, the divine eye; and in the last watch of the night, his intellect fathomed Dependent Origination.

Now while he was musing on the twelve terms of Dependent Origination, forwards and backwards, round and back again, the ten thousand worlds quaked twelve times, as far as to their ocean boundaries. And when the Great Being at the dawning of the day, had thus made the ten thousand worlds thunder with his attainment of omniscience, all these worlds became most gloriously adorned. Flags and banners erected on the eastern rim of the world let their streamers fly to the western rim of the world; likewise those erected on the western rim of the world, to the eastern rim of the world; those erected on the northern rim of the world, to the southern rim of the world; and those erected on the southern rim of the world, to the northern rim of the world; while those erected on the level of the earth let theirs fly until they beat against the Brahmā-world; and those of the Brahmā-world let theirs hang down to the level of the earth. Throughout the ten thousand worlds the flowering trees bloomed; the fruit trees were weighted down by their burden of fruit; trunk-lotuses bloomed on the trunks of trees; branch-lotuses on the branches of trees; vine-lotuses on the vines; hanging-lotuses in the sky; and stalk- lotuses burst through the rocks and came up by sevens. The system of ten thousand worlds was like a bouquet of flowers sent whirling through the air, or like a thick carpet of flowers; in the intermundane spaces the eight-thousand-league-long hells, which not even the light of seven suns had formerly been able to illumine, were now flooded with radiance; the eighty-four- thousand-league-deep ocean became sweet to the taste; the rivers checked their flowing; the blind from birth received their sight; the deaf from birth their hearing; the cripples from birth the use of their limbs; and the bonds and fetters of captives broke and fell off.

When thus he had attained to omniscience and was the centre of such unparalleled glory and homage, and so many prodigies were happening about him, he breathed forth that solemn utterance whih has never been omitted by any of The Buddhas:--

278. "Through birth and rebirth's endless round,
Seeking in vain, I hastened on,
To find who framed this edifice.
What misery!-- birth incessantly!

279. "O builder! I've discovered thee!

This fabric thou shalt ne'er rebuild!

Thy rafters all are broken now,

And pointed roof demolished lies!

This mind has demolition reached,

And seen the last of all desire!"

The period of time, therefore, from the existence in the Tusita Heaven to this attainment of omniscience on the throne of wisdom, constitutes the Intermediate Epoch.

x. FIRST EVENTS AFTER THE ATTAINMENT OF BUDDHASHIP.

Translated from the Mahā-Vagga, and constituting the opening sections.

Hail to that Blessed One, that Saint and Supreme Buddha!

At that time The Buddha, The Blessed One, was dwelling at Uruvelā at the foot of the Bo-tree on the banks of the river *Nerñjarā*, having just attained the Buddhaship. Then The Blessed One sat cross-legged for seven days together at the foot of the Bo-tree experiencing the bliss of emancipation.

Then the Blessed One, during the first watch of the night, thought over Dependent Origination both forward and back:--

On ignorance depends *karma;*

On *karma* depends consciousness;

On consciousness depend name and form;

On name and form depend the six organs of sense;

On the six organs of sense depends contact;

On contact depends sensation;

On sensation depends desire;

On desire depends attachment;

On attachment depends existence;

On existence depends birth;

On birth depend old age and death, sorrow, lamentation, misery, grief, and despair.

Thus does this entire aggregation of misery arise. But on the complete fading out and cessation of ignorance ceases *karma*; on the cessation of *karma* ceases consciousness; on the cessation of consciousness cease name and form; on the cessation of name and form cease the six organs of sense; on the cessation of the six organs of sense ceases contact; on the cessation of contact ceases sensation; on the cessation of sensation ceases desire; on the cessation of desire ceases attachment; on the cessation of attachment ceases existence; on the cessation of exitence ceases birth; on the cessation of birth cease old age and death, sorrow, lamentation, misery, grief, and despair. Thus does this entire aggregation of misery cease.

Then The Blessed One, concening this, on that occasion, breathed forth this solemn utterance,--

"When to the strenuous, meditative Brāhmaṇa

There come to light the elements of being,

Then vanish all his doubts and eager questions,

What time he knows THE ELEMENTS HAVE CAUSES."

Then The Blessed One, during the middle watch of the night, thought over Dependent Origination both forward and back:--On ignorance depends *karma*...Thus does this entire aggregation of misery arise. But on the complete fading out and cessation of ignorance ceases *karma*...Thus does this entire aggregation of misery cease.

Then The Blessed One, concerning this, on that occasion, breathed forth this solemn utterance,--

"When to the strenuous, meditative Brāhmaṇa

There come to light the elements of being,

Then vanish all his doubts and eager questions,

What time he knows HOW CAUSES HAVE AN ENDING."

Then The Blessed One, during the last watch of the night, thought over Dependent Origination both forward and back:--On ignorance depends karma...Thus does this entire aggregation of misery arise. But on the complete fading out and cessation of ignorance ceases karma...Thus does this entire aggregation of misery cease.

Then The Blessed One, concerning this, on that occasion, breathed forth this solemn utterance,--

"When to the strenuoous, meditative Brāhmaṇa

There come to light the elements of being,

Then scattereth he the hordes of Māra's army;

Like to the sun that lightens all the heavens."

End of the account of what took place under the Bo-tree.

Then The Blessed One, after the lapse of seven days, arose from that state of exalted calm, and leaving the foot of the Bo-tree, drew near to where the Ajapāla (that is, the Goatherd's) banyan-tree was; and having drawn near, he sat cross-legged at the foot of the Ajapāla banyan-tree for seven days together, experiencing the bliss of emancipation.

Then a certain Brāhmaṇa, who was of a proud and contemptuous disposition, drew near to where The Blessed One was; and having drawn near, he exchanged greetings with The Blessed One. And having passed with him the greetings of friendship and civility, he stood respectfully at one side. And standing respectfully at one side, the Brāhmaṇa spoke to The Blessed One as follows:--

"Gotama, what is it constitutes a *Brāhmaṇa*? and what are the Brāhmaṇa-making qualities?"

Then The Blessed One, concerning this, on that occasion, breathed forth this solemn utterance,--

"The Brāhmaṇa who his evil traits hath banished,

Is free from pride, is self-restrained and spotless, Is learned, and the holy life hath followed,

'T is he alone may claim the name of Brāhmaṇa;

With things of earth he hath no point of contact."

End of the account of what took place under the Ajapāla-tree.

Then The Blessed One, after the lapse of seven days, arose from that state of exalted calm, and leaving the foot of the Ajapāla banyan-tree, drew near to where the Mucalinda tree was; and having drawn near, he sat cross-legged at the foot of the Mucalinda tree for seven days together, experiencing the bliss of emancipation.

Now at that time a great cloud appeared out of season, and for seven days it was rainy, cloudy weather, with a cold wind. Then issued Mucalinda, the serpent-king, from his abode, and enveloping the body of The Blessed One seven times with his folds, spread his great hood above his head, saying,--

"Let neither cold nor heat, nor gnats, flies, wind, sunshine, nor creeping creatures come near The Blessed One!

Then, when seven days had elapsed, and Mucalinda, the serpent- king, knew that the storm had broken up, and that the clouds had gone, he unwound his coils from the body of The Blessed One. And changing his natural appearance into that of a young man, he stood before The Blesse One, and with his joined hands to his forehead did reverence to The Blessed One.

Then The Blessed One, concerning this, on that occasion, breathed forth this solemn utterance,--

"How blest the happy solitude
Of him who hears and knows the truth!
How blest is harmlessness towards all,
And self-restraint towards living things!
How blest from passion to be free,
All sensuous joys to leave behind!
Yet far the highest bliss of all
To quit th' illusion false--'I am.'"

End of the account of what took place under the Mucalinda-tree.

Notes and References :

1. This entire story is related by The Buddha to his disciples, and describes how, in his long-ago existence as the *Brāhmaṇa* Sumedha, he first resolved to strive for the Buddhaship. In stanzas 12-16 he speaks of himself, that is, of Sumedha, in the third person, but elsewhere in the first.
2. Only six of the ten noises indicative of a flourishing town are here mentioned. For the complete list, see *Mahā-Parinibbāna Sutta*. No. 16 of *Dīgha Nikāya* Chapter vi page 53[16]
3. Probably gold, silver, pearls, gems (such as sapphire and ruby), cat's eye, diamond, and coral; or perhaps the wheel of empire, the elephant, the horse, the gem the empress, the treasurer, and the crown-prince.
4. Lust, hatred, and infatuation. Compare page 54, and also the "Fire-sermon," *Mahā-vagga*(i.21[1])
5. The two eyes, ears, and so forth, as enumerated in *Visuddhi magga* (chap. vi)
6. The Himalaya mountains. *Himalaya and Himavant* are Sanskrit words of almost identical singnification. The former means "snow-abode", and is a compound of *hima*, "snow", and *ālaya*, "settling down place" or "abode." *Hima-vant* meams "snowy."
7. Native gloss: *Jātaka*, vol. i., p.7,1.14: *Exempted from the five defects*: The following are the five defects in a walking-place: hardness and unevenness: trees in the midst; dense underbrush; excessive narrowness; excessive width. For if the walking-place be on hard and uneven ground, then any one who uses it hurts and blisters his feet, so that he fails of concentration of mind, and his meditation is broken up; while he who walks at ease on a soft and even surface succeeds in meditation. Therefore hardness and uneveness of surface are to be reckoned as one defect. If a walking-place have trees in it, whether in the middle or at the end, then any one who uses it is liable, if not careful, to strike his forehead or his head aginst them. Therefore trees in the midst are a second defect. If a walking-place be overgrown with a dense underbursh of grass, vines,

and so forth, any one who uses it in the dark is liable to tread upon snakes and other creatures and kill them, or they may bite and injure him. Thus a dense underbrush is a third defect. If a walking-place be excessively narrow, say only a cubit or half a cubit wide, then any one who uses it is liable to stumble at the broders and stub his toes and break his toe-nails. Therefore excessive narrowness is fourth defect. If a walking-place be excessively wide, then any one who uses it is liable to have his mind wander and fail of concentration. Thus excessive width is fifth defect. A walking- place should be a path a cubit and a half in breadth, with a margin of a cubit on either side, and it should be sixty cubits in length, and it should have a surface soft and evenly sprinkled with sand.

8. Ibidem, 1.30. *And having all the virtues eight*: Having the eight advantages for a monk. The following are the eight advantages for a monk: it admits of no storing-up of treasure or grain; it favors only a blameless alms-seeking; there one can eat his alms in peace and quiet; there no annoyance is experienced from the reigning families when they oppress the kingdom with their levies of the precious metals or of leaden money; no passionate desire arises for furniture and implements; there is no fear of being plundered by robbers; no intimacies are formed with kings and courtiers; and one is not shut in any of the four directions.

9. Native gloss: *Jātaka*, vol.i.,p.8,1.27: *For cloaks possess the nine defects*: ...For one who retires from the world and takes up the life of an anchorite, there are nine defects inherent in garments of cloth. The great cost is one defect; the fact that it is got by dependecne on others is another: the fact that it is easily soiled by use is another, for when it has been soiled it must be washed and dyed; the fact that when it is much worn it must needs be patched and mended is another; the difficulty of obtaining a new one when needed is another; its unsuitableness for an anchorite who has retired from the world is another; its acceptableness to one's enemies is another, for it must needs be guarded lest the enemy take it; the danger that it may be worn for ornament

is another; the temptation it affords to load one's self down with it in travelling is another.

10. The bast, or inner bark of certain trees, was much used in India as cloth, to which indeed it bears a striking resemblance.---Native gloss: *Jātaka*, vol.i.,p.9,1.2: *Which is with virtues twelve endued*: Possessing twelve advantages. For there are twelve advantages in a dress of bark. It is cheap, good, and suitable, this is one advantage. You can make it yourself; this is a second. It gets dirty but slowly by use, and hence time is not wasted in washing it; this is a third. It never needs sewing, even when much used and worn; this is a fourth. But when a new one is needed, it can be made with ease; this is a fifth. Its suitableness for an anchorite who has retired form the world is a sixth. That it is of no use to one's enemies is a seventh. That it cannot be worn for ornament is an eighth. Its lightness is ninth. Its conducing to moderation in dress is a tenth. The irreporachableness and blamelessness of searching for bark is an eleventh. And the unimportance of its loss is a twelfth.

11. Native gloss: *Jātaka*, vol.i., p.9,1.11: *My hut of leaves I then forsook,So crowded with the eight defects*: ...(L.36) For there are eight evils connected with the use of a leaf-hut. The great labor involved in searching for materials and in the putting of them together is one evil. The constant care necessary to replace the grass, leaves, and bits of clay that fall down is a second. Houses may do for old men, but no concentration of mind is possible when one's meditation is liable to be interrupted; thus the liability to interruption is a third. The protection affected against heat and cold renders the body delicate, and this is a foruth. In a house all sorts of evil deeds are possible; thus the cover it affords for disgraceful practices is a fifth. The taking possession, saying."This is mine," is sixth. To have a house is like having a companion; this is a seventh. And the sharing of it with many others, as for instance with lice, bugs, and house-lizards, is an eighth.

12. Ibidem, p.10,1.9: *And at the foot of trees I lived. For such abodes have virtues ten:....* The following are the ten virtues. The smallness of the undertaking is one virtue, for all that is necessary is simply to go to the tree. The small amount of care it requires is a second; for, whether swept or unswept, it is suitable for use. The freedom form interruption is a third. If affords no cover for disgraceful practices; wickedness there would be too public; thus the fact that it affords no cover for disgraceful practices is a fourth. It is like living under the open sky, for there is no feeling that the body is confined; thus the non-confinement of body is a fifth. There is no taking possession; this is a sixth. The abandonment of all longings for houshold life is a seventh. When a house is shared with others, some one is liable to say, "I will look after this house myself. Begone!" Thus the freedom form eviction is an eighth. The happy contentment experienced by the occupant is a ninth. The little concern one need feel about lodgings, seeing that a man can find a tree no matter where he may be stopping,---this is a tenth.

13. Translated from the prose of the *Jātaka*, vol.i., p. 10, last line but one: At his [Dipaṁkara's] conception, birth, attainment of Buddhaship, and when he caused the Wheel of Doctrine to roll, the entire system of ten thousand worlds trembled, quivered, and shook, and roared with a mighty roar; also the Thirty-Two Prognostics appeared. [For the Thirty-Two Prognostics, see page-40.]

14. Native gloss: *Jātaka*,vol,i.p.13,1.31: As he lay in the mud, he opened his eyes again, and gazing upon the Buddha-glory of Dīpaṁkara, The Possessor of the Ten Forces, he reflected as follows: "If I so wished, I might burn up all my corruptions, and as novice follow with the congregation when they enter the city of Ramma; but I do not want to burn up my corruptions and enter *Nirvāṇa* unknown to any one. What now if, I like Dīpaṁkara, were to acquire the supreme wisdom, were to cause multitudes to go on board the ship of Doctrine and cross the ocean of the round of rebirth, and were

afterwards to pass into *Nirvāṇa*! That would be somthing worthy of me!"

15. Native gloss: *Jātaka*, vol.i. p.14.1.20: For it is only a human being that can successfully wish to be a Buddha; a serpent, or a bird,or a deity cannot successfully make the wish. Of human beings it is only one of the male sex that can make the wish; it would not be successful on the part of a woman, or of a eunuch, or of a neuter, or of a hermaphrodite. Of men it is he, and only he, who is in a fit condition by the attainment of saintship in that same existence, that can successfully make the wish. Of these in a fit condition it is only he who makes the wish in the prefence of a living Buddha that succeeds in his wish; after the death of a Buddha a wish made at a relice-shrine, or at the foot of a Bo-tree, will not be successful. Of those who make the wish in the presence of a Buddha it is he, and only he, who has retired form the world that can sucessfully make the wish, and not one who is a lay man. Of those who have retired form the world it is only he who is possessed of the Five High Powers and is master of the Eight Attainments that can successfully make the wish and no one can do so who is lacking in these excellences. Of those, even, who possess these excellences it is he, and only he, who has such firm resolve that he is ready to sacrifice his life for the Buddhas that can successfully make the wish but no other. Of those who possess this resolve it is he, and only he, who has great zeal, determination, strenuousness, and endeavor in striving for the qualities that make a Buddha that is successful. The following comparisons will show the intensity of the zeal. If he is such a one as to think: "The man who, if all within the rim of the world were to become water, would be ready to swim across it with own arms and get to the further shore,---he is the one to attain the Buddhaship; or in case all within the rim of the world were to become a jungle of bamboo, would be ready to elbow and trample his way through it and get to the further side,---he is the one to attain the Buddhaship ; or, in case all within the rim of the world were to become a *terra firma* of thick-set javelins,

would be ready to tread on them and go a foot to the further side,---he is the one to attain the Buddhaship; or, in case all within the rim of the world were to become live coals, would be ready to tread on them and so get to the further side,---he is the one to attain the Buddhaship,"--- if he deems not even one of these feats too hard for himself, but has such great zeal, determination, strenuousness, and power of endeavor that he would perform these feats in order to attain the Buddhaship, then, but not otherwise, will his wish succeed.

16. Better known as Magallāna and Säriputta, repectively.
17. Ficus religiosa.
18. There have been many beings who, like Sumedha here, were to become Buddhas, and who were therefore called Bodhi-sattas or "Future Buddhas." The certainty of their ultimate" Illumination," or Buddhaship, was always foretokened by certain presages. The "dwellers of ten thousand worlds" describe in the following stanzas what these presages were, declare that they are reappearing now, and announce to Sumedha their prophetic inference that he will attain Buddhaship.
19. This refrain is added to these stanzes in the *Buddha-Vaṁsa*. In the *Jātaka* it is omitted.
20. The four cardinal points of the compass, the four intermediate points, the zenith and nadir.
21. See *Visuddhi-Magga,* chapter i.
22. The Vessantara Birth-Stroy is the last of the five hundred and fifty.
23. I despair of giving in metre more than the general drift of these two lines. See Hardy. *"Manual of Buddhism,"* chap.ii.s.11.
24. *Abhidhammattha-Saṅgaha* (v. 2-6 and 10)
25. The stroy of the Future Buddha's existence as the Wise Hare is given further on under the caption, "The Hare-Mark in the Moon." It is the only one of the numerous Birth-Stroies above mentioned that is to be found in this book. The stanza quoted, however, is not taken from that account, but from another work called

Cariyā-Piṭaka, which is wholly in poetry. The *Cariyā-Piṭaka* consists of Birth-Stories, and, besides the Wise Hare, gives several others of those here mentioned. Some are also briefly alluded to in th ninth chapter of the *Visuddhi-Magga*; but of course the grat treasure-house for Birth-Stories is the Jātaka itself.

26. That is, "How long is she to live after conceiving me?" And the answer is, "Ten lunar [that is, the nine calendar] months of my mother's pregnancy, and seven days after my birth."

27. In making up this number the Future Buddha is to be counted as number 1, and four urns of teasure together as number 7.

28. The Nālaka course of conduct is given in the Nālaka Sutta of the *Sutta-Nipāta*, and consists of a number of precepts for leading the holy life.

29. See p. 39. They presumably were the spokesmen for the sixty four, as here for the one hundred and eight.

30. *Dīgha-Nikāya*

31. The Future Buddha puns upon the word "happy" in Kisā Gotami's verses. The word in Pāli is *nibbuta* and is in form a past passive participle of a verb which perhaps does not occur in Pāli in any finite form, but which appears in Sanskrit as *nirvṛ*. Now there is a Pāli verb of which the third person singular peresent indicative a *nibbāyati*, and from this verb is formed the verbal noun *nibbāna* (Sanskrit, *Nirvāṇa*). *Nibbuta* is constantly made to do duty as past passive participale to this verb, so that what would be the true form (*nibbāta) is never found*. The Future Buddha therefore puns when he pretends that Kisā Gotami was using *nibbuta* as the participle of *nibbāyati* , and was urging him to *Nirvāṇa*. The verb *nibbāyati* means "to be extinguished," as the flame of a candle! and when used as a metaphysical term, refers to the fires of lust, desire, etc. And as when fire is extinguished coolness results (as consummation devoutly to be wished in a hot climate like India), the verb acquires the further meaning of "be assuaged." "become happy." And in like manner the verbal noun *Nirvāṇa* (in Pāli *nibbāna*). meaning both

literally and metaphorically "becoming extinguished." comes to stand for the *summum bonum*.

I add a restraslation of the passage, to show the punning meanings given by the Future Buddha to the words, *nibbuta, nibbāyati.* and *Nirvāṇa*:---

"*Nirvāṇa* hath that mother gained,
Nirvāṇa hath that father gained
Nirvāna hath that woman gained
Who owns this lord so glorious!"

On hearing this the Future Buddha thought, "In beholding a hand-some form the heart of a mother is made happy (*nibbāyati*), the heart of a father is made happy, the heart of wife is made happy. This is what she says. But wherein does happiness (*nibbuta*) consist?"And to him whose mind was already averse to passion, the anwer came: "When the fire of lust is assuaged (*nibbuta*) , that is happiness (*nibbuta*); when the fire of hatred and infatuation are assuaged, that is happiness; when pride, false belief, and all other passions and tornents are assuaged, that is happiness. She has taught me a good lesson. Certainly, happiness (*Nirvāṇa*) is what I am looking for. It behooves me this very day to quit the household life and to retire form the world in quest of happiness. I will send this lady a teacher's fee."

32. In India it is coustomary to hang doors at the height of about two feet form the ground for the sake of coolness and ventilation. The threshold is thus exposed even when the door is shut.

33. The Buddhists recognize no real devil. *Māra,* the ruler of the sixth and highest heaven of sensual pleasure, approaches the nearest to our Satan. He stands for the pleasure of sense, and hence is the Buddha's nautral enemy.

34. About the first of July.

35. I think the conception here is that a round portion of the earth, in which the Future Buddha stood, turned around like a modern rail-road turn-table, thus detaching itself form the rest and turning the Future Buddha with it.

36. An *usabha* is 140 cubits.

37. A garment new, a new-built house,
A new umbrella, and a bride,---
The new is good; but long-kept rice
And long-kept servants men do praise.

Form the Sanskrit of the *Nītipradīpa*, 15, as given by Bohtlingk, *Indische Sprūche*, 3410.

38. These are the five donations great:
The gift of treasure, gift of child,
The gift of wife, of royal rule,
And last, the gift of life and limb.

—Form the *Abhidhānappadīpikā*, 421.

CHAPTER 2

THE QUEST OF THE HISTORIC ŚĀKYA-MUNI

—Dr. Kenneth J. Saunders

After nearly a century of Western scholarship the quest of the historic Śākyamuni still goes on, and controversy is vigorous. Of no historic figure are so many divergent views held and defended. Nor is Eastern thought less at variance. Buddhists themselves hold many different views about their Master. "The diamond-throne of the original enlightenment", says Okakura Kakuzo "is now hard indeed to discover, surrounded as it is by the labyrinths of gigantic pillars and elaborate porticoes which successive architects have erected, as each added his portion to the edifice of faith."[1] That is true as well as beautiful. And it is not only because of the elaboration of Buddhism by later sects that it is hard to find the Founder: it is because those who claim to be nearest to him are themselves widely divided in their attitude towards him. Not only is there the wide gulf between the so-called "Mahāyāna" and "Hinayāna,": between Sanskrit and Pāli versions : in the Pāli Canon itself there are several stages of Buddhology which await critical evaluation; and until we have some clear evidence as to what was central in the Founder's person and mission the whole question remains in confusion. *Was* the house of Buddhism a "House of Faith"? To Mrs. Rhys Davids and to many a modern Neo-Buddhist it was a house of scientific thought; and the Buddha is revealed sitting upon a diamond-throne of dialectic, "Surely a notable milestone in the history of human ideas," says Mrs. Rhys Davids (in commenting upon the Buddhist formula of causation 'that being present this becomes; that being absent this does not become,') "That a man reckoned for ages by thousands as the Light not of Asia only but of the world,and the Saviour from sin and misery, should call this little formula his Norm or Gospel, or at least one aspect of that Gospel."[2] This view, which clearly is only one phase of Mrs. Rhys Davids' interpretation, has been lately attacked by Dr. Berriedale Keith who maintains that "given the psychological conditions of the time, it would have been a miracle had the Buddha been capable of the rationalism imputed to him...It was the age of the growth of the great gods Śiva and Viṣṇu in their various forms, and Buddha's success was due to the fact that he either had claims to divinity or his followers attributed it to him, and won general acceptance for the view. It is conceivable that divinity was thrust upon him against his will, but every ground of probability supports the plain evidence of the texts that he himself had claims which necessarily conferred upon him a place as high as the rank of the greatest of gods."[3] These two positions may be said to express the extremes of Western scholarship in its attempt to discover the historic Śākyamuni. For one he is Rationalist, for the other Deity. The one emphasises reason as essential to his disciples, the other faith.

These views are not new, but they are here more emphatically stated than has been usual, and the issue is joined. It is long since Kern insisted that Buddhism "is professedly no rationalistic system but a super-human law founded upon the decree of an omniscient and infallible Master."[4] And recently L. de la Vallee Poussin has argued that "Buddhism, which does appeal to reason and which will later reason freely, place intuition, Jñāna, above all. It is in ecstasy that one sees things truly.[5] "Buddhism", says Dr. Sten Konow, "is essentially a *"jñāna-mārga."*

The confusion thought in which Western scholarship finds itself may be partly explained by the misinterpretation of Jñāna, and partly by the statement of Hermann Oldenberg, who said nearly fifty years ago.: "The Indian mind was wanting in that simplicity which can believe without knowing, as well as in that bold clearness which seeks to know without believing, and therefore the Indian had to frame a doctrine, a religion and a philosophy combined, and therefore perhaps, if it must be said, neither the one nor the other , Buddhism."[6]

Buddhism is, infact, a Middle Path in this as in every-thing else. Not only it is a Middle Path between the way of the world and the way of the ascetic, it is also a Middle Path between the way of the rationalist and the way of the man of faith; and in placing the emphasis most truly we shall probably do well to follow the clue given us by Senart---a view held by Śaṅkara and familiar to Indian thought--- that Śākyamuni was essentially a Yogī, an early Mystic who because he himself had realised the ineffable experience of the conquest of *Tanhā*, spoke with authority to the conscience and heart of man: and because he was also a thinker seeking to explain this great experience and an ethical teacher seeking to reform men explained it as the cessation of *Tanhā* and went on to the further interpretation that it means also *Bhava-Nirodha*, or escape from *Saṁsāra*. Himself more interested in the experience of *Nirvāṇa* than in the explanation, he was yet an Indian teacher seeking to lead others to *Mokṣa*. to use the categories of Indian thought, and to set forth *Nirvāṇa* as freedom from Saṁsāra. What is central there is *jñāna*, intuition, mystical experience of Turth: and Śākyamuni is the great Yogī.

Many Western writers have trembled on the verge of this interpretation. Most of them have fallen back upon the conclusion that here was an early Socrates, or an early Hume. There is truth in these positions; what makes them false is that inveterate tendency of the "either or". With one recent Indian statement,that of Dr. B. Barua, that Buddha was essentially a philosopher, some may be found to agree; but Dr. Barua[7] himself goes on to quote that very vital passage in which the Teacher says "There are things profound, hard to realise, hard to understand, yet tranquilising, sweet, not to be grasped by logical reason, subtle, intelligible only by the wise. It is for these things that the Buddha must be rightly praised. "Here then is a key passage: it is not for his morality or moral teaching, not for his use of logical reason, not for his philosophical achievements that the founder is to be praised, it is for that apprehension of mystical truth which is the Buddhist equivalent of the *Neti, neti* of the *Upanishads,* and expression "from which words turn back"---and which later Buddhists of the Mahāyāna recognizing it as the essence of Buddhism -- call *Śunyatā* the Void, the Ineffable. It is the language of all Mystics from Śākyamuni to Eckhart.

It is in other words as a Yogī who grasps things by intuition that Śākyamuni claims originality; and yet if we are to accept the passage in *Majjhima Nikāya*, ii 19, as early and authentic he calls himself a *Vibhajjavādin*, that is an Analyst, rather than an *Ekamsavādin* or Synthetist. This also may be true. For the Mystic may also have in him something of the rationalist; and if he is to communicate his experience he must seek at any rate to make it intelligible to others. The age was not as Dr. Keith allows himself to argue "a barbarous age", it was one of mystical seers like those of the *Upanishads*, and of a vigorous dialectic like that of the sixty- two schools mentioned in Buddhist texts. The Indian Renaissance was at its height. Some, at any rate, of these were philosophers, and some were rationalists. Dr. Keith is the last scholar to ignore such rationalism as that of the Sāmkhya. Senart's view that Śākyamuni was an early Yogī has long been before us: in 1889 he said emphatically "Buddhism is not a philosophic sect: it is a system of Yoga."[8] And in 1900 he worked out this view,[9] and showed that we have in the four *Dhyānas* of Buddhism (a central doctrine and practice common to Northern and Southern Buddhism, and therefore very old) an even older Indian practice, which is of the essence of *Yoga*. The famous Buddhist practice of *Brahma-Vihāra* carries in its very name the proof of its origin, and Patañjali in his *Yoga- Sutras* uses the very works of the Pāli texts a proof that he looked upon these practices of *Mettam*-Benevolence, *Karuṇā*-Compassion, *Muditā*-Sympathy, and *Upekhā*- Balance or Detachment, as common property, not distinctively Buddhist, but belonging to Yoga as such.

The four stages, again by which the Buddha analyses the disease of the world, and lays down the essential treatment known as the "Four Noble Truths" of Buddhism, are the old stages of medical diagnosis which we find coming up again in the *Yoga Sūtras;* and as the technique of meditation leading to ecstasy is the same, so are the powers of *Iddhi* to which they lead, remembrances of past lives, power to pass through space, and so on.

Much might be said on this subject; but here it may suffice to note that in the great works of art of the Andhra and Gupta periods exemplified in the solitary Buddha in the jungles of Anurādhapura and in the even more deserted Dear Park at Sārnāth, the artists have left to us the clear proof that they thought of him as a Yogī, seated with eyes closed, regulating his breath, with head and trunk in one line, and with hands folded in meditation. Here in fact is *Samādhi* which is the crown and goal of the Eight-fold Noble Path. This Path, though it begins with right views, is in fact a Path for the Mystic, and ends in right ecstasy. It is in fact a rational Mysticism.

And as these old masterpieces of Buddhist art may be looked upon as strong rocks amidst the shifting sands of the Texts and the surging waves of the Schools, so when we look at the modern practice of the Buddhist Monk, whether in Ceylon with its strange meditation upon skeletons, or in some Zen temple in Japan, or in the Chan meditation-school of China and Korea, we find that the living heart of Buddhism, amidst much that is dead and corrupt, is this practice. It is this and this alone which keeps alive the old faith which, because it is essentially Yoga, is able to attach to itself almost any outward observance. Yoga is in fact, as Poussin has said, a technique "in itself strange to all morals as to all religions and philosophic theory, but from this technique there can be separated out, and to it there can be added, morals, theology and devotion."[10]

At the core then of early Buddhism was the Solitary, the great Seer the Yogī Śākyamuni, surrounded by a small group of others who had caught his spirit, and entered into some of these difficult practices. At the circumference were all sorts of lay-people, to whom he could not communicate even an idea of such things. For them he had a different teaching, a different technique and to them he offered a different goal. "Whatsoever householder desires to be reborn in a heaven let him attach himself to me with faith and devotion," says the *Majjhima Nikāya*, "but whatsoever monk would realise Nirvāṇa let him tread the Noble Eight-fold Path,"; for the way of the Mystic is a difficult and elusive way, open only to those who have the original spiritual genius to tread it, and who are prepared to give their whole time and attention to its pursuit. The layman *may* attain *Nirvāṇa*; it is very unlikely that he will ever attempt it. That his interpretation of this profound experience of *Nirvāṇa* is what it is, is due to the fact that Śākyamuni was an Indian of the Sixth century before Chirst, and could only explain it in terms of current thought; that he was a great original thinker is evidenced by the fact that he had the courage to interpret it ethically rather than metaphysically, and to urge upon men that what mattered was the moral emancipation rather than the monistic interpretation. And even to the laity like Sigālo, whom we find worshipping the gods of the four quarters, he insists that the true worship of the gods is righteous living; to honour Mother and Father, to treat one's household aright, this is to pay respect to the gods. To the specialist to meditate upon the great virtues or graces of Kindness, Compassion and Sympathy, this is the true Mysticism; and it will lead on to that *Upekhā*, or Yoga, which is Balance, Harmony and Poise. The world is out of joint because men are following false views, and obsessed with false pursuits. This is the meaning of *Dukkhaṁ*, and over against it Śākyamuni holds out the alluring vision of that Yoga--Calm, *Sānti*, Peace, which he has himself experienced. This and this alone is *Sukkhaṁ*--Joy, Harmony. From the ordinary Yogī this great one differed in that his experience was profound and ethical -- and that he established the practice on a rational basis. From the seers of the *Upanishads* he differed in bringing into daily life some of the glamour or the Ineffable and in insisting more strongly that the way of salvation is a Way of Purity.

Note and References :

1. Kakuzo, Okakura, *The Ideals of the East p. 60*

2. Rhys Davids, Mrs. *Buddhism* p. 89.

3. Keith, A.B. *Buddhist Philosophy* p. 29

4. Kern, H. *Indian Buddhism,* p. 50

5. Poussin, L.de la Vallee, *The way to Nirvāṇa,* p. 15

6. Oldenberg, H. *Buddha, His Life His Doctrine, His Order* p. 6.

7. Barua, Benimadhab, *Prolegomena to A History of Buddhist Philosophy,* quoting *Dialogues of the Buddha,* ii 33-36.

8. Revue des Deux Mondes.

9. See Buddhism et Yoga. Revue d'Histoire des Religions,1900, volume II p. 345.

10. Ponssin op. cit, p. 12.

CHAPTER 3

MAHĀVĪRA AND BUDDHA

—Kamta Praśad Jain, M.R.A.S.

'How to emancipate Man from the trammels of the world', has been the subject of a rational speculation to Indian philosophers from time immemorial. The Jainas say that it was their first Tīrthaṅkara, Lord Ṛṣabha, who showed the Right Path to the suffering humanity at the very dawn of civilisation of *karmabhūmi*--millions of millions years ago in the present cycle of time in this part of earth called *Bhārat-Kṣetra*.[1] The Hindu Purāṇas, too, testify it.[2] The Dharma thus preached by the first Lord of Mankind was soon lost in dark oblivion and the Tīrthaṅkaras one after another followed Him. Not only Tīrthaṅkaras but many other philosophers also, appeared; they held and preached their own peculiar views. Most of these were from the *Brāhmaṇas*. And the Path first propagated by Lord Ṛṣabha and other predecessors of the last two Tīrthaṅkaras: Pārśva and Mhāvīra, lost its dominant sway and the Brāhmaṇical cult came into force. The bloody sacrificial rituals were the marks of the period; but soon followed a voice condemning them and the philosophical predominance, again, found its way in the fold of Goal-Seekers. Man was conceived by one and all as a being in bondage in his abode---the world, a pool of pain and misery; but people differed in tracing out the way to get out from it. One sect mostly comprising *Brāhmaṇa* teachers of old, thought that the final emancipation is attainable only through true knowledge.[3] It ignored the direct utility of a practical aspect of the philosophy. While the other, which had unto its fold all the unorthodox *brāhmaṇas* and *samaṇas*, utilised the necessity of the same.[4] It constituted that Right Knowledge and Right Conduct together with Right Faith shall make us free. Thus it was eight or nine hundred years before Christ that India had a troop of philosophers or wandering sophists, who, in the language of Dr. Rhys Davids, "spent eight or nine months of every year wandering about precisely with the object of engaging in conversational discussions on matters of ethics and philosophy, nature lore and mysticism. Like the sophists among the Greeks, they differed very much in intelligence, in earnestness and in honesty."[5]

When such were the conditions in India and the philosophical controversy wrought a havoc, not only amongst the wandering sophists but within all the social quarters also, then there appeared two heroes of the day. The darkness, in which the atmosphere plunged, took to its heels before these two luminous stars who came of *Kṣatriya* nobles. Buddha and Mahāvīra are both said to have flourished from amongst the *Ikṣāku-Vaṁśīya-Kṣatriyas.* Buddha's ancestors were known at the time as *Śākyas,* while those of Mahāvīra as *Nāthas or Jñātris.*[6] Śuddhodana, the father of Buddha, was a democratic chief of the clan of the *Śākyas;* so was the father of Mahāvīra--Rājāh Siddhārta of the clan of the *Jñātris.*[7] Buddha was born at Kapilavastu, the metropolis of the *Śākyas;* Mahāvīra in the city of Kuṅdanagara, which was a flourishing suburb of Vaiśālī and an important seat of the *Jñātri Kṣatriyas.* Buddha's mother died soon after his birth; Mahāvīra's parents lived to see him a grown up man; his birth caused an increment of their wealth, fame and merit (*puṅya*); so they named him as Mahāvīra Vardhamāna.[8] Buddha married a lady named Yaśodharā; Mahāvīra lived a householder's life in celibacy, practising the first vows of a Jaina layman.[9] Mahāvīra's parents professed the religion of Tīrthaṅkaras, similar seems to be the case with the parents of Buddha, though they are said to have been the followers of the previous Buddhas.[10] Buddha while enjoying the life of a worldly man got disgusted with it, seeing the misery and affliction of old age; he imbibed the spirit of renunciation and became an ascetic during the life-time and against the will of his father at the age of about 29; Mahāvīra while passing a pious householder's life and meditating upon the true nature of things, gained *vairāgya* and so doing adopted the vows of a *Nirgrantha muni*, with the consent of his parents, when he hardly completed 30 years of his age.[11] Buddha is said to have been born with the thirty-two *lakṣaṇas* or characteristics of a *mahāpuruṣa* and he had an amiable character;[12] Mahāvīra was born possessed of three kinds of of knowledge, viz., the sensuous (*mati*) the scriptural (*śruta*) and the clairvoyant (*avadhi*); and from the very moment of his birth his body was perfectly pure; no stain no sweating was ever found in it, rather it gave a sweet and fragrant smell; no excretions from his organs; the flesh and blood of his body were purely milk-white: his words and behaviour were always pleasing and beneficial to all the living beings; his beauty was indescribable and incomparable; his bodily strength was great and no cut was ever possible to it; and his body was symmetrically built.[13]

As an ascetic, Buddha's course of adherence was not a fixed one.[14] He is said to have followed every cult of asceticism, prevailing at the time. After giving up home, he walked off in search of a teacher and living a few days with the *Vānaprasthas*, he went over to ascetic Ārāḍa Kālāma, who was a professor of the Sāṅkhya views.[15] But he thought, "What Ārāḍa has declared, cannot satisfy my heart." 'So he went to Ṛṣi Udra Rāma. But once more leaving Udra Ṛṣi he went on in search of a better system and came at last to mount Kia-ke (Gayā--the forest of mortification), where was a town called pain-suffering forest (Uravilva?). Here the five *Bhikkhus* had gone before. When he beheld these five, virtuously keeping in check their senses, holding to the rules of moral conduct, and practising mortification,[16] he quietly gave himself up to thought. And afterwards "having finished their attentions and dutiful services,"[17] he occupied a spot besides the *Nairañjarā* river and "with full purpose of heart (he set himself) to endure mortification, to restrain every bodily passion, and give up thought about sustenance. With purity of heart to observe the fast rules, which no worldly man (active man) can bear, silent and still, lost in thoughtful meditaiton, and so for six years he continued."[18]

This course of Buddha's thoughtful mortification, for six years,as described above is in harmony with the penance given and thoughtful, (*upavāsa* and *dhyāna-maya*), silent and still (*Mauna* and *kāyotsarga*) life of a Jaina *muni*,[19] and as such it bears testimony to the Jaina view that Buddha was a Jaina *muni* at a certain stage of his ascetic life. The Jaina author says that he was a great learned disciple of the Jaina saint Pihitāshrawa, who ordained him as Muni Buddhakīrti in the Saṅgha of Śrī Pārśva, at the town of Palāsha, near the river *Sarayu;* but after a time taking the food of flesh and dead fish and putting on the red cloth, he preached his own *Dharma,* saying that there is no harm in taking such food.[20] We cannot reject this statement of the Jaina author altogether. The Jaina author points the place, where Buddha first got ordained as a Jaina *muni* quite accurately. The Jaina and Buddhist both agree to it, for each names the place to be a forest-town besides a river. (See above). And the Buddhist author, too, names his ordination as a Jaina muni, in the from of finishing "attentions and dutiful services." But however the latter assertion of the Jaina author demonstrates no historical fact, rather it points to the Buddhist belief[21] which according to the Jainas, is not a right path.

Furthermore there remains no doubt about this assertion of the Jaina author, when we find Buddha himself declaring to have practised the very preliminary austerity of a Jaina *muni,*[22] i.e. the practice of uprooting and pulling out the haris of beard and head, which is the *keśa-loñcakiriyā* of a Jaina *samṇa*[23]. Thus Buddha followed no fixed course of *samanaship.* At a time he was a *Vānaprastha,* and at another a Jaina *muni.*

Mahāvīra, on the other hand, followed the course of a *Nirgranṭha Sādhu,* as it was prevalent at the time. The *Digambaras* say that the eternal and natural attire of a Jaina *muni* is nothing besides nakedness and Mahāvīra adopted it; but the *Śvetāmbaras* dissent from it, though they ascribe nakedness to the first and the last Jaina Tīrthaṅkaras, after a year and a quarter from the date of their respective renunciation.[24] But a thoughtful glimpse at their sacred literature induces us to believe that their *Ācāryas,* too, prescribed nudity as an essential step towards goal.[25] In their *Ācārañga Sūtra* it is praised in nice words and not only Ṛṣabha and Mahāvīra are said to have practised it, but all the Tīrthaṅkaras are described to have borne its troubles.[26] In fact *Śvetāmbara* author exhorts the clothed monk to adopt nakedness. He says,..."one should be clad with one or no garment---aspiring freedom from bonds.[27] Only for that novice, who cannot bear the troubles of nakedness, a clothed course is allowed, according to *Śvetāmbaras,*[28] otherwise the same author exhorts the adoption of nakedness again and again. Obviously the freedom from bonds is only attainable, when one has no connection with external things as well. A Jaina *muni* must completely subdue all his emotions and desires for worldly things--- shame amongst others. In the words of the Irish author "being rid of clothes, one is also rid of a lot of other worries too: more important to a Jaina, no water is needed in which to wash them." Really our knowledge of the sensual perception of good and evil keeps us away from salvation. "To obtain it we must forget nakedness. The Jaina Nirgranthas have forgotten all knowledge of good and evil".[29] Therefore they require no clothes to cover their nakedness. This is the apparent reason, why the *Śvetāmbara* author supports nakedness. Rather the Jina- Kalpi[30] and *Sthavirakalpi* divisions of the *Nirgranthas* by the Śvetāmbaras bear testimony to our argument, if we take these words into consideration in their literal sense. And it is obvious that the Jaina technical words are moreover used in their literal sense.[31] Hence it could not be ignored in this case particularly. These words signify their literal meaning respectively, (1) of the *kalpa* of Jīnas and (2) of the *kalpa* of *Sthaviras.* In other words, they denote that *Jīnakalpi* (naked) *Nirgranthas* are to be found in the *kalpa* of Jinas, viz, 4th. era of *Awasarpiṇī* and *Utsarpiṇī* divisions of time and the *Sthavira-kalpi* (clothed) ones in the periods void of Jinas Tīrthaṅkaras. Hence Mahāvīra and his predecessors, who flourished in the 4th era, cannot be said to have passed the life of a clothed monk. Rather Mahāvīra adopted the *Nirgranthadikṣā* (nakedness) from the very day of his renunciation.[32]

As to the nakedness of the *Nirgrantha sādhus* at all times, it may be pointed out that Buddhist and *Brāhmaṇical* Sanskrit literatures abound with references to Jaina *munis* as naked monks.[33] Of course the Buddhist names the 'one-cloth-wearing' and 'white-clothed' *nigganṭha--sāvakas* as well.[34]. But quite wonderfully, this too, coincides with the *Digambara śāstras,* which describing the eleven stages of character development and self-realisation for a layman, treat the layman of the eleventh stage as an *'Eka-vastra-dhārī* (wearing one cloth): while all the *Vratī-srāvakas* are enjoined to wear the white clothes.[35] Moreover Buddhists' knowledge of their contemporary *nigganṭhas* does not end here, but curiously they also describe their important ascetic practices quite correctly.[36]

In view of these facts it would not perhaps be sound to accept Mahāvīra as exception to this important practice of Jaina *munis.*

Really it seems to be a fact that nakedness was held necessary for the attainment of *samanaship* in ancient times all over the world, In Hindu *śāstras*, too, it is not less highly spoken of. Śukācārya on whose arrival at the court of Parikṣit all the many thousands of *Ṛṣis* including his father and grand-father stood up, was a *Digambara.*[37] Śiva is a *Digambara* and so has been said the god Dattātrya.[38] The Holy Bible, too, describes nudity as a mark of saintship, as is apparent from the following passages:

"And he stripped off his clothes also, and prophesied before Samuel in like manner, and lay down naked all that day and all that night. Wherefore they said, 'Is soul also among the Prophets'? (Samuel xix. 24)

"At the same time spake the Lord by Isaiah, the son of Amoz, saying, go and loose the sackcloth from off thy loins and put off thy shoe from thy foot. And he did so, walking naked and barefooted." (Isaiah. xxi.2)

"Nudity was also a sign of world renunciation amongst the Arabs about whom Washington Irving says in his 'Life of Mahomet'.

'The Towaf, or procession, round the Caaba was an ancient ceremony observed before the time of Mahomet and prohibited this exposure and prescribed the Ihram or pilgrim dress.'... The seamless coat of Christ (St. John, xix, 23) is suggestive of bare skin esoterically."[39] Hence in the light of these facts it must be admitted, that at a certain time nakedness was held to be a mark of sainthood among the ancient people of different creeds and countries. In India at the time of Mahāvīra, the *Ājīvika* and *Acelaka* recluses, too, went naked.[40] Even to-day the Jaina *Nirgranṭha sādhus* discard all clothes and there are *naṅgā* (naked) *sādhus* also amongst the Hindus.

Hence it is significant that Mahāvīra renounced the world, in the manner of a naked *nirgranṭha muni,* and instead of wandering about in search of a teacher or a course of *samanship,* as Buddha did, he instantly began to practise the rules of a *nirgranṭha* monk after paying obeisance to the previous *Siddhas* (Liberated Ones) and pulling out his haris into five handfuls. After this he remained two days absorbed in deep thought and then he had his first meal, as *samaṇa,* at the hands of a certain Kula-nṭpa of Kulanagara.[41] There after wandering about in silence, one day he resolved to practise penance for full twelve years.[42] Accordingly he gave himself up to deep meditation and during that period he swerved not in the least from his position. And the second month of summer during the thirteenth year of his penance, brought forth the ripe and unique fruit of his hard perseverance. Mahāvīra became a *Jina,* a *Tathāgata,* a Tīrthaṅkara, or an omniscient Teacher.[43] This blessed thing happened on the northern bank of the river *Ṛjukūlā,* outside the town of Jṛmbhakagrāma, under a śāl tree. Now he was a *Kevalin,* omniscient and comprehending all objects. He knew all conditions of the whole world of al! living beings. Then as a profound Teacher he preached the ancient truth all round.[44] Indrabhuti Gotama, a renowned orthodox Brāhmaṇa, was first converted and acquiring the *Manahapary-jiñān,* he became the first and foremost apostle of Lord Mahāvīra.The Jainas say that he composed and kept in his memory the Teachings of Mahāvīra.[45] The thing noteworthy in this connection is that not only Buddhist canon speak in good and reliable terms about the omniscience and teachings of Mahāvīra, but Hindu literature also corroborates the fact.[46] Buddha has also given his assent to this fact in pleasing words. On one occasion he said:-

"There are, brethern, certain recluses (*Acelakas, Ājīvikas, Nigaṇṭhas,* etc.,) who thus preach and believe: whatsoever an individual experiences, whether it be happy or painful, or neutral feeling, all has been caused by pevious actions. And thus from the cancelling of old actions by *tapas,* and by abstaining from doing new actions, there is no influx into future life; by this non-influx *karma* is destroyed, and so ill is destroyed, and so feeling is destroyed, and so all pain will become worn away: This, brethern, is what the *Nigaṇṭhas* (jains) Say.....Is it true, I asked them, that you believe and declare this?.... They replied....Our leader, Nātaputa, is all-wise..... out of the depth of his knowledge he tells us: Ye have done evil in the past. This ye do wear away by this hard and painful course of action. And the discipline that here and now, by thought, word, and deed, is wrought, is a minus quantity of bad *karma* in future life...... thus all *karma* will eventually be worn away, and all pain. To this we assent. (Majjhima, ii, 214 ff. cf. i. 238)" ----ERE. VOl. II. p 70.

Similar were the teaching and assertion of the Jainas, as is evident from the Jina *śāstras*[47]. But 'notwithstanding the above mentioned assent when faced with the severity of --- *pariṣā-Jaya* (mortification), which signifies cheerfully enduring all kinds of hardships incidental to asceticism, and finding them only leading to enfeeblement and emaciation, but not to the enlightenment that he sought, Buddha declared:--

"Not by this bitter course of painful hardship shall I arrive at that separate and supreme vision of all sufficing, noble (*Aryan*) knowledge, passing human ken. Might there be not another path to enlightenment?" ERE. Vol. ii, p. 70.

'He thenceforth began to look after the welfare of the body once more. At last the middle course that he was looking for occured to him under famous Bo tree.'[48] The Buddhists say that he gained a full sight of the supreme knowledge and became a *Tathāgata* then and there. According to these assertions, Indian at that time possessed these two luminous stars who made her rejoin with a rational theme.While Buddha caused a necessary reform in the social conditions of the country in general and among the wandering ascetics in particular and founded a religion of his own, with the sole object of relieving the humanity of the apparent misery.[49] Mahāvira, quite in reverse to this, founded no religion or creed of his own, but he preached the self-same ancient Truth which was preached by his twenty three predecessors, and demonstrated every question pertaining to the material as well as spiritual elevation of all the living beings in a scientific light. The Truth, thus propagated, got home in the hearts of all the Goalseekers and they were successful in sinking their differences easily. The Jainas say that even the beasts were given place in the preaching hall of Mahāvīra. A glimpse at the mode and course of their respective preaching and teachings will convince one of the credibility of this position of ours and also, that of the fineness and quality of their acquired knowledge. It is admitted that both the Teachers were possessed of supernatural powers,[50] but while Buddha had recourse to them in converting his early disciples and wrought miracles,[51] Mahāvīra never sought aid of the kind in his preaching. Besides he never let go any kind of point whatsoever without full elucidation, but Buddha, on the other hand, evaded even such important questions as the existence of world and soul which are quite essential in a rational speculation.[52] Taking these into our consideration and examining the quality of Buddha's knowledge, we can easily proceed on, with our position thus made clear. As for this we will have to content ourselves with the following passage from the orthodox Buddhist canon, like 'Milinda-Pañha'. There in reply to the question about the omniscience of the Buddha, the Buddhist author says that "the insight of knowledge was not always and continually (consciously) present with him. The omniscience of the Blessed One was dependent on reflection. But if he did reflect he knew whatever he wanted to know."[53] Thereupon King Milinda tells him that "Buddha cannot have been omniscient, if this all- embracing knowledge was reached through investigation." And the Buddhist author acknowledges it to a degree, saying : "If so, Great King, our Buddha's knowledge must have been less in degree of fineness than that of other Buddhas. And that is a conclusion hard to draw."[54] Hence it is clear that an omniscient knowledge should be all-comprehensive and ever present with its possessor, and as such we should say for the sake of simple truth that Buddha's knowledge could not compete with this. Consequently this seems to be the evident reason why Buddha himself did not accept to be the foremost *Arahat* (Omniscient Teacher). Rather he simply evaded the question in his usual way, when asked or ascribed so at occasions.[55] But after all it is a fact that Buddha got a certain kind of inner knowledge under the Bo-tree. From the Jaina point of view, it was most probably a kind of *Avadhijñāna* (*vibhaṅgā* one perhaps), while that Mahāvīra was full *Kevaljñāna* (omniscience), as we have seen above.

Well, any how after this famous event in the life of Buddha, he was styled by his votaries, as *Tahāgata*, Buddha or the Blessed *Arahat*. So the titles or epithets of Buddha and Mahāvīra are almost the same but Mahāvīra's epithe of Tīrtnaṅkara is peculiar to him. The Buddhists use it for a heretic teacher.[56] Further we know about Buddha that after his *"sambodhi,"* he did not begin to preach at once for he was in fear of his doctrine not being accepted by people so he decided to remain quiet and enjoy the peace of mind in silence for a time.[57] But in the end he became victorious over his weakness and resolving to preach his *'Dharma* far and wide, he started at once for Benares.[58] There he met the former ṛṣis of his acquaintance. At first they believe him not and addressed him in the familiar term, 'Friend, Buddha assured them of his Buddhahood and asked them to call him with the epithet, *"Tathāgata."*[59] Thereupon they acknowledged him as their teacher.[60] And Kaundiny Kulaputra, the foremost among them first acquired the inner sight in the 'Norm', and became the first apostle of Buddha.[61]

Buddha's Norm, which he preached for the first time at Benares was most probably nothing else than a protest against the caste system of the Hindus and the severe asceticism of the Jainas, not as a new metaphysical system at least, not in its inception.[62] The following assertion of Buddha leaves no doubt about it:-

"There are two extremes, O *Bhikkhus*, which he who has given up the world, ought to avoid. What are these two extremes? A life given to pleasures, devoted to pleasures and lusts, this is degrading sensual vulgar, ignoble and profitless, and a life given to mortification, this is painful, ignoble and profitless. By avoiding these tow extremes, O *Bhikkhus*, the *Tathāgata* has gained the knowledge of the Middle Path, which leads to insight, which leads to wisdom, which conduces to calm, to knowledge, to *sambodhi*, to *Nirvāṇa*" (*Mahāvagga*, i, 6, 17.)

Now it is evident that Buddha assumed the position of a moderate preacher or reformer. His chief aim was to make an end of pain, at any rate, for his own self and for the individual who was willing to accept his teachings.[63] So the Norm was, truly speaking 'a compromise between rigid asceticism on the one hand and the life of unrestrained licentiousness, under the guise of *Karmayoga*, (the doing of all worldly actions but without attachments to their fruits) on the other.' Buddha never thought it necessary to inquire about the scientific validity of his teachings. He was far from entering into a true philosophical discussion. To him what mattered was the avoidance of pain in any form.[64] If asceticism itself led to pain, how could it lead to its destruction?

"*Dukkha* is evil," said the Enlightened One, "and must be removed. Excess is *Dukkha*. *Tapa* is a form of excess, and multiplies *Dukkha*. It does not even lead through suffering to any gain, it is unprofitable" --- (ERE. Vol.II. p. 70).

But in fact, Buddha was trying to perfect himself in *sannyāsa* without ever having passed through the prescribed stages of a householder's preparatory course and as such, it must have never led him to the desired goal. It he had known it and would have comprehended the necessity of a ladder to reach the top, we might have expected something else from him than the above condemnation. Mahāvīra sought the goal by gradual steps and he got it. Really Mahāvīra, too, had condemned such asceticism, as, in the absence of faith and knowldge of right sort, only led to distress and pain.[65] He had styled it as a foolish and childish practice, for he knew quite well that the observance of vows and the suffering of hardships in asceticism were essential to separate the *Karmic* filth from the soul. Of course this course seems irksome and unpleasant only when looked at from a distance. But when one is imbued with the Right Faith, one realises at once the necessity of a well-regulated life and actually longs for the perfection of character through suffering and selfdenial.[66] Buddha, too, was not inclined to give it up in whole. He has also prescribed it, but in a very loose form.[67]

In this way the early events of the lives of Buddha and Mahāvīra differed quite widely, and their after-life as Teachers, also, does not point any similarity. Buddha began to preach when he was thirty-five years old and abhorring philosophical discussions, he exerted great force to root out the craving of desire and care for nothing else, as is pointed above.Mahāvīra, on the other hand, preached his *'Samaṇa Dhamma'* at the age of forty-two.[68] And the course of their wanderings, too, was different. Finally Mahāvīra got his *mukti* at Pāvā,[69] during the life-time of Buddha,[70] at the age of seventy-two. Buddha, on the contrary, lived a few years after him and is said to have died at Kuśīnārā when he was eighty years old.[71] Dr. Hoernle says that Buddha lived after Mahāvīra about five years more.[72] Accepting it as such, we find that Buddha was born three years before Mahāvīra and when he began to preach his Norm, Mahāvīra was a novice and of about thirty-three years of age. The reliability of the fact is already evident from the calculations of Dr. Hoernle, still it can be proved further, when the reason for a gap of events between fifty and seventy years of Buddha's life is traced out. Rev. Bigandet styles this period as almost completely blank.[73] Hence let us try to find out the obvious reason which caused this gap. Knowing that Mahāvīra began to preach when Buddha was already in the field as a teacher and was about forty-five years of age, according to above calculations, it is quite probable that within the rest five years Mahāvīra's preaching would have predominated that of Buddha, because we have already noticed that the knowledge (omniscience) of Mahāvīra was of a finer and greater degree than Buddha's and as such, his teachings were all profound. Really quite in accordance with this the Jaina author, too, describes this fact.[74] But Buddhist author also says that before the rising glory of Buddha all the other teachers lost their predominance.[75] though at the same time he acknowledges the predominating glory of Mahāvīra.[76] So it seems to be true that as the faith of the Buddha was patronised afterwards by King Ajātaśatru, perhaps just at the time of or after the great Decease of Mahāvīra,[77] and at a later period *Niganṭhas* were persecuted by King Padma of *Ājīvikas,*[78] the order of Mahāvīra must have suffered and its glory of the time of Mahāvīra must have faded to a degree. Hence the Buddhist author's statement, too, holds water along with that of the Jaina author, i.e., before the unique dazzling glory of Mahāvīra's omniscience all other creeds were lost. Thus the apparent reason for the gap of events between fifty to seventy years of Buddha's life is the surpassing glory of Mahāvīra as an omniscient Teacher. The Buddhist canon also bears testimony to it. The schism caused by Devadatta in the Buddha's order was solely a demand for a more restrained and strict ascetic life and avoidance of meat diet.[79] Nevertheless it is a truth that there was no other rival of Buddha than Mahāvīra, who did hold the importance of and preached the doctrines of Asceticism and *Ahiṁsā*, just since a decade before this schism, which occured when Buddha was of about seventy-two years,[80] and Mahāvīra of about sixty-nine years. And 'it follows from the evidence of *Abhayarājakumāra-Sutta* of the *Majjhima Nikāya* that Mahāvīra was aware of the fact of dissension between Buddha and Devadatta.[81] Jaina *śāstras*, too, support this view in as much as they describe that just after the death of Śrenika Bimbisāra, Ajātaśatru became an adherent of the creed of Mahāvīra, and his mother Cellanā went to the *Samosarana* of Mahāvīra, where she took the vow of a nun and remained under the guidance of Candanā.[82] This shows that Mahāvīra was still in the field as a Teacher and the Buddhist schism occured at this very time; and this coincides with the opinion of Dr. Kern as well.[83] Therefore it is significant that at this time the teachings of Mahāvīra must have predominated amongst the people around.[84] Hence Devadatta demanded for a reform which was necessary according to time. Besides, when Mahāvīra breathed his last at Pāvā, we see that the disciples of Buddha rejoiced at the event and thought it most important.[85] They hurried at once to Buddha at *Sāmagāma*, who seeing that much benefit could be acquired then, delivered a sermon. And actually Buddha and his disciple Sāriputta derived much benefit out of this important event in the annals of the Jainas.[86] This, too, corroborates the fact that Mahāvīra's appearance in the field as an omniscient Teacher caused the gap mentioned above. Of course in one passage of Buddhist canon we find Buddha described as the youngest among the living teachers[87] but in another we see that Buddha evades the question and gives no definite reply.[88] This might mean that as in age he was really older than Mahāvīra at least, but as a teacher he was younger, because all other prevalent schools of thought were pre- Buddhistic in their existence. Hence judging from these documentary evidences, the above relations between the lives of Buddha and Mahāvīra would seem to have substantial historical accuracy.

Now there remains the question of the date of the Great Decease of Mahāvīra. There are two prominent opinions about it. One assigns it to 527 B.C.[89] and the other to a later period of 468 B.C.[90] The first is accepted by all the Jainas as well, but the latter has no place elsewhere than the fold of scholars. We think the prevalent date of 527 B.C. holds much credit, when it is evident that Buddhists ascribe the event in the life-time of Buddha[91]. But even in this there seems to have crept a a mistake owing to miscalculations. The documentary evidences in support of this opinion are said to be (1) *Gāthā* No. 850 of Śrī Trilokasāra of the *Digambaras,* (2) *Āryavidyāsudhākara,* (3) The introduction of the *Paṛṛāwali* of *Sarasvatī gaccha,* and (4) The introduction of *Gurwāwali,* 'A' of the same as examined by Dr. Hoernle in the Indian Antiquary. Now in the latter two evidences of the above, it has been established in clear words that after 470 years since the *Nirvāṇa* of Mahāvīra, King Vikrama was born, viz : सत्तरिचदुसदजुतो तिचकालाविक्कमो इवइजन्मो' ।And it is quite well known that the date 527 B.C. has been arrived at by assuming the beginning of Vikrama era after 470 years from the *Nirvāṇa* of Mahāvīra, but in fact the matter is that Vikrama's era dates from his ascension to the throne at the age of eighteen, after subduing the Sakas.[92] Hence eighteen years should be added more in the prevailing era of Mahāvīra. Dr. Jacobi also draws our attention to this fact, in a private letter and says "the Vikrama era does not date from the जन्म of Vikrama, but from the राज्य of Vikrama, or from the eighteenth year after his birth. By this reckoning the *Nirvāṇa* should be placed eighteen years earlier or 545B.C." The former two evidences of the above do no also hinder us in any way from forming this correct and more sound opinion, because in them it is not said that the era of Vikrama began after 470 years since the Nirvāṇa, rather they denote the existence of King Vikrama at the time. Hence taking the date of *Nirvāṇa* to be 545 B.C. we find it to coincide with our above date of the relations of Buddha's and Mahāvīra's lives, as well, because the orthodox Ceylonese date of Buddha's demise rightly falls later than Mahāvīra's and in 543 B.C., which has also become more reliable under the new light of the Khārvela Inscription.[93] Hence it is safely conceivable that the accurate date of Mahāvīra's *Nirvāṇa,* which has been accepted by and is prevailing amongst the jains is 545 B.C The date of Buddha's demise can also be taken safely as 543. B.C.

In this way by looking side by side at the events of Buddha's and Mahāvīra's lives, we have demonstrated their differences fully, and now we can easily form a safe idea about their separate identities and mutual connections as contemporaries. The acquaintance with the above facts will also dispel the false notion about the origin of Jainism from Buddhism, which still prevails in certain quarters.

Now so far having dwelt on the lives of the Buddha and Mahāvīra, we shall now proceed to consider the aspect of their respective teachings.

Inquiring at the very outset about the *Dharma* of the Buddha, we find that, "it denotes the Laws of nature : man's body falls under the rule of decay; it equally applies to the law of impermanence enunciated by the Buddha; whatever comes into being is subject to the law of destruction."[94] Mahāvīra, also proclaimed the *Dharma* to be the very nature of things: "*Vastu svabhāvodharmaha.*"[95] Though these definitions are somewhat similar yet in fact they are applied by both the Teachers in different senses. At the hands of Buddha it had not that full treatment which it enjoyed near Mahāvīra. Truth compels us to admit that the philosophical conceptions of Buddha are lacking both in system and maturity. Rather he took the philosophical discussion to be a cause of further bondage.[96] Hence scientific answers to such questions are quite far from him. They were styled by him as Indeterminates. When he is asked: 'Is the world eternal? Is this alone the truth,and any other view mere folly He quite definitely replied that, "that, Poṭṭhapāda, is a matter on which I have expressed no opinion." 'Then in the same terms, Poṭṭhapāda asked each of the following questions : (1) Is the world not eternal? (2) Is the world finite? (3) Is the world infinite? (4) Is the soul the same as body? (5) Is the soul one thing and the body another? (6) Does one who has gained the truth live again after death? (7) Does he not live again after death? (8) Does he both live again and not live again after death? (9) Does he neither live again, nor not live again after death? And to each question the Exalted One gave the same reply.[97] Consequently whenever such a critical position arrived, Buddha gave no elucidation on the point. And Dr. Keith makes us believe that his 'refusal is perfectly categoric; he insists that he made no undertaking to instruct his disciples in these matters. He is instead a physician who gives such instruction as leads to the freeing of man from bondage.[98] Really by leaving these matters unexplained, he allowed the people to frame their own conceptions. And such a position was quite necessary for a 'Norm' Preacher.

It seems that Buddha looked at the nature or things from only the particular aspect of their empiric existence. He clearly asserts that 'there are no eternal substances in the world, nor are there substances which perish utterly, but that the whole world is a process of becoming, anything in time could not be the true reality.[99] And there is also no such things as soul.[100] Even the material phenomenon has not been fully explained by him.[101] But we are, however, made to understand that there are four material elements, earth, fire, air, and water. The ether, also, at times is counted in the list.[102] Still the manner in which Buddha conceived these elements is not explained and "what is clear is that every material thing is a compound (*saṁkhāra*) which may, as in the case of body, endure for a long time, but will nevertheless ultimately pass away. Things are impermanent (*Anicca*), in early Buddhism they are not literally momentary, a refinement of later thought.[103]

Moreover the world was a matter of mere experience to Buddha. He declined to answer the speculative questions on its infinity and duration. But it is evident that in admitting the above four material elements, Buddha had to accept the realistic aspect as well.[104] And so we may safely assume the indefinitencess of his position.

Besides these four elements, Buddha included in them, the *Nirvāṇa* element (the state of release) and the conception of consciousness, to subsume under it pleasure and pain and thus began his philosophical career with a doctrine of six elements, all real whose interaction explained the existence of world.[105]

Herein the influence of *Brāmaṇical* and Jaina doctrines is quite evident, for both the systems were already in existence at the time of the advent of Buddhism.[106] The Four material elements were accepted from the *Brāhmaṇical* tradition,[107] and they were framed in such a way as to resemble the Jaina conception of the universe. Jainas, too, describe six substances to constitute this universe, but these are quite different from the above, as well see below. Besides, we already know that Buddha's definition of *Dharma*, also, possesses a degree of resemblance with that of the Jainas. Its division into internal (*ajjhattika*) and external (*bāhira*) aspects.[108] is also outwardly synonymous with the *niścaya* (real) and *vyavahāra* (material) aspects of *Dharma* as accepted by the Jainas.[109] But herein too the difference is apparent in as much as the Buddhist division has its connection only with the outer and mental conditions of the empiric world[110] and the individual, that of the Jainas along with these, with the real aspects of the things, as well. Hence it is obvious that Buddha only endeavoured a little to explain his position about the conception of the universe in the *vyavahāra* (material) *dharma* of the Jainas.

Mahāvīra in accordance with his definition of *Dharma*, demonstrated the eternal truth about all the existing things. He said that this universe is eternal, without beginning and end.[111] It is nothing but the sum-total of substances which have been existing from eternity and shall remain so for ever. In this universe nothing new is created, nor is anything destroyed. Only there are modifications of substances, which cause the beginning,duration and end of a particular condition of the universe.[112] Hence there is no need of any creator. the Jaina thinker, Prabhācandra expressly condemns the assumption of a creator in the following way:-

"The theists maintain that God as the Creator has knowledge, will to act and active effort, that He need not be an embodied Being. But this is impossible. One who is a disembodied Being cannot know through senses, etc., -- as for instance an emancipated Soul (who although emancipated is never a creator).

"It is not proper for a kind Being to be an author of pain and to furnish animals with bodies for feeling them."[113] (*Prameya- Kamala-Mārtaṇḍa*).

Further the substances of this eternal universe are primarily described as *jīva* (soul) and *ajīva* (non-soul). The *lakṣaṇa* or differential of living substance (soul- Jīva) is upayoga, attention, consciousness, attentiveness.[114] And the non-living substance (*Ajīva*) is all the rest, which is void of this differential and is of five kinds: (1) Matter-*pudgala*, (2) Space-*ākāsa*, (3) Time-*kāla*, (4) Medium of motion --- *Dharmāstikāya*, and (5) Medium of rest *Adharmāstikāya*. Thus in all Mahāvīra made us enumerate six kinds of substances, which compose this universe. With the lengthy descriptions of these six substances the whole Jaina canon is filled, but here viewing them in short, we find that the (1) conscious immaterial substance is soul and is in infinite number, (2) matter is *rūpī* (material) and its special attributes are touch, taste, smell, and colour. Its atoms and molecules are infinite and distinct, but they are found in numerable and innumerable numbers as well, (3) space is one grand infinite immaterial and indispensable substance. Its two divisions, *Lokākāśa* (Universe) and *Alokākāśa* (Non-universe), are based on *Dharma* and *Adharma*. Souls and matter move on and rest up to the confines of the universe only, because *Dharma* and *Adharma*, which are respectively causes of motion and rest, do not exit outside *Lokākāśa*, (4) time is an immaterial and immovable substance, which is an auxiliary cause in bringing about modifications of and in all the substances. The being or continuing to exist, i.e., the continuous change in the attributes of substances at every moment is done by *niścaya kāla* (real time substance) and the modifications, their movements and long and short duration are the bases of *vyavahāra kāla*, i.e. of time, from a practical point of view, which is based upon the motion of matter, Sun, Moon, earth, etc., in space. 'The number of time-units or instants or time atoms *(kālāṇus)* is innumerable. Each time-atom occupies one point of space, thus the space of the universe which has innumerable spatial points, covered entirely by time-atoms,' (5) the medium of motion is one immaterial substance, co-extensive with the universe. Its function is to support the motion of souls and matter, and (6) the medium of rest is also one immaterial substance and co-extensive with the universe. It is an auxiliary cause for the rest of souls and matter.[115]

Among these, only soul and matter are the chief factors and the rest follows them. We are told that "they perform mainly four actions, viz, they occupy space, undergo change, and are at motion or at rest. Every action must have two causes, one principal, primary or root-cause, and the other the auxiliary cause. The primary and essential cause of a gold-ring, is the gold of which it is made; but the auxiliary or secondary causes are several, e.g., fire the goldsmith's tools, etc., etc. So the primary causes of these above four actions of soul and matter are the soul and matter themselves, but the auxiliary causes are the above said four immaterial substances. Thus this universe is composed of six real, uncreated substances *(dravyas)* and all the manifestations of this universe are due to modifications of soul and matter with the help of the other four substances.[116]

Obviously we can now easily see the wide differences in the primary teachings of Mahāvīra and Buddha. Though the latter's mode of expression and systematising his creed generally resembles those of Mahāvīra's, still Buddha's teachings were based on Non-self *(Anattā)* system, while Mahāvīra preached the very *Dharma* of the previous Tīrthaṅkaras who held the necessity of the soul conception, i.e., Ātma or *Anekānta-Vāda*. But on the other hand, the five *Saṁkhāras* of Buddha could not be found anywhere in the teachings of Mahāvīra.

Buddha declared that these *saṁkhāras* are produced by the ignorance of four noble truths of pain or misery, its origin, its destruction and the way to that end.[117] As regards the differentia and function of *saṁkhāra*, Dr. Keith rightly holds that "*saṁkhāra*, like the sanskrit *Saṁskāra*, is a term of varying, but consistent and intelligible meaning; it denotes the making ready or complete something for an end -- an idea emphasised in the compound *Abhisaṁkhāra*, and also the result of the activity when achieved. Hence it has no exclusive application to the psychical sphere; the movement given to a potter's wheel is styled an *Abhisaṁkhāra;* the wheel rolls on so long as the impression thus communicated lasts. Hence *Saṁkhāras* may be divided, as often, between those of the body , speech or thought; expiration and inspiration are *Saṁkhāras;* when Buddha decides to attain *Nirvāṇa* he lets go his *Āyusaṁkhāra*, his disposition to live, and the motive force which but for his decision would have continued to keep alive his mortal frame; it is inconceivable that nothing more is meant than that the Buddha laid aside merely a subjective process. The same point arises regarding the *Saṁkhāras* which affect the form of rebirth of the dead; a monk who forms a resolve to be born in a noble family achieves this result from the *Saṁkhāra* thus framed; here again we cannot believe that the rebirth is a pure figment of the creative imagination, just as little as it is credible that a man who has the disposition to pay a visit (*gamikābhisaṁkhāro)* has merely the idea of himself as on a journey. Such a conception is clearly far from the texts, which frankly tell us that a man forms the *Saṁkhāra* of the body when a body exists, and it is incredible that the body, which is described as the ancient deed made ready *(abhisaṁkhatam)* and made real by mental activity *(abhisaṁcetayitam)* is really to be understood as merely the ancient act conceived or presented to consciousness as existing. The difficulty of Franke's view appears still more clearly when it is remembered that the *Saṁkhāras* are one of the five Khandas which constitute the individual of Buddhism; they rank alongside of material form (*rūpa)* or body, feeling (*vedanā), *perception *(saññā),* and intellect or consciousness *(viññāna),* and there is clearly no room here for the concept of ideas; rather they are the dispositions which lead to rebirth, precisely parallel to the *Saṁskāras,* which in the Sāṅkhya system represent the predispositions of the individual resulting from the impressions left by former thoughts and deeds. In the chain of causation the *Saṁkhāras* play the same role; they are not the creation of ignorance of the illusory character of the world; something much simpler is meant; by reason of his ignorance of the doctrine of misery as taught by the Buddha, the unfortunate man commits action and so produces dispositions which lead on to fresh birth.[118]

Hence the Buddha is reported to have said:--"*Ajñāna* (ignorance) begets *Saṁskāra* (tendency); this leads to *Vijñāna* (apprehension); from it emerge *Nāma* (name) and *Bhautika Deha* (material body) from them come the *Ṣaṭ- Kṣetra* (six spheres or centers), from the contact of the senses and their objects, there arises *Vedanā*(affection), *Vedanāleads* to *Tṛṣṇā* (longing to get) this to *Upādāna* (appropriation), this to *Bhava* (being), this to *Janma* (birth), this to *vāddhakya* (old age) *Maraṇa* (death), *Dukkha* (pain), *Anuśya* (despair). Thus flourishes the kingdom of Pain"

Consequently the *saṁsāra-pravāha* of the Buddha is apparently based on the law of cause and effect. Hence there are unbroken and eternal cognitive series in the world, and so, it can be styled to be an idea of transmigration theory which is accepted in the Jaina philosophy as well. The difference is evident that according to Buddhists, in beginning, if there be any, there everything in form and mode was ignorance,[119] but no such things has been accepted by the Jainas.

Here if we try to know what takes birth, when there is no such thing as soul, we unfortunately find that this too, has been left unsolved by the Buddha. What he points out is that an individual takes birth. This individual is only an aggregate of material form (rūpa), or body feeling (*vedanā*, perception (*saṁjñā*), dispositions (*saṁkhāras*), and intellect or consciousness (*vijñāna*).[120] It is not a person (*satta*)--no permanent individuality in the least. Just as it is by the condition precedent of the co-existence of its various parts that the word 'chariot' is used, so also is the individual. Individual is not a real thing in itself. As chariot is an aggregation of its wheels, axles, etc., so is the individual.

Now in accordance with the above chain of causation becoming continues; and in a true sense there is no being or individual, except a becoming.[121] And to connect the link between all old and a new becoming the descent of the consciousness into the womb of the mother, preparatory to rebirth, is accepted in the *Mahānidāna-Sutta*.[122] Dr. Keith, too supports it and says that "the phrase 'descent of consciousness' certainly implies a continuity of consciousness between the old and the new lives, and it may imply that this consciousness was accompanied by some form of body, if we take the word 'descent' literally, in fact the schools differed on this point and Buddhaghoṣa is consistent with his own view in negativing the question of a corporeal accompaniment of consciousness. But this has nothing to do with the far more important animistic implication, namely, that there is a continuity of consciousness, which the Buddha seems frankly to admit."[123]

In this way though the Buddha tried to work out his position without a permanent real 'being.' assuming the consciousness to appear itself in the aggregates in the manner of the Sāṅkhya system, but ultimately he had to accept the continuity of the consciousness in the series of becoming. Thus the absurdity of the point is quite apparent. Without any real basis, the castles are being built in the air. Still the Jaina idea is quite evident in this conception as well. According to the Jainas, desire is the sole cause of bondage which has its origin from *karmic* delusion.[124] Consequently the real being (soul)whose differentia is consciousness suffers worldly pain and misery and being in bondage transmigrates. In this transmigration it carries with itself a subtle material body of *karmic* molecules, which cause a new birth of the embodied conscious being. Thus apparently a similarity seems to find a place here too.

Now the thing which derives consciousness to its new birth and determines its form, said Buddha, is that of action. Dr. Keith again assures us that "on this topic the Canon is emphatic and as clear as the nature of the subject permits; the force of action cannot be evaded by any device, excuses are vain, punishment is certain and inevitable, save only if the necessary intuition is found to break the chain of existence; then, though the law of action is broken for the future, the deeds of the past must be worked out in a form in which their seriousness is lost; the man guilty of many murders is repaid by a few blows.[125] This suggests that between consciousness and dispositions there is a transition from the old to a new life"[126]

Hence obviously misery arises from action *(karma)* and it from passion or infection.[127] Thus "thirst is the *Upādāna* when consciousness passes to a new existence and in this sense we have the doctrine that the five aggregates constituting the individual are the objects grasped."[128] All foolish individuals who always take pleasure in their thirst pursuits, remain entangled in the pool of misery. But it must be remembered that the chain does not explain fully the working of action *(karma)*. It is also one of the Indeterminates of Buddha. Buddha only asserts the operation of karma, but shows no way about its actual working.[129] And this seems to be the apparent reason that conflicting views are found on the point, even in such an orthodox work as Milinda Pañha. At one place its author clearly asserts that "No, O King it is not all suffering that has its root in karma. There are eight causes by which suffering arises, by which many being suffer pain. And what are the eight? Superabundance of wind, and of bile,and of phlegm, the union of these humors, variations in temperature, the avoiding of dissimilarities, external agency and *karma*. From each of these there are some sufferings that arise and these are the eight causes by which many beings suffer pain. And therein whosoever maintains that it is *karma* that injures beings, and besides it there is no other reason for pain, his proposition is false."[130] But at another he conflicts it saying: "It is precisely the effect of *karma*, which overcomes all the rest, and has them under its rule; and no other influence is of any avail to the man in whom karma is working out its inevitable end."[131] But this much, however, is clear that *saṁsāra*, according to Buddha, is a continuous flow, without any beginning and end and is unsubstantial, dependent on action *(karma)*. And action itself has not been described as merely an ethical or moral act done by a person; it is a Law Universal. It requires no foreign intervention to produce its *phala* (effect). It is independent. Hence the necessity of a Creator found no place even near Buddha.

Thus apparently the *karma* theories of Mahāvīra and Buddha, with regard to their nature and operation, are wonderfully the same. But this similarity, too, is, however, in words only. There lies a fundamental difference between the both. According to Mahāvīra, the *karma* is a real and material thing---the cause of the bondage of an unemancipated soul.But Buddha thought it to be the ethical act of a person and an unsubstantial law. Thus it seems quite evident that Buddha borrowed this theory from the Jainas and used also their technical term *Āśrava* and *Samvara*, but not in the same literal sense, as found in Jainism.[132]

Mahāvīra, contrary to Buddha, preached the theory of *Ātmavāda*. He said, "the soul is in combination with matter from time immemorial. Though in its pure essence the soul is an independent personification of Perfect Knowledge; Perfect Perception, Perfect Power, and Perfect Bliss; but this combination has caused its delusion and impurity, which make it transmigrate in many different mundane existences from eternity. The soul, thus involved in transmigration suffer a multitude of afflictions. This association with matter makes them burn with unquenchable thirst of sense-produced desire and infatuations. They have got with them a subtle *karmic* body of meritorious and demeritorious *karmic* matter; in which every moment karmic molecules inflow, according to the activities of mind, speech and body;[133] and at the same time, old ones are cast off. The *karmic* matter is inhered in the soul but for a time only. As soon as the embodied soul sees the true nature of the things and acquires Bheda Vijñāna (Discriminating Inner Sight), it gives up all attachment to the worldly affairs and false delusions and becomes absorbed in self-concentration and penances. Thus it gets itself freed from the bonds of *karma*." The famous Jaina saint Kundakundācārya asserts it so and says:--

"The Soul and the *Karma-Matter* permeate each other, through and through. At the proper time they separate; up till that they generate pleasure and pain which are experienced by the souls."[134]

Hence it is the *karma,* which causes all activities in cosmic phenomena.[135] What a being soweth, so he reapeth. And as this embodied being is working together with the rest five substances, all conditions of the universe are dependent on it. Its operation extends throughout the universe and the flow of *saṁsāra* also, depends on it. Its effect is, also irresistible. It could not be maintained otherwise even accepting the apparent fruitlessness of *karma,* seeing that a sinful man is prosperous and that an honest man suffers untold miseries. The Jaina thinker has already said that "the prosperity of a vicious man and the misery of a man devoted to the worship of the *Arahat* are but respectively, the effects of good and bad deeds done previously. The vice and the virtue of their present lives will have their effects in their next lives. In this way, the law of causality is not infringed."[136]

Really Mahāvīra gave an elaborate and scientific discourse on the Law of Karma and the same is well-described in the Jaina metaphysical books like *Gommaṭsāra* and *Pañcāstikāyasāra* etc. The rationality of its operation and nature cannot be denied in the least. It is a natural Law of Cause and Effect. But it should be remembered that the soul operates in its won nature and causes its own *Bhava* or state. It is not the direct cause of the modifications in the *karma*. And the "*Karma* also is the cause of its own state or modification, working in and through its own nature."[137] Ācārya Nemicandra has made their mutual relationship quite clear, saying that "from the practical or empirical standpoint *(vyavahāra)* the soul is the cause of *karma*-modifications. From the imperfect ontological stand-point *(asuddhniścaya-naya)*, the soul is the cause of its own conscious dispositions. According to the purely metaphysical view *(śuddha-niścaya-naya)*, it is the cause of its own pure, essential states."[138]

Thus observation shows that the soul involved in impurity is unable to enjoy its attributes of perfect nature. In its impure state the dispositions--attachment, envy, etc., arise in it and further cause its bondage. Saint Kundakunda points so and says that "Bondage is due to *bhāva* (dispositions) and the *bhāva* which is attended with lust *(rati)*, attachment *(rāga)*, repulsion *(dveṣa)*, and stupefaction *(moha)*."[139]

So it is clear that what causes the attraction of the *karmic* molecules, which are filled in this universe, are the dispositions *(bhāva)*, viz. wrong belief (mithyādarśana), unrestraint *(avirati)*, recklessness *(pramāda)*, intense passions *(kashāya)* and the activity of body, speech and mind *(yoga)*.[140] These dispositions according to good and bad actions attract the meritorious or demeritorious *karmic* matter. Consequently there are two kinds of *karma Bhāvakarma* and *Dravyakarma*. The dispositions are former and the *karmic* matter which is attracted is itself the *Dravyakarma*.[141] This inflow of karmic matter is styled *Āsrava* and is the third *tatta* (principle) of the Jainas---the first two being *Jīva*, which constitute six *dravyas*.

Now the fourth *Tattva Bandha*, too, naturally arises in this rational speculation. It is nothing else than the union of attracted *karmic* matter with the Soul, which will automatically get combined with it.[142] The duration of this of passions present at the time of inflow. During this period of duration of *karmic* matter produces good or bad effects according to its nature, and having borne its proper fuit it falls off gradually.

So far the attraction and operation of *Karma* is defined but the next Tattva announces the motive of getting rid of these notorious *karmas*. For this, it is quite essential that the channel through which the *karmic* inflow is caused should be barred. This barring prevention is the *Saṁvara* the fifth *Tattva*.[143] Control of mind, speech and body with their objects, sensual desires and passions, etc., stop the further inflow. Hence there remains only the necessity of getting rid of those karmas which are in bondage with soul, before their maturity. This shedding off is the sixth *Tattva, Nirjarā*[144] and it is a kind of artificial and premeature fruition of *karmas*. It is achieved by means of giving up desires and practicing penances producing pure self-realization and concentration thereby. Finally the total freedom from the *karmas* is the *summum bonum* the true state of the soul. It is *mokṣa*---liberation, the last Tattva.[145] The liberated soul reaching a pure and blissful abode *(Siddha Śilā)* at the farthest end of the universe remains for ever pure and absorbed in its own true and perfect nature---All-Knowledge, All-Perception, Infinite Power and Infinite Bliss.[146]

The Karma matter which plays such an important part is mainly divided into following eight kinds:--

(1) *Jñānāvarṇiya* or the knowledge-obscuring *karma;* it suppresses the power of cognition.

(2) *Darśanāvarṇiya* or Perception-obscuring *karma;* it obscures the power of Perception.

(3) *Mohanīya* or Deluding *karma;* it undoes the right faith and right conduct of a soul.

(4) *Antarāya* or opposed *karma;* it interferes with the free functioning of a soul.

(5) *Vedaniya* or Affective *karma;* the result of it is the feeling of either pain or pleasure.

(6) *Nāma* or State-determining *karma;* it gives the soul the various factors of its objective individuality---celestial beings, man, animal, body, voice, etc.

(7) *Gotra* or Family determining karma; this brings the soul into a high or low family and determines its surroundings.

(8) *Āyu* or Age-determining karma; it determines the span of a soul's particular life.

These eight are again sub-divided into different sub-classes and there are 148 sub-classes in all.[147] The inflow of any particular sub-class will account for the state or condition of a soul at the time; even the very bones of an animal's body are determined by a *karma*, called *Asthi-Nāma-karma*. For a full description of these, reader is referred to the aforesaid Jaina metaphysical books.

Further these embodied souls migrating in this world, pass through four grades of life. These are *Deva*, *Manuṣya*, *Ṭriyañca* and *Naraka* and are styled *Gatis.*[148] The *Deva-gati* is the condition of existence in heavens, where the embodied souls enjoy great felicity and pleasure; though they are not quite rid of pain and misery. The second is the existence in human life. The lot of human beings is both pleasure and pain, but the pain has a great proportion with them. The *Triyañca- gati* embraces all such other forms of life as birds, brutes, insects, plants, metals, water,[149] fire, air, etc. This gati is more full of pain and misery.The last *Naraka-gati* is the life in hells, where the intolerable sufferings prevail all the time. Again these are all divided into sub-classes and have birth and death for their characteristics. The meritorious and demeritorious deeds of a soul in any of the above grades do follow it automatically in the next incarnation. Thus there is no fear of loosing the *pūṇya'* acquired in the present life.

However the inmates of heaven and hell enjoy the full spans of their lives, as dtermined by their Āyukarma.[150] The bodies of hellish beings though cut into pieces and destroyed under the influence of hell-tortures, yet they are not totally destroyed.[151] They continue in the same form until their *Āyukarma* is fully worked out and shaded off. Among the Triyañcas, there are two kinds of beings. viz (1) *Amanaska--without* mind and (2) *Samanaska* --with mind.[152] These, again into the movables and immovables. The soul embodied in the from of water, fire, air , earth and vegetable are immovable. They cannot move from the objects of their fear and are only one-sensed. The movables are birds, brutes, etc.[153] The *Manuṣya* are broadly divided into *Āryas* and Mlecchas.[154]

All the embodied beings have a certain kind of vitality, according to their grades of life. This vitality is a form of consciousness as manifested through the body of a mundane soul and is of ten kinds, i.e., the five senses (touch, taste, smell, sight, hearing), three powers of mind, body and speech, age and respiration.[155] Thus embodied souls are capable of accumulating the quantity of *karma* and of creating the intensity of passions only in accordance with their vitalities. And so there are designed six kinds of thought-colours which denote the intensity of passions and the worldly natures of karmic influence on the souls, known as *khata-lesyas.*[156] These could not be compared with the six *Abhijātis,* i.e., division of souls according to their colours, of Makkhali-Gosāla. In Jainsism no colour has been accepted to have risen in a mundane soul. All souls in their true nature are homogeneous and of same stuff. Hence it should not be confused with the above conception of *Ājīvikas.*

Buddha, on the other hand, has described six kinds of the existence of individuals.[157] They are the inmates of heaven and hell, men and animal, and *pretas* and *asuras*. The souls in the form of water, fire, wind and earth have no place in Buddhism; though life in vegetable form seem to have been accepted.[158] But a detailed scientific account of any of these is not available. This much we know that meritorious and demeritorious deeds done through ignorance cause the aggregation of individual in these existences to undergo pleasure or pain.

As to the spheres of situation of these existences, Buddha said that this universe consists of innumerable world systems with their earth, sun moon, heavens and hells.[159] Mahāvīra, too, maintained that there are innumerable world systems, with their earth,sun and moon; but the hells and heavens are the same for them all; because according to him, the universe, wrapped in with three kinds of air (vapourous, gross and thin), is divided into three regions, upper (ūrddhva), middle *(madhya)*, and below *(Adha)*,[160] The middle region possesses all these world systems, while the upper and lower regions are heavens and hells respectively. Buddha's dividosn of Universe into three regions *(avacaras)* worlds *(loka)* or layers *(dhātu)*, being the realms of desire *(kāma)*, material form *(rūpa)* and that of absence of form *(arūpa)*,[161] emboldens us to assume the probability of its formation under the influence of Jaina tradition. Besides the situation of hells and its description, tortures, no total-destruction of its inmates, Vaitarni, Simbali tree, etc. and styling it as *Duggati* and the layers of *pretas* and *asuras* are described mostly in accordance with the Jainas.[162] But, of course, that number of them differs in each system. According to Mahāvīra, they are seven and their regions are called:--

(1) Ratnaprabhā in hue like jewels and is hot

(2) Sarkarāprabhā in hue like sugar and is hot.

(3) Vālukaparabhā in hue like sand and is hot.

(4) Paṅkaprabhā in hue like mire and is hot.

(5) Dhūmaprabhā in hue like smoke and is hot only its 2 lacs hell layers and rest is cold.

(6) Tamahprabhā in hue like darkness and is cold.

(7) Mahātamahprabhā in hue like pitch darkenss and is cold. In all these there are in different numbers 84 lacs huge holes known as *Vilās,* in which hellish beings are born and live.[163]

While Buddha held them broadly-speaking to be eight, though he maintained many minor hells besides them as well. Perhaps they might have been sub-hells of the following eight, in identity with those of Mahāvīra's as described above:-

"Sañjīa, Kālasūtra, Saṅghāta, Raurava, Mahāraurava, Tapana, Pratāpana and the very deepest, Avīci." In the old system of the Northern Buddhists, there are, besides the eight hot hells, as many cold hells also.[164]

Thus we see that Buddhist and Jaina conceptions of hell have much in common and this might be due to the early belief of Buddha as a Jaina muni.

Happily the descriptions of the heavenly beings and their abodes also differ very slightly in both the systems. Mahāvīra says that there are four kinds of *Devas*: *Bhavanvāsī* (Residential), *Vyantara* (Peripatetic), Jyotiṣka (stellar) and *Vaimānkika* (Heavenly).[165] Every class has ten grades: *Indra, Sāmānika, Tryāstrimsa* (minister, priest, etc.) *Pārisada* (Courtiers), *Ātma-Rakṣaka, Lokapāla, Anika* (Army), *Prakīrnaka* (people), *Abhiyoga* (that grade of celestial beings who form themselves into conveyances) and *Kilbhiska* (the servile grade).[166] In Buddhist Canon, too, the first kind is known as *Bhummadevas,*[167] second as the *Pretas* and *Asuras* of *Apāyas,*[168] third as the sun, moon etc.[169] and the fourth the residents of seven abodes of gods in *Kāmāvacaraloka* and others[170]. The last named are the heavenly beings in true sense according to the Jainas. Their *vimānas* are situated just above the mount Meru in couples and are sixteen in all.[171] Above these are *Graiveyaka, Anudisa, Anuttara* and *Sarvārth-*

Siddhi heavens.[172] The residents of these are males and have no sexual desires. These are called *Ahamindras*. Buddha's heavens of *Rūpaloka* had the same meaning with him.[173] The *Lukāntika- devas* of the Jainas, who have their abode in the *Brahmaloka* situated in the highest part of the fifth heaven and who have elevated their souls so high on the Right Path that they shall attain Liberation (*Nirvāṇa*) in their very next incarnation of human being.[174] seem to be quite identical with the Buddhist gods of *Brahma-loka*, who reach this abode after practising a great meditation.[175] But the number of the abodes of heavenly beings in Buddhist Canon, however, is not a fixed one. We find it even seven, eight, sixteen and seventeen as well.[176] Now leaving it, as it may be, we see without any doubt that apparently a great resemblance, also, pervails between them and those of the Jainas. A full justice to them cannot be expected here for the sake of brevity. Still it is clear that the Buddhists and the Jainsas both agree that individuals have birth in heavens in consequence of their meritorious deeds done previously; but the Jainas deny the fact that the heavenly beings could attain *Nirvāṇa* from their various abodes.[177] But the meritorious deeds even of a soul in lower grades of life will entitle it to attain heaven. We are told a frog in its deep devotion to Mahāvīra breathed its last under the feet of King Śrenika's elephant and attained *Devagatī*.[178] A similar parable is narrated in the Buddhsit book, "*Visuddhi-Magga*."[179] It is also co-extensive in both the religions that heavenly beings suffer pleasure and pain according to their good or bad dispositions; but those gods, who are in a way free from attachment, do not feel any grief, though they are conscious of it.[180] Besides, both agree as to the Devas having the power of changing their form but the Buddha seems to deny the *Avadhijñāna* in them[181].

Thus the embodied souls suffer pleasure and pain again and again through delusion in the above grades of life. The adoration of Truth and Self-contemplation shall make them acquire the discriminating sight (*Bheda-Vijñāna*). And that once acquired, the soul will remain making its progress on the Right Path. Truly the Jaina thinker says:--

"He, who has acquired discrimination between the Self and not- Self, through the teaching of the perception, by repeated meditation on the natue of things, or by direct inner

Self- perception, that great soul enjoys the happiness appertaining to salvation constantly".[182]

Mahāvīra has declared the three-fold Path of Right Belief, Right Knowledge and Right Conduct, for the release of embodied souls from transmigration which path is styled as *'Ratna-Traya'* (Three Jewels) *Dharma* in the Jaina *Śastras.*[183] Right Belief, according to the *vyavahāra-naya* (practical view-point, for there are described two points, real and practical, of looking at things, the latter being an auxiliary cause for the real)[184] is the belief in the aforesaid Tattvas. Knowledge of the aforesaid *Tattvas* is the true Practical Knowledge. Due observance of the prescribed vows and rules is the Practical Right Conduct.[185] While these above mentioned three jewels from the real view-point are respectively the belief, knowledge and attainment of the true and pure nature of soul itself. Real Right Conduct is nothing other than Self-absorption.

Practical Right Conduct is twofold : (1) less rigid for householders and (2) strictly austere, the direct cause of liberation, to be pursued by ascetics and saints.[186] The householder begins with the acquisition of Right Faith and Knowledge and takes to the partial observance of five vows of Non-Injury (*Ahiṁsā*), Truthfulness (*Satya*), Non-Theft (*Acourya*), Chastity (*Brahmacarya*) and Non-Attachment (*Aparigraha*).[187] Then he gradually improves his observance of the vow, step by step, through what hare technically known as *Pratimās,* till he also becomes a saint (*Śramaṇa*). These *Pratimās* are eleven in number and mark the spiritual progress made by the soul from time to time and signify the imprvement made in the next step from the preceding one.[188] These constitute various kinds of rules such as *Guṇavratas* (observance of making perpetual and daily vow to go to certain directions and to certain distances only[189] and avoidance of useless talk,act or thought of sinful things), *Śikṣāvrata* (limitation in the articles of diet and enjoyment for the day, worship at fixed times and charity), *Sāmāyika* (regular meditaion), *Prosda* (fasting on the 8th and 14the days of lunar fortnight)[190] etc., tec., After completing these pratimās the householder reaches the state of sainthood and then he begins the practice of *Mahā-Vratas.* He observes all the above vows in full. And we are told that for self- realisation both saints and laymen, follow their respective six essential daily duties. For the saints, they are:--

"Equanimity, i.e. the condition of mind free from worldly love and hatred, penitence for past faults, intention not to commit faults in future, praising the Holy person, bowing to the Holy ones, and renunciation of bodily attachent."

And for laymen, they are described as follows:-

"(1) Worship of the Holy ones---the Conquerors of *Karmas*--by their spiritual qualities. The idols of *Arahats* represent the feature of self-contemplation, thus impressing on the worshiper's mind the pure nature of the Self; (2) Service to the Preceptors and listening to their preachings; (3) Some minor vows for control of mind and senses such as : -- To-day I shall refrain from going to the theatre; I shall have only two meals during the day; shall not use scents etc., etc. These are small self denials to strengthen self-control and to speed one on the realisation of self-absorption; (4) Reading Holy books; (5)Contemplation--i.e. twice a day, morning and evening or only once, sitting in lonely place and meditating upon the nature of Holy Ones or one's own soul thereby acquiring equanimity by renouncing attachment and hatred to worldly things during the time devoted to contemplation (6) Charity---practise charity of food, medicine knowledge and fearlessness. The six daily duties induce pure thought in saints and laymen and enable them to reach Self-absorption -- a state where real Right Belief, Right Knowledge and Right Conduct are present in one interfused condition. It is the path of shedding off much *karmic* dirt and making the soul pure and free."[191]

The progress towards Self-absorption is technically styled as *Gunasthānas*[192], which are 14 in all. In the 13th stage (*Gunasthāna*) the Saint destroys those of the four *karmas*--*Jñānāvarṇiya, Darśaṇāvarṇīya, Mohanīya, Antrāya*-- which obstruct the true nature of soul and attaining Omniscience he becomes an *Arahat--Sayogakevalī* or *Sakalparmātmā*, i.e. Vibrating Perfect Soul or Living God.[193] These are of two kinds, *Sāmānyakevalī* and *Tīrthaṅkara.*[194] The *Sāmānyakevalīs* effect their own salvation and preach and tour in an ordinary manner, without any *samosarana* of 12 *sabhās* (preaching hall) while Tīrthaṅkaras have the *samosarana* and from there, teach the afflicted people the way to their deliverance from the pangs of the world and address the *Tīrtha*, or the assembly of the four great groups of people -- the monks, the nuns, the householders and ladies.[195] Nemicandrācārya says, "One who is an *Arahat*, has destroyed the four kinds of the *Ghāti Karma*. He is possessed of the four Infinities, viz., of Perception, of Knowledge, of Happiness and of Power. He is embodied in a glorious body. He is pure."[196] He is free from the eighteen faults,--hunger, thirst, fear, envy, attachment, delusion, thought, old age, disease, death, sorrow, sweating, pride, langour, surprise, birth, sleep and grief.[197] His body shines like the brilliance of a thousand suns. He is free from all desires, uttely pure and absolutely spotless. He is the first among the five Great Beings whom the Jainas worship daily.[198]

Now when the visible Lord reaches the 14the stage, He becomes *Ayogakevalī--Non* vibrating Perfect Soul, Perfect God. 'This is attained when there is before the *Sayogakevalī's* liberation just enough time to speak out the five letters अ इ उ ऋ लृ. In this stage--a very brief one indeed--the vibration of the holy body ceases, and the soul attaining peace and bliss becomes one with itself and leaving the body is called Siddha'[199] The Siddha never returns to world, but remains absorbed in his own essence for ever.

The Siddha is an adorable God. Though he has nothing to do with the world and its activities, yet he is a source of goodness and self-contemplation to the aspirants. The Ācārya says:--

"The Siddha has no body which is constituted of the eight modes of *karma*. He sees and knows the *Loka* (the Universe), and the *Aloka* (the Non Universe). He is really completely disembodied, but (from the practical point of view) he is supposed to have a size of his soul (slightly less than his last corporeal frame). He stays at the summit of *Lokākāsa*."[200] After getting freed from the *karmas* he naturally proceeds into an upward motion, in the same manner as a clay-coated gourd, being washed off, bobs to the surface.[201]

In this way Mahāvīra prescribed the scientific path for the release of embodied beings. To sum up, he declared that the soul suffers pain and misery in this world, owing to its own delusion and folly, under the influence of *karmic* matter, which is assimilated with it since eternity. And when it discriminates its own nature and that of not-self, real and unreal, it realises the Truth, and starts to tread on the threefold Right Path, with such perseverance that at a time all misery and pain are left behind and it becomes a perfect Master to enjoy the bliss of final Beatitude. Thus the independence of the Soul is quite evident in the system of Mahāvīra.[202]

Turning to Budda, we find him declaring that:--

"All foolish individuals, O king, take pleasure in the senses and in the objects of sense, find delight in them continue to cleave to them. Hence are they carried down by that flood (of human passions), they are not set free from birth, old-age and death, from grief, lamentation, pain, sorrow and despair--they are not set free, I say, from suffering. But the wise, O king, the disciple of the Noble Ones neither takes pleasure in those things, nor finds delight in them nor continues cleaving to them. And inasmuch as he does not, in him craving ceases, and by the cessation of craving, grasping ceases and by the cessation of grasping, becoming ceases and when becoming has ceased birth ceases and with its cessation old age, death, grief, lamentation, pain, sorrow and despair cease to exist. Thus the cessation brings about the end of all that aggregation of pain. Thus is it that cessation is *Nirvāṇa*."[203]

Hence Buddha's highest aim was complete passing away and for this very end he preached his norm path of renunciation[204] which constituted the eightfold path of right views, right aspirations, right speech, right conduct, right livelihood, right effort, right mindfulness and right rapture, that is, mental tranquillity[205]. Thus this eightfold path is intended to stop the wheel of Life and is prescribed for monks and nuns only. In it are included various rules and vows for the *Sākyan Samaṇas*. The most important *Sīlas*, too, find place in it, which are somewhat identical with the twelve *śīlas* of the Jainas (5 *Anuvratas*, 3 *Guṇavratas* and 4 *Śikṣāvratas*). The eight *śīlas* (precepts) of the Buddhist ascetics are : (1)non-injury, (2) non-stealing (3) abstinence from impurity and unlawful sexual intercourse, (4) truthfulness (5) abstinence from intoxicating drinks, (6) not to eat at forbidden time and at night,(7) refraining from dancing, singing, and using garlands, scents, ornaments, etc. (8) to sleep on mat spread on ground.[206] This first four of these quite agree with the first four *anuvrates* of the Jainas, but their fifth precept is more comprehensive than the corresponding one of the Buddhists. And the rest three, also appear as an abridged shape of the four *Śikṣāvratas* of the Jainas. This agreement is so striking that we cannot doubt, if the Buddha have borrowed them from the Jainas,who were already in existence at the time of the foundation of Buddhism.[207] It is supported by the narration of the formation of Buddhist precepts and the rules of Order, as given in the *Mahāvagga* and *Cūlavagga*. It is obvious from this that they were framed as necessity arose. And such rules as abiding at one place during the riny reason (*vassā*) and the appointment of the *Uvājhyāyas* and *Ācāryas*, etc., are clearly stated to have been adopted under the influence of the *Titthiyas*, which include the *Nigaṇṭhas* (Jainas) too.[208] Besides it is notable that the divion of ascetics into *Uvājhyāyas* and *Ācāryas*, etc., is only traceable in the Order of *Nigaṇṭhas* (Jaina ascetics) and the observance of *vassā rule* is a distinct feature of them.[209] Hence the Buddhist author here apparently had the meaning of *Nigaṇṭhas* in using the word *Tittiyas*. Thus it is conceivable that the Buddists borrowed materials from the Jainas in framing the rules and precepts of their Order.

It should, however, be remembered that though the above precepts of both the systems bear a resemblance, yet they are not so comprehensive in Buddhism as in Jainism and so they cannot be compared with the *Mahāvratas* of a Jaina *muni*. Hardly they cope with that much field as is covered by the *Anuvratas* of a lay Jaina. A comparative account of them will leave no doubt about it, but owing to the scarcity of space at our disposal, we confine ourselves only to compare the *Ahiṁsā* vow of the both. Apparently it has the same meaning with them both, but a Buddhist *Samana*, even observing it, will not hesitate to take meat and fish if offered to him.[210] A Jaina layman, on the contrary, will not touch them, though he observes this *ahiṁsā* vow in a less rigid manner than a Jaina *muni*.[211] This also bears out the credibility of the view expressed above for we know that Buddha aimed at making his "Norm" less rigid than that of the *Niganṭhas.* Thus Buddha's moral code is viewed in short.

The aspirant, who acquires faith in Buddha, *Dhamma,* and *Saṅgha* (particularly in Buddha) and shakes off his delusion of egoity, he gains inner-sight and becomes an *Arahat,* as is apparent from the facts of first converts of Buddha.[212] And having become an *Arahat,* he continues his pursuit of the eightfold path. Rhys Davids assures us that "the victory to be gained by the destruction of ignorance (of Individuality) is, in Gotama's view, a victory which can be gained and enjoyed in this life, and in this life only. This is what is meant by the Buddhist ideal of *Arahantship* --the life of a man made perfect by insight, the life of a man who has travelled along the "Noble eightfold path" and broken all the "fetters" and carried out in its entirety, the Buddhist system of self culture and self-control".[213]

Now when the aspirant has fully mastered the noble eightfold path and has elevated himself in meditaion etc., Buddha said, to him appears the light of th best of Aryan knowledge. This is the *Nirvāṇa* of Buddha and is attained before the bodily death of sage. It brings with it happiness of the highest order.[214] But Buddha is silent about the state after it. If ever he breaks his silence on the point it is not definite-sometime quite nihilism and on others something real; but the former holds the foremost ground, as we have seen in the aforementioned quotation from an orthodox Buddhist book.

Apparently the *Arahatship* and the *Nirvāṇa* of Buddha are identical with *Kshāyika -Samyaktva* and *Arahatship* of the Jainas respectively but in an outward shape only. The *Arahat* of the Buddhists has not the same identity as the *Arahat* of the Jainas. Rather it is comparable with the *Nirvāṇa* of the Buddhists, which seems to coincide ouwardly with the Jaina description of the *Sayogakevalī*[215], though there also lies a great difference between them. Therefore it is certain that the *Arahatship* is the highest aim of and most revered by a Jain aspirant; while the Buddhahood is the same for a Buddhist follower. In Buddhism *Arahatship* has not the same place and meaning as in Jainism.

In this manner we have attempted to get a glimpse of the respective lives and teachings of Buddha and Mahāvīra, and we find that a wide full of dissimilarities divides them to a great distance from each other. Mahāvīra's life is a model of perfect and ideal man and his teachings are more systematic and rational, appealing to the heart and intellect alike. Buddha's life is, however, of that of a healer and reformer of mankind only and his teachings have no fremost value with his votaries.[216] But a great noteworthy thing is that though Buddha aimed at bringing into his fold all the different sects and creeds and constituted his systems after taking something from, and resembling to a degree, all the prominent schools of thought of the time and even paid no heed to its validity,[217] but still it gave not the true healing balm to the suffering humanity and a principle of adversity in diversity. Yet it should not be oversighted that Buddha had a very clear perception of the misery of unemancipated life, of which he drew in words a most faithful picture.

Mahāvīra aimed at defining the very nature of things and a true path for the emancipation of all living being of any grade quite in a scientific way. And as such his principle of *Syādvāda* was quite peculiar to him and was a very successful attempt to explain the exact reality of an object. The universe being itself a complex of innumerable elements and aspects and our knowledge being imperfect, we cannot grasp the whole of it from our limited standpoints. Hence ours are the only partial side-views and could not be relied upon. Therefore Jain thinker has propagated the seven modes of speech viz. "from some point of view a substance is, is not, is and is not, is unpredictable,and is not and is unpredicable."[218] These seven modes of speech describe the relation between a substance and its conditions according to their various aspects.

For a full description of this important principle of Jainism a study of *Āpta-mimāṁsā*, *Syādvādamañjarī* and *Saptabhaṅgitaringinī* is necessary. Thus it is an omniscient teacher who attributes to the substance impartially. Hence the necessity of *Syādvāda* is quite obvious. But the Nyāya of Buddha contains no such thing. And owing to the lack of this very important principle, the Buddhist idea of entire impermanence could be styled only one-sided, as we have already pointed above. However here again viewing it comparatively, we find Buddhists saying that there is every-thing impermanent in this world; and he exhorts:-

"Look upon the world as a bubble, look upon it as a mirage, the king of death does not see him, who thus looks down upon the world."--(Dhammapada, xiii, 170)

Further it is said emphatically:-

"All created things perish, he who knows and sees this becomes passive in pain, this is the way to purity."-- (ibid. xx. 277).

But in the system of *Syādvāda* no such thing could be found. Mahāvīra rightly warned his disciple that:-

"He should not believe that (this world) is without beginning or without end, eternal or not eternal, according to the argumentation (of heretics)." --(JS. Pt. II. p. 405).

All such questions, He declared, must be decided with the help of the *Syādvāda*, "which in an admirable way removes all difficulties, e.g., the world is eternal as far as that part is concerned which is the substratum of the idea (*sāmānya*) 'world'; it is not eternal as far as its everchanging state is meant." (Ibid. f. n.). Hence the substance is defined as "*Sada-dravya-lakṣaṇam.* 29. *Utpāda-vyaya-dhrouvya-yuktam sat* 30-5 *Tattvārtha-Sūtra.*" It means that the substance is that which is eternal; and the eternal is that in which are found the conditions of birth, decay and duration at every moment. The Jaina Canons give a full explanations to these views and so they should be studied for a thorough elucidation. Herein a full justice cannot be done to them. It is enough to point out that in the teachings of Mahāvīra things are viewed and explained in all their aspects, which is quite necessary and natural in a scientific treatment of the things. In the similar way the position of Self is defined. In this system of *Syādvāda* no such teaching finds place solely from a single view-point, as Buddha taught:--

"Look upon the world as void, O Mogharagan, being always thoughtful having destroyed the view of oneself (as really existing) so one may overcome death; the king of death will not see him, who thus regards the World."---(Sutta-Nipāta, Vol. X.p. 208)

Quite in reverse to this Mahāvīra taught that:--

"the Self is ever One, Eternal, Pure, and All-knowing in its essence. The rest are all outside the Self, non-eternal and brought about as results of action."--(Saint Amitgati's *Samayika*. 20).

Hence, "the Self encased in the body undergoes various sorts of sufferings, because of this connection; therefore those who desire Deliverance of their Selves should avoid this corporeal contact either through mind or speech or action."---(Ibid. 28)

Thus the Self though unperishing and eternal, yet passes away on death, owing to its association with the karmas, into some other form of life and continues to suffer pain and misery until its emancipation. Now no such assertion is found in Buddism. So rightly the Jaina saint Mallisena praised Mahāvīra:--

"अन्योन्य पक्षप्रतिपक्षभावात् यथा परे मत्सरिण: प्रवादा: ।

नया न शेषानपिशेषमिच्छन् न पक्षपातौ समयस्तथति ॥"

i.e., "Showing how the same thing may be viewed equally from innumerable standpoints, your position is not partial like that of those who are rancorous of each other, because their position happens to be opposed."

Now *Syādvāda,* if rightly applied to life, stands firmly for religious tolerance, too, along with the intellectual impartiality. And it is not curious that after the preaching of Mahāvīra, most of the prevailing creeds disappeared. Thus we reach to the end of our treatise.

Notes & References :

1. *Ādipurāṇa* of Jinasena
2. *Bhāgavata,* 5, 4,5,6
3. *Sāṅkhya Sūtras,* 21-24, *Nyāya-Sātras,* 1; 1;1 and *Vaiśeṣika Sātras,* 1;1;4
4. To the Jains, Buddhists and other wandering teachers it was a great necessity to pass a practical life full of thought and true knowledge. Buddha's Norm Path (*Mahāvagga,* 1,6) and the following aphorism of the "Jaina Bibble" can be referred to in this connection "सम्यग्दर्शनज्ञानचारित्राणमोक्षमार्गः" ।१ ।१ । तत्वार्थसूत्र
5. *Buddhist India,* p. 141
6. LB. pp. 5-10 and JS.pt. I, p. 191
7. Law B.C., *Some Kṣatriya Tribes of Ancient India,* p. 123
8. JS. pt. I. p. 192.
9. The *Śvetāmbara* Jains describe him to have married a princess by name Yaśodharā, but the Digambaras flatly deny this. They say that the father of Yaśodharā wanted to give her in marrigage to Mahāvira, but he did no accept this offer, viz:-
"भवान्त्र किं श्रंणिकवेत्ति भू० तिं नृपेन्द्रसिन्हाथ कनौयसौपतिं ।
इमं प्रसिद्ध जितशच माख्यया प्रतावन्त' जित शच्चु मण्डलम् ।।६ ।।
जिनेन्द्र वौरत्य समुद्भवोत्सवे तदागतः कुंडपुरं सुहृदद्दतः ।
सुपूजितः कुण्डपुरुय भूभृता नृपोऽययारमण्डल तुल्ये विक्रमः ।।७ ।।
यशोदयायां सुतया यशोदया पवित्रयां वैर विवाह मंगलम् ।
अनेक कन्या परिवारयऽऽरुहृत्सभौक्षितुं तु 'गमनोरुथ' सदा ।।८ ।। हरिवंश पुराणः ।।"
10. Jainsim was prevalent before Mahāvīra is now a proved fact. The references to the Jainas (*Nigaṇṭhas*) in Buddhist literature bear testimony to this as it is shown by Jacobi in the Introduction to the Jaina *Sūtras*. It is well- known that there were then mainly two opposite sects, i.e. *Samaṇas* and *Brāhmaṇas*. The *Sutta Nipāta* describes the *samaṇas* as of four kinds (vv. 83-88). Really these with the exception of the 4th kind actually coincide with the living teachers of the Jains, whose religion is styled as *samaṇa- dhamma;* (*Kalpa-Sūtra* p. 83), viz (1)*Arahat Jina,*

(2) *Nirgranṭha Ācārya*, (3) *Nirg. Upādhyāya*, and (4) *Nirg. Sādhu*. These, with *Siddhas*, are styled as Pañca *Parmeshtīs*, whom the Jainas worship daily and the following ancient formula corroborates the existence of these FIVE GREAT BEINGS from the very beginning of Jainism:-
"NAMO ARHANTĀ NAMA, NAMO SIDDHĀ NAMA,NAMO ĀYIRYĀ NAMA, NAMO UYAJJHĀYĀ NAMA, NAMO LOYE SABBA SĀHU NAMA." This coincidence, too, supports the pre- Buddhistic existence of Jainism. Siddhārtra professed this religion. The *Lalitavistara* describes tha Buddha used to wear in boyhood some peculiar marks, such as, *Śrīvatsa, Svastika, Nandyāvarta* and *Vardhamāna*. The former three of these are the *cihnas* (marks) of Jaina Tīrthaṅkaras, Śrī Śītalnāth, Supārśvanāth and Arahanāth and the last is itself the very name of the last Tīrthaṅkara. Hence it makes us bold to guess the Jaina belief of Buddha's parents.

11. JS. pt. I.p. 256, but here the *Śvetāmbara* author describes the parents of Mahāvīra to be dead,, but the *Digāmbaras* say that they were alive at this time. See Guṇabhadra's *Uttara-Purāṇa*.
12. LB. p. 12 ff.
13. JS. pt. I. pp. 256-257
14. LB. p. 130 ff.
15. Ibid, 131.
16. Ibid, 141
17. Idem.
18. LB. p. 141
19. JS. pt. I. pp. 39-41
20. Devasenācārya of the 8th century A.D. describes it thus:--
"सिरिपासणाहतित्थे सरयू तौरे पलासणयरत्थो ।
पिहिय सवत्स सिस्सो महासुदो बुड्ढकित्तिमुर्णा ॥६ ॥
तिमि पूरूासणोहिं अहिगयपवज्जायोपरिब्भट्टो
रत्तबरं धरित्ता पवट्टियं तेाण एयंतं ॥७ ॥
मंसस्स णत्थि जौवो ज़हाफले दहिय-दुड्व९ सक्करए ।
तन्हा तं वंछित्ता तं भक्खंतो ण पाविट्टो ॥८ ॥

अणो करेदिकम्मं अणो वं भुंजदौदिसिङ्गंतं ।
परिकप्पिऊणणूणं वसिकिच्चाणिरययुववणो ॥"१० ॥ दर्शनसार ॥

In the last gāthā the "Kṣaṇika-Vāda" of Buddha is referred to and as such is clear that the Jaina author is writing precisely about Buddha.

21. Fish and flesh if not specially procured, were acceptable to Buddhist monks is apparent from these passages: *Mahāvagga* VI, 31, 11 and 14; VI, 23, 2, VI 25,2; *Mahā-pari-nibbāna Sutta* IV, 17-18; and Sutta-Nipāta 241 (p.40)
22. See the Discoures of Gotama tr. by Silācāra, 1, 97-99 quoted by Mr. K.J. Saunders in his "Gotama Buddha" p. 15
23. See *The Mūlācārā* I, 29, and the JS. pt. I. p. 56
24. JS. pt. I. p. 79.
25. Ibid, p. 56.
26. JS.pt. I. p. 57
27. Ibid p. 71
28. Ibid., p. 73
29. *The Heart of Jainism*, p. 35
30. JS. pt. I., p. 57 f.n. In the original texts of the *Śvetāmbara Āgama*, no such division is found. Thus its authenticity is open to doubt.
31. ERE Vol. VII. p. 472
32. Śvetātāmbaras say that a celestial robe was given by Indra and Mahāvīra wore it (garment of gods) for a year and few mounths more, but wearing it, he looked like naked and after that period he threw away even that. On this, Rev. Dr. Stevenson comments that *Śvetāmbara* "Jainas do not understand properly what it means, or do not wish to explain it. It might have meant he became a *Digambara*, had this not been opposed to what follows." (*Kalpa-Sūtra*, p. 85 f.n.). Thus to a rational mind, it gives no reliable explanation; rather encourages us to say that Mahāvīra became a naked *muni* from the very day of his rennciation. The meaning of *Jinakalpi* and *Sthavirakalpi* are different with the *Digambara* Jainas from the above.

33. Buddhist references are : *Divyāvadāna* p. 165; *Jātaka-mālā*, S.B.B. Vol. I., p. 145; *Viśākhāvatthu, Dhamma-padaṭṭha-kathā* (P.T.S.), Vol. I., pt. II., p. 38; 4 *Dialogues of the Buddha*, pt. III., p. 14; *Mahāvagga*, 8 15; 3; 1; 38; 16, *Cūllavagga*, 8, 28, 3, *Samyutta-nikāya*, 2,3,10,7. And the Brahmanical references are : *Varāhamihira- Samhitā*, 19, 61 and 45, 58 *Mahābhārata*, 3, 26-27, *Rāmāyaṇa Bālakāṇḍa*, 14, 22 commentary by Bhūṣaṇa.

34. Ind. Antiquary, Vol. 43.

35. 'सद्देथा प्रथमः अश्रु मूधैजान अपनायेदने ।
सित कौपोन सं आनः कतरियावाक्षुरेण वा ॥३८ ॥
तद्दत् द्वितीयः किन्त्वायिं संज्ञा लुंचप्तसौकवान् ।
कौपौनमाव युग्धत्ते यतिवन्द्रति भासनम् ॥४८ ॥ सागर धर्मामृत् ॥
"उत्कृष्टः श्रावको भवेत् द्विविधः वस्त्रैकधरः प्रथमः कौपौन परिग्रहोऽन्यास्तु ॥"
स्वामिकीति केयानुप्रेक्षा ।

36. "Dialogues of the Buddha" (S.B.B.) in its "Kassapa-sihanāda--sutta" gives a list of ascetic practiees, which the author says, are "in the opinion of some samaṇas and Brāhmaṇas, as samanaship and Brahmanaship." Really these are intended for the Jaina nirgranthas; as will be apparent from their comparison with the practices given for Jaina monks in the Jaina śāstra Mūlācāra of early centuries of Christian era, viz :

Buddhist Author.	**Jaina Author.**
1. He goes naked.	It is one out of the 28 root characteristics of a Jaina muni and is described thus:— 'वत्थाजिणवक्कणेथ' अहव पत्तादिणा असंरण । णिव्भूसण णिग्गंयं अञ्चेलकं जगदि-पूज्ज ॥३० ॥
2. He is of loose habits (performing his bodily functions and eating food in a standing posture, not crouching down as well-bred people do)	This constitutes the 24th (Non-bathing) 26th (Non-brushing of teeth), and 27th (Taking meal in a standing posture) (31-32-33) mūla-guṇas.

3. He licks his hands clean, etc.	It is known that Jaina muni takes food in the hollow of his hands and sips the placed food without taking it into morsels and turning it from jaw to jaw. (JS., pt. I., p. 57). The Buddhist author here seems to point this practice.
4. When on his rounds for alms, etc.	It is described in full in commentary on Aishana samiti; viz :— 'भिक्षावेलायां ज्ञातवा प्रशान्ते धूम मुशलादि शब्दे गोचरं प्रविशेन्मुनिः । तत्र गच्छन्नाति द्रुतंए न मन्दंए न विलम्बितं गच्छेत् ।
5. He refuses to accept food brought (to him, before he has started, etc.).	In Aishana samiti the recluse is allowed to take only pure food, void of 46 doṣas (defilements) and in procuring it he will have no concern of mind, speech and body and it must not be specially prepared for him. If he accepts food brought to him, he will be taking it, knowing that it has been specially prepared for him and thus cause defiling. So it is not allowed. (śloka 13)
6. He refuses to accept (food, if told that it has been prepared) especially for him.	In it too the Kārita and Anumodanā doṣas are apparent.
7. He refuses to accept any invitation, etc.	The same is the case here.
8. He will not accept food taken from the mouth of the pot or pan, etc.	It is "Sthāpita or Nyasta doṣa."

9. He will not accept food within the threshold, (lest it should have been, etc.).	These are "Prādushakara Doṣa."
10. He will not accept food placed among the sticks, etc.	
11. (He will) not (accept food) placed among the pestles (lest it should, etc.).	It is the Unmisra-Ashana-Doṣa.
12. When two persons are eating, etc.	It is Aneshwara-Vyaktāvyakta-Aneeshārtha-Doṣa.
13. He will not accept food from a woman giving suck, etc.	These are described among 35 Dāyaktāvyakta-Ashana-Doṣas.
14. He will not accept food from a woman in intercourse with a man, etc.	It seems Abhighāt-Udagama-Doṣa.
15. He will not accept food collected.	It seems Pādāntara Jiva sampāta or Daushaka Dosha.
16. He...food where a dog is standing.	It seems Pāni-jantu-Badha-Doṣa.
17. He...food where flies are swarming	
18. He...fish, nor meat, nor strong drind, nor intoxicants, nor gruel.	It requires no corroboration; viz :— "खौरदहिसप्पिलेन गुडलवणाण खजं परिञ्चयण । तित्ताकटुकसाय विलम धरसाण चज 'चयण' ॥१५५ ॥ चत्तारि महावियड़ोय होंति णवणौद मज्जमांस मधु । कखामसंगदेप्पासंजम कारौओं एदाओ ॥१५६ ॥
19. He is a "one-houser", etc., etc.	It is the Vrata-Parisankhyata Practice.

20. He takes food only once a day, or once every two days, etc., etc.	it is the Sākānkṣānakṣhāna vrata.

For a full comparative treatment of the subject, see the Jaina Hostel Magazine, Vol. VI, No.2, and the Vīra, Vol. II., pp. 580-588, and the Indian Historical Quarterly Vol. II. pp. 702-704 as well.

37. The Jaina Itihāsa Series. pt. I. p. 13
38. Idem
39. Supplement to the *Confluence of Opposites*, p. 27
40. See Dr. Barua's "The Ājīvikas," pt. I
41. For a full view on the point, please refer to my books "Bhagavāna Mahāvīra." and "Bhagwāna Mahāna Mahāvīra aur Mahātmā Buddha." It is too probable that the "kūla" might mean the "kula" (family or clan); because Mahāvīra renouncing the world remained fot two days in the Vanakhanda forest, adjoining his birth place. Hence a Rājā (Feudatory Chief) of his own clan (kula) might have entertained him in his own birth place Kūlanagar- Kṣatriyakhanda of Kundanagara).
42. JS. pt. I., p. 200
43. Ibid p. 201
44. JS. pt. I., p. 201
45. JS. pt. II., p. 41 n. 2 And Uttarapurāṇa pp. 614-616.
46. Buddhist references are : Majjhima, 1, 238 an 92-93; Aṅguttara, iii, 74; 'Buddhist scholar and saint of the standing of Dharmakīrti, actually cites the insances of Śrī Ṛṣabhadev and Śrī Vardhamāna Mahāvīra, the 1st and the last of the Jain Tirthaṅkaras, as endowed with omniscience, while illustrating some of his syllogistic prepositions.' (The Nyāyabindu, Ch. III. quoted in the "Science of Thought") Brahmanical references; Pañcatantra, ed. Keilhorn, V.1.
47. JS. pt. II., Intro p. xv.
48. Jain, C.R. *Confluence of Opposites* p. 14
49. BP., p. 62
50. BP.,pp. 30-31
51. *Mahāvagga*, I, 7, 8, I, 15-20 and BP. p. 29

52. *The Dialogues of the Buddha-Poṭṭhapāda Sutta-* (S.B.B.), p. 254 and BP pp. 36 and 63.
53. Questions of King Milinda iv, i. 29 SBE. Vol xxxv, p. 154
54. Idem
55. *Samyutta-Nikāya*, pt. I., pp. 78-79 and Mahāparinibbāṇa-Sutta, SBE, Vol. xi p. 14
56. JS. pt.I., Intro. xx
57. *Mahāvagga*, 1,5,1
58. LB p. 188
59. *Mahāvagga*, I., 6, 9-15.
60. Ibid. I., 6, 47
61. LB. p. 172
62. Jain, C.R. op. cit p. 149
63. BP. p. 62
64. Co-p. 150 and BP., p. 121
65. परमट्ठिन्रिय अठिदो जो कुणदि तवं वदं च धारयदि ।
    तं सव्व वाल तवं वालकं विति सव्वराइ ॥१५९ ॥
    वदणियमाण धरंता सीलाणितहा तवं च कुव्वता ।
    परमट्ठ वाहिराजेण ते होंति अक्षाणी ॥१९० ॥ श्रीकुन्दकुन्दाचार्य ।
66. Divine Discousrse, p. 8
67. These passages from the Buddhist Canon speak for themselves: Suttanipāta, pp. 60, 63, and 146, 148; *Dhammapada*, Ch. I. etc.
68. JS. pt. I., p. 269
69. Idem
70. *Sāmagāma Sutta* M., Vol II. (P.T.S), p. 243 and Pāṭika sutta of Dīgha Nikāya, III., p. 1
71. LB., p. 283. ff. or Buddhist Suttas pp. 99-101.
72. Ājivikas, Hastings' ERE
73. Life and Legend of Gautama quoted in Saunders' Gotama Buddha, p. 54
74. "तव जिन शासन विभवो जयति कखावपि गुणानुशासन विभवः ।
    दोषकशासन विभवः स्तुवंति चैनं प्रभा क्वशासन विभवः ॥१३७ ॥
    अनवद्यः स्याद्दादस्तव दृष्टेष्टा विरोधतः स्याद्वादः ।

इतरी न स्याद्वादोसदित्य विरोधात्मुनीश्वराऽस्याद्वादः ॥१३८ ॥
त्वमसि सुरासर महितोगुत्तिकसत्त्वाशय प्रणमा महितः।
लोकत्रय परम हितोऽनावरण ज्योतिरुज्जवलुङ्काम हितः ॥१३९ ॥
—वृहद् स्वयंभूस्तोत्र

75. Fausboll's Jātaka, Vol II., p. 128
76. *Historical Gleanings*, p. 78
77. *Jaina Gazette*, XXI., pp. 254
78. *The Āivikas*, pt. I., p. 58
79. Saunder's K.J. *Gotama Buddha* pp. 72-73
80. *Historical Gleanings*, p. 25
81. Ibid p. 79
82. Śrenika Caritra.
83. Kern's *Indian Buddhism* pp. 38-39
84. In Cullavaga (vii, 3, 14), it is accepted in these words that "the peop;e believe in rough measures" and so they condemned Buddha with luxury and abundance (viii, 3, 16)
85. Pāsādika-Suttanta, *The Dialogues of the Buddha*, pt iii., p. 112
86. *Some Kṣatriya Tribes of Ancient India* p. 154
87. *Historical Gleanings*, . 24
88. *Sutta-Nipāta*, S.B. E. Vol. X. p. 87
89. *Life of Mahāvīra* by Manikchand Jaini. and JS., pt ii, Intro.
90. Indian Antiquary, Vol. 43
91. *Majjhima Nikāya*, II., p. 143
92. 'Madanakossa' and 'Bhārata-ke Prācīna Rājavamśa.'
93. Bhārata-ke-Prācīna-Rājavamśa, pt. ii. p. 34; JBORS, IV., 364 ff; Ind. Ant., xlviii, 25 ff. 29 ff. and xlix 43 ff.
94. BP., pp. 69-70
95. "धम्मोवत्थुसहावो, खमादि भावो य सदविही धम्मो ।
रयणत्तयं च धम्मो, जीवाणं रक्खणं धन्मो ॥४७९ ॥ स्नामीकीर्तिकेयातुप्रेक्षा ।
96. *Buddhism: Its History and Literature*, p. 39
97. *Dialogues of the Buddha*, S.B.B., II. p. 254
98. BP. p. 62

99. BP. p. 64
100. BP., p. 13 and *Milinda Pañha,* II., 1, 1, p. 40
101. Ibid. p. 92
102. Idem
103. Idem
104. Ibid, p. 95
105. Ibid. pp. 94-95
106. JS. Vol. I xxxiv; *Historical Gleanings,* p. 76; *Buddhist India,* p. 143
107. BP. p. 92
108. Ibid p. 74
109. *Tattvārtha-Sūtram,* S.B.J., II, p. 15
110. BP., p. 74
111. In Buddhist book "Sumaṅgala-Vilāsinī" (P.T.S. p. 119) this belief of the Jainas is described and ascribed to them.
112. Tattvā Sūt : SBJ. II, p. 120-121
113. The Buddhist book "Sumaṅgala-Vilāsinī" describing Jain beliefs, corroborates thsi differentia of soul, viz, "Arūpī attā saññī," (P. T.S. 119)
114. See also JS., pt. II. 244
115. Umāsvāmī's Tattvārtha-Sūtra, Ch. v.
116. The Principles of Jainism, p. 4
117. S. ii. 4
118. BP. pp. 50-51
119. *Milinda-Pañha,* II, 33 (S.B.E.) p. 81
120. *Milinda-Pañha,* II. i.e. SBE Vol. xxxv. p. 45
121. Buddhism : Its History and Literature, pp. 120-124,
122. Dīgha-Nikāya, ii. 63
123. BP., p. 80
124. Buddha, too, accepts it, though the meaning of delusion is different with him. Futher the number and characteristics ofthe senses, he gives the same as are in Jainism. His definition of mind, also bears a resemblance to that of Jainas. cf. Tattvārtha Sūtra, Ch. VI

125. This seems to be another version of Jaina conceptions of Samkramans, Atikramana, etc., of the Karmas.

126. BP. p. 102

127. Ibid., p. 105

128. Ibid. pp. 103-104

129. Ibid. p. 109

130. *Milinda*, iv., 1, 63

131. Ibid. iv 4,3

132. ERE, Vol. VII p. 472

133. *Majjhima Nikāya*, Vol. I., p. 372

134. जीवा पुग्गल काया अघोचा गाढ़गदृण परिवङ्का।
काले विजुज्जमाणा सुहद्धुक्रवंदिन्ति भुञ्जन्ति ॥९७ ॥—पञ्चास्तिकायसार।

135. The Buddha's chain of Causation on the contrary gives no idea about the physical aspects of the World. It is essentially an explanation of misery BP. p. 112

136. 'याहिंसावतोपिसमृद्धःअर्हत्पूजावतोपिदारिद्राप्तिःसाक्रमेणप्रागुपात्तस्यपापानुवश्चिनः पुण्यस्यपुण्यानुवन्धिनः पापस्य च फलम्। तत् क्रियोपात्तंतु कर्मजन्मान्तरे फलिष्यतीतिनाव नित्त कार्यकारणभाव व्याभिचारः ॥'

137. Pṅcästikāyasāra, 61-62. In 'Ishtopadesa' too we find that "karma works in its won cause ; the soul works for its own good; who is there in the world that will nto work for his own good when he has the power to do so.' 31

138. पुग्गलकन्मादोण कत्ताववहारदो दुण्ञ्श्चयदो चेदण,कन्माणदामुङ्कणया सुङ्कवाणम् ॥८ ॥
द्रव्य संग्रह

139. भावनित्तोबन्धोभ वीरदिरागद्वेषमोहजुदो—पञ्चास्तिकायसार।

140. Tattvārtha-Sūtram, SBJ., Vol. II., p. 155; Cf. Yoga with *Majjhima Nikāya*, Vol. I., p. 372.

141. *Dravya-Saṁgraha*, 2, 29

142. Tattvā: Sūtr. p. 157ff.

143. Tattvārtha Sūtram, p. 175

144. Idem

145. Ibid. X, 2. S.B.J. Vol. II, p. 194

146. Ibid. p. 198

147. *Tattvārtha Sūtram*, S.B.J. Vol. II. pp. 159-169

148. Ibid. p. 57
149. The Buddhist books, viz, Sumaṅgala-vilāsinī p. 168 and Miinda Pañha, IV, i. 54 too, make mention of this belief of the Jainas.
150. *Tattvā Sūt* p. 78.
151. Cf. Buddhist view expressed in B.C. Law's Heaven and Hell in Buddhist Perspective, p. 102.
152. Tatt. Sū S.B.J. Vol. II. p. 62. Mana (mind) is the faculty of distinguishing right and wrong. It is styled as objective mind and is in the region of the heart, like an eight petalled flower, made of very fine mind molecules subjective mind is the Soul's capacity to make use of the objective mind.
153. Idem
154. Ibid. p. 92
155. Tattvā : Sūt : S.B.J. Vol.II. p. 64
156. Ibid. p. 57
157. Law B.C., *Heaven and Hell in Buddhist perspective,* p. 92
158. Milinda Pañha. IV. 3,7
159. Law B.C., *Heaven and Hell in Buddhist Perspective,* p. 93
160. Tatt: Sūt : SBJ. Vol. II. p. 83 and Dravya Saṃgraha. SBJ. Vol. I
161. Law B.C. op.cit., p. 93
162. Cf. Buddhist tradition (Ibid. p. 92) to Jaina one (Tattvā: Sūt : SBJ Vol. II. p. 79 ff).
Nigoda is that place, which is filled with the infinite number of the Nigoda Jīvas. The Nigoda Jīvas, in the Jaina teory, is that from of life, which is lower and more miserable than even that of single-sensed beings. Here even the sense of touch is not manifest, and the souls inhabit a part of another's body. The span of their life is very short; they are said to undergo eighteen births and deaths in one śvāsa or breath. These Nigoda Jīvas supply souls in place of those who have reached Nirvāṇa. For a full view of them the Jaina books, e.g., the Pañcāstikāya-Sāra, etc., should be consulted.
163. Tattvārtha -Sūtram SBJ Vol. II. pp. 79-81

164. Law B.C., op. cit p. 94
165. *Tattvārtha Sūtram,* SBJ. Vol. II. p. 96
166. *Tattvārtha-Sūtram,* SBJ Vol. p. 97. Buddhist, too, describe a certain kind of grades in heavenly beings and they have a separate heaven of the name of Trayastriṁsa. (Heaven and Hell in Buddhist Perspective, p. 14 ff).
167. Law, B.C. op. cit, p. 7
168. Ibid p. 93.
169. Ibid. p. 31
170. Ibid. p. 2
171. Tatt: Sūt : SBJ Vol. II. p. 101
172. Ibid p. 102
173. Law B.C. op. cit., p. 90 ff
174. *Tatt. Sū*: SBJ Vol. II. p. 104. These are of eight classes: Sāraswat, Āditya, Vahni, Aruṇa, Gardatoya, Tuṣita, Avyābādh and Ariṣṭa.
175. Law, B.C. opcit p. 2
176. Ibid, p. 34
177. *Tatt: Sut*: SBJ. II. p. 199-200
178. Śrenika Carit
179. Law, B.C. op. p. 19
180. Ibid. p. 12 and Tattvārtha Sūtram SBJ II. p. 97
181. In Buddhism no such division of jñāna is found.
182. Divine Discourse. p. 24.
183. *Tattvārtha-Sūtram,* SBJ. II. p. 1
184. Ibid. p. 45
185. Ibid. p. 4 ff
186. Ibid. p. 137
187. Tatt : Sūt., p. 137 These are also ascribed to jainas in the Buddhist book, Majjhima-Nikāya Vol II. pp. 35-36
188. Ibid. pp. 142-143.
189. The Buddhist Canon, too, mentions this practice of Jainas, followed by a Jaina layman (sāvaka) at the time of Buddha. See The Aṅguttara-Nikāya III, 70, 3.

190. Prosada is also referred to in the above passage of Aṅguttara Nikāya and it runs thus" On the Upesatha day they exhort a Sāvaka thus: "Well, sir, take of all your clothes and declare: I belong to nobody, and nobody belongs to me."- It agrees with the Jaina view on the point, and it means that he becomes quite naked. Of course the laymen are enjoined to put off all their garments, and to remain in a Pratimāyoga; but during the period of night only. See the Sāgāra- Dharmāmrata. 7., 7. p. 421.

191. *The Principles of Jainism* pp. 12-15

192. *Tattvārtha-Sūtram,* SBJ. Vol II. p. 194

193. Ibid. p. 197.

194. *Divinity in Jainism* p. 37

195. These householders and ladies are not to be understood as the ordinary followers of Mahāvira, rather they are the Vrati- Srāvakes, who follow the preparatory stage of a layman, and always remain with the Order of Lord--even on his preaching tours. King Śrenika and many thousand believeers in Dharma believers in Dhamra were quite separate from them.

196. *Dravyasamgraha.* 50

197. *Divinity in Jainism,* p. 38

198. Idem

199. *Tattvārtha-Sūtram,* SBJ. II. p. 197

200. *Dravyasamgraha.* 51

201. *Tattvārtha-Sūtram,* SBJ. II. p. 198.

202. स्वस्मिन्सदभिलाषित्वादभीष्ट ज्ञापकत्वतः ।
स्वयं हितप्रयोक्तृत्वादत्मैव गुरुरात्मनः ॥३४ ॥ इष्टोपदेशः
Cf. i.e. "Because of its internal longing fot the attainment of the highest Ideal, because of its understanding of that Ideal,and because of its engaging itself in the realisation of its Ideal, because of these the soul is its own preceptor." Divine- Discourse, p. 25.

203. *Milinda-Pañha,* III. 4.5, SBE. Vol. XXXV. p. 106

204. Ibid, II. 1, 5, p. 49.

205. B.P. p. 119

206. Rhy Davids' *Buddhism,* p. 139. The first five of these are bindingon the Buddhist layman too.

207. Jacobi has made it known in his Introduction to the Jaina Sūtras, that Mahāvīra and Buddha, both borrowed these precepts from the Brahmanical sources. But it is an open question still, that the Brahmanical out predates Jainism. So far the documentary and all other evidences corroborate the existence of Jainism alongside of Brahmanism. (See Svet; Conferenece Herald- Vol. X pp. 252-253.)

208. Mahāvagga, I. 25 6 ff.

209. JS. I. p. 262

210. *Mahāvagga,* VI, 31, 11 and 14; VI, 23, 2; VI, 25, 2.

211. The Householder's Dharma pp. 25-26

212. BP. p. 122

213. *Buddhism : Its History and Literature* p. 163.

214. BP. p. 61

215. Cf: Buddha's assertion : "He who has overcome doubt, is without pain, delights in Nibbāna, is free from greed, a leader of the world of men and gods, such a person Buddhas call, a maggajins (that is, victorious by the way)"-*Sutta Nipāta,* SBE Vol. XII. p. 16

216. BP. , pp. 14-15

217. This is the obvious reason that a great change took place afterwards in Buddhism. Rhys Davids remarks that "the soul theory step by step gained again the upperhand. The caste system was gradually built up into a completely organised system. The social supremacy of the Brahmans by birth became accepted as an incontrovertible fact. And the inflood of popular superstition..." (The Dialogues of the Buddha. SBB. p. 142.)

218. *Tattvārtha Sūtram,* SBJ. II. p. 16

CHAPTER 4

SOME ANCIENT INDIAN KINGS

—Dr. Bimala Churn Law, M.A.; B.L., Ph.D.

An attempt has been made here to give a brief but interesting account of the life and career of some kings of Ancient India. The materials gleaned from Pāli books throw a flood of new light on the social, religious and political aspects of the period in which these kings lived and worked.

BIMBISĀRA

Bimbisāra,[1] according to the *Sumaṅgalavilāsini*, a commentary on the *Dīgha Nikāya*, was so named because his appearance was like that of gold (*bimbi*-golden). He was also called Seniya because he had a large army (Mahatiyā Senāya Samannāgatā). The *Mahāvamsa*[2] states that Bimbisāra was anointed king by his own father when he was only 15 years old. A mention is made of Bhātiya as the name of the father (*Dīpavamsa*, 3,52) who was defeated by Brahmadatta, king of Aṅga. But this defeat was, later on, avenged by Bimbisāra. The *Mahāvagga* (S.B.E., XVII, p. l) offers a reasonable evidence of prove that the kingdom of Aṅga came under Bimbisāra's sway. The *Soṇadaṇḍa Suttanta* of the *Dīgha Nikāya* while mentioning the bestowal of Campā, the capital of Aṅga, as a royal fief on the *Brāhmaṇa* Soṇadaṇḍa, indubitably proves that Aṅga was annexed by Bimbisāra. The annexation of Aṅga was indeed a turning point in the history of Magadha. It marked "the first step taken by the kingdom of Magadha in its advance to greatness and the position of supremacy which it attained in the following century, so that Bimbisāra may be regarded as the real founder of Magadhan imperial power."[3] The *Mahāvagga* of the *Vinaya Piṭaka* (II p.1) tells us the Bimbisāra was the lord of 80,000 townships, the overseers of which used to meet in an assembly held by the king. Bimbisāra strengthened his position by matrimonial alliances with the two neighbouring States, *viz.*, Videha and Vaiśālī. He took one consort from the royal family of Kośala and another from the influential Licchavi clan at Vaiśālī.[4] A third queen of Bimbisāra as mentioned in the *Therīgāthā* commentary (p.131), was Khemā, daughter of the king of Madda in the Punjab. The *Mahāvagga* says that Bimbisāra had 500 wives (VIII. i. 15). The Jātakas[5] tell us that Bimbisāra married Mahākośala's daughter, Kośaladevī who was given by her father a village of Kāśī yielding a revenue of a hundred thousand for perfumeries used in baths. Thus it is reasonable to hold that these diplomatic marriage relations were of great political importance for the history of Mahgadha. They paved the way for the expansion of Magadha and enabled Bimbisāra to add a part of Kāśī to his dominions.

Seniya Bimbisāra was a righteous man and righteous king (*Dhammika dhammarājā, Dīgha Nikāya,* I.p. 86). He was benign to priests and laymen, to town-folk and country-folk alike (Ibid, II. p. 202). He had the rare power of understanding the character of men by their voice. Once the king heared the voice of an ill-clad man named Kumbhaghosaka who earned his livelihood by working for hire and remarked that he must be a rich man. But the royal servants ascertained from the man that he was poor. Whenever the king saw the man, he remarked that the man was wealthy but the royal servants learnt from the man himself that he was poor. One day a maid-servant told the king that she would find out the mystery. Accordingly with her daughter she went to Kumbhaghosaka's house and by employing tricks she succeeded in causing Kumbhaghosaka to part with a few pieces of the buried treasure which ultimately came to the hand of the king. Bimbisāra summoned Kumbhaghosaka and caused him to tell the king that he had 40 crores of wealth which his father had kept buried underground. The king then had this buried treasure brought to his royal court by carts and bestowed high honour upon Kumbhaghosaka. The king appointed him to the post of treasurer and gave his daughter in marriage to Kumbhaghosaka (*Dhammapada Commentary,* Vol. I., p. 232 foll.)

GOTAMA BUDDHA AND BIMBISĀRA.

The account of Bimbisāra's conversion, as given in the commentary on the *Tirokuḍḍa-Suttaṁ in the Khuddakapāṭha,* reveals the fact that Buddhism conveys the idea of salvation from *preta* life by the giving of offerings to *bhikkhus.* This Buddhist idea brought about a change which was injurious to the *brāhmaṇas* inasmuch as people began to make offerings of the *bhikkhus* and the *brāhmṇas* could no longer get their dues which they used to enjoy until Hinduism was partly overshadowed by Buddhism[6]. We read in the *Paramatthajotikā* on the *Khuddakapāṭha* that certain *pretas* finding their confreres to attain salvation from the spirit life due to the offering of gifts to *bhikkhus* by their relatives, appeared before Kassapa Buddha and enquired when they would be relieved of the *preta* life. Kassapa Buddha prophesied that they would be released of the *preta* life on the offering of gift for their sake to the *bhikkhus* by one of their relatives who would be reigning in the time of Gotama Buddha as a king named Bimbisāra. These *pretas* awaited the advent of Gotama Buddha. In course of time Gotama Buddha came of the noble Śākya family. In his youth, he renounced the world and turning from door to door he gradually came to Rājagṛha and one day on his begging round in the city he was seen by certain royal officers who informed the king of the arrival of an ascetic of charming deportment. The king sent for the ascetic who declined to come to the king. Thereupon the king himself came to the ascetic, was pleased to see his deportment and having learnt that he was a prince of the noble Śākya family and son of Śuddhodana, his father's friend, he tried to induce him to give up the ascetic life and to accept half of his kingdom. Gotama refused the offer and told the king that he had renounced all for the sake of attaining Supreme Enlightenment. The king then had the promise from Gotama that the latter would see the king just after his attainment of *bodhi.* A few years after Gotama attained *Sambodhi* and about six months after his attainment of Buddhahood he entered Rājagṛha. The king being informed of the arrival of Gotama Buddha left the palace with 1,20,000 Brāhmṇas householders to receive the Buddha. The Buddha delivered a sermon. King Bimbisāra and the *Brāhmaṇas* listened to the Buddha's teachings and then and there they attained the first stage of sanctification. The king invited the Buddha to take food in the palace the following day and came back to the palace and made every arrangement for delicious food and drink. The next morning the king informed the Buddha that everthing was ready for him. The Buddha and his disciples came to the palace and were offered delicious food and drink by the king himself. Meanwhile the *pretas* in accordance with the prophecy of Kassapa Buddha, came to the spot (where the Buddha with his disciples was being fed) in the expectation that the offerings by the king would be given for their sake; but the king in his anxiety to select a suitable place for the Buddha and his disciples forgot to mention *"Idaṁ vo ñātinaṁ hotu, sukhitā hontu ñātayo"* (Let the merit of this offering be beneficial to my deceased relatives and let them be happy). The *pretas* were disappointed and made a troublesome sound round the palace at night. The king was frightened and the following morning he came to the Buddha who told him that he should not be afraid and that the sound was caused by his deceased relatives who were disappointed for not having received the merit of the royal offerings which, they were told by Kassapa Buddha, would relieve them of their *preta* life. The Buddha advised the king to make another offering for their deceased relatives. The king did so. The *pretas* were relieved of their *preta* life and received heavenly enjoyments. Thereafter the king selected Veluvana pleasure garden as the most suitable residence for the Buddha and the *bhikkhus*. He offered the Veluvana to the Buddha who accepted it. (Commentary on the *Tirokuḍḍa Suttaṁ of the Khuddakapāṭha*). Bimbisāra had a deep regard for the Buddha who was five years older than the king.[7] Along with his children, wives, people and courtiers, he put his faith in the Samaṇa Gotama (*"Sameṇaṁ khalu bho Gotamaṁ rājā Māgadho Seniyo Bimbisāro saputto sabhariyo sapariso Sāmaccopāṇehi saraṇaṁ gato"*[8]). He became a stern adherent of the Buddhist faith and staunch follower of the Buddha. Once the Buddha while staying at Rājagaha intended to visit Vaiśālī. The king caused the ground from Rājagaha to the Ganges, a distance of five leagues, to be made smooth and a rest house to be constructed at the end of each league. He caused flowers of the five colours to be spread knee-deep, and flags and banners and standards to be set up, he caused two white parasols, a lower and a higher to be held over the head of the Exalted One; likewise he caused a white parasol to be held over the head of each monk. Along with his retinue he honoured the Teacher with flowers and perfumes and lodged him for one night in each rest house, giving rich offerings to him. In five days he conducted the Blessed One to the bank of the Ganges and got the Buddha boarded on a boat well adorned (*Dhammapada Commentary*, Vol. III. p. 439).

Bimbisāra had many sons of whom we get the names of five in literature, namely, Kuṇika, Ajātasattu, Abhaya,[9] Vimala-Kondañña,[10] Vehalla and Sālavat,[11] but he was not at all happy in his old age. He passed his last days in deep misery. He was so very unlucky that he had to lose his life at the hand of his son Ajātasattu begotten on the Kosalan princess. He had, we are assured by some of the Buddhist writers, a premonition that his end would be brought about by his own son, but out of affection he could not take any step to avert this evil. Buddhaghosa in his commentary on the *Dīgha Nikāya* has conjured up a myth to explain the conduct of the parricidal prince. He avers that Ajātasattu was even before his birth an enemy of his father, King Bimbisāra, The circumstances that preceded Ajātasuttu's birth and augured the impending evil, were appalling. When the would-be parricide was in his mother's womb, the queen, it is said, felt a craving for sipping blood from the right arm of the king. She, however, dared not speak out her inhuman desire. Worried by this she looked pale and emaciated. The king asked her the cause of her getting weak. At last she spoke out and the king then sent for his surgeon who drew blood out of his right arm for the queen. The blood was diluted with water and the queen was asked to drink up the horrible potion. The soothsayers, however,warned that the child would be an enemy to the king and would kill him in consequence of the queen's drinking the king's blood. The queen horrified at the prospect, tried to effect miscarriage but she was prevented by the king who urged that such a single act would be abhorred by the people of Jambudīpa; in fact voluntary abortion was against all national tradition of India. The queen again, it is said, thought of destroying the child at the time of delivery. The attendants took away the child as soon as it was born. When the child had grown up, he was presented before the queen whose maternal affection towards the lad got the upperhand and she could no longer think of killing the lad. In due course the king made him his viceregent. Not long days passed when the prophecy of the soothsayers was fulfilled. Ajātaśattu deposed his father and kept him confined in a room which was very hot and full of smoke and none else was allowed to enter into that room except Ajātaśattu's mother who used to take some food for the unfortunate king but she used to bring food for Bimbisāra concealing it in several parts of her body but she was found out and was ordered not to enter the room with any kind of food. Thenceforth she used to enter king's apartment with her body besmeared with a mixture of honey, butter, ghee, and oil. Bimbisāra got some sustenance by licking her body. This too was detected by the ever vigilant Ajātaśattu and she was forbidden to enter the room and asked to see the king from outside. The queen now reminded Bimbisāra that it was she who had requested him to kill Ajātaśattu while in the womb. She further told him that it was the last occasion on which she would be permitted to meet him and she begged his pardon and took leave. Bimbisāra was now prevented from taking any food but he was still alive and the commentator informs us that the inhuman practices of Ajātaśattu increased in their barbarity. Bimbisāra, it is said, was meditating on the fruition of the path and was walking up and down and his appearance became very bright. Ajātaśattu was informed of this and he ordered that his walking up and down must be stopped and ordered his barber to go and cut the feet of his father and put salt and oil thereupon and then to heat them on the fire of Khadir charcoal. The barber went to Bimbisāra who thought that his son had realised his folly and had become kind to him. The barber when asked by the king about his mission, intimated to him the order of king Ajātaśattu. The barber carried out we are told, the ghastly operations required by the royal order. Bimbisāra breathed his last with the words, "*Buddha, Dhamma and Saṁgha.*" (*Sumaṅgalavlāsinī*, pt, I. pp. 134-137). The Vinaya Piṭaka gives a short account of an attempt made by Ajātaśattu to kill his father with a dagger. Persuaded by Devadata, the recalcitrant brother of the Buddha, Ajātaśattu entered with violence at an unusual hour the king's chamber with a dagger fastened on his thigh to kill his father, but the ministers who were in attendance in the private chamber saw that and seized him. On searching his person they found a dagger and asked him the reason of his running apace with a dagger to the royal chamber. The prince told the ministers that he was going to kill his father. The matter was bought to the notice of the king who asked his son the reason of his being ready to take away the life of his father. The prince said that he had coveted the throne. The king then handed over the kingdom to prince Ajātaśattu (Vinaya Texts, III, pp. 241-243). The concluding portion of the *Sāmaññaphala Suttanta* says that Ajātaśattu deprived his father of his life (*pitaram jivitā voropesi*, D., I.p. 85). The details may or may not be true but the fact that Bimbisāra was put to death by Ajātaśattu is an historical truth, the tradition is so very strong and persistent with regard to this matter. According to the Ceylonese chroniclers, this event took place eight years before the death of the Buddha, at the time when Bimbisāra had been on the throne for fifty-two years (*Dīpavaṁsa*, III, 56-60; *Mahāvaṁsa*, II, 29, 30).

AJĀTASATTU

Ajātaśattu, according to the *Sumaṅgalavilāsinī*, the Commentary on the *Dīgha Nikāya*, was an enemy to King Bimbisāra while yet in his mother's womb. (*Ajātaśattu* literally means an enemy unborn). Ajātasattu while in the womb desired to suck the blood of the right arm of King Bimbisāra. From this fact it was inferred that he was so called because he was an enemy of the king before his birth (*Ajātasattu*). While Ajātasattu was a prince, Devadatta intended to win over the prince to his side and to lower the Blessed On in the estimation of the people. With this end in view he "folded up his sleeping mat, and set out, fully bowled and robed, for Rājagaha; and in due course he arrived at Rājagaha. Then he laid aside his own form, and took upon himself the form of a child clad in a girdle of snakes, and appeared on the lap of prince Ajātasattu." The prince got frightened and was alarmed. Then the figure spoke out that it was Devadatta. The prince asked Devadatta to appear in his own form. Devadtta laid aside the form of the child, appeared there before the prince with his inner and outer robes on, and with his bowl in his hand. The miracle pleased the prince so much that he became a devout follower of Devadatta. One day Devadatta said to prince Ajātasattu, "In former days, prince, people were long-lived but now the span of their life is short. It is quite possible, therefore that you may die while a prince. So kill your father and become the Rājā."(*Vinaya Texts.* III. p. 241; cf. *Dhammapada Commy.* I. pp. 139-140). Ajātaśattu succeeded in occupying the throne after killing his father. The first thing that Ajātaśattu did just after ascending the throne was to fulfill his desire while a prince to take the great palace of the treasurer Jotika which he saw with his father king Bimbisāra from the lowest to the topmost storey. The palace was entirely made of seven precious minerals which illumined it so much that there was hardly any use of the light of a lamp or the light of fire. Th unique beauty of the palace pleased the prince so much that he thought lightly of his father for dwelling in a house of wood and resolved then and there to be a possessor of this jewelled palace in the near future (*Dhammapada Commy,* Vol. IV. p, 211 foll). To achieve his object Ajātaśattu marched with his retinue. The jewelled wals of Jotika's palace reflected Ajātaśattu and his retinue.But Ajātaśattu misunderstood the reflection and took it to be a reality thinking that the treasurer was also ready with his men to fight with him. He did not therefore venture to approach the palace. He was seen and disbanded by the guard of Jotika's palace. Ajātaśttu fled and took refuge in a monastery in which he found to his utter surprise Jotika listening to the Buddha and asked him how it was that after giving orders to his men to fight with him (Ajātaśattu) he had come to the monastery. The treasurer enquired whether the king had set out to take his house. The king replied in the affirmative. The treasurer told him that a thousand kings could not take his house against his will. The treasurer tested the king's weakness in taking off the rings on his fingers. He then took off the rings himself and gave them to the king. Afterwards Jotika intended to retire from the world and asked the royal permission to become a monk. The king permitted him to become a monk with the thought that it would be an easy matter for himself to get possession of his palace. --- (*Dhammapada Commy.*, Vol iv, pp. 221-223).

On the day Bimbisāra died a son was born to Ajātaśattu. Two reports conveying the news of the death of his father and the birth of his child were received by his ministers at the same time. The ministers first of all handed over the letter conveying the news of the birth of his child to king Ajātasattu. On receipt of the letter the king's mind was filled with filial affection and at that moment all the virtues of his father rose up before his mind's eye and he realised that similar filial affection had filled his father's mind when his father received the news of his own birth. Ajātaśattu at once ordered the release of his father but it was too late. The ministers handed over the other letter and on hearing of his father's death, he cried and went to his mother and asked her whether his father had any affection for him. The mother replied, "When a boil appeared on your finger, you were crying and none could pacify you and you were taken to your father when he was administering justice at the royal court. Your father out of affection put your finger with the boil into his mouth and the boil was burst open. Out of filial affection he swallowed up the blood and pus instead of throwing them away." Ajātasattu heard this and wept hot tears. The dead body of his father was burnt. Shortly afterwards Devadatta went to Ajātaśattu and urged him to order his men to go and kill the Buddha also. Devadatta sent Ajātasattu's men to kill the Buddha and himself took several steps to bring about his death. He himself went to the top of the *Gijjhakuṭa* mountain and hurled at the Buddha a big stone, then he set the mad elephant Nālagiri against the Buddha but all his attempts were baffled. All his gain and fame were lost and he became very miserable (*Sumaṅgalavilāsinī*, pt. I. pp. 138-139). After Ajātasattu murdered his father, Kośaladevī died of grief. On her death Ajātasattu continued to enjoy the revenues of the Kāśī village. But Pasenadi, king of Kośala, determined that no parricide should enjoy a village which was his by right of inheritance and made war upon Ajātasattu. The result was that sometimes the king of Kośala won, and sometimes the king of Magadha. Once the Kośala monarch was defeated and had to save his life by fleeing away from the field of battle. At last as the result of another combat he succeeded in taking Ajātasattu prisoner and gave his daughter Vajirāin marriage to his captive nephew. The Kāśī village was given to Vajirā.Thus Kāśī once again came under the sway of Ajātasattu, and the two kingdoms, Magadha and Kośala, were once more closely united by materimonial alliance. (*Saṁyutta Nikāya*, I. 82-85)[12]. Afterwards Ajātasattu felt that the Licchavis had formed the greatest bar to the realisation of his idea of Magadhan expansion and we find him taking the dreadful resolve, "I will root out these Vajjians, I will bring out these Vajjians to utter ruin." (*Buddhist Suttas*, S.B.E., Vol. XI, pp. I. & 2). Ajātasattu was not on friendly terms with the Licchavis. He was under the impression that his foster brother, Abhaya, son of Bimbisāra by Ambapālī (a courtesan of Vaiśālī) had Licchavi blood in him and he liked the Licchavis very much. At this time, the Licchavis were gaining strength day by day, and Ajātasattu thought that if Abhaya sided with them it would be very difficult for him too cope with the Licchavis. So he made up his mind to do away with them. In the *Sumaṅgalavilāsinī*, we read that there was a port near the Ganges extending over a *yojana*, half of which belonged to Ajātaśattu and the other half to the Licchavis, and their orders were obeyed in their respective yojanas. There was a mountain not far from it, and at the foot of the mountain, there was a mine of precious substance *(mahogghabhaṇḍa)*.Ajātasattu was late in coming there and the avaricious Licchavis took away the precious substance. When Ajātasattu came and learnt that all the precious substance had been taken away by the Licchavis, he grew angry and left the palace. This happened also in the succeeding year. Having sustained a heavy loss he hought that there must be a fight between him and the Licchavis. He realised, however, that the Licchavis being numerically stronger, he would fail to carry out his purpose. So he conceived the design of destroying the independence of the Licchavis by sowing seeds of dissension. Formerly the Licchavis were not luxurious but very strenuous and exerting, so Ajātasattu could not get an opportunity of usbduing them. He sent Vassakāra, one of his ministers, to the Buddha, who predicted that in future the Licchavis would be delicate, having soft hands and feet, would use very luxurious and soft beds with soft pillows made of cotton, would sleep till sunrise.[13] and further declared, "By no other means will the Vajjians be overcome but by propitiating them with tributes or dissolving the subsisting union." Vassakāra returned from the Buddha and stated to the king what the latter had said about the Licchavis. The rājā did not agree to propitiate the Vajjians with tributes as that would diminish the number of elephants and horses. So he decided to break up their union and Vassakāra advised him to drive him (Vassakāra) from the kingdom so that he might tell the Vajjians that in defending the cause of the Vajjians he had been driven off by Ajātasattu.A meeting was convened and Vassakāra interdicted royal discussion. The king drove him off. He came to the Licchavis who appointed him to the post of Judicial prime minister. Very soon he acquired a reputation for his able administration of justice and in no time by employing various tricks he succeeded in bringing about a complete disunion among the Licchavis so much so that none of them turned up when the tocsin was sounded. Vassakāra informed Ajātaśattu of the disunion of the Licchavis and asked him to attack the Licchavis at once. Ajātasattu marched with his army. The Licchavis disregarded the call of tocsin and offered no resistance to the king. Ajātasattu entered Vajśālī by the wide open gates and went back after putting the Licchavis to great calamities. He seems to have succeeded in causing the Licchavis to accept his suzerainty and to pay him revenue, leaving the internal management to themselves. In the *Uvāsagadasāo,* Ajātasattu is said to have made use of two deadly weapons, the *Mahāsilākaṇṭage* and *Rahamusala,* in his war with the Licchavis. The first seems to have been some engine of war of the nature of a catapult which hurled big stones.

The second was a chariot to which a mace was attached and which by running about effected a great execution of men (Vol. II. app. p. 60). the war with the Licchavis ending in the victory of Ajātasattu resulted in a further expansion of the Magadhan kingdom. But this expansion could not satisfy Ajātasattu nor could it pacify his perturbed mind. Ajātasattu was at first, as already said above, an adherent of Devadatta, a base and wicked false believer and foe of the Buddha. He honoured Devadatta so much that he had a monastery built for Devadatta at Gayāsīsa and every day brought to him five hundred kettles of perfumed three-year old rice prepared with all the choicest flavorings. (*Jātaka,* I.

67). Following Devadatta's wicked counsels Ajātaśattu slew the good and virtuous old king, his father, who had attained the fruition of the first stage of sanctification. He heard one day that Devadatta had been swallowed up by the earth and he was frightened lest he should have to meet with the same fate. He began to pass his days in peacelessness and wanted to see the Buddha; but he could not venture to go to the Buddha alone owing to his sinful deeds. So he devised that on the day of the *Kattikā* festival he would burst forth in praise of the moonlit night and ask his minister as to the name of the teacher whom he (the king) might see to enjoy peace of mind (*Jātaka,* I, 319-320; v., No. 530) The *Sāmaññaphala suttanta* of the *Dīgha Nikīya* tells us that the Magdha king Ajātasattu, while seated one night on the upper terrace roof of his palace, being surrounded by his ministers, was moved by the beauty of the moon-lit night. He declared that the moon lit night was really very pleasing. He thought of approaching a *Samaṇa* or a *Brāhmaṇa* who could bring solace to his perturbed mind (cf. *Sumaṅgalavilāsinī,* I , 141-142). He asked his ministers to name a recluse or a *Brāhmaṇa* who would be able to pacify his disturbed mind. His ministers mentioned one after another with eulogistic remarks the names of Pūraṇa Kassapa, Makkhali Gosāla, Ajitakesakambali, Pakuḍhakaccāyana, Sañjaya Belaṭṭhiputta and Nigaṇṭha Nāthaputta. But Ajātasattu said nothing to his ministers. He asked Jīvaka, the physician who took his seat not far from the king, the cause of his silence. Then Jīvaka spoke out in praise of the Buddha. Ajātasattu was greatly moved to hear of the virtues of the Buddha. In royal pomp he came to the Mango grove and enquired of the Buddha about the effect of leading the life of a recluse.. The Buddha gave a long discourse on the subject. Ajātasattu was sorely penitent to hear it so much so that he confessed his parricidal sin. Then on the assurance of the Blessed One that he (Ajātasattu) would attain self-' restraint in future for his having looked upon his fault as fault and rightfully confessed his guilt. Ajātasattu left the mango-grove (See also *Sumaṅgalavilāsinī,* pp. 158. foll.) The Blessed One passed away, as Buddhaghosa informs us in his commentary on the *Vinayapiṭaka,* in the eighth year of Ajātasattu's reign. (*Samantapāsādikā,* I. p. 72). After the Buddha's *parinirvāṇa* in the forest of the Mallas between the twin sāla trees, his relics were distributed as we learn from the *Mahāparinibbāṇa Suttanta*. Ajātasattu sent a messenger to the Mallas saying, "The Exalted One was a Kṣatriya and so am I. I am worthy to receive a portion of the relics of the Exalted One. Over the remains of the Exalted One will I put up a sacred cairn and in their honour will I celebrate a feast." (D. II. p. 164. cf *Paramattahadīpanī* on the *Petavatthu*, pp. 212- 215). Ajātaśattu received a share and made a cairn over the remains of the Exalted One and celebrated a feast. (*Dīgha Nikāya*, II, p. 166). Ajātaśattu built Dhātu caityas all round Rājagaha, his capital city. (*Mahāvaṁsa*, p. 247). At his own cost he repaired eighteen Mahāvihāras at Rājagaha, deserted by the *bhikkhus* after the *parinirvāṇa* of the Buddha. (*Samantapāsādikā*, I, 9-10). He erected a *pandal* at the entrance of the Sattapanni cave near the Vebhāra mountain for the *bhikkhus* taking part in the First Buddhist Council. He supplied the *bhikkhus* with requisites. (*Samantapāsādikā*, Vol. I., p 10). Like his father Bimbisāra, Ajātasattu too had a firm faith in the Buddhist doctrine. Once some thieves employed by some naked ascetics struck the Elder Maggallāna to death. Ajātasattu who was a stern adherent of the Buddhist faith had the murderers captured by his spies, placed them waist-deep in pits which he had dug in the palace court, caused their bodies to be covered over with bundles of straw, and then caused the bundles of straw to be lighted. When he knew that they had been burnt to a crisp, he caused their bodies to be "plowed with iron plows and thus caused them all to be ground to bits". (*Dhammapada Commy.*, Vol. III, p. 67). The punishment inflicted on the criminals, while showing as it does Ajātasattu respect towards the Buddhist Elders, giver us a picture of the administration of criminal justice by Ajatasattu. The principle of "Life for life and limb for limb" was adopted by Ajātasattu in a way which was more inhuman than hanging. Ajātasattu, as we learn from the *Samantapāsādikā*, a commentary on the *Vinaya Piṭaka*, reigned for twenty-four years (Vol.; I. pp. 72-73). He had to share the same miserable fate with his father. As he put his father to death so was his life taken away by his own son Udāyi Bhadda (*Mahāvaṁsa* chap. IV).

The *Dīgha Nikāya* indubitably asserts that Udāyi Bhadda was the son of Ajātasattu and probably also his successor (Vol. I, p. 50). The Ceylonese Chronicles[14] inform us that Udāyi Bhadda succeeded his father on the throne. This is confirmed by the *Samantapāsādikā* (p. 73), and the *Sumaṅgalavilāsini* (I. 153-154). In the face of so much clear evidence, it is reasonable to hold that Udāyi Bhadda was the son and successor of Ajātaśatru. He reigned for sixteen years (*Samantapāsādikā*, pp. 72-73; *Mahāvaṁsa*, ch. IV). That he was very wicked is apparent from the fact that his father Ajātasattu wished that his son Udāyi should be quiet and restrained like the *Bhikkhusaṁgha* (I, p. 50). He was killed by his son Anuruddha who had to share the same miserable fate at the hand of his own son. Muṇḍa, Anuruddha and Muṇḍa reigned for 18 years. Muṇḍa's son Nāga Dāsaka slew his father and reigned for 24 years. He was banished by the citizens who anointed the minister known as Susunāga king. Susunāga reigned for 18 years. His son Kālāsoka reigned for 28 years. (See *Mahāvaṁsa* Ch. IV; *Samantapāsādikā*, I. 73).

AŚOKA

Aśoka was the grandson of Chandragupta. He was the foremost of his hundred and one brothers in virtue and power.[15] He reigned without coronation for four years.[16] He was at first called Candāsoka on account of his evil deeds; later on he became known as Dhammāsoka on account of his meritorious deeds. Like his father he used to give alms to sixty thousand *brāhmaṇas;* but soon he became disgusted with them on account of their disorderly conduct. He fed religious mendicants of different sects to test their conduct.[17] Aśoka fell in love with a girl named Devī, daughter of a seṭṭhi of Vedisā. He had, by her, a son named Mahindra and a daughter named Saṅghamittā.[18] Both the son and the daughter obtained ordination after hearing the *dhamma* practised by Nigrodha.[19] Aśoka received a very great shock when he lost his devoted wife Asandhimittā in the twelfth year of his reign. Four years after her death he married a girl named Tiṣyarakṣā[20]

Aśoka obtained some miraculous power,e.g., his power was extended to one *yojana* under the earth and to one *yojana* in the sky. Gods used to bring sixteen pots of water for him from the *Anotatta* lake; out of these, he used to distribute eight pots among the *bhikkhus*, two pots amongst the *bhikkhus* versed in *Tipiṭaka* and two pots to the chief queen Asandhimittā; and four pots he kept for his own use. Gods used to bring for him celestial drink.[21] Aśoka followed the doctrine of the heretics for three years and in the fourth year of his reign, he was established in the Buddhasāsana. His father Bindusāra was devoted to the *brāhmaṇas*.[22] Ariṭṭha was sent to Aśoka by Devānampiyatissa, king of Ceylon, to bring Saṅghamittā and a branch of the Bo-tree. The mission of his taking Saṅghamittā to Ceylon was to give ordination to the females of the palace of Ceylon.[23] Aśoka was greatly mortified after giving a branch of the Bo-tree to Ariṭṭha.[24] He sent the following present to Devānampiyatissa (I) Chattṁ (umbrella) (2) *Cāmar* (a tail- fan), (2) *Khagga* (sword), (4) *Moli* (helmet), (5) *Ratna* (jewel), (6)*Pādukam* (slipper) and many other articles necessary for the coronation ceremony, e.g., conch, Ganges water, water-pot, palanquim sandal, etc.[25]

It is to be noted that Aśoka came from Ujjain where he was a sub-king to Puspapura when he heard of his father's illness. He brought Puspapura (Pāṭaliputra) under his sway.[26] Aśoka's income from the four gates of Pāṭaliputra was great. The king used to get 4,00,000 *kahāpanas* daily from the four gates. From the Sabhā 1,00,000 *kahāpanas* were daily received, thus 5,00,000 *kahāpanas* in total he used to spend for the *Buddhasāsana*.[27]

Heretics entered the *bhikkhusaṁgha* in disguise and the *bhikkhus* failed to bring them under their control. Hence the *bhikkhus* neither performed *uposatha* ceremony nor the *Pavāranā* ceremony for seven years. Knowing this Aśoka requested the *bhikkhus* dwelling in Aśokārāma to perform *uposatha* ceremony. The *bhikkhus* refused to do so with the heretics. An officer was sent by the king to the *bhikkhus* and he knowing this grew angry and killed many *bhikkhus*. The king was informed of this and became very sorry. The king was doubtful as to who would be responsible for this great misdeed. Aśoka brought Moggaliputtatissa with great honour who removed his doubt by saying that the king would not be responsible.[28] Aśoka received his ordination from a Sāmaṇera named Nigrodha with whom he came in contact. Daily he used to give him food sufficient for eight *bhikkhus*.[29] Nigrodha offered this food to his preceptor and Aśoka further promised to supply food sufficient for thirty-two *bhikkhus*. Nigrodha established the king in three refuges and five precepts. Aśoka offered four kinds of requisites to sixty thousand *bhikkhus* at Aśokārāma in a grand scale.[30] He built 84,000 *caityas* in 84,000 towns to show reverence to 84,000 *dhammakhandas* praised by the Tathāgata.[31] In his reign the third Buddhist Council was held at Pāṭaliputra with Moggaliputtatissa as its President. In it the whole *Tripiṭaka* except the *Kathāvatthu* was recited and Moggaliputtatissa compiled the *Kathāvatthupakaraṇa*. It was Moggaliputtatissa who told Aśoka that he was the foremost amongst the *Paccayadāyakas* but later on he became the foremost of the *Sāsanadāyakas* after making his son *bhikkhu* and daughter *bhikkhunī* in the ninth year of his reign. Aśoka made arrangements in his kingdom to provide medicines for the *bhikkhus* so that they might not die for want of medicine.[32] It is a well-known fact that Aśoka sent missionaries to the various countries, e.g. (I) Majjhantika Thera to Kāshmir and Gandhāra, (2) Mahādeva Thera to Mahimsakamandala. (2) Rakkhita There to Banavāsi, (4) Yonakadhammarakkhita to Mahāraṭṭha, (5) Mahārakkhita to Yonakaloka, (6) Majjhima Thera to Himavantapadesa, (7) Sona and Uttara to Suvannabhumi and (8) Mahinda, Itthiya,m Uttiya, Samvala and Bhaddasāla to Tambapanni.[33]

PASENADI

Pasenadi was the son of Mahākosala, king of Kosala. He was educated at Taxila, Mahāli, a Licchavi prince, and a Malla prince of Kusinārā were his class mates (D.C., pt. I.m pp. 337-338). Pasenadi ascended the throne of Kosala after the death of his father. Bāvari who was the son of the chaplain of Pasenadi's father, became Pasenadi's chaplain. The king bestowed on him honour and wealth. In his youth the new king had learnt *sippa* from Bāvari who informed his royal patron that he would renounce the worldly life. He took ordination and lived in the royal garden. Many *brāhmaṇas* became his disciples. Pasenadi served him morning and evening with the four requisites. Afterwards Bāvari with his disciples went to the Dakkhināpatha as he was unwilling to stay in the royal garden any more (S. Commentary, II., pp. 579 foll).

The Sākyas became the vassals of King Pasenadi of Kosala who received homage from them and they treated him in the same way as the king treated the Buddha. (*Dīgha Nikāya*, III., p. 83). King Pasenadi had a great admiration for the Buddha. The *Jātaka* commentary furnishes us with an account of the matrimonial relation established between Pasenadi, king of Kosala and the Sākyas of Kapilavastu. It says that at Sāvatthī in the house of Anāthapiṇḍika there was always unfailing food for five hundred Brethren and the same with Visākhā and the king of Kosala. But in the king's palace, 'various and fine as was the fare given,' no one was friendly to the Brethren. The result was that the Brethren never ate in the palace, but they took their food and went off to eat it at the house of Anāthapiṇḍika or Visākhā or some other of their trusted friends.

One day the king said. "A Present has been brought, take this to the Brethren," and sent it to the refectory. An answer was brought that no Brethren were there in the refectory. "Where are they gone?" asked he. "They were sitting in their friends' houses to eat," was the reply. So the king after breakfast came to the Buddha and asked him, "Good sir! What is the best kind of food?" The food of friendship is the best, great king,' said he' 'even sour ricegruel given by a friend becomes sweet." 'Well, sir, and with whom do the Brethren find friendship? 'With their kindred, great king, or with the Sākya families.' Then the king thought what if he were to make a Sākya girl his queen-consort: then the Brethren would be his friend, as it were, with their own kindred. So rising from his seat, he returned to the palace and sent a message to Kapilavatthu to this effect, 'Please give me one of your daughters in marriage for I wish to become connected with your family.' On receipt of this message the Sākyas gathered together and deliberated. "We live in a place subject to the authority of the king of Kosala; if we refuse a daughter, he will be angry, and if we give her, the custom of our clan will be broken. What are we to do?" Then a Sākya chief named Mahānāman said to them, "Do not trouble about it. I have a daughter named Vāsabhakhattiyā whose mother is a slave woman, Nāgamuṇḍā by name; she is some sixteen years of age, of great beauty and auspicious prospects, and by her father's side noble. We will send her, as a girl nobly born." The Sākyas agreed, sent for the messengers, and said that they were willing to give a daughter of the clan, and that they might take her with them at once. The messengers knew that the Sākyas were very proud of their birth, so they could not believe their words. They told the Sākyas that they would take one who would eat along with them (Sākyas). The Sākyas assigned a lodging for the messengers and then wondered what to do. Mahānāman told them not to worry about it but to get the dish ready and to bring Vāsabhakhattiyā dressed in her finery and to produce a letter as soon as he would take one mouthful saying that such a king had sent this letter which would require your immediate attention, The Sākyas did so. The messengers saw Vāsabhakhattiyaā eating with Mahānāman and were firmly convinced that she was his saughter for they could not divine the secret. So Mahānāman sent away his daughter in great pomp. The messengers brought her to Śāvatthī and said that this maiden was the true-born daughter of Mahānāman. The king was pleased, caused the whole city to be decorated and placed her upon a pile of treasure, and by a ceremonial sprinkling made her his chief queen. She became dear and beloved to the king. (Fausboll, *Jātaka,* Vol. IV. p. 144 foll.) In course of time, a son was born to Pasenadi and Vāsabhakhattiyā. This son was named Viḍuḍabha who massacred the Sākyas later on when he knew that they had deceived his father by giving him a slave girl to marry.

Pasenadi had a fight[34] with Ajātaśattu for the village of Kāśī. At first Pasenadi was defeated but later on he succeeded in defeating his sister's son Ajātaśattu and having him captured. Then he married his daughter Vajirā to Ajātaśattu and gave her the Kāśī village for bath and perfume money.

The *Dhammapada commentary* gives us a glimpse of the administration of criminal justice by Pasenadi Once some thieves were caught and brought before the king of Kosala. He ordered them to be bound in ropes and chains and kept in prison.[35] In the *Dīgha Nikāya* we read that Pasenadi, king of Kāsi- Kosala, used to collect taxes from the inhabitants of Kāsi- kosala. He used to enjoy the income not alone but with his subordinates.[36]

On a certain festival day King Pasenadi while marching sunwise round the city seated on the back of an elephant, saw the beautiful wife of a certain poor man who was looking down on the royal pomp from the top of a seven-storied palace. The king was fired by lustful desire for the woman. He had the husband of the woman summoned before him, appointed him a servant and gave him a shield and a sword. The king tried to find faults with him so that he might punish the man with death and could have his wife. But the man used to discharge his duties so satisfactorily that it was scarcely possible for the king to punish the man. At last he ordered the man to bring red earth, which are to be had of the dragons only. Before attending to the royal requisition the servant came home, took his meal and gave that choicest portion of the meal to a traveller. Then he cast a handful of rice into the water while rinsing his mouth. The fish partook of the handful of rice. By offering food to a traveller and the fish, the servant acquired merit. He stood on the bank of the pool and addressing the dragons, he said that he would transfer the merit to the white and blue. The king of the dragons appeared in the guise of an old *brāhmaṇa*. He was assured of the merit; he then brought red earth and water lilies both white and blue to the servant who transferred all his merits to the king of the dragons. The servant came back to the palace with red earth and water lilies. He found the doors closed, threw the red earth on the threshold and hung the flowers over the door. He shouted loudly asking the citizens to witness that he had executed the royal order. Then he left the royal service and took refuge in the monastery. But that very night Pasenadi heard a terrible sound, "*Du sā nā so*" and had not a wink of sleep. The following morning he enquired of a *brāhmaṇa* as to the significance of the sound. The *brāhmaṇa* frightened the king by saying that it signified death. But he assured the king at the same time that this danger could be averted if the king would sacrifice one hundred of every description of living beings. The king , afraid of death, ordered his men to arrange for a sacrifice. All sorts of living beings were got ready; meanwhile Queen Mallikā seeing so many living creatures, enquired of the matter and learnt every thing. The queen reprimanded the king for his foolishness in relying on the *brāhmaṇa's* words and told him that it was impossible for one to save one's life by sacrificing other lives. She took him to the Buddha who explained the meaning of the sound. The king was satisfied with the answer, paid obeisance to the Teacher, came back to his palace and ordered the releases of these living beings got ready for sacrifice. (*Dhammapada Commy*. II. p. I. foll).

Many a tale is told in the Pāli literature about Pasenadi's dealings with Buddha and his disciples. The *Samyutta Nikāya* tells us that Pasenadi before accepting Buddha's discipleship saw Buddha at Jetavana. Pasenadi asked him thus "Six heretical teachers, e.g., Pūraṇa Kassapa and others, who are senior to you in age and in point of the time of ordination, do not care to call themselves Buddhas. How is it that you though younger in age call yourself a Buddha?" Buddha replied, "A *kṣatriya*, a serpent, fire, and a *bhikkhu* though younger in age should not be disregarded." Pasenadi heard this reply and became his disciple. (S. I., pp. 68-70). Pasenadi was a king of charitable disposition. He gave two towns known as Ukkhaṭṭha and Sālavatikā respectively to two *brāhmaṇas* named Pokkharasādi and Lohicca, as royal gifts with power over it as if they were kings (*Dīgha Nikāya*, I., pp. 87 and 224). He made an incomparable gift and thus became famous for his charity. Once while the Buddha was residing at Sāvatthī in the *ārāma* of Anāthapiṇḍika at Jetavana, Psenadi made gifts for a week on an immense scale, not to be compared with the charity practiced by any body in his kingdom. These gifts were known as *'asadisadāna'* (incomparable charity) (*Vimānavatthu Commentary*, pp. 5-6). Pasenadi had religious instructions from the Buddha on several occasions. He was told that one who is born must meet with decay and death[37] that the self of one who commits three kinds of sin is unprotected[38] and it becomes an enemy to him,[39] that one how is in possession of great wealth often becomes attached to world,[40] that *lobha* (avarice), *dosa* (hatred), and *moha* (delusion arise in a person and trouble him[41] and that earnestness is the only virtue which gives happiness in this life as well as in after life.[42] Pasenadi used to take a pot of rice which was sufficient to hold sixteen seers of rice. He reduced his meal to one *nāli* under Buddha's instruction.[43]

CAṆḌA PAJJOTA AND UDENA

Caṇḍa Pajjota was the king of Ujjain. He was a contemporary of Gotama Buddha. Beal points out in his *Romantic Legend of Sākya Buddha* (p.29) that Pradyota was called bright lamp, his son was named Pūrṇa and the king's personal strength was very great. We learn from the *Theragāthā* commentary that Mahākaccāyana was the chaplain of King Caṇḍa Pajjota who asked him to bring the Buddha. Mahākaccāyana went to the Master who taught him *dhamma* with such effect that at the end of the lesson he with his seven attendants was established in *Arahantship* with thorough grasp of letter and meaning. Thus accomplished he invited the Buddha on behalf of the king, saying "Lord! King Pajjota desires to worship at your feet and hear *Dhamma*." the Buddha told him and his seven attendants to satisfy the king by their mission. Thus bidden they returned to the king, satisfied his desire and established him in the Buddhist faith. Since his conversion to the Buddhist faith Buddhism became the State-religion of Avanti.

The *Dhammapada* Commentary furnishes us with a romantic story of the manner in which the matrimonial alliance was established between the two royal families of Kausāmbi and Avanti.

Once Udena, king of Kosambī, was informed by a woodman that a white elephant was moving on the bank of a lake. Udena versed in the art of charming elephant desired to capture the elephant. He set out with his men to capture it. He recited his spell, played his lute but in vain. Udena pursued the elephant. He could not understand that it was not a living being but a wooden elephant containing armed men inside its belly. The more he pursued the elephant the more the latter continued its flight. Thus King Udena was disbanded from his men and was easily captured by the men of King Caṇḍa Pajjota of Ujjain. King Udena was imprisoned. On the third day, Udena said to the keepers, "Where is your king? Why is he acting like a woman? He has captured a royal adversary and he should either release him or kill him." The keepers said these to their king who came to Udena and questioned him whether he had said so. King Udena answered in the affirmative. Then Caṇḍa Pajjota said that he would release him provided he would teach him the art of charming elephants. King Udena consented to teach the art to anybody who would be agreeable to pay homage to him. The king of Ujjain declined to pay homage to the king of Kosambī and asked the latter to teach the art to a hunchbacked woman who would pay homage to him. King Udena agreed. King Caṇḍa Pajjota asked his daughter to sit inside a curtain. Thus arranged Pajjota's daughter Vāsuladattā began to learn the art from Udena who remained outside the curtain. A few day passed but Vāsuladattā could not learn the art. One day Udena rebuked her saying, "You hunchbacked woman! You have no intelligence. You won't be able to learn it." "What do you mean by a hunchbacked woman, you wretched leper?" asked Vāsuladattā. Udena lifted the curtain and saw the beautiful girl and fell in love with her. The girl too fell in love with Udena at first sight. Then they decided to leave the palace. Vāsuladattā deceived her father by exacting from him the permission of going out of the palace at night to obtain medicinal herb that would facilitate the learning of the art. One night Vāsuladattā eloped with Udena who brought her to Kosambī and made her his chief consort. (*Dhammapada Commentary, I.*, 191 foll)

The *Dhammapada* commentary narrates the account of the birth and the attainment of sovereignty of Udena, son of Parantapa, king of Kosambī. One day Parantapa and his queen who was then pregnant, were basking themselves in the rays of the newly risen sun. The queen put on the crimson blanket of the king and had a royal signet on her own finger. A monster bird took the blanket to be a piece of meat, and bore off the queen through the air. The queen afraid of death kept silent lest her voice should frighten the bird and cause it to drop her. The monster bird settled on a banyan tree. The queen immediately clapped her hands and frightened the bird away. After freeing herself from the cruel clutches of the monster bird she experienced double danger at one and the same time at the close of the day. A severe storm arose causing nature restless and travail came upon her at the same time making her restless too. She was alone and had no one by her side. The queen suffered the terrible night. The following morning at daybreak nature became silent and the queen gave birth to a bonny son. The child was named Udena, because he was born at the time (*utu*) of a storm, at the time when she was upon a mountain and at the time when the sun just rose. An ascetic while picking up bones from the foot of trees heard child cry, looked upwards and saw the queen. Then after an exchange of the password of the *Kṣatriya* castem, the queen came down and the child was taken down by the ascetic. The queen ordered the ascetic not to touch her. Both of them came to the hermitage; the ascetic provided the queen with every necessary thing. A few days after, a sinful thought due to self-preservation crossed the queen's mind. She began to display herself in a state of nature and seduced the ascetic to violate his vow of chastity; thenceforth the ascetic and the queen began to live together as husband and wife. One day as the ascetic was noticing a "conjunction of a constellation with one of the lunar mansions, he saw the occultation of Parantapa's star," and told the queen that Parantapa, king of Kosambī, was dead. The queen shed tears; questioned by the ascetic she told him that Parantapa was her husband and that she was weeping because her child would have been a king if he had been at Kosambī by this time. She was then assured by the ascetic that her son would get the throne of Kosambī. The ascetic taught Udena elephant charms and Udena very soon learnt the art successfully. Then Udena went to Kosambī on the back of an elephant long with several thousands of elephants.

He stopped at the entrance of the city and challenged the citizens either to give battle or to give him the throne. The citizens refused to give either. Thereupon Udena showed the royal blanket and the signet to the citizens and told them that he was the son of king Parantapa whose queen was taken away by a monster bird. He mentioned the names of commander-in-chief, etc. The citizens were satisfied with his proof and anointed him King.

King Udena saw Sāmāvatī, daughter of the treasurer Bhaddavtiya, through the window and fell in love with her at first sight. He told the treasurer to give his daughter in marriage with him. The treasurer refused at first sight but ultimately at the desire of his daughter consented to the marriage proposal. Then Udena sent a royal retinue to the treasurer's house to bring Sāmāvatī to the palace. Sāmāvarī was brought to the palace and was made the chief consort.

(*Dhammapada Commy.*, *Udenavatthu*, Vol. I., p. 161 foll).

A *brāhmaṇa* named Culla Māgandiya brought her niece named Māgandiyā to King Udena who on seeing her fell deeply in love with her, fonferred the ceremonial sprinkling on her, provided her with a retinue of five hundred ladies-in-waiting, and raised her to the dignity of chief consort. The king of Kosambī had thus three chief consorts with a retinue of fifteen hundred nautch girls. (*Dhammapada* Commentary, I, pp. 199- 203; cf. Ibid, Vol. III. P. 193 foll.)

In the Pālī Buddhist canon King Udena of the Vamsas is said to have been a contemporary of the Buddha and to have survived the latter. King Udena was at first indifferent or even unfriendly towards Buddhism, but later on he is said to have felt a loving admiration for the Buddha. In the Pālī canon we read that Piṇḍola Bhāradvāja dwelt at Ghositā rāma in Kausāmbī. He was the son of the chaplain to King Udeṇa of Kausāmbī. He entered the Order in Rājagaha and followed the method of the teacher with regard to temperance and diet. He then acquired six-fold *abhiññā*. (*Psalms of the Brethren*, p. 111) King Udena approached Piṇḍola Bhāradvāja and asked the cause of young *bhikkhus* having black hairs on the head leading the life of pure *brahmacārīs*. Bhāradvāja replied, "It is the command of the master that *bhikkhus* should regard as mother a lady who has reached the age of a mother, should regard as sister one how has reached the age of a sister and should treat as daughter one who has reached the age of a daughter." The king further questioned Bhāradvāja, "Mind is unsteady when it is bent upon attaining something. It is for this reason that it might become tempted to get the three classes of women referred to above. Is there any other cause of a *bhikkhu* leading a pure *brahmacarī* life? Bhāradvāja replied, "The Buddha instructed the *bhikkhus* to meditate upon the bodies as full of impurities" The king further asked, "Do they who do not meditate upon the impurities of the body find it difficult to lead the pure life of a *brahmacārī*?" Bhāradvāja replied that the *bhikkhus* were instructed to control their senses. The king admitted that when he entered the *harem* with his senses uncontrolled, he used to think of various sensual pleasures, but when he entered with his senses controlled, he did not get the opportunity of thinking of sensual pleasures at all. (S., IV. pp. 110-112).

Notes and References :

1. The *Tibetan Dulva* says that Bimbisāra was so called because he was the son of Bimbī, Queen of King Mahāpadma of Rājagrha (Rockhill, *Life of the Buddha*, p. 16.
2. Geiger's Translation, p. 12
3. Smith, V. A. *Early History of India*. 4th Ed., p. 33
4. For a detailed critical account of Bimbisāra's marriage with a Licchavi girl and the parentage of the mother of Ajātaśatru, see Law, B.C., *"Some Kṣatriya Tribes of Ancient India,"* Ch. I VI,pp. 106-197 & Ch. III. p. 136
5. Nos 239, 283 & 492.
6. The *Petavatthu* and its commentary also furnish us with an account of the spread of Buddhism and its influence over *Brāhmaṇism* the time of the Buddha. *Brāhmaṇas* began to give offerings to the *bhikkhus* for the sake of their dead relatives in the expectation of enabling them to obtain freedom from the spirit life.
7. *Dīpavamsa*, III., verse 59
8. *Dīgha Nikāya*, I. p. 116
9. For an account of the birth of Abhaya, son of Bimbisāra by a Licchavi woman, see : *"Some Kṣatriya Tribes of Ancient India*, Ch. I. VI pp. 108 110 The son of Bimbisāra by Ambapālī, a courtesan of Vaisālī is called Vimala-Kondañña in Pālī literature and not Abhaya.
10. *Psalms of the Sisters*, p. 120; *Psalms of the Brethren*, p. 65
11. *Psalms of the Brethren*, 269
12. Cf. *Vaḍḍhakisūkara, Kummā Sapiṇḍ, Taccha Sūkara and the Bhaddasāla Jātakas.*
13. *Saṁyutta Nikāya* (P.T.S.) pt. II p. 268
14. *Dīpavaṁsa*, V., 97; Mahāvaṁsa, IV. I
15. *Mahāvaṁsa*, ch. V
16. *Samantapāsādikā*, Vol. I p. 41
17. *Mahāvaṁsa*, ch. V.
18. Ibid., Ch. XIII
19. Ibid, Ch. V.

20. Ibid., Ch. XX
21. *Samantapāsādikā*, Vol. I p. 42
22. *Samantapāsādikā*, I.pp. 44-45
23. *Mahāvaṁsa*, Ch. 18
24. *Mahāvaṁsa*, Ch. 19
25. *Samantapāsādikā*, I, p. 75
26. *Mahāvaṁsa*, Ch. V.
27. *Samantapāsādikā*, I. p. 52
28. *Samantapāsādikā*, I. pp. 53-54, cf. *Mahāvaṁsa*, ch. V.
29. *Samantapāsādikā*, p. 47
30. Ibid., p. 48
31. Ibid., 49
32. Ibid., p. 52
33. *Samantapāsādikā* pp. 63--64
34. *Saṁyutta Nikāya*,I. 82-85
35. Part. IV. pp. 54-55
36. *Dīgha Nikāya*, I. pp. 228-229
37. *Saṁyutta Nikāya*, I., p. 71
38. Ibid. p. 73
39. Ibid.pp. 71-72
40. Ibid. pp. 73-74
41. Ibid. p. 70
42. Ibid. pp. 86-87
43. Ibid pp. 81-82

CHAPTER 5

BUDDHIST COUNCILS

–Dr. Ramesh Chandra Majumdar M.A; Ph.D.

THE FIRST COUNCIL

1. THE ACCOUNT IN CULLAVAGGA

According to the Buddhists of all schools a Great Council (*Saṅgiti*)of the Buddhists was held almost immediately after the death of the Buddha. Our authorities.[1] however, widely differ regarding the details of this First Great Council. It would, therefore be well to take as a basis of our discussion the very circumstantial account that has been preserved in the Eleventh Khandhaka of the *Cullavagga* of the *Vinaya Piṭaka*.[2]

It began in the irreverent conduct of a monk called Subhadda.[3] While the death of the Great Master caused universal mourning, he struck an altogether different note. "Enough Sirs." said he, "Weep not, neither lament! We are well rid of the great *Samaṇa*. We used to be annoyed by being told ,"This beseems you, this beseems you not.' But now we shall be able to do whatever we like; and what we do not like that we shall not have to do."

The Venerable Mahā Kassapa took this to be an alarming indication of the possible laxity of discipline among the monks in the absence of the Great Teacher. He therefore requested the other monks to meet and "chant together the *Dhamma* and *Vinaya*, before what is not *Dhamma* and what is not *Vinaya* are spread abroad, and what is *Dhamma* and what is *Vinaya* are put aside".

Four hundred and ninety-nine *Arahats* were accordingly chosen, and Ānanda, although he had not yet attained the state of *Arahatship*, was added to the number, at the request of the assembled monks, and in view of his special knowledge of *Dhamma* and *Vinaya*. It may be added that Ānanda reached the state of *Arahat* at the close of the night preceding the first session of the Assembly.

The town of Rājagṛha was selected for the meeting, as there was abundance of lodging places and plenty of alms. It was then arranged by a special resolution of *Saṁgha* that the five hundred selected Bhikkhus would spend the rainy season at Rājagṛha in order to chant the *Dhamma* and the *Vinaya*, and that no other *Bhikkhus* should go there during that period.

The meeting actually took place in the second month of the rainy season. The procedure adopted was quite simple. The Venerable Mahā Kassapa questioned Upāli regarding *Vinaya* and Ānanda regarding *Dhamma*, and elicited from them full information about both. A specimen of these questions may be given here.

'Venerable Upāli, where was the first *Pārājika* promulgated?'

'In Vesālī, Sir.'

'Concerning whom was it spoken?'

'Concerning Sudinna, the son of Kalanda.'

'In regard to what matte?'

'Sexual intercourse.'

"Thus did the venerable Mahā Kassapa question the Venerable Upāli as to the matter, as to the occasion, as to the individual concerned, as to the (principal) rule, as to the sub- rule, as to who would be guilty and as to how would be innocent, of the first Pārājika." Similarly Mahā Kassapa questioned Ānanda through the five *Nikāyas*.

After the chanting of *Dhamma* and *Vinaya* was over Ānanda represented to the *Bhikkhus* that the Great Buddha had told him at the time of his death, that the *Saṁgha* might, if it should so wish, revoke all the lesser and minor precepts. There was, however, a wide difference of opinion as to what constituted the lesser and minor precepts, where upon the Assembly agreed, on Mahā Kassapa's proposal, to follow all the precepts laid down by the Buddha, 'not ordaining what has not been ordained, and not revoking what has been ordained'.. The Assembly, however, took Ānanda to task for not ascertaining from the Blessed One which were the lesser and minor precepts, and Ānanda had to confess his fault. Ānanda was similarly charged by the Assembly, and had to confess his fault, for (1) stepping upon the Blessed One's rainy season garment in order to sew it; (2) causing the dead body of the Blessed One to be first saluted by women who profaned it by their tears; (3) not requesting the Buddha to remain on earth for a *kalpa* even when a plain hint was given by the Buddha of such a desire on his part; and (4) exerting himself to procure admission for women into the Buddhist Church.

Ānanda then told the Bhikkhus that the Buddha had said at the time of his death. "Let then the *Saṁgha*, Ānanda, when I am dead, impose the higher penalty on Channa the Bhikkhu." Fortunately, in this case, Ānanda had already ascertained from Buddha what the higher penalty meant. The Bhikkhus accordingly imposed on Channa the terrible punishment which meant practically a social boycott. Channa, however, repented of his sins and attained the state of Arahata, whereupon the penalty was removed. This ended the business of the First Council.

2 ACCOUNTS IN OTHER AUTHORITIES

In order to understand properly the other view-points it would be necessary to analyse the account of *Cullavagga* into its constituent parts and discuss each of them in the light of other authorities. For the sake of convenience we might divide the whole story into the following topics:

(a) The motive or object of summoning the Council.

(b) The preliminary arrangements about the Council

(c) The Scriptural work attributed to the Council.

(d) The part played, by Ānanda.

(a) The motive or object of summoning the Council.

The irreverent words of Subhadda have been alleged in Cullavagga as the motive of summoning the Council. This is not however, universally agreed to. Some authorities agree in the main, but differ in details; other authorities ignore this motive altogether and suggest entirely different reasons for the convocation of the Council.

The Mahīśāsaka, Dharmagupta, Mahāsāṁghika Vinayas, the Sudarśana-vinaya-vibhaāṣā (Nanjio, 1125) and the *Vinayamātṛkā-sūtra* agree with Cullavagga, though the name of the irreverent monk is given as (Śu)bhānanda in the first, second and fifth, Mahallaka in the third, and Subhdramahallaka in the fourth.[4] In *Mahāvaṁsa*, the irreverent conduct of Subhadda is regarded as only one of the many reasons which induced Mahā Kassapa to convoke the Council.[5] Hiuen Tsang has improved upon the account of Cullavagga. In his account, not one monk, but many expressed satisfaction at the death of Buddha. Mahā Kassapa, having heard this, was deeply moved and afflicted, and he resolved to assemble the treasure of the law (*Dharmapiṭaka*) and bring to punishment the transgressors.[6] Buddhaghoṣa has followed closely on the lines of Cullavagga.[7]

But a good many authorities altogether ignore the Subhadda-episode as the motive of Mahā Kassapa in summoning the Council. The Sarvāstivādins, for example, are silent about it,[8] while no mention is made of it in the *Dīpavaṁsa*,[9] the *Tibetan Dulva*[10], *Prajñāpāramitāśāstra*, the life of Aśoka, the Transmission of the *Dharmapiṭaka* (Nanjio 1363) or in the record of the compilation of the three *Piṭakas* and the miscellaneous *Piṭaka*.[11]

As to other motives and objects for summoning the Council, some very general ones have been suggested by the *Mahāvaṁsa*[12]. The *Dīpavaṁsa* says that the five hundred Theras as composed the *Vinaya* and *Dharma*, *as they knew the doubts of the people*. The *Tibetan Dulva* describes the situation as follows: "Mahā Kāśyapa heard, after the death of the Buddha, people remark that whereas 80,000 *Bhikkhus* had died at the same time as Śāriputra, 70,000 on Maudgalyāyana's death and 18,000 more when the Buddha had died, the words of the Blessed One had vanished like smoke; and that as all the mighty *Bhikkhus* had utterly passed away, the *Sūtrānta*, the *Vinaya*, and the *Mātṛkā* of the Blessed One were no longer taught. When he heard people thus censuring, blaming, and slandering, he told what he had heard to the *Bhikkhus*, and concluded by saying that they must assemble in that place (i.e. at Kuśinārā). The *Bhikkhus* assented to this proposition"[13]

Hiuen Tsang, after narrating the irreverent conduct of the monks as described above, proceeds thus: "And now the King of the Law having gone from the world, both men and *Devas* were left without a guide, and the great Arahatas moreover were cleaving to (the idea of their) *Nirvāṇa*. Then the great Kāśyapa reflected thus: "To secure obedience to the teaching of the Buddha, we ought to collect the *Dharma-piṭaka*". Some authorities refer to the intervention of the gods in order to induce Mahā Kassapa to summon the Council, while, lastly, several others record that he spontaneously resolved to assemble the Council. "It is for the laymen" said he "to occupy themselves with the relics of the *Tathāgata*, for us to tabulate the law.[14]" According to the *Mahāvastu*, five hundred monks wanted to die voluntarily after the death of their master, but Kasspa opposed the procedure, saying that it is necessary to compile the law lest the heretics would say that the law of Buddha vanishes like smoke.[15]

(b) *The preliminary arrangements about the Council.*

All authorities agree that Mahā Kassapa took the initiative, and summoned the Assembly. Some supernatural elements are introduced by later authorities. Thus, according to Hiuen Tsang, Mahā Kassapa ascended mount Sumeru and sounded the great gong to summon the Councilors.[16] The *Tibetan Dula* ascribes the same part to Pūrṇa and further introduces the somewhat fantastic episode of Gavampati, who, when summoned to attend the Council, consumed himself by means of his magical powers and passed into the state of *parinirvāṇa*.[17]

But although Mahā Kassapa took the initiative and chose the *Bhikkhus,* his actions were, according to Cullavagga, sanctioned by formal resolutions of the *Saṁgha*. This important detail is omitted in some authorities.[18] Other authorities make it quite clear that there was at first a general assembly of the *Bhikkhus* who flocked from all the regions at the invitation of Mahā Kassapa, and the five hundred *Bhikhhus* who took part in the Council were chosen by this body. Thus the *Dīpavaṁsa* says "The congregation of *Bhikkhus,* seven hundred thousand in number, assembled ......They all, having made enquiry and determined which were the most worthy, elected by vote of the congregation five hundred Theras."[19] Most authorities agree with Cullavagga that the number of

Councilors was 500 but Hiuen Tsang puts it as 1,000. All authorities agree that the Council was held at Rājagṛha, in the Sattapaṇṇi Cave, with the exception of *Tibetan Dulva* which substitutes Nyagrodha Cave instead. This last named authority states an additional ground for selecting Rājagṛha *viz.* that as Ajātaśattu was a very firm believer, he would provide the *Saṁgha* with all the necessaries.[20]

(c) *The Scriptural work attributed to the Council.*

The account in *Cullavagga* is followed by *Mahāvaṁsa.* According to Hiuen Tsan and *Tibetan Dulva,*[21] Ānanda first recited the *Dhamma,* then Upāli recited *Vinaya* and lastly, Mahā Kassapa himself recited the *Abhidhamma.*[22] The last named authority adds various episodes, and, further, the sections of *Vinaya* and *Dharma* which it puts in the mouths of Upāli and Ānanda do not always agree with those stated in *Cullavagga*

Buddaghoṣa while agreeing generally with *Cullavagga* refers specifically to all the constituent parts of the *Pāli Vinaya* and *Suttapiṭakas* as being recited in the Council.[23]

According to all these accounts, however, the whole business of the Council was practically conducted by the three *Theras* named above, while the other Councillors remained more or less passive listeners. The *Dīpavaṁsa,* on the other hand, gives a more circumstantial account, and makes all the *Theras* take an active part in the proceeding. "The *Bhikkhus* composed the collection of *Dhamma* and *Vinaya* by consulting Upāli about the *Vinaya* and by asking the *Thera* called Ānanda regarding the *Dhamma. Thera* Mahā Kassapa and the great teacher Anuruddha, *Thera* Upāli of powerful memory, and the learned Ānanda, as well as many other distinguished disciples who had been praised by the master ... made this first collection."[24]

Among these other distinguished members Vaṅgīsa, Pūrṇa, the junior Kassapa, Kātyāyana and Koṭṭhita are mentioned in diverse sources. The account in the *Mahāvastu* is entirely different. According to it, Kātyāyana is the chief speaker in the Council and the subject of his discourse was the exposition of the *'Daśabhūmis'* i.e. ten degrees of *Bodhisattvas.*[25] It must be remembered, however, that the *Mahāvastu* preserves the traditions of the *Lokottaravādins,* a sect belonging to the *Mahāsāṁghikas,*[26] who broke away from the Orthodox Church.

(d) *The part played by Ānanda.*

The part played by Ānanda in the First Council is confusing in the extreme. Although he is regarded as the chief authority on *Dhamma,* he is at first refused admission into the Council on the ground that he has not yet attained the state of *Arahata*. Further, although he attains the *Arahatship* he is charged, after the close of the Council, with several offences for each of which he has to confess his fault.

The account in the *Tibetan Dulva* differs in some material respects from *Cullavagga*. As soon as the proposal of the Council was mooted by Kassapa, the assembled monks inquired if Ānanda would be admitted into the synod. Kassapa was unwilling to make an exception in favour of Ānanda, but agreed to admit him if they were willing that he (Ānanda) should be appointed to supply the *Saṁgha* with water. This having been formally approved by the Assembly, Ānanda proceeded to Rājagṛha. Ill luck, however, accompanied him. Having arrived at Rājagṛha Kassapa "requested Aniruddha to examine if any one out of the five hundred was still subject to passions, anger, ignorance, desire or attachment." Aniruddha discovered that this was the case only with Ānanda and so Kassapa excluded him from the Assembly. Ānanda was naturally mortified and protested against this decision. "Bear with me, venerable Kassapa" said he, "I have neither sinned against morality, the doctrine, nor against good behavior.. Be forbearing, then, O Kassapa." Kassapa then brought forward several charges against Ānanda, similar,if not identical to those mentioned in *Cullavagga.* Ānanda replied as best he could, but Kassapa refused to admit him so long as he had not destroyed his passions and become an *Arahata.* Thereupon Ānanda mournfully departed for Vṛji, but erelong he attained the state of *Arahata* and took his rightful place in the Assembly.[27]

Apart from mioner discrepancies to be noted hereafter there is one essential difference between the accounts given in *Cullavagga* and the *Tibetan Dulva*. According to the former, Ānanda was allowed to take part in the Assembly without any objection, and was brought to trial only after the business of the Council had ended. *The Dulva,* however, places Ānanda's trial before the Council and makes his admission to that body dependent upon his acquisition of *Arahatship*. The *Cullavagga* is followed in this respect by the *Vinayas* of the Mahīśāsakas and of the *Mahāsāṁghikas*. Hiuen Tsang omits the 'charges' but makes the acquistion of *Arahatship* a condition precedent to Ānanda's admission into the Assembly. It may be added that no reference is made to Ānanda's guilt in *Dīpavaṁsa, Mahāvaṁsa,* Buddhaghoṣa's Introduction to *Samantapāsādikā,* and *Mahāvastu*.

There can be hardly any doubt that the account in *Cullavagga* is in this respect less reasonable than the other versions, and is besides involved in a self-contradiction. After the account of the Council the *Cullavagga* refers to the penalty imposed upon a monk named Channa for some faults committed by him. But as soon as Channa reached the state of *Arahat* the penalty was automatically removed from him. This is in strict accordance with the orthodox view that *Arahatship* involves the exemption from all guilts. Judged by this standard, it seems incongruous that Ānanda should have been brought to trial for his offenses, long after he had attained the position of an *Arahata.*[28]

Nothing in the whole account of the Council is so difficult to explain as the episode of Ānanda. He is referred to in the most flattering terms and regarded as indispensable by almost all the authorities.[29] And yet he is not only denied admission to the Coucil but charged with a variety of offences, and sometimes even forced to accept the function of menials. As regards the charges against him there are two more,in addition to the five stated above on the authority of Cullavagga.[30]

6. Ānanda did not give clear water to the Buddha to drink, although he thrice asked for it.

7. After the death of the Buddha, Ānanda showed man and women of low habits the hidden parts of *Tathāgata*.

Ānanda made a suitable reply to all these charges. (1) He forgot to ask the Buddha about the lesser and minor precepts as he was overcome with grief at the prospect of losing the Buddha. (2) He had to tread upon the Buddha's garment while sewing it, as there was no friendly *Bhikkhu* to help him. (3) He caused the body of the Buddha to be saluted by women first, as he thought they should not be kept beyond due time, and that if they saw the Blessed One, many of them would conceive a longing to become like him. (4) He was possessed by the Evil One when he refrained from requesting Buddha to remain on earth for a Kalpa. (5) He exerted himself to procure admission for women into the Church out of consideration for the venerable Gautamī who nursed the Buddha in his infancy. (6) He could not give clear water to Buddha as five hundred waggons had just then crossed the neighboring river and made it muddy. (7) He thought that women, being naturally sensual, would cease to be so, if they but saw the privy parts of the Blessed One.[31]

The replies of Ānanda would appear generally satisfactory to most persons,and except one or two important ones, such as the admission of women into Order, most of the other offences would seem to be trivial in the extreme.

3. HISTORICAL CHARACTER OF THE COUNCIL.

What historical value are we to attach to the accounts of the First Council sketched above? This question has been discussed by eminent scholars and different opinions have been expressed by them.

The opinion which now holds the field was the one so strongly expressed by Professor Oldenberg nearly half a century ago. He held the story of the First Council as not history, but pure invention, and, moreover, an invention of very ancient data.' Strange as it may seem this view, which goes counter to the unanimous tradition of the Buddhist world, both ancient and modern rested mainly on an *argumentam ad Silentio*. Oldenberge pointed out that the story of the irreverent conduct of Subadda is narrated in nearly identical words in the *Cullavagga* and *Mahāparinibbāna Sutta*, but although it is described in the former as the immediate cause of summoning the Council, no allusion to the Council is made in the latter. "This silence" says Oldenberg "is as valuable as the most direct testimony: it shows that the author of the *Mahāparinibbāṇa Sutta* did not know anything of the First Council".[32]

That a most dogmatic view of this character, based on nothing but the flimsiest grounds, should have held the field for nearly half a century only testifies to the great respect which the name of Oldengerg commanded among generations of scholars. It is true that Rhys Davids raised a mild protest against the dogmatic character of the theory, but he hastened to add that "the conclusion drawn by Oldenberg is at least the easiest and readiest way of explaining the very real discrepancy that he hs pointed out."[33] Kern, too, pointed out that the motive alleged in *Cullavagga* (i.e. the irreverent conduct of Subhadda) is not only absent from the *Mahāparinibbāṇa Sutta* but likewise from the *Dīpavaṁsa*, and hence Oldenberg's argument falls to the ground. But nev :theless Kern hastened to add that his remark in no wise invalidates the conclusion that the dogmatical story of the First Council, as told in *Cullavagga*, is comparatively young.' Rockhill, too demurred against the view of Oldenberg and held that the authenticity of the Council of Rājagṛha has been doubted on insufficient grounds,[34] but he did not push his contentions any further. The first bold attempt to expose the weakness of Oldenberg's argument was made by Professor L.De La Vallee Poussin. "Never,"said he, "and the mere thought of it disconcerts them, never will they believe that the silence of a *sūtra* about a dogma or an ecclesiastical event can furnish anything but an hypothesis. They read again two three times Prof. Oldenberg's remark about the absence of allusion to the First Council in the *Mahāparinibbāṇa* ......still they are not quite sure they have read correctly."[35]

In view of the different accounts of the First Council, culled from various authorities, it is now a comparatively easy task to refute the opinions of Prof. Oldenberg. It has been pointed out that the story of the irreverent conduct of Subhadda has not been described or alleged as the motive of summoning the First Council in good many authorities. *The Tibetan Dulva*, for example, narrates the story of Subhada, in very much the same way as the *Mahāparinibbāṇa Sutta*, but makes no allusion to the First Council as resulting from it. Are we to conclude, then, with Oldenberg, that the author of this book did not know anything of the First Council? But fortunately we can easily demonstrate the falsity of this assumption ,for, in the eighth page after that, it contains a most detailed account of the First Council. Thus we see that the peculiarity which Prof. Oldenberg noticed in the *Mahāparinibbāṇa Sutta* is shared by many other later texts, and it therefore hardly stands to reason to characterise the account of the Council as a forgery. On the other hand,some recension of th *Mahāparinibbāṇa Sutta* actually contains an accounts of the Council.[36] Thus the whole argument of Professor Oldenberge loses its weight.

Further, Prof. Oldenberg proceeded on the assumption that the account in *Cullavagga* is the authentic account of the First Counci. This might have been excusable in his days in view of the imperfect knowledge of Buddhist literature, but is no longer so. It will be apparent from a comparison of the different accounts given above, that the *Cullavagga* has no claim to be regarded as the parent-stock from which the other accounts have been derived. It is equally clear, that judged from the point of view of general credibility, the accounts in *Cullavagga,* at least in some respects, the case of Ānanda for example, are less reliable than others. One cannot help thinking that the importance of *Cullavagga* has been much exaggerated in this respect. It can only be regarded as containing one of the many versions about the story of the First Council which were current at the time of its composition.

The original source from which these different versions have been compiled will probably never be known. Still it is against all accepted canons of criticism to dismiss the unanimous tradition of the First Buddhist Council as nothing but an invention of a later date. Probably all fair-minded critics will admit that there must be some basis of truth in a matter agreed to by all the sects of the Buddhists, in spite of their fundamental diferences in other essential matters.

If therefore we accept, what Minayeff propounded long ago, that there was really an assembly of the Buddhists shortly after the passing away of the Master, the question resolves itself into a discussion about the nature of the meeting and the business performed in it.

That the assembly was held in the Sattapaṇṇi cave at Rājagṛha may be accepted in view of the unanimity of the tradition. It is impossible to rely on the number of assembled

Bhikkhus given in any account, but it is probable that a large number of eminent *Bhikkhus* attended the session. We may agree with *Cullavagga* that Kassapa, Ānanda and Upāli took the leading parts in the discussion, but it seems to be certain that that authority has unduly belittled the importance of the other members present. The *Dīpavaṁsa,* although a much later work, seems to contain a more genuine account in this respect, when it assigns due importance to the other members. It would indeed appear from a perusal of *Cullavagga* that the other members formed more or less a dumb show. This is neither probable nor reasonable, and adds one more evidence infavour of rejecting *Cullavagga* as the primitive source of the varying accounts of the First Buddhist Council. As to the business of the meeting, the four things of primary importance seem to have been the trial of Ānanda, punishment of Channa, the recital of Scriptures, and the decision as to the minor or lesser precepts.

Minayeff and Prof. L.De Le Vallee Poussin both agree in regarding all these excepting the recital of scriptures, as bearing the mark of high antiquity. They go even further and regard the discussion of these episodes as the cause of summoning the assembly. The reasons advanced by these scholars for regarding the episodes of Ānanda, Channa and the lesser precepts as genuine can be readily appreciated. Ānanda, being the favourite desciple of the Buddha, must have been an object of jealousy to many, and, as too often happens in such cases, the withdrawal of the protecting hand must have been a signal for bringing trivial charges against him. As regards Channa, the Church was bound to carry the punishment ordered by the Master. As to the precepts which the *Bhikkhus* were to observe, it was absolutely necessary for the Church to decide the question on one way or the other for the very existence of the organisation. These episodes are natural and almost inevitable consequences of the death of the Master, ---on the other hand they are of too trifling a character to be invented in later times. These considerations seem to me to be enough to regard the episodes as historical.

But while regarding the First Council as a historical one, and believing in the authenticity of the episodes referred to above, Minayeff does not concede that the recital of Scriptures formed any business of that meeting. But almost all the arguments which can be advanced in support of the other episodes apply with equal force in this respect also. What, for instance, can be more natural than that the disciples of the Great Master should make an effort to collect his sayings and teachings immediately after his death in order to guide themselves? In the absence of a written book, and any recognised leader, the necessity of such a collection is almost a paramount one. In this connection we have got an episode in some versions of the story which seems to be of great significance.It is said that immediately after the recitation of the Scriptures was over the monk Purāṇa arrived at Rājagṛha with five hundred brethren. When asked to associate himself with the *Dhamma* and *Vinaya* as had just been recited, he replied: "The *Dhamma* and the *Vinaya* have been well chanted by the *Theras*. However, in the way in which I have heard and received the law from the mouth of *Bhagavat* himself, in that manner I purpose to retain it in my memory."[37] This was a danger signal for the Church. The attitude of exclusiveness displayed by Purāṇa and the irreverent conduct of Subhadda may perhaps be regarded as typical of a large section of the monks. And this rendered it all the more necessary that there should be a general agreement among the *Bhikkhus* on the main and essential points of the doctrine and disciplinary rules.

Besides, the convocation of a general Council for this purpose, " from being unusual,may be regarded as quite in consonance with the democratic Constitution which the great Master imparted to his Church. The example of the republican tribes, after which the Constitution of the Buddhist Church seems to have been designed,[38] must also have furnished a model to the *Bhikkhus*. In that critical hour of the Church when the guiding hand of the Master was no more and the spirit of insubordination and irreverence was gradually raising its head, nothing seems to be more natural and reasonable that the eminent *Bhikkhus* should meet in a conclave,and arrange the disciplinary and doctrinal matters as best they could, in order to substiture something for the Departed Master as the guiding authority of the Church. And when the course of events, so natural and reasonable in itself, is supported by the unanimous tradition of the Buddhist world, it is difficult not to regard it as authentic, at least in its main outline.

It is quit true that we shall not be justified in regarding the present Canon as arranged in its entirety in the First Council. But once we concede that the essentials of doctrine and disciplinary matter were discussed in the First Council,it is fruitless, in the present state of our knowledge, to inquire as to what portions of *Vinaya, Sūtra* and *Abhidharma* were recited there. It may be conceded that the First Council framed the nucleus out of which the elaborate and well-arranged *Tripiṭakas* arose in later time, as a result, probably, of efforts of generations of scholars. But the question as to which portions of the existing literature formed the original nucleus must be decided by textual criticism and no amount of historical discussion can solve the problem. It seems to be certain, however, that the present Pāli Canon has little claim to be regarded as that nucleus.

THE SECOND COUNCIL

1. THE ACCOUNT IN CULLAVGGA

In pursuance of the method already adopted in the case of the First Great Council, we shall begin with th account of the Second Council as given in *Cullavagga*.

About a century after the death of the Master dispute arose regarding the validity of 'ten points'[39] in the Buddhist doctrine which were upheld by the monks of Vaiśālî. It happened in this way. Yasa, the son of Kākaṇḍaka, arrived in Vaiśālī and stayed at Mahāvana in the Kūṭāgāra hill. On *Uposatha* day, the monks of Vaiśālī placed a copper pot full of water in the midst of the *Bhikkhu Saṁgha*, and asked the lay disciples to put some coins in it. The contribution, they said, "will be wanted for the *Saṁgha*, for the provision of various utensils." The venerable Yasa openly protested against this for he held that the use of gold and silver was forbidden to the *Bhikkhus*,a and forbade the lay disciples to pay anything. They, however, did contribute, but Yasa refused to take any share of the collection when offered to him.

The monks of Vaiśālī were angry and carried out against Yasa the *Paṭisāraṇiya-kamma* (Act of Reconciliation), for upbraiding and reviling the laity.[40] According to this Act

Yasa was to go and ask pardon of the laity. Accordingly Yasa went to the laity, but instead of asking pardon he defended his own points of view by quoting the sayings of the Buddha. His eloquent sermon brought over the laity to his side, who declared in one voice 'that there is but one (meaning Yasa) who is a real *Bhikkhus,* the rest are no *Bhikkhus.'*

The monks of Vaiśālī, thereupon, determined to carry out against Yasa 'the *Ukkhepaniya-kamma'* or Act of suspension for 'not acknowledging and for not atoning for an offence.' This would virtually mean the expulsion of Yasa from the *Saṁgha.*

The Venerable Yasa then proceeded to Kauśāmbī and sent messengers to Avanti and other countries in the West and the South, inviting the *Bhikkhus* to come and decide what is true and what is not. From Kauśāmbī Yasa went to the Venerable Sambhūta Sāṇavāsī who was living on the Ahogaṅga hill.[41] He explained to him the ten doctrinal points wrongly held by th *Vajjian Bhikkhus* of Vaśālī and requested him to take up the question before "what is not *Dhamma* is spread abroad, and what is *Dhamma* is put aside."

Sambhūta Sāṇavāsī agreed. In the meanwhile, apparently in response to the invitations sent by Yasa, about sixty *Arahatas* from the Western Country, and about eighty-eight from Avanti and the Southern Country assembled on the Ahogaṅga hill.

These monks held "that the legal question involved was hard and subtle", and wanted to enlist the support of the Veneable Revata who was distinguished alike by his learning and personality. The Venerable Revata moved from one place to another in order to evade the *Bhikkhus,* but they at last got hold of him at Sahajāti.[42]

The Venerable Yasa then put before Revata the ten points one after another and asked his opinion. A specimen of this question and answer may be quoted:

Yasa--'Is the horn-salt-license, Lord, allowable?

Revata---'What, Sir,is this horn-salt-license?

Yasa--'Is it allowable, Lord, to carry about salt in a horn with the intention of putting it into food which has not been salted?'

Revata---'No, Sir, it is not allowable.'

In this way did Revata declare as invalid each and every one of the ten points held by th *Vajjian Bhikkhus* of Vaiśālī. Thereupon Yasa requested Revata to take up this question "before that which is not *Dhamma* is spread aboard and that which is *Dhamma* is put aside." And Revata agreed.

The Venerable Yasa had thus stolen a great march over the monks of Vaiśāli. But they were not idle. They fully appreciated the importance of Revata and wanted to gain him over to their side. With this object they got together a large quantity of bowls, robes and other requisites of a monk, and proceeded by boat to Sahajāti, where Revata dwelt.Revata, however, refused to receive any gift. They then approached his disciple Uttara, who, after a great deal of persuasion, accepted one robe only, and agreed to intercede on their behalf to his master and request him in the following words: "Let the venerable *Thera* (meaning Revata) say thus much in the meeting of the *Saṁgha* --"It is in the regions of the East that the Buddhas, the Blessed ones, are born. It is the *Bhikkhus* of the East who hold opinions in accord with the *Dhamma*, whereas the *Bhikkhus* of the West do not."

Revata, however, sent Uttara away, saying "Thou urgest me to that which is against the *Dhamma*."

Then Yasa and the monks assembled by him met together to decide the question. But Revata very wisely suggested that the dispute should be settled where it arose. And so they all went to Vaiśāl.

Fortunately, there was living in Vaiśālī, at that time, the oldest *thera* in the world named Sabbakāmī, who had been ordained by Ānanda exactly 120 years ago. He was approached by Sambhūta Sāṇavāsī and on being questioned about the validity of the ten points gave his verdict against them.

Then the monks, seven hundred in number, met in a Council to decide the question. It shortly became apparent, however, that the large assembly was merely wasting time in pointless talk and fruitless discussion. Revata accordingly proposed, in full conformity to the rules laid down by the Buddha,[43] to refer the whole question to a Committee. The Committee was agreed to and it was constituted in a surprisingly modern fashion. It consisted of four monks of the East, viz, Sabbakāmī, Sālha, Khujja-sobhita and Vāsabhagāmika, and four monks of the West, viz., Revata, Sambhūta Sāṇavāsī, Yasa and Sumana. The *Bhikkhu Ajita* was appointed seat-regulator, corresponding, though remotely, to the position of the Secretary, of the Committee, and the Vālika Ārāma was fixed as the place of meeting.

When the Committee met at Vālika Ārāma, Revata proposed that he would put the questions before the Venerable Sabbakāmī, and this was agreed to.

Then followed the questions and answers of which a specimen is given below.

Revata--Is the horn-salt-license. Lord, allowable?

Sabbakāmī--What, Sir, is this horn-salt-license?.

R--Is it allowable Lord, to carry about salt in a horn with the intention of putting it into food which has not been salted?

S-No, Sir, it is not allowable.

R-Where was such a claim rejected?

S-At Sāvatthi, in the *Sutta Vibhaṅg*.

R-Of what offence is the person, who does so, guilty?

S-Of *Pācittiya,* in eating food which has been put by.

R-Let the venerable *Saṁgha* hear me. This first point having been examined into by the *Saṁgha,* has been found to be false *Dhamma* and false *Vinaya,* and not contained in the teaching of the Master. Thus do I cast the first vote.

In this way, all the ten questions having been disposed of Revata concluded:

"Let the venerable *Saṁgha* hear me. These ten points having been examined into by the Saṁgha, have been found to be false *Dhamma* and false *Vinaya,* and not contained in the teaching of the Master.

Sabbakāmī also agreed that the question was settled and settled once for all. Nevertheless he suggested that Revata should repeat his questions in the full Assembly and he would give reply to them. This was accordingly done and the decision arrived at by the Committee was endorsed by the whole Assembly. Thus concluded the session of the Great Council.

2. DIFFERENT VERSIONS OF THE ACCOUNT.

A. The Ceylonese Tradition.

The *Dīpavaṁsa* has preserved two accounts of the Council. The first is a brief summary of *Cullavagga* and may be regrded as the account proper, as it is concluded with the words: "Here ends the history of the Second Council." The second account of the Council is given in connection with the history of the different Buddhist sects, and contains much additional information. This is evidently of later origin. But both these accounts as well as those contained in *Mahāvaṁsa* and Buddhaghoṣa's Introduction to *Samanta-pāsādikā* follow closely on the lines laid down by *Cullavagga*[44] The essential differences may be noted as follows.

(a) As regards the eight *Theras* who formed the Committee, the Cullavagga merely says about Sabbakāmī that he was ordained by Ānanda exactly 120 years ago. But the Dīpavaṁsa and the *Mahāvaṁsa* add the information that all the eight *Bhikkhus* had seen the Buddha, that two of them, Sumana and Vāsabhagāmika, were pupils of Anuruddha and the rest were pupils of Ānanda.

(b) In the second account of *Dīpavaṁsa* we find the numbers of *Bhikkhus* on both sides exaggerated beyond all probability. "Twelve thousand Vajjiputtas of Vaiśālī," we are told, "assembled and proclaimed at Vaiślī the ten indulgences......In order to subdue them, many pupils of the Buddha, twelve hundred thousand sons of the Jina, assembled." But the account concludes with a reference to the eight Bhikkhus, and the 700 *Arahatas* selected by them. The *Mahāvaṁsa* puts the number of *Bhikkhus* on the side of Yasa as eleven hundred and ninety thousand. Later, on, however, it gives the number as one hundred and twelve thousand, from whom 700 were chosen by Revata to form the Council. Buddhaghosa also puts the number of assembled *Bhikkhus* as 12,00,000 though he refers to the Council of 700.

(c) We learn from the *Dīpavaṁsa* and *Samanta- pāsādikā* that at the time of the council , Aśoka, the son of Suṣunāga, was ruling at Pāṭaliputra. The *Mahāvaṁsa* not only corroborates this and traces the genealogy of Kālāśoka from Ajātasattu, but adds that the king took an active part against Yasa's party, till he was dissuanded from his evil course by a dream and the persuasion of his sister.

(d) We learn from the *Dīpavaṁsa* that after the Second Council had rejected the ten indulgences, the *Bhikkhus* of Vaiśālī held another Council. It was attended by ten thousand monks and was therefore called the Great Council (*Mahā-Saṁgīti*). The members of this Assembly, who were the first schismatics, made in altogether new redaction of the Buddhist Scriptures.

(e) In describing the *Bhikkhus* who came to Ahogaṅga hill in support of Yasa, the *Mahāvaṁsa* uses the word *Pāveyyakā,* instead of *Cullavagga's* Pāṭheyyakā. The former would mean the *Bhikkhus* from Pāvā, while the latter means *Bhikkhus* from 'Paṭheyya' a kingdom situated to the west of the Kosala country.[45]

(f) According to *Cullavagga,* the Bhikkhus of Vaiśālī merely carried out the Act of Suspension against 'Yasa'. *Mahāvaṁsa* tells us that they "came to thrust him (Yasa) out and surrounded the Thera's house."

(g) According to the *Mahāvaṁsa* the seven hundred *Theras* meeting in the Vālika Ārāma under the leadership of the Thera Revata "compiled the *dhamma*" (*akaruṁ dhamma-saṅgaham).* This has been construced as a 'collection or redaction of the Scriptures.' But this does not seem to be the real meaning. The term is to be taken in the same sense in which the words 'rehearsal of the *Vinaya*' are used at the end of the account in *Cullavagga.* All these terms apparently mean the setting or rehearsal of *Dhamma* or *Vinaya* so far as the ten points under dispute were concerned. Buddhaghoṣa, however, says that after the ten points were decided, the 700 *Bhikkhus* discussed the *Vinaya* and *Dharma* inthe same way as was done in the First Council, and made a new redaction of these into *Piṭaka, Nikāya, Aṅga* and *Dhammaskandh.*

B The Chinese and Tibetan Versions.

The too brief account of Hiuen Tsang does not differ materially from *Cullavagga,* except by way of omitting many details. Thus he mentions only five of the eight Arahatas.[46] and omits altogether the name of the Venerable Sabbakāmī who, according to *Cullavagga,* acted as the President. He places the Council exactly 110 years after the death of Buddha, and concludes his account in very much the same way as *Cullavagga,* merely pointing out how the doctrines held by the monks of Vaiśālī were declared erroneous, and without making any reference to the compilation of Scriptures. But. Mr. Watters has translated a passage at the beginning of Hiuen Tsang's account of the Council which contradicts this view. According to this translation the pilgrim refers to the Commemorative *stūpa* at Vaiśālī as "the place where the 700 eminent sages made the second comilation (viz, of the *Dharma* and *Vinaya*)"[47] Julien and Beal, however, rendered the passage differently, viz., "the place where 700 sages assembled together."

Fā-Hien also states that the assembled Bhikkus "examined afresh and collated the collection of disciplinary books, i.e. *Vinaya Piṭaka.*"[48]

The *Mahāsaṁghikas* go one step further and name one Daśabala as having drawn up the *Vinaya* for the Council.[49]

But the Chinese version of the Second Council does not mention anything beyond the condemnation of the ten indulgences.[50]

The *Tibetan Dulva*[51] gives a brief account of the Second Council. While differing in details, it agrees substantially with the narrative as given in *Cullavagga*. It, however, gives a quite different version of the ten indulgences, and omits the preliminary discussion of the question by the Committee of eight. But the eight *theras* are mentioned together with their dwelling places, and Yasa is said to have visited the other seven *theras* and discussed the question separately with them. It adds that originally 699 *arahatas* formed the assembly, and all these were contemporaries of Ānanda. The number of 700 was completed by the addition of Kuyyasobhita of Pāṭaliputra, who was aroused from his meditation by the *Devas* and mysteriously made his appearance before the Assembly just before the proceedings began. The account in *Dulva* concludes as follows "When they (i.e. the 700 *arahatas*) had examined and condemned the ten indulgences they beat the *ghaṇṭā* (i.e. the bell) and having assembled all the *Bhikkhus* at Vaiśālī, Yasa informed them of the proceedings and decision of the

Council." It does not say anything about the revison of the Scriptures or the subsequent assembly of the *Mahāsaṁghikas.*[52]

3. HISTORICAL CHARACTER OF THE SECOND COUNCIL

Anyone who carefully reads the varying accounts of the Second Council, as given in different authorities, cannot but come to the conclusion that, barring unessential details, there is a fair amount of agreement as to the essential part of the story. The dispute about ten doctrinal points which the monks of Vaiśālī regarded as vaild, and their rejection by a general assembly of Buddhist monks are the essential points of the story, and fortunately they are subcribed to by all our authorities. Nay more; these authorities are equally agreed about the names of the main actors in that strange episode, howsoever they might differ as to details about them. This consensus of opinion among different authorities, who evidently drew their inspiration from widely varying sources, certainly raises the presumption that there was a historical nucleus around which the legend of the Second Council has subsequently grown up.

Kern, however, thought otherwise.[53] He summed up his conclusions in the following sentence: "We could not discover in these accounts anything but dogmatic fictions for which didactic mythical stories of older times have furnished the materials." Apparently he changed his views later on. For we find the following sentence in his later work. "*Manual of Buddhism*" (p. 109) "The Council on *Vinaya* in Vaiśālī has an historical base" Oldenberg, however, all along held the same view and remarked as early as 1879, that "it is an account which, with its pedantic snatching after trifles, bears the stamp of being in the highest degree trustworthy"[54] The latter writers have more or less subscribed to this view, and the historical character of the Second Council is generally maintained.

It is not difficult to get an idea of what exactly took place in the Second Council. For this purpose it is only necessary to eliminate the episodes which are obviously of later growth. Let us take, for example, the Southern version. It has been noted before that *Dīpavaṁsa* gives two versions of the Council, one being a faithful summary of *Cullavagga* while the other contains much additional information. The same spirit of making additions to old authentic tradition is clearly perceptible in the accounts given in *Mahāvaṁsa* and *Samanta-pāsādikā*. As there is no doubt that all these different versions are based on *Cullavagga*, which is the oldest authentic text, we are justified in regarding all material variations from that primitive source as bearing the stamp of unauthentic additions in later ages. We can thus sweep away, at one stroke. (1) the legendary number of the members of the Assembly, ultimately reaching the astounding figure of 12,00,000 (2) the introduction of king Asoka, son of Susunāga, (3) the story of the *Mahāsaṅgīti*, i.e., a separate Council held by the monks of Vaiśālī and (4) the comilation afresh of the Buddhist Scriptures not to speak of the many lesser details such as are given above on p. 190, paras (e) and (f)

After this preliminary spade is over, we can have a clear perception of the main events in the story, and on a comparison of *Cullavagga* with the Northern versions we are forced to admit the substantial correctness of the main outline as given in the former.The points for critical discussion, then resolve themselves into the following questions:--

(a) The time of the Council

(b) The main actors in the Council

(c) The ten points which formed the subject-matter of discussion in the Council.

(a) The Southern version, as we have seen, places the Council just a century after the *Nirvāṇa*.The northern versions generally give the date as 110 A.B. but some authorities place the Council even so late as 210or 220 A.B. The last two dates fall near or within the reign of Aśoka and are apparently due to a belief that the Council was held in his time. This belief has, however,no basis in fact, and we are therefore justified in ignoring it. The difference between the other versions is so slight that we may reasonably conclude that Council was held about 100 years after the death of Buddha, in round numbers.

(b) As to the principal actors in the Council, there is a fair degree of consensus of opinion among our different authorities about their names. Hiuen Tsang and the *Tibetan*

Dulva give some additional information about their residence. This is shown in the following table:

Name	Residence as mentioned in *C.V.*.	*Dulva*	Hiuen Tsang
1. Sabbakāmī	Vaiśāli	Vaiśāli	
2. Khujja Sobhita	(of the east)	Pāṭliputra	Pāṭaliputra
3. Vāsabha-gāmika	(of the east)	Saṅkāśya	
4. Sālha	(of the east)	Sonaka	Vaiśālī
5. Revata	Soreyya	Sahadsha	Han-no(or Sa-han no)
6. Sambhūta Sāṇavāsī	Ahogaṅga hill	Māhīsnatī	Mathurā
7. Yasa	nil	Sonaka	Kosala
8. Sumana (of the west)			

As will be seen from the above list, Hiuen Tsang omits the names of three *Arahatas*, Nos. 1,3, and 8. the *Tibetan Dulva* omits No. 8, Sumana, but introduces a new name, Ajita, who lived at Śrughna.[55]

As regards the residence, there is haldly any agreement except in the case of Sabbakāmī and Khujja Sobhita. Sometimes the two soruces are contradictory; thus while Vāsabha-gāmika is represented in *Cullavagga* as belonging to the east, his residence is placed at Saṅkāśya, far to the west, in the *Dulva*. The conclusion is thus almost forced upon us that while there was a fairly accurate tradition about the names of the chief actors, there was no equally trustworthy information, available to succeeding generations, regarding their places of residence.

The same thing may be said of the age of these actors. In the *Cullavagga* Sabbakāmī is said to be a pupil of Ānanda and of 120 years' standing from the data of his *Upasampadā*. The *Mahāvaṁsa* proceeds a step further and makes all the eight theras contemporaries of the Buddha, Vāsabhagāmika and Sumana being pupils of Anuruddha and the remaining six, pupils of Ānanda.[56] In the *Dulva* we find the last step in this process of legendary reconstruction, and all the 700 *arahatas*, who took part in the Council, are said to be contemporaries of Ānanda.[57]

It is not difficult to perceive in the above a gradual transformation of the actors of the Council into semi-mythical hoary-headed *Arahatas* whose authority and influence were supposed to have been derived from the Blessed One himself. The absurdity of the assumptions lies on the very face and he who runs can read it. But the story of the Second Council is not indissolubly bound up with this fabulous age of the actors. As matter of fact, the fable, as we have seen, is of gradual growth. It would be extemely unfair, then to challenge the historical character of the Second Council simply on the ground of the impossibly old age of its principal actors. It is equally futile to argue, with Kern, against the historical character of the Council on the ground that the list of principal actors does not include any of the Patriarchs of the Buddhist Church,for the list of Patriarchs is contained in only late authorities and Kern has himself proved its unhistorical character.[58]

(c) Lastly, we come to the ten points which formed the subject- matter of discussion in the Second Council. The *Cullavagga* describes them as follows.

(1) The Horn-salt-license' (Is it allowable to carry about salt in a horn with the intention of putting it into food which has not been salted?)

(2) The Two-inch license (Is it allowable to eat the midday meal beyond the right time, provided only that the shadow has not yet tuned two inches?)

(3) Village-trip-license. (Is it allowable for one who has once finished his meal, and refused any more, to eat food which has not been left over, on the ground that he is about to proceed into the village?)

(4)The Circuit license. (Is it allowable for a number of *Bhikkhus* who dwell within the same circuit, within the same boundary, to hold separate *Uposathas*?)

(5) The Indemnity-license. (Is it allowable for a *Saṁgha*, which is not legally constituted, to perform an official act, on the ground that they will afterwards obtain the sanction of such *Bhikkhus* as subsequently arrive?)

(6) The Precedent-license. (Is it allowable to do a thing on the ground that "My preceptor has practised this" or "My teacher has practised that"?)

(7) The Churn-license. (Is it allowable for one who has once finished his meal and has refused any more, to drink

milk, not left over from the meal, on the ground that it has left the condition of milk and has not yet reached the condition of curds?)

(8) Drinking Toddy. (Is it allowable to drink spirits which have not yet become spirits and have not yet acquired intoxicating properties?)

(9) Unfringed seat.[59]

(10) Gold and Silver. (Whether the *Bhikkhus* could accept gold and silver as present).

The ten points, as enumerated and interpreted in the *Cullavagga,* do not however, agree with those mentioned in other texts. Some schools like the Dharmagupts and the Mahīśāsakas accept the technical names but give quite different interpretations.[60] On the other hand the Tibetan version of the ten points is almost entirely different from that of *Cullavagga.*[61] It would appear that whereas there was a common tradition about ten disciplinary points having been discussed in Vaiśālī, there was no such unanimity of views as to what those ten points actually were. Consequently, in subsequent times, each sect or community sought to utilise the tradition for settling local disputes by simply including the points which agitated their own narrow world among the traditional ten points of Vaiśālī.This seems to be the way in which the traditional ten points came to assume various forms.

It is also not unlikely that the Council of Vaiśālī was merely the precursor of many other similar, more or less general ,Assemblies,in which other disputed points of discipline or doctrine were discussed, and that later traditions have jumbled them all up into one story. Whatever may be the reason, the result is extremely unfortunate. For we cannot now be quite sure as to the matters which created such a profound agitation in the Buddhist world within a century of the Master's death, and therby we miss a brilliant opportunity of studying the primitive Buddhism in its actual working.

Further, a decision on these ten points has an important bearing on the history of the growth of Buddhist Canon. It is obvious, in spite of what Oldenberg says to the contrary, that if we accept the ten pints as given in *Cullavagga,* we can hardly accept the present *Pāli Vinaya* texts as anterior to the Council of Vaiśālī. For many of these ten points have been so clearly decided in the existing *Vinaya* texts that it would be an insult to the understanding of the *theras* of old if we believe them incapable of coming to a decision about them without so much ado. It is to be remembered that each of these points was discussed, not on its merits, but only as to whether or not it was in accordance with the doctrines as preached by the Buddha. If the *Vinaya Texts* existed then in anything like its present shape, most of the points of discussion would never have arisen at all[62], and the monks could hardly agree that the legal question involved therein "was hard and subtle" (see ante). One instance only need be quoted in support of this contention. Take for example the *avāsakappa* which was disposed of as follows in the Council of Vaiśālī according to *Cullavagga*.

"Revata-Is the 'circuit-license' Lord allowable?

Sabbakāmī-What, Sir, is this circuit-license?

R-Is it allowable Lord, for a number of *Bhikkhus* who dwell within the same circuit, within the same boundary, to hold separate *Uposathas*?

S-No. Sir, it is not allowable.

R-Where was such a claim rejected?

S-At Rājagaha, in the *Uposatha Saṁyutta*.

R-Of what offence is he, who does so, guilty?

S-Of Dukkhaṭa, in neglecting the *Vinaya*"

But consider for a moment the following passage in *Mahāvagga*: "At this time two halls of *Uposathas* had been instituted in a certain parish. The *Bhikkhus* assembled in both halls because (some) thought. 'The *Uposata* will be held here', and (the other): 'The *Uposath* a will be held there' This was reported to *Bhagavat* who said "Let no one establish two halls of *Uposatha* in the same parish....I order the suppression of one of the two and I desire that the *Uposatha* be held (only) in one place."

In the face of such instances no unbiassed reader would accept the dictum of Oldenberg that the text of the *Vinaya*, as we have it, "does not know of the propositions discussed at Vaiśālī.[63] It is equally difficult to believe that in the face of such clear ruling in the *Vinaya* texts, the matter would have formed a subject of dispute in a learned assembly of *Bhikkhus*. Again, Oldenberg has truly observed: "'We may with full assurance infer that if the discussions as to what was permitted and what forbidden, which we have before us in the *Vinaya*, were established after the time of this Council, it was next to unavoidable, that in appropriate passages, it should be directly stated how the *Bhikkhus* were to act with regard to the points so hotly disputed at Vesālī."[64] As a matter of fact, however, the *Vinaya* has made explicit statement about many of these points. This topic is not, however, relevant to our present discussion and we need not, therefore, labour the point any further.[65]

The sum up. The story of the Second Council seems to be based upon a genuine historical tradition. It was held at Vaiśālī about a century after the death of Buddha in order to settle some disputed points of discipline on which there were apparently no clear decisions extant. It was largely attended by the Buddhists from all parts of northern India,and the principal parts were played by eight *Bhikkhus* notably Revata, Sabbakāmī and Yasa. The result of the Council was the condemnation of the view held by the *Bhikkhus* of Vaiśālī. This might have led to a schism in the Church and the evolution of one or more new sects, but of this we have no clear evidence.

THE THIRD COUNCIL

The story of the Third Council is given in the *Dīpavaṁsa*, *Mahāvaṁsa*, and Buddhaghoṣa's Introduction to *Samanta-pāsādikā*.[66] It is not referred to in *Cullavagga*, and is unknown to the Buddhists of northern India, Tibet and China. This fact at once raises great suspicions to the historical character of the Third Council,and the doubt is more than confirmed when we proceed to discuss the details given in the late Siṁhalese authorities.

There is hardly any doubt that all the three authorities are indebted to a common source for information on this point. All the three give pretty long rambling accounts of the circumstances leading up to the Council. These accounts are full of unnecessary and impossible details, and contain reference to miraculous happenings. It will suffice here to give a short outline of the essential features of the story as gleaned by a comparison of the three texts.

It appears that the bounty of Aśoka had increased the riches of the Buddhist monasteries while it had reduced to great straits the followers of heretical cects, so much so, that the latter found it difficult even to procure a livelihood. The result was that the heretics in large numbers passed themselves as Buddhist *Bhikkhus* and dwelt even in the royal monastery with the latter. "They proclaimed their own doctrines as the doctrine of the Buddha and carried out their own practices even as they wished." On account of the large number of these heretics the Buddhist *Bhikkhus* proper could not maintain discipline in the *Saṁgha*, with the dire consequence that for seven years neither the *Uposatha* ceremony nor the *Pavāraṇā* could be held in any monastery in the whole of Jambudvīpa.

At that time 60,000 *Bhikkhus* dwelt at Aśokārāma in Pāṭaliputra. When the emperor heard that the *Uposatha* ceremony had been stopped in his own *ārāma*, he sent an officer to settle the matter. The officer went thither and announced to the *Bhikkhus* the king's command to carry out the *Uposatha*. Some *theras* boldly replied that they could not carry out the *Uposatha* festival with the heretics. This was too much for the foolhardy official who immediately drew his sword and cut off the heads of several *theras* who had protested. But when he found the *Bhikkhu* Tissa, brother of Aśoka, reported the whole matter to him. Aśoka deplored this action of his officer and was very much disturbed in mind at the idea that the guilt of his official might devolve upon him. He asked several *Bhikkhus* whether the guilt belonged to him or to his officer, but no uniform reply was received, some attaching the blame to him, others exonerating him of any guilt. Then the king asked of the *Bhikkhus* whether there was any eminent *Bhikkhu* in India who could give a decisive reply to this question. They all in one voice referred to Tissa Moggaliputta.

This Tissa Moggaliputta is held out as the divine majestic figure round whom centred all the important events leading up to the Third Council. It is related that even at the time of the Second Council the *theras* taking part in that assembly foresaw that the hretics will be dominant about a century later, and that a *Samaṇa* descending from *Brahmā's* world will be born in human race to destroy the heretics, his name being Tissa and surname Moggaliputta.

Aśoka sent for Tissa Moggaliputta, and after great difficulties succeeded in bringing him to Pāṭaliputra. There he first established his greatness by a display of supernatural powers, and then staisfied the king by his decision that the guilt of killing the *Bhikkhus* did not attach to the king as the latter had no evil intent.

On the seventh day after this Aśoka held an assembly of all the *Bhikkhus* on the earth.' Then 'seated with Tissa Moggaliputta on one side behind a curtain, he called to him in turn the Bhikkhus of the several confessions', and after each sect had expounded its wrong doctrine, Tissa had no difficulty in exposing its false character. The king there upon expelled these sects from the order. Lastly came the upholders of the Vibhajja- doctrine and Tissa Moggaliputta held that that was in consonance with the real teaching of Buddha.

After the order was thus purged of all heretical sects, the *Uposatha* ceremony was held again, and Tissa Moggaloputta proclaimed the treatise called *Kathāvattu*. Then he chose a thousand learned *Bhikkhus* and held a Council in Aśokārāma. There he compiled the true *Dharma*, even as Mahākassapa and Yasa did before him and the convocation was finished in the space of nine months.

Such is the brief outline of the story which the later Siṁhalese authorities have handed down to posterity. The story stands self-condemned. It is impossible to hold that thousands of heretics entered into the *Saṁgha* and were not detected for years; that the *Uposatha* ceremony was stopped for seven years even in his own *ārāma* in Pāṭaliputra and Aśoka did not know anything fo it till at the end of that long period; and lastly, that the name and fame of such a great *Arahata*, as Tissa Moggaliputta is represented to be, could possibly remain unknown to Aśoka till the 18th year of his coronation. Then again the upshot of the whole affair was an authentic declaration that the *Vibhajjavādins* were the only true followers of the Buddha, and if we remember that all the three accounts that we possess really originated from the *Vibhajjavādins* of *Mahāvihāra*, whereas the whole affair is completely ignored by the rest of the Buddhist world, we are bound to entertain very grave doubts about the Coucil at Pāṭaliputra. Even if any Council was held it was admittedly a party-meeting of the *Vibhajjavādins* alone, and could by no stretch of imagination be called a general Council. But whether even such a party-meeting was ever held to compile the *Dhamma,* may be doubted in the absence of evidence of a more reliable character. It must be remembered that Hiuen Tsang who has recorded so many traditions about Aśoka has not a word to say about this Council, and that not the slightest reference to it is made in the numerous inscriptions which that emperor has bequeathed to us.

In courses of his description of Pāṭaliputra Hiuen Tsang has told us a very interesting story regarding the origin of a stūpa called "The Institution of the Gong-call tope" We are told that once in bygone days the heretics of Pāṭaliputra had excelled the Buddhists by means of their learning and scholarship. As a result, heated discussions often took place between the rival parties, and these were attended by loud shouts and wild beating of gongs. At last the king arranged a public discussion to decide the respective merits of the parties with the condition that if the heretics proved successful the Buddhsist monasteries should not be allowed to call mettings by gong-beating. The Buddhists, being defeated, had to put up with this humiliation for twelve years. Then Deva, a disciple of Nāgārjuna, came to Pātaliputra and arranged a public discussion. In the course of twelve days he refuted the propositions of the heretics and vanquished them utterly in argument. The king and his ministers being satisfied raised the *stūpa* in question as a memorial.[67]

it is not difficult to perceive striking resemblances in essential points between this story and that of the Third Council.Both refer to the predominance of heretics over the Buddhists in the city of Pāṭaliputra, a consequent period of humiliation for the Buddhists, seven years in one case and twelve years in another, and the final discomfiture of the heretics and the triumph of the Buddhists by the efforts of a great *Bhikkhu,* Deva in the first case and Tissa Moggaliputta in the Second. In both the king plays a more or less passive part.

It seems reasonable to hold that a long-drawn struggle between the heretics and the Buddhists, out which the latter finally emerged as triumphant, was the nucleus of both the stories, to which different personalities were introduced in later times.

THE FOURTH COUNCIL

It is held by all the Buddhist sects with the exception of the Ceylonese monks, that a Council was held under the patronage of King Kaniṣka. Thus while the Ceylonese look upon the Council of Aśoka as the third and the last, the same view is taken about the Council of Kaniṣka by the remaining Buddhist world.

The most circumstantial narrative of this Council is given by Heuen Tsang. It may be summarised as follows:-

'Kaniska, the Buddhist king, was much perplexed at the different and contradictory interpretations of the Buddhist Scriptues caused by conflicting tenets of sectarians. He then expressed to the venerable Pārśva a desire to have the *Tripiṭaka* explained according to the tenets of the various schools. Pārśva having agreed, Buddhist *Bhikkhus* were summoned from all quarters. As the number of *Bhikkhus* who had assembled in response to the invitation were very large, Kaniṣka selected, out of them 499 *Bhikkhus* noted for their learning. To this was added the venerable Vasumitra who acted as the President. This Council of 500 composed 100,000 stanzas of *Upadeśa-śāstras,* explanatory of the canonical *sūtrās,* explanatory of the *Abhidharma.* These treatises were written out on copper plates. Kaniska had these enclosed in stone boxes and deposited them in a *stūpa* specially erected for the purpose.[68]

There are differences in points of detail in the various accounts of the Council that where the Council was held. Hiuen Tsang places it in Kashmir, while according to Tibetan authorities it was in Jālandhara. As to the personnel of the Council, the Tibetan Life of Buddha says that 500 *Arahatas* under Pārśva and 500 *Bodhisatvas* under Vasumitra held the Council, while Tārānāthe proceeds one step further,and speaks of 500 *Arahatas,* 500 *Bodhisatvas* and 500 *Paṇḍitas.* There can be hardly any doubt that the original 500 was duplicated and triplicated in the hands of later writers.

As to the work of the Council, Tārānātha gives a some what different version. Having referred to the internal dissensions in the Church which resulted in the rise of 18 different sects, Tārānātha adds that all these 18 sects were acknowledged by the Fourth Council as holding the true doctrine. According to him the Council further put to writing the whole of *Vinaya* and the portions of *Sūtra* and *Abhidharma* which had not yet been written out. The other portions of the last two, which already existed in a written form, were corrected. According to the Tibetan Life, the Fourth Council collected the canonical books. These three accounts, although different, are not self-contradictory and may be reconciled without much difficulty. If, as Hiuen Tsang says, elaborate commentaries were made on the *Tripiṭakas*, it was obviously necessary in the first place to collect together the canonical books themselves. So far we can agree with the views in Tibetan Life but it is difficult to believe the statement of Tārānātha that the whole of *Vinaya* yet remained unwritten and was merely transmitted orally even as late as the first century A.D. As to the reconciliation of the 18 different sects, the best way of doing that was obviously by means of ingenious commentaries which would satisfy rival sects by putting different interpretations on the same passage, exactly as was done in later times in the case of the *Brāhmaṇical Smṛtis*, the same passage in *Manusaṁhitā*, for example, being quoted to support almost diametrically opposite views.

We may thus hold he canonical texts, and to prepare elaborate commentaries on them, with a view to reconcile the tenets of different sects, as far as possible.

But the Fourth Council, like the Third, can hardly claim to be a general Council of the Buddhists at large. As noted above, it is completely ignored by the Ceylonese Buddhists. It also appears that the *Mahāyānists* took no part in it. It was at best a Council of the *Hīnayānists* of northern India. But within this narrow sphere it did a great deal of good by putting a stop to old quarrels and dissensions. It was well that the *Hīnayānists* thus closed up their ranks, for times was not distant when their position was going to be seriously challenged by the new *Mahāyāna* sect. That the *Hīnayānists* were in a position to make a common cause against their new rival was in no small measure due to the work done in the Council of Kaniṣka.

Notes and References :

1. The account of the First two Councils given below is mainly based on the following authorities, but incidental references will be made to other texts.
    1. Cullavagga of the *Pāli Vinaya,* and the canonical texts of other Buddhist sects
    2. *Mahāvaṁsa.*
    3. *Dīpavaṁsa.*
    4. Buddhaghoṣa's Introduction to *Samanta- pāsādikā.*
    5. *Mahābodhivṁsa.*
    6. *Mahāvastu.*
    7. *Tibetan Dulva.*
    8. Hiuen Tsang's Record of Western Countries,
    Kern (Histoire Bk. IV) has given prominence to the Tibetan version contained in "Tibetische Lebensbeschreibung sakyamunis" by Schiefner (St. Petersburgh, 1848). But as the work on which it was based was composed by a Tibetan Lama of the seventeenth century, it can hardly be regarded as authoritative. Besides, the authentic version in the *Dulva* (Tibetan *Vinay*) is now available in Rockhill's Translation. Hence no reference has been made to Schiefner's book. It appears, however, on a comparison of the two texts, that Schiefner's account follows closely on the lines of that in the *Dulva.*
2. Vinaya Text, Vol. II., pp. 284 ff.
3. This Subhadda is not identical with the monk of the same name who was the last desciple converted by Buddha shortly before his death. Oldenberg's view that they were identical is wrong.
4. The information is given by M. Suzuki who has dealt with the Chinese sources in his article "The first Buddisht Council" (Monist, XIV, 1904, pp 252-283). Cf. Ind. Ant. 1908 p. 2 fn 5.

5. Mahāvaṁsa, Transl. Geiger, Chap. III pp. 14-15 "......bethinking him (Mahākassapa) of the evil words of th aged Subhadda and also bethinking him that he (the Master) had given him his garment and had (thereby) made him equal with himself, and (bethinking him) that the sage had commanded the establishing of the holy truth, and (lastly) that the Sambuddh's consent existed to make a compilation of the holy *dhamma,* appointed to this end five hundred *Bhikkhus...*"
6. Beal-Records Vol. II. p. 162
7. *Samanta-pāsādikā,* Introduction, *Vin. Text* Vol. III. p. 284
8. According to Suzuki (op. oit).
9. *Dipav*-Ch. IV-pp. 133-135.
10. Rockhill-p.148.
11. Ind. Ant. 1908. p. 2 fn. (5)
12. cf. the passage quoted in fn. 2 at p. 30
13. Rockhill pp. 148-149
14. Cf. Ind. Ant. 1908 p. 2 fn (5).
15. *Mahāvastu* pp. 69 ff.
16. Beal-Records Vol. II. p. 162.
17. Rockhill-op cit.
18. E.g. *Mahāvaṁsa,* op cit.
19. *Dipav*. Op. cit
20. Rockhill op. cit.
21. Rockhill op. cit
22. The Dulva refers to Mahātṛkā. According to Kern it really means Indices (Anukramaṇī) though some took it in the sense of *Abhidharma* (histoire-p. 264 fn. 3)
23. Introduction to *Samanta-pāsādikā,* Vin. Text. III. p. 289
24. *Dipav*. op cit.
25. *Mahāvastu,* I, pp. 76 ff.
26. On the *Mahāsāṁghikas* see later, in connection with the account of the Second Coucil.
27. Rockhill op. cit.

28. For the long discussion on this point by Minayeff, Oldenberg and Prof. L. De la Vallee Poussin Cf. Ind. Ant. 1908, pp. 10 ff.

29. *Mahāvastu* seems to be the only exception. It practically ignores Ānanda's part in the Council and assigns the leading position to Kātyāyana.

30. For the different charges and sources of information about them cf. Ind. Ant. 1908. pp. 4 ff. Almost all the charges are contained in the *Dulva* (Rockhill, pp. 152 ff). There are only two exceptions viz (1) that Buddha asked Ānanda three times to serve him as one who offers things(?) to Buddha but he declined him (Dharmagupta) and (2) that when Buddha preached in parables Ānanda made some superfluous remarks on them (*Sarvāstivādins*). Neither of these is, however, very intelligible. As regards the charge of having first admitted the women to venerate that body, and having it profaned by their tears, this last element is omitted in some authorities e.g. the *Mahāīsāsakas*. As to the treading upon garment, according to most authorities it was done while sewing, but according to some while washing it (*Sarvāstivādins*). According to the *Dulva*, Ānanda rested his feet for whole day' on the garment.

31. The replies of Ānanda are taken from *Cullavagga* and *Dulva*.

32. *Vin Text* Vol. I. pp. XXVI ff.

33. S.B.E. Vol., p. XIII

34. Rockhill,p. vii

35. Ind. Ant. 1908, p. 9. I may add that 15 years ago I made and eqully emphatic protest against the views of Oldenberg, although unaware at that time of the writings of Prof. Poussin.

36. "The *Mūlasarvāstivāda-nikāya-saṁyukta- vastu* (Nanjio 1121) makes that M.P.S. followed by the account of the Council" Ind. Ant. 1908, p. 8 p. fn. 36

37. Ind Ant. 1908. p. 5. The episode of Purāṇā is not, however, found in all versions. It is absent e.g. in *Cullavagga*.

38. Bhandarkar - Carmichel Lectures, Vol. I., pp. 179 ff.

39. These ten points will discussed fully later on.

40. This was apparently based on the directions laid down in *Cullavagga* I. 20. Among the offences for which such an act could be carried out against a monk is included "speaking to the laity in dispraise of the *Saṁgha,*" and "revilling and finding fault with the laity". The last offence is intended though the first one is also not inapplicable in the present case.

41. The hill was probably situated somewhere near the Upper Ganges Valley. (cf. Mv. VII I.I. fn).

42. During excavations at Bhiṭā (near Allahabad) a seal containing the legend "*Sahijitiya nigamasa*" in letters of the 3rd or 4th century B.C. was found in a building of the Mauryan epoch. 'Sahijiti' may be identified with 'Sahajāti' of the text and would the correspond to Bhiṭā or a place in the neighbourhood. (A.S.I., 1911-12 p. 29)

43. Cf. *Cullavagga,*IV,14 19

44. The account in Mahāvaṁsa is a close summary of *Cullavagga.* The othr account are very brief and omit the details.

45. Cf.S.B.E. Vol. XVII, p. 146 fn I.

46. For the indentification of the *Arahatas* mentioned by Hiuen Tsang with those in *Cullavagga* cf. Watters ")n Yuan Chwang." Vol. U. pp. 74-75.

47. Watters, op. cit p. 72.

48. Legge, Fā-Hien, p. 75

49. Watters, op cit., p. 75

50. Rockhill,op. cit., p. 180

51. Ibid pp. 171-180.

52. In addition to those given above there are slightly varying versions of the Second Council in a large number of texts (cf. e. g. Kern "Histoire du. Bouddhisme"- Vol.II., p. 288), but no great importance attaches to them. The same may be said of the account of Tārānātha. It tells us that the *Arahata* Dhitika who usually lived at Kauśāmbī and was regarded as the head of the *Bhikkhus* fell ill. The monks of Vaiśālī consequently rejected his authority and declared the ten points to be legal. After

Yaśas and 700 other *Arahatas* had condemned these practices as illegal a second compilation of the canon took place at Kusumapurī under the patronage of King Nandin of the Lichchhavi race.' It thus substitutes Kusumapuri or Pāṭaliputra for Vaiśālī and King Nanda for Aśoka. Evidently the story deserves but little credit.

53. Kern op. *cit*. p. 290

54. Introduction to *Vinaya Piṭakam*, p. XXIX

55. A *Bhikkhus* Ajita is mentioned in *Cullavagga* as the Seat-regulator i.e. Scretary. but not a member, of the Committee (See ante).

56. op. cit. p. 24

57. op. cit.p. 179.

58. op. cit. p. 120 ff.

59. The *Cullavagga* does no explain this. But from the Tibetan sources we learn that it means: "to use a new mat without patching it around the edge (with the wiath of) a Sugata span (equal to a cubit and a half)" Rockhill -op cit., p. 172.

60. These have been fully discussed by Prof. Le De la Vallee Poussin,Ind. Ant. 1908 p. 89 ff.

61. Rockhill op. cit. p. 171 ff. Ind. Ant. 1908,p. 104 ff.

62. Oldenberg, of course, maintains the contrary view-but Professor Poussin seems to have completely demolished his contentions (Ind. Ant. 1908, pp. 89 ff).

63. Introduction to *Vinaya Texts* p. XXXVI

64. Introduction to *Vinaya Texts* p. XXXvi.

65. For an illuminating discussion on this point that reader is referred to Ind. Ant. 1908, pp. 89 ff.

66. *Dipav*. VII 34 ff. *Mahāvaṁsa*- V.; *Vinaya Texts*, Vol. III, p. 306 ff.

67. Beal-Vol Ii. pp. 96 ff.; Watters -Vol. II p. 100-101.

68. Watters-Vol. I. p. 270; Beal Vol. I, p. 151.

CHAPTER-6

DUKKHA

—*Dr. Harcharan Singh Sobti, M.A., LL.B; Ph.D.*

Man has his roots in the past identified as heritage. All that is part of the heritage, at any point of time, is not necessarily conducive to achieve results favourable for the humanity, at large. Therefore, it becomes imperative to see what ought to be disinherited. The heritage finds its manifestations through various forms forming part of the contemporary living. The Buddha through his alive response to the contemporary modes of thinking and living articulated his views on living beings and their final destiny. To appreciate the Buddha's reactions and responses he had displayed towards his contemporary thinkers, is our primary concern, at the moment.

2

Ancient India contemporaneously known as *Jambūdīp*[1] consisted of generally accepted five-fold zonal division. Rājeśekhra (880-920 A.D.) in his book *Kāvyamimāṁsā*[2], *a treatise on poetry, has indentified these zones, viz:*

(i) *Madhyadeśa* (Central India).

(ii) *Udiya* (Northern India) known a *Uttarapatha*.

(iii) *Prāca (Eastern India) also called Pūrvadeśa.*

(iv) *Dakshināpatha (Deccan).*

(v) Aparānta (Western India) also identified as *Pāścadeśa*.

Madhyadśea or in Pāli *Majjhimadesa*, birth place of Buddhism that covered the area of eastern *Uttara-Pradeśa* and Bihār,[3] and comprising of as many as fourteen *Mahājanapadas*[4] *or republics e.g. Kāsi, Kosala, Kuru* and *Pañcāla* etc., during the

6th century B.C. compared with other areas, witnessed a phenomenal upsurge of religious fermentation and spiritual awakening. A number of teachers, both householders and recluses, kept themselves consistently engaged in enquiring into the nature of reality and continued to preach their doctrines among the people. Their only purpose, no doubt, was to bring the people close to reality as they had contemplated. We find repeated references made to Six Contemporaries of the Buddha in Pāli Canon[5] deemed to be quite formidable, and are thus grouped as 'heritical (*titthya*) teachers'. They exercised, one can gather from scriptural evidences, enormous psychic influence on the modes of living and thinking of their respective followers.

One among the six 'heretical teachers' was Pūraṇa Kassapa, who preached the doctrine of non-action.[6] He is mentioned to have stated his doctrinal standpoint to Ajātasattu, the king of Magadha, in the words that:

"To him who acts, O King or causes another to act...to him who kills a living creature, who takes what is not given, who breaks into houses, who commits dacoity....or highway robbery or adultery or who speaks lies, to him thus acting there in no guilt. If with a discus with an edge sharp as a razor he should make all the living creature on the earth one heap one mass of flesh, there would no guilt thence resulting, no increase of guilt would ensue. Were he to go along the south bank of the Ganges, striking and slaying, mutiliating, and having men mutilated, oppressing and having men oppressed, there would be no guilt thence resulting, no increase of guilt would ensue. Were he to go along the north bank of the Ganges, giving alms, and ordering gifts to be given, offering sacrifices, or causing them to be offered, there would be no merit thence resulting, no increase of merit. In generosity, in self-mastery, in control of the senses, in speaking truth there is neither merit, no increase of merit."[7]

Obviously, the doctrine amounts to ethical neutrality i.e. man's actions are neither moral nor immoral. Also, Pūraṇa Kassapā's doctrine of ethical necutrality was a frontal attack on *sīla*, the moral code of Buddhism. Pūraṇa Kassapa is also interpreted to have adhered to the doctrine of *adhicca-sammuppāda*[8]. "The Buddha in the *Brahmajāla Sutta*" suggests B.M. Barua. "distinguished the logical standpoint of Pūraṇa

Kassapa from his own, as a hypothesis of fortuitous origin (*adhiccasamuppāda)* from what he called the theory of causal-genesis (*paticca- samupāda)*[9]. 'Elsewhere he *[the Buddha]*" rightly adds Barua, " describes the former as a theory of non-causation (*ahetu- appaccyayvāda)*.[10] The doctrine of *adhicca-samuppāda* only prepares us to inculcate an idea that whatever comes into being was previously non-existent. Alternatively expressed, it means that every becoming (*bhava*) is a result of chance (*saṅgati*), therefore, absolutely devoid of any link whatsoever.

Makkhali Gosāla, another contemporary of the Buddha, was no way lesser influential than Pūraṇa Kassapa. As alleged by his opponents, he commercialized his knowledge of astrology to earn his livelihood and was therefore despised having founded the sect of Ājivakas,[11] Allegations apart, one thing clearly emerges that his knowledge of astrology did influence his own mode of thinking, when he advocated the doctrine of Fate or *Niyati*. "The cardinal point of the doctrines of its founder, Makkhali Gośāla, writes A.L.Basham, while expressing his views on Ājivakism, "was a belief in the all-embracing rule of the principal of order, *Niyati*, which ultimately controlled every action and all phenomena and left no room for human volition, which was completely ineffectual".[12] Evil *kamma*, declared Gosāla, not at all, serves as a base or cause for Suffering.[13] Also, an escape from evil *kamma* needs not to have base or cause.[14] Rather, there, is hardly any base of cause for anything whatsoever. Everything, according to Gosāla, is pre-determined. All beings, according to aforementioned doctrine of *niyati*, are governed for their growth, by the principle of Fate (*niyati*), chance (*Sangiti*) Nature (*bhāva*).[15] The denial of freedom of Will, with Gosāla, takes an extreme posture. "The powerful (*balaṁ)*, vigorous (*viriyaṁ*) and those full of energy (*parakkama*)", asserts Gosāla, "like the frail (*avasā*) weak (*abalā*) and timid (*avariya*), all are governed by the one and the same principle of *niyati*, *saṅgati* and *bhāva*.[16]

And, a ball of string is made to serve as a simile to convey the whole idea, thus:

"Just as when a ball of string is cast forth it will spread out just as far, and no farther, than it can unwind, just so both fools and wise alike, wandering in transmigration exactly for the allotted term, shall then, and only then, make an end of pain."[17]

Makkhali Gosāl's doctrine of strict determinism, only theoretically leads to fatalism. L.D. Barnett's observation is quite convincing when he writes, that "man is not a logical creature: he does not abstain form effort although he may believe the issue to be pre-determined..."[18] Therefore, keeping in view the practical side of man's functioning it would be erroneous to submit to the notion of denial of freedom of Will. Man is not absolutely dispossessed of freedom of Will, his Will or volition does operate, but, in no way transcending the limits of Universal Law binding over things and beings, alike.

Next is Ajīta Kesakambalī, who not only influenced his own followers so as to bring them into his fold, but, also had some impact on the mode of teaching of the Buddha, though in a negative way. The body, according to Kesakambalī consists of four elements viz. earth, water fire and air. These consitutents of the body, after its dissolution, merge to their respective genetic sources under the law of regression. Earth returns to earth, watar to water, fire to fire and senses disappear into *ākāsa*.[19] Ajīta Kesakambalī therefore, was through and through materialist and consequently believed and preached that there is no life after death.[20] He was an unambiguous annihilationist (*uccheda vāīdinī*).

The doctrine foremost in importance, for us, and attributed to Pakudha Kaccāyāna, yet another contemporary of the Buddha, is that of *Sassatavāda* or eternalism. Kaccāyāna in the *Sāmaññaphala Sutta* is stated to hold the view that earth, air, water, fire (these four elements), *sukkha* and *dukkha* and lifeforce (jiva), these seven,[21] are neither created nor caused to be crated, hence exist eternally. Kaccāyāna is called Empedocles[22] (492-432 B.C) of India, the latter only replaces love and hatred instead of *sukka* and *dukkha*.

Sañjaya Belatthiputta also reckoned as significant among the contemporaries of the Buddha was identified as sceptic who preached uncertainty about all matters man could be interested in. Whenever questioned, say for example, about the existence of another world,[23] he would always refrain from committing to either of the positions, generally held

Man does not relish uncertainty about things and beings, and so desires, otherwise. But, one thing is abundantly clear that the notion of uncertainty certainly destroys the premise of dogmatic thinking and renders speculations substnceless. May be that uncertainty about all matters creates conditions to bring about tranquillity of mind.

Nigaṇtha Nātaputta, identified as no other than Mahāvira, the founder of Jainism as stated in *Sāmaññaphala Sutta* preached *Cātuyāma-saṁvara*[24] or 'four-fold Self- restraint'. This doctrine of Mahāvira, comments B.M. Barua, means that "the way to self-possession, self-command and imperturbability consists 'a four-fold self-restraint' such as restraint in regard to all water, restraint as regard all evil, and restraints by way of the purification of sin and feeling a sense of ease on that account."[25] Further, quoting from Pāli sources, Barua adds that "in Mahāvira's view the established path to the realm of highest bliss lies through abstinece from killing, abstinece from the adultery, from lying and such austere practices (*tapoguṇa)* as nudity, penance, confession and the rest."[26] The second set of principles, in part, stated to have been preached by Mahāvira, is no other than Sīla, also popular with the Buddhists.

3

To understand, the doctrinal standpoints of 'heretical teachers,' we have, no doubt, depended on the Buddhist records. The reputation might have been "unfairly blackened" using L.D. Barnett's expression "by the *odium theologicum* of their rivals,"[27] the Buddhist monks in the present case. Our main concern, at the moment, is to ascertain the Buddhist position. Confrontation of the Buddha with his contemporary teachers and vice a versa, is helpful in the sense that it is through these discourses and discussions, we learn about the prevailing 'climate of opinion'. The contemporary milieu, so to say, helps us not only to appreciate the mode of teaching but also the message of the Buddha. The Buddha's doctrine of *paticcasmuppāda* can be better understood, referred to earlier, when juxtaposed to Pūaṇa Kassapa's hypothesis of *adhicca-samuppāda*. Again, when once a wandering ascetic Vacchagotta visited the Buddha and inquired from him as regard to the existence or non-existence of 'self' (*attā*), the Buddha kept silent and Vacchagotta as if annoyed, left. After Vacchagotta had left, Ānanda asked the Buddha as to why did he remained silent and Buddha clarified, saying:

"If, Ānanda, when asked by the wanderer: "Is there a self," I had replied to him: "There is a self", then, Ānanda, that would be siding with the recluses and *brāhmins* who are eternalists. But if, Ānanda when asked: "Is there not a self" I had replied that it does not exist. Ānanda, would be siding with those recluses and *brāhmins* who are annihilationist."[28]

The Buddha was not only refraining from associating himself with either the eternalists like Pakudha Kaccāyāyna or annihilationist like Ajīta Kesakambalī, but was also silently subscribing to middle position.

The proposed doctrines of 'heretical teachers', more or less speculative, therefore, evasive in nature and thus deviating from the existential problem of human Suffering instead of guiding the people to overcome their ignorance (*avijjā)* the root cause of Suffering bewildered them, all the more. The resultant path prescribed by them, necessarily, failed to satisfy the spiritual hunger of the multitudes of their followers and the problem of man's emancipation from ignorance continued to remain intact and alive. It was in the background of such a 'climate of opinion' that the Buddha emerged carrying a light of practical wisdom to dispel the darkness of ignorance. He was exclusively concerned with the existing problem of life and advised his followers not to alineate themselves from existing reality. He confronted the basic problem---the problem of Suffering-and searched for methods and means for its eradication. The Buddha like a physician (and not like a philosopher)diagnosed the disease, discovered the remedy only thereafter prescribed a prescription, (forming into a Path), leading the beings, when put into practice, from the state of perpetual Suffering to the state of eternal bliss, 'to be realized by the wise in their own interior'.

4

But, there is a peculiar tendency among both the followers and scholars of religions to indulge in things and ideas discarded by the founders of the religions, as spiritually unrewarding. The Buddha, in a way, was critical of similar practices then prevailing when, besides refuting the charge of preaching 'extirpation of existing creature (*Sato Sattassaucchedaṁ*)' and reiterating his pragmatic view of things, he not only attacked misreading of his intentions, but also summed up the kernel of teaching, saying:

"Though this is what I affirm and what I preach, yet some recluses and *brāhmins* wrongly, erroneously and falsely---charge me in defiance of facts, with being an annihilationist and with preaching the disintegration, destruction and extirpation of existing creatures. It is just what I am not, and what I do not affirm, that is wrongly, erroneously and falsely charged against me by these good people, who would make me out to be an annihilationist. Both in the past and to-day, I have consistently preached Ill (Suffering) and the ending of Ill."[29]

Pāli Canon is believed to constitute a coherent whole and all that consists in it, whether attributed to the Buddha himself or to *theras or therīs,* form an integral part of the teachings of the Buddha. The theme of the Buddha's Sermons, therefore, can be identified not only in ditferent forms, but also through different channels contained in the Canon. For instance, Sāriputta in the *Mahāhatthi-padopma Sutta* describes one of the caridinal principles of Buddhism i.e. Four Noble Truths (*cattāri ārya saccāni*), making use of the simile of footprint of an elephant, thus:

"Just as the foot of every creature that walks the earth will go into the elephant's foot-print which is pre-eminent for size, even so, sirs, are all the right states of mind comprised with the Four Noble Truths which are Noble Truth of Ill (Suffering) the Noble Truth of Origin of Ill and the Noble Truth of the Way that leads to the Cessation of Ill".[30]

Sāriputta, in a formentioned passage, without having a 'close fist' reveals what the Buddha aimed at, in other words, his total concern that concerns singular problem the problem of Suffering and its solution.

5

The Buddha, in his very First Sermon, *Dhamma-Cakkappavattana Sutta*, delivered at Isipatana, now called Sārnāth, near Benares, and addressed to the *Pañcavaggiyā Bhikkhus.*[31] categorically stated that:

"Birth is attended with pain (or is painful) decay is painful, death is painful. Union with the unpleasant is painful, painful is separation from the pleasant; and any craving that is unsatisfied, that too is painful. In brief, the five aggregates which spring form attachment (the conditions of individuality and their cause) are painful."[32]

And, the Buddha indentified this part of his Sermon as *dukkhaṁ ariyasaccaṁ*: Noble Truth of Suffering."[33]

Some of the key-expressions, found in the above passage, we propose to analyze. Better to begin, in a way, from the beginning, we call birth, and which is bracketed with Suffering (*Jāti pi dukkhā*). What is, after all, meant by the expression 'birth'? The Buddhist scriptures are certainly not silent on the question. We find the problem posed and solved in the *Saṁyutta Nikāya*, which reads as under:

"And what, brethren, is birth? That which, of this and that being is this and that group, is birth, continuous birth, descent, reproduction, appearance of component factors, acquiring of sense-spheres. This is called birth."[34]

An expression, 'of this and that being in this and that group', deserves special attention. Normally, when we refer to birth we mean to convey the idea of birth of human beings. But in Buddhism the phenomenon of birth enfolds any living creature, inhabiting any one of the five realms of existence that constitute *Saṃsāra*[35]. Thus, according to Buddhist tenets. LIFE IS ONE and it extends the range of limit of LIFE to as vast as *Saṁsāra*. This also explains the transit of LIFE from one realm to another. We learn from *Jātaka* stories that the Buddha passed through the various forms of life, covering a very vast range of animal and bird-life; sometime as a stag and sometime as a quail; and so on so forth. This means, that every living creature can ascend to the peak of *arahathood* or in later Buddhism to Buddhahood. Here, in the context of grades of life, Copleston's attempt to draw distinction between a Buddha and one who has only attained *Nibbāna* is quite revealing. "It is only, indeed, in the human stage."writes Copleston "that the highest achievement, that of a Buddha, is possible;

but *Nirvāṇa* is accessible to all, to the superior deities and to men directly, and ultimately to all that lives;.[36] The precept of non-killing, and Compassion for animal and bird life, derives its moral sanction from this very fact of phenomenal existence.

Nothing that exists in phenomenal world exists in isolation. This, and precisely this is the spirit that pervades throughout the *Paṭiccasamuppādd*.[37] or the Doctrine of Dependent Origination. It would suffice to mention, at this stage of our enquiry into the domain of dukkha, that 'birth' is only one link or *nidāna* in the grand scheme of the Chain of Twelve links, (*dvadasaṅgapaticca-sammuppāda*) worked out in the said doctrine. The old age and death also form other links of the same chain. The basic idea set forth in this doctrine is that everything for its origination or arising, inevitably, depends upon something else. One hardly needs any support from scriptures to conform to the self-evident fact of existence that old age and death are dependent upon birth.

Birth, old age and death, as a normal course, constitute integral parts of the continuous process of change, that, in Buddhism takes the form of Doctrine of *Aniccā* or Impermanence that in itself is only one aspect of the Doctrine of Three Marks of Existence, or *Tilakkhaṇa, dukkha* and *anattā* being the rest of the two.[38] One of the fundamental causes of Suffering lies in the impermanent nature of things or transitoriness of their character. *Yaṁ aniccaṁ taṁ dukkhaṁ:* whatever is transitory that amounts to Suffering"[39] is the dictum quite often pronounced in the Buddhist scriptures. The idea finds its expression in the *Majjhima Nikāya*, in the following form:

"What do you think, Almsmen?

Is visible form (body) permanent or impermanent?

Impermanent, Sir.

And is the impermanent, a weal or a woe?

A woe, Sir."[40]

Another important expression is *Pañcaupādānakkhandha pi dukkhā :.*[41] 'Five aggregates constitute suffering'. Now, in the light of Buddha's assertion, we can well appreciate why do these five aggregates generate Suffering? We know, that old age means decaying of organism and death is its final dissolution. In other words, old age and death have reference to the bodily organism which we know from our experience the way it under-goes the gradual process of decaying: it grows weak, withers, it is exhausted, senses lose their vitality. The description speaks of the body being plagued with transitoriness. The transitory nature of body is also explained through the nature of constitutents it is composed of. The matter consists of four chief elements, namely, earth, air, water and fire, which are subject to the iron law of Universal Flux, yet, another expression subscribing to the idea of transitoriness. Now, when the four chief elements can not escape from the Universal Law of Flux, it is hard to imagine that anything formed by these can. The body has to share the fate of all these things which come into existence by virtue of the combination of these elements. This also explains the nature of *Saṅkhārā* described as "*Sabbe Saṅkhārā aniccā' ti*: Transient are all conditioned things (or Productions)."[42] This idea of transitoriness is so fundamental that 'a time will come' as contemplained in the Buddhist Canon,[43] when all these elements, and, hence the entire world which is compounded of these elements, shall abide by the same law to its ultimate destruction.

So far we have described the transitory nature of things termed as *Saṅkhārā* or Production, including bodily organism with all its constituting factors. And, we have only stated that Suffering has its root-cause in transitoriness also described as *aniccā* or impermanence. This premise needs little elaboration. The bodily organism does not come into existence on its own, or it is not at all the result of accidental combination of four basic elements. What brings these elements together to bring forth a kind of production we call bodily organism? In order to meet the demands of this query the Buddhist scholars invariably identified *chanda* or wil as a factor that brings these elements together and it is by virtue of an exercise of Will, we gain body. This does not happen only in the case of *Saṅkhārā*, somethimes referred to as mental productions, but the whole gamut of personality falls within its range of influence. To substantiate their views on the subject, these scholars have, time and again, fruitfully made use of these utterances, as: *Chandamūlakā āvuso sabbe dhamma:* In the Will all things are rooted."[44] "Again, *Pañcaupānakkhandhā Chandhamūlakā:* Five Aggregates are rooted in the Will."[45] Though indirectly, refer to another very significant Buddhist term *taṇhā* or craving. The Will that serves as a cause for *bhava* (Becoming), seems to be identical in its meaning with the craving, in the sense, that the latter is also described as cause of rebirth. The Buddha, while pronouncing "*dukkha samuddyaṁ ariya saccanṁ*: Noble Truth of Suffering"[46] held *taṇhā* in its threefold mode of operation---i.*kāmataṇhā*, ii.*bhava taṇhā* and iii. *vibhava taṇhā* the sole responsible for *punnabhava* or rebirth and which, as already analyzed, is bracketed with Suffering. It is, in fact, this craving that the Seeker on the path of the Buddha is instructed to annihilate.

It is the Will, pregnant with *taṇhā* (craving), that is the root-cause of Suffering. It is our common experience that we feel happy, when we find our Will fully executed. In other words, happiness stems from the satisfaction of our Will. The perpetual happiness is only possible if neither the Will nor the realm of existence in which it operates, is subject to impermanence. Whereas, the fact is that Will and the realm in which it is exercised, both are governed by the Law of Universal Flux. We find, as a consequence of pervading this Law in the phenomenal existence, the impediments in the way of satisfaction of our Will. We desire the state of affairs to exist permanently, which are conducive to yield the fruit of happiness. And, the fact is contrary to our desire. We experience change of circumstances, we do not relish. The change, irrespective of our liking or disliking occurs. In fact, nothing is permanent, but change. It is the change that rules as Sovereign over the territory of phenomenal existence. Earlier, we have referred to a discourse, describing 'what is transitent amounts to suffering.' Under the Law of Universal Flux, both the animates and inanimates are subject to perpetual change, and, thus, the state of permanence is only illusion. The Will, intune with this illusion only, begets Suffering. When this illusion is predominant; as a result, Suffering predominates.

The existing state of Suffering can also be explained in terms of the Doctrine of *Anattā*. The doctrine, in its essence,refers to a state, combining both, physical and mental, *that one is not*, and this doctrine is beautifully summed up in *Saṁyutta Nīkāya* in the following words:

"Then is it proper for one thus to regard what is impermanent, woeful, by nature, chageable:---'This is mine, this am I, this is the self of me'? asked the Buddha, 'Surely not, 'Lord', Ānanda replied.[47]

We know from our experience that the five aggregates e.g.*rūpa, vedanā, saññā, saṅkhārā and viññaṇakkhandha'* that constitute our personality, function, most of the time, contrary to our Will, or desire, so to say. We fall sick, grow old and die, in spite of wishing, otherwise . A stream of unpleasant ideas flows in our mind, and quite often, we fail in our attempt, to stop it. In the *Majjhima Nikāya,*[48] while explaining the Doctrine of Anattā to Aggivessana, the Buddha has referred to the position and power of a ruling king and contrasted with a person who presumes that 'Body is my Self' and unlike a king possesses no power to control his body as the former does posses within his kingdom. Obviously, anything over which one has no control cannot belong to one-self. And, to identify one-self with that which does not belong to oneself, can hardly yield anything except Suffering. This is, in short, the substance of discourse, entitled the *Cūla-Saccaka-Sutta,* in which the Buddha, in a public discussion, brings round the Jain, Saccak, clarifying the existential status of *khandhās,* and we quote:

What say you, Aggivessana? Is material shape (*rūpa kkhandha*) permanent or impermanent?

Impermanent.

Is that which is in permanent an III or reverse?

An III.

Is it proper to regard what is impermanent and an III and the creature of change, as being mine, or I or, my Self?

No. 49

The same argument is put forth and the conclusion drawn to the satisfaction of Aggivessana, in the case of remaining aggregates. Again, when the bodily organism, which in itself is nothing, but an organic form of the four basic elements, does not belong to one Self, it is difficult to contemplate that anything else that exists in the pheomenal world, consisting of four elements, can be identified with Self.

This means, that entire functioning of human personality consisting of six sense organs e.g. eye, ear, nose, body, tongue and mind, and also things other then these, and existing in the phenomenal world, are to be (identified) as *anattā*, and to identify Self with anything that is transient, yields only a bitter fruit of Suffering.

Notes & References :

1. For detailed descriptions of naming of ancient India, see: Law, *B.C. Historical Geography of Ancient India*, pp.8-11, (Introduction).
2. Dalal, C.D. and Shastry R.A. (Eds.) *Kāvyamīmāṅsā of Rājāekhara*,pp.93-94.

   Tatra vārāṇasya parataḥ pūrvadeśaḥ

   ....

   Māhiṣmatyā parataḥ Dakshināpathaḥ

   ....

   Devasabhāyā parataḥ paśchātdesaḥ

   ....

   Prithadakāt parataḥ uttarāpathaḥ

   ....

   Vinasanaprayāgayoḥ Ganga----Yamunāyosca antaraṁ Antravedi
3. Sharma R.S. *Material Culture and Social Formations in India,p.89.*
4. A. i, 213; iv,252,256,260.
5. References made to six 'heretical teachers' in *Tipiṭaka*, are detailed as under:

   (i) Pūraṇ a Kassapa: D i. 52, 53; S.i,65; S.iii, 68,69;S.iv.398; S.v.126; A.iii.383; A.iv.428.

   (ii) Makkhali Gosāla: D.i.53; M.i.231, 238, 438.S.i.66,68; S.iii.211; S.iv.398; A.i.33f,286; A.iii,376, 384.

   (iii) Ajit Kesakambali; D.i.55; M.i.515; S.i.98; S.iii.207; S.iv.398.

   (iv) Sañjaya Belatthiputta: D.i.27,58; Vin.i.39,42;A.i.286.

(v) Pakuddha Kaccāyān. D.i.56; M.i.198,250,517; M.ii.4;S.i.66,68;Sn.p.91.
(vi) Nigaṇṭha Nātputta: D i.57; D,iii,119,M.i.91 ff;371,373 ff; M.ii.31,214 ff; S.i.66; S.ii,214;S.iv. 298 ff, 398; A.i.220; A. iv 180ff; A.v.150.

6. D.i.53; akiriyaṁbyākāsi.

7. D.i.52-53: *karato kho, Mahārāja kārayato.....pāṅaṁatimapāyato, adinnaṁ ādiyato, sandhiṁ chindato, nillopaṁ harato.....paripanthe tiṭṭhato, paradāraṁ gacchato, musā bhaṇato karoto na karīyaṭ pāpaṁ, Khura-pariyan-tena ce pi cakkena yo imissā paṭhaviyā pāṇe.....eka maṁsa....puñjaṁ kareyya, n' atthi tato- nidānaṁ pāpaṁ, n' atthi pāpassa āgamo. Dakkhinañ ce pi Gaṅgātīraṁ āgaccheyya hananto ghātento chindanto chedāpento pācanto pācento, n'atthi tato---nidānaṁ pāpaṁ, n' atthi pāpassa āgamo. Uttarañ ce pi Gaṅgātīraṁ gaccheyya dadanto dāpento yajanto yajāpento n' atthi tatonidānam puññaṁ, n' atthi puññassa āgamo. Dānena damena saṁyamena saccavajjena n'atthi puññaṁ n'atthi puññasa āgamo.*
   Rhys Davids T.W.,*Dialogues of the Buddha*, Part I, pp.69-70.

8. D.i.28-29.

9. Barura, Benimadhab, *History of Pre-Buddhistic Indian Philosophy*, p.279.

10. Ibid. cf.S iii.69

11. Rhys Davids, *op.cit.p.221* (Introduction *to Kassapa Sihanāda Sutta*).
   "Those who claimed to be especially strict in their rules as to means of livelihood."

12. Basham, A.L., *History and Doctrine of the Ājivikās*, p.3.

13. D.i. 53: N' *atthihetu........n' atthi paccayo sattānaṁ saṁkilesāya."*

14. D.i.53: *"Ahetu---a 'paccāya suttā visujjhati."*

15. D.i.53; *"Niyati---saṅgati-bhāva- pariṇatā."*

16. D.i.53: *"N'atthi purisakāre, n' atthi balaṁ, n' atthi viriyaṁ n'atthi purisa-thāmo n'atthi purisa- parakkamo Sabbe sattā avasā abalā aviriya niyati- saṅgati-bhāva-pariṇatā."*

17. D.i.54: *"Seyyathā pi nāma sutta-gule khitte nibbeṭhiyamānam eva phaleti, evam eva bāle ca paṇdite ca sandhāvitvā saṁsaritvā dukkhass' antaṁ karissanti."* *Rhys Davids, op.cit.p.* 73.

18. Foreword to Basham *op.cit.p.xii.*

19. D.i.55: *"Cātum-mahābhūtiko ayaṁ puriso; yadā kālaṁ karoti paṭhavī pathavi--- kāyaṁ anupeti anupagacchati,.....ākāsaṁ indriyāni saṁkamanti......"*

20. D.i. 55: *"N' atthi ayaṁ loko, n'atthi parloko,......... Na honti param maraṇā."*

21. D.i.56: *"Katame satta? Paṭhavi-kāyo āpo-kāyo tejo- kāyo vāyo-kāyo sukhe dukkhe jīva- sattame.....Satt'ime......kāyā akaṭā akaṭā-vidhā animmitā animmitā vañjhākūṭaṭṭha esika ṭṭhāyiṭṭteitā......"*

22. Empodocles (492-432 B.C.) of Acragas-modern name of Acrages is Sicily in Greece, hence a pre-Socratic philosopher who is said to have written two long poems.....(i) On Nature and (ii) Purifications. The Second poem is a religious-mystical poem on Personal Salvation.

23. D.i. 58: *"Atthi paro loko"? ti iti ce taṁ pucchasi, "atthi paro loko" ti 'iti ce me assa, "atthi paro loka" ti te naṁ vyākareyyam. Evaṁ pi me no, Tathā ti pi......me no. Aññathā ti pi no. No ti pi me no. No no ti pi me no.....'*

24. D.i.57: *".......Nigaṇṭho cātu-yama-saṁvara-saṁvuto hoti. Kathañ ca....Saṁvuto hoti?.....Nigaṇṭho Sabba-vāri-vārito ca hoti, Sabba-vāri-yuto ca, Sabba-vāri-dhuto sabba vāri-phuttho ca...yato...evam...saṁvutto hoti, ca-ayam vuccati....nigaṇṭho gatatto ca yatatto ca thitatto ca ti." cf.* M.ii.35-36.

25. Barua, op.cit., p. 378; Rhys Davids, op.cit., pp.75-76.

26. Ibid.p.379. cf.S.i.66.

27. Foreword to Basham, op.cit., p.xii.

28. S.iv.400: *"Ahṁ Cānanda, Vacchogttassa paribbhājakassa 'atthttā' ti puṭṭho samaṇo 'athtta' ti byākareyyam, ye te, Ānand, Samaṇa brāhmaṇa sassatavāda tesametaṁ Saddhiṁ abhvissa. Ahṁ Cānando, Vacchagottassa paribbhājakassa 'natthta' ti puṭṭho samaṇo 'nathtā, ti byākareyyam, ye te, Ānanda samaṇabrahmaṇa ucchedvāda tesametaṁ saddhiṁ abhvissa."* .....Woodward, Part iv, p.282.

29. M.22: (*Alagaddūpama-Sutta*) or 'Simile of the Watersnake.' In this *sutta*, a monk learning thS doctrine of the Buddha, contrary to its spirit, is censured and his mental act is described like catching a snake by the tail (M.i.133-134) M.i.140:

Evaṁ vādiṁ kho maṁ bhikkhave, evamakkhāyiṁ e' ke samaṇabrahmaṇa asata tucchā musā abhūtena abbhāci-Kakhantivanayiko samaṇo goto, sato sttassa ucchedaṁ vināsaṁ vibhavaṁ paññāpeti. Yathā cāhaṁ na, bhikhave, yathacāhaṁ na vadāmi, tathā maṁ te bhonto samaṇabrāhmaṇā asatā tucchā musā abhūtena abbhācikarkhanti vanayika samaṇo Gotamo, sato sattassa ucchedaṁ vināsaṁ vibhavaṁ paññāpeti'ti. Pubbe cāhaṁ bhikkhave, etarahi ca dukkhaṁ ceva paññāpemi, dukkhassa ca nirodhaṁ.

Chalmers, Vol.1.p.99

cf.M.26: (*Ariyapariyesana-Sutta): M.i.161-163.* In this *Sutta* the Buddha talks about two quests: the Ariyan and the Unariyan quest.

30. M.28; M.i., 184-85: *Seyyathāpi, āvuso, yāni Kānici jaṅgamānaṁ pāṇānaṁ pada jātāni sabbāni tāni hotithopade Samodhānaṁ gacchanti, hatihapadaṁ tesaṁ aggamakkhayāti yadidaṁ mahantattena; evameva kho, āvuso, ye keci kuslā dhammā sabbete catūso ariya saccesu saṅigaham gacchanti. Katamesu catūso? dukkhe ariya sacce dukkha smudaye ariyasacce, dukkhanirodhe ariyasacce, dukkhanirodha gāminiyā paṭipādaya ariyasacce.* Chalmers Vol. I. p.133.

31. The name of these *Bhikkhus* are: i. *Kondañña; ii. Bhaddiya iii. Vappa; iv. Mahānāma; v. Assaji.* These five *Bhikkhus*, at one time, had joined with Gotama in his austerities at Uruvelā. When Gotama, after realizing the futility of ascetic practices had abandoned the path of self-modification, quite popular with the recluses, and adhered, to the Middlepath, all the five deserted him, as if Gotama had gone astray. After Gotama attained Sambodhi and became the Buddha, he could find them with his Buddha-eye, where they were. He went there and preached to them the Dhamma and they became his disciplies.

32. S.V. 421.(*Dhammacakkappavattana-Sutta): Jāti pi dukkhā, jarā pi dukkha, vyāhdi pi dukkho, maraṇaṁ pi dukkhaṁ,*

appiyehi sampayogo dukkho piyehe vippayogo dukkho, yaṁpicchaṁ na labaṭhi taṁ pi dukkhaṁ saṁkhittena pañcaupādānākkhandha pi dukkhā.
Rhys Davids, T.W.Vol.XI (S.B.E.) p. 148.
For an idea of the ommnipresence of *dukkha* see the story Kisā Gotamī: Rhys davids, Mrs. *(trs.) Psalms of the Early Buddhists-1*, pp.106-110.

33. *Vinaya P. (Mahāvagga): Dhammacakkappavattnaṁ.*

34. S.ii. 3: Rhys Davids, C.A. F. Part II, p.3.

35. For details see; Sobti, Harcharan Singh, *Nibbāna in Early Buddhism*, pp. 20-25.

36. Copleston, R.S., *Buddhism-Primitive and Present*, p.103.

37. D. 15; (*Mahānidāna-Sutta*); D.ii.55.

38. A.iii, 134. In this discourse the Buddha, while staying at the Veluvana, the bamboo grove at Rajagha, rather emphasized the point that whether Buddhas arise or do not arise, the existence continues to be marked with the three characteristics viz.*anīccā,dukkha* and *anattā*.

39. S.iv.1.

40. M.22: (*Alagaddūpama-Sutta*): M.i.138: Chalmers, Vol.1,p.97.

41. The expression *Pañcaupādānakkhandha consists of three components: pañca+upādāna+khandha, Pañca* means five. *Upādāna* stands for clinging and *Khandha* refers to aggregates which are five in number viz., *rūpa, vedanā, sañña, viṇṇāṇa* and *saṅkhārā* that constitute the corporeal organism of man. The aggregates, when associated with *upādāna* cause Suffering. When *upādāna* is eliminated there remain *pañca khandhas* intact, but, now free from Suffering.

42. Dhp.277. Also, for detailed analysis pertaining to the transitory nature of *saṅkhārā* see. *A iv, 100-103,* where reference to the appearance of Seven Suns is made and which shall result in the total disappearance of all that is produced also termed as *saṅkhārā,*

43. *Saṅkhāra* is derived from the verb *Saṅkharoti* that means to make or put together. It refers to anything produced hence synonymous with production. The terms *saṅkhārā*

or Production can be used, therfore, for anything existing in the phenomenal world, since, everything is produced.

44. A.V., 107 *Chandamūulka āvuso Sabbe dhammā.*

45. M. 109. (*Mahā-Puṇṇama-Sutta*): M. iii.16.*Ime kho bhikkhu pañcaupādāna-kkhandhā Chandamūlakā.*

46. Vinaya P. (*Mahāvagga*) (*Dhammacakkappavattana-Sutta*)

47. S.iii.186:
Yaṁ panāṇiccaṁ dukkhaṁ viparināmadhammaṁ: api nu taṁ anupādāya uppajjevyuṁ saṁyojanaminive-savinbandhajjosānā" ti?
"No hetaṁ, bhante."
Woodward, part III, p.154.

48. M.35: (*Cūla-Saccaka-sutta*): M.i.231.

49. Ibid., M.i.232-233. Chalmers, Vol.I.p.166.

CHAPTER-7

THE BUDDHIST CONCEPTION OF *MĀRA*

—Dr. Bimal Churn Law, M.A.; B.L; Ph.D.

Māra, the spirit of evil of the Buddhists, the enemy of the Good Law, appears to have been the personification of an abstract conception of the Buddhist religion. The Buddhacarita-kāvya of Aśvaghoṣa tells us that he who is called in the world Kāmadeva, the owner of the various weapons, the flower arrowed, the Lord of the course of desire, is the Buddhist Māra, the enemy of liberation (Book 13). In other words, Māra is the personification of Kāma that thwarts the aspirant after the highest stage, *Nibbāna*. *Māra* is of different kinds: - *Khandha Māra* (*Māra* of the elements of being), *Kilesa Māra* (*Māra* of sin), *Maraṇa Māra* (*Māra* of Death), *Devaputta Māra* (*Māra* of the gods), and *Abhisaṁkhāra Māra* (*Māra* of the accumulation of *Kamma*) (Childers' Pāli Dictionary, p. 241).The Śikṣā-*samuccaya* of Śāntideva mentions the four, except *abhisaṁkhāra*. (Tr. Bendall & Rouse, p. 192). In the *Mahāvaṁsa,* he is described as one having thousand hands (Ed. Geiger, Ch. 30, Verse 75). Women is not competent to acquire the state of *Māra* (*Vibhaṅga*, p. 337). It is interesting to note on the authority of the Buddhist and Jaina texts that *Māra* is the originator of *Māyā* or attachment. (Cf. *Sūtrakṛtāṅga*, *Jaina Sūtras*, pt. II., S.B.E., Vol. XLV, p. 244) and the person who falls a victim to *Māyā* is conquered by *Māra*. His daughters are desire (*tanhā*), discontent (*arati*), and passion (*rāga*),[1] the ultimate categories of evil in its psychological system. The fight of the Bodhisattva with *Māra* is a struggle against the fetters and hindrances that stand in the way to *Nibbāna*. He does not resemble the evil spirit of the Zoroastrain

Ahriman who is a spirit of equal power with Ormuzd, the principle of good. In the Zoroastrain system every good is opposed by its correspoinding evil, and Ahriman, the spirit of evil, has existed opposed to Ormuzd since the commencement of the world. With the Satan of the Old Testament, *Māra* has not much in common, though there are some points of resemblance. Like *Māra,* Satan goes forth to tempt Job, to test his loyalty to God whose permission he obtains before commencing his evil activities.

Scholars like Windisch,[2] Beal,[3] Kern,[4] Rockhill[5] And Sir Charles Elliot[6] have given us very little information regarding *Māra* and his activities.

Oldenberg's treatise on *Māra* is indeed the pioneer work in this field.In the following pages an attempt has been made to collect from the Buddhist literature materials which remained hitherto unnoticed and which throw some new light on the subject. The Buddhist conception of *Māra* is in many respects the same as that of the Hindu *Kāmadeva.* Like *Kāmadeva, Māra* has his flowery arrow and there are many more points of resemblance; in fact, *Māra* is one of the names by which Kāmadeva is designated in *Brāhmanical* literature. *Māra* bears many names in Pāli literature; he is called, for example *Kaṇha* (black), *Adhipati* (chief), *Antagu* (destroyer), *Namuci* (non-deliverer), *Pamattavandhu* (friend of the passionate)[7] and at the same time he is also designated Maccu (death)[8], perhaps because death and ruin overtake one who is caught in the snares of *Māra. Anatthakāma* (wishing ill), *Ahitakāma* (wishing injury) and *Ayogakhemakāma* (wishing unsafety) are the epithets of *Māra.* (*Majjhima* Nikāya, Vol. I, p. 118).

Kāma (sensual pleasure) forms the first army of *Māra; arati* (discontent) is his second army; *khuppipāsā*(hunger and thirst), the third; *tanhā* (desire), the fourth; *thīnamiddha* (sloth and torpor), the fifth; *bhiru* (fear), the sixth; *vicikicchā* (doubt), the seventh; *makkho* (disdain to others) and *thambho* (self-adulation) the eighth; *lābha* (gain), *siloka* (fame), sakkāra (honour), *micchāladdhayaso* (wealth obtained by improper means), *attānaṁsamukkaṁsanā* (self-praise) and *paresaṁ avajānanā* (speaking ill of others)-all these constitute *Māra's* army (Niddesa, Vol, I. p. 96; cf. Sutta-Nipāta, Padhāna Sutta).

Diṭṭhadhammika kāmasaññā (i.e. the idea of sensual pleasure in present life) and *saṁparāyi kakāmasaññā* (i.e., the idea of sensual pleasure in future life) form the kingdom, state and food of *Māra* (*Majjhima Nikāya*, Vol. II., pp. 261-262).

The snare of *Māra* (*Mārabandhanaṁ*) means that a meditative person through two kinds of meditation, becomes freed from the snares of *Māra* which consist of births in *Kāmāvacara*, *rūpāvacara* and *arūpāvacaralokas.*[9] One is entangled in the snares of *Māra* if one has any attachment for a beautiful form, etc.[10] Māra is the chief of those who are possessed of *adhipatta* (influence)[11]. He who has attachment is entangled by *Māra.*[12] In the *Dhammapada* we read that Māra will certainly overthrow a person who is unrestrained in his senses, immoderate in his food idle and weak.[13] A person's mind is always attempting to come out of the kingdom of *Māra.*[14] Those who can restrain their mind and check its propensities can escape the snares of *Māra.*[15] One should fight with Māra with the weapon of wisdom.[16]. One can go beyond the sight of Māra, King of Death, by destroying the flowery arrow of *Māra.*[17] *Māra* cannot find those who are pious, leading a strenuous life and emancipated by perfection of wisdom.[18] One can make oneself free from *Māra* if one has attained the noble eightfold path.[19] Those who meditate on the impurities of the body can cut off the snares of *Māra.*[20] *Māra* cannot destroy the *Dhammacakka* (wheel of law).[21]

One should destroy the army of *Māra* with strenuous exertion.[22] One whose mind is not protected, who has false belief and is idle, comes under the control of *Māra.*[23] The *Nettipakaraṇa* mentions the fact that *Māra* could not detect the consciousness of Godhika.[24] *Māra* went to search for Vakkali's consciousness but he could find no trace of it because Vakkali passed away comletely before the quest of *Māra.*[25] The *Visuddhimagga* tells us that a wise man who finds delight in forest hermitage, that is, who has freed himself from the ties of the world, is fit to overcome *Māra* with his army.[26] A yogī who remains fixed in his seat spending his whole time in meditaion, can subdue *Māra.*[27] The *Niddesa* relates a conversation that is supposed to have taken place between a *bhikkhunī* named Vajirā and *Māra*. Vajirā said to *Māra* thus, "There is no *sattā*(being) here who can come under your control. This is no being but a heap of dirts (Vol.

I., p. 439, cf. *Kathāvatthu*, Vol. I. p. 66; *Abhidhammāvatāra*, p. 88).

There is a reference to the Buddha's subjugation of *Māra* at the foot of the Bodhi tree at Gayā. (*Ibid*. p. 455). The Buddha assured his disciples thus. "Oh, *bhikkhus*, if you live within the country of your father (i.e. the Buddha), you will not be overcome by *Māra*. (*Niddesa*, Vol. I, p. 475). *Māra* has no share in *jarā* (old age), *vyādhi* (disease), *maraṇa* (death) and *pubbakatapāpakammam* (Kathāvatthu, Vol. II. pp. 457-458). The *Itivuttaka* tells us that *Māra* is conquered by a person who is free from attachment and who has risen triumphant over all sufferings and will not be born again (p. 58). A fool, a person devoid of merit, and one who earns his livelihood by following low professions are reborn in hell. (Ibid. p. 59) Those who are under the domain of passion, delusion and anger, are ignorant of the *ariyadhammas* and subject to *Saccāyadiṭṭhi* (heresy of individuality). They cannot liberate themselves from the clutches of *Māra*. (Ibid, p. 92). The *Aṅguttara Nikāya* asserts that one who follows the *dhamma* can conquer *Māra* (Vol. I. p. 150).

The *bhikkhu* who puts forth the right effort and who has conquered the kingdom of *Māra*, is not subject to rebirth and death. He can conquer *Māra* with this army and can destroy the power of *Namuci* and live fuil of bliss. (*Aṅguttara Nikāya*, Vol.II. p. 15)

An *ariyasāvaka* endowed with the seven kinds of *saddhamma* and the four *jhānas*, is one who has passed beyond the influence of *Māra*. (Ibid. Vol. IV. pp. 108-109). In one of the *Jātakes*, we read that Yudhiṭṭhila and Yuvañjaya passed beyond the kingdom of *Māra*, which was made up of rāge (passion), *dosa* (fault), and *moha* (delusion). (Fausboll, *Jātaka*, Vol. IV. p. 123).

Māra stood up as an antagonist of the Buddha trying to prevent his attainment of *Nirvāṇa*. *Māra* in his great and ineffectural struggle to bring down the Buddha, used all sorts of arms, both phycical and spiritual. The *Nettipakaraṇa* tells us that *Māra* hurled a huge stone at the Buddha from the top of the Gijjhakuṭta mountain. (p. 34) When Siddhārtha was going out of th city of Kapilavastu for the great renunciation, he was met by *Māra* at the gate. He urged

Prince Siddhārtha not to leave the city as he (Buddha) would become an universal monarch on the seventh day if he stayed in it, but all *Māra's* efforts were in vain. *Māra* then tried the effect of threats on him and pointed out that he would bring him to grief if the least thought of lust disturbed his mind. In vain did he seek for seven long years to detect any defect in the conduct of the Buddha. After the lapse of five years, the Buddha acquired omniscience. When the Buddha was sitting at the foot of the *Ajapālanigrodha* tree, in the fifth week of his attainment of bodhi, *Māra* came and told him that he was now beyond his power. The three daughters of *Māra* named *taṇhā, arati* and *rāga* tried to tempt the Buddha in various way but all were in vain. (*Dhammapada* Commentary, Vol. III, pp. 195-196). Again we are told that when the Buddha was going for alms to a *Brāhmin* village named Pañcasāla, *Māra* resolved that he should not get any alms there. *Māra* entered the bodies of the villagers and inclined their minds not to offer any alms to the Buddha who came back to the village-gate with his empty bowl. *Māra* taunted him by putting the question whether he had received any alms. The Buddha replied that he was fully aware of his mischievous intention. Thereupon *Māra* urged him again to go and seek for alms with the sinister object that the Buddha might be insulted all the more. The Buddha retroted that he would live on *pīti* (joy) like the *ābhassaradevas* if he received no alsm. (*Dhammapada Commentary*, Vol. III. pp. 257-258). The same commentary also records another passage at arms between the Buddha and *Māra;* we are told that a god belonging to the *Māra* world entered into the bodies of five hundred young women of whom the great and wealthy lady of Sāvatthī, Visākhā Migāramātā, was in charge. As *Māra* got possession of them, they began to laugh and clap their hands in the presence of the Buddha, who, however, became aware of the fact that all this was the act of *Māra*. By his supernatural powers the Buddha created darkness and the women were entirely nonplussed and were overtaken by fear. A short while afterwards they came to their senses. Then the Buddha removed the darkness and brought in light and the ladies became ashamed of their light conduct (Ibid. Vol. III, pp. 101-102).

The *Dhammapadaṭṭhakathā* narrates another story recounting how *Māra* tried to catch the Buddha in his toils. the Buddha said on one occasion that the kings were in the habit of oppressing their subjects, thus causing untold misery to them. He further said that if he had been the ruler, he would have ruled his kingdom without any such oppression. *Māra* ordered him the sovereignty of a kingdom with a view to put him to trouble. The Buddha, however, saw through his evil motive and gave out his intention to him and said, "the four means of obtaining supernatural power have been well meditated on. If necessary, I can even change the Himālaya mountains into gold. Therefore I can rule the subjects well without exacting any tax from them." He further said that *Māra* need not tempt him (*Dhammapada Commentary*, Vol. IV, pp. 31-32), as all such attempts were bound to be fruitless. Once *Māra* in the shape of an elephant attacked Rāhula Kumāra while he was lying down in the latrine of the Buddha, being driven out by the *bhikkhus* in the *Jetavana vihāra*. *Māra's* intention was to terrify Rāhula and thereby to cause pain to the mind of the Buddha. The Exalted One, however, recognised *Māra* and told him at once and retorted, "*pāra* is obtained by sinless *arahatas*. You are *Māra* and you have nothing to do with *pāra*". (Ibid, Vol. IV pp. 140-141).

The *Majjhima Nikāya* records that *Māra* entered into the bowels of Mahāmoggallāna who felt his stomach to be heavy. Trying to find out the cause, he sat down to meditate and came to know that *Māra* had entered into his body. He asked *Māra* to leave him and not to disturb *Tathāgata* and his disciples. *Māra* came out of his mouth and stood on the bar of the door. Mahāmoggallāna related to him (*Māra*) his deeds in time of the Buddha Kakusandha, the trouble he gave to Vidura, which ultimately led him to hell where he suffered for many years. (Vol. I., pp. 332 foll).

The *Aṅguttara Nikāya* records a conversation which the Buddha is supposed to have held with *Māra* three months before his *parinibbāṇa*. *Māra* said, "Let the Blessed One now pass away , this is the time for him to pass away. You said that you would not pass away until your disciples were trained properly,until they had grown restrained, fearless, learned, beholders of *dhamma*, followers of the *dhamma* and the right path, till they were able to teach and preach and also to refute the teaching of others. Your disciples are now competent to do all this work and it is time for you to pass away". *Māra* also said the same thing regarding the *bhikkhunīs.*The Blessed One replied, "Don't be anxious. The *Tathāgata* will pass away after the lapse of three months" (Vol.IV., pp. 310-311). The *Saṁyutta Nikāya* informs us that *Māra* in the guise of a *devatā* named Vetamvarī came to the Buddha and told him thus, "He who hates *tapa* (austerity) and does not like to stay alone, who is addicted to *rupas* or beautiful forms and wishes to go to the regions of the blessed (*devaloka*) is competent to give advice regarding the attainment of the next world." The Buddha recognised *Māra* in the guise of a god and explained to him that "*rūpa* (from) in this world in the next and in the sky is praised by *Namuci*, It is nothing but a bait". (Vol. I. p. 67.) One night while the Buddha was at Veluvana, *Māra* in the guise of a big snake, went to terrify the Exalted One how, however, recognised him at once and said, "He who lives in a solitary place and has self-restrint, has no reason to be afraid of any terrible sight and can bear the bite of snakes, etc." (Ibid., Vol. I. pp. 106-107). On another occasion, *Māra* said to the Buddha, "the term of life of a human being is long. It should be enjoyed to the full extent." The Buddha retorted that the contrary was the truth. (Ibid., Vol. I. p. 108). *Māra* disturbed the Buddha while he was delivering a discourse on *dhamma* to a large assembly at *Jetavana* by saying, "You have your opponent, why are you roaring like a lion? You have not yet conquered your opponent, why should you call yourself a conqueror?" The Buddha replied, "He who has become fearless, does roar in this way. The *Tathāgatas* who are endowed with ten powers, are veritable conquerors of the world." (*Saṁyutta Nikāya*, Vol. I. p. 110) *Māra* came to the Buddha while he was lying at ease after having received injury to the finger of his leg due to the stone thrown at him by Devadatta, and said, "You have no wealth, how is it that you are lying at ease. Are you absorbed in poetry or indolence?" The Buddha replied., "I have enough wealth, I am lying at ease with compassion for all beings. Those who are pierced with arrows, etc., are lying at ease, why should I not lie at ease being free from all spears?" (Ibid pp. 110-111). Again *Māra*, in the guise of a fiery bull, wanted to break the bowls of the *bhikkhus* placed outside in the sun while the *bhikkhus* were attentively listening to the religious instructions given by the Buddha on *upādānakkhandha* at Sāvatthī. A *bhikkhus* shouted that a bull had come and it might break the bowls. The Buddha said that it was *Māra* that had come in that guise and not a real bull (Ibid. ,p. 112). While the Buddha was delivering a discourse on *Nirvāṇa* at Sāvatthī, *Māra* in the guise of a ploughman came and told him, "Have you seen my bulls?" By this query *Māra* disturbed the Buddha and *bhikkhus* and their attention was distracted. (Ibid., p. 115). *Māra* told his daughters to overpower and defeat the Buddha. They made every attempt to do so but in vain (*Ibid.*, Vol. I. p. 127).

A study of the Tibetan version of the account of *Māra's* fight with the Buddha is interesting and instructive.

Before his attainment of *Nirvāṇa* Buddha intended to destroy his antagoinst *Māra*, the Buddhist Satan. He addressed the *bhikkhus* and said that he would put an end to *Māra*, the master of lust. He then issued from his forehead a ray of light that illuminated the world. The earth quaked. *Māra* heard the following message:-"The being who is very pure, who has led a religious life form many ages, who is the son of Suddhodana and who has given up his kingdom, desires to favour other beings with his nectar like teachings. Be careful as he is coming to-day before the Bodhi-tree. When he will be free, he will help others to be free, he will rejoice and make others rejoice. He will pass away from this world of affliction and will help others to do so. He will thoroughly destroy the three apāyas[28] to have the city filled up with *Devas*. If the self-born religion comes, it will uproot the city of the devil and the devil will then be quite helpless, knowing not whither he should go". *Māra* got frightened to hear the message. He dreamt thirty two different kinds of dreams, viz, I. his place has been overshadowed by darkness. 2. He runs away through fear. 3. He sees that he is leaving his crown. 4. He sees the feathers of goose, crane, peacock etc., falling. 5. He sees that musical instruments, e.g., drums, conches, kettle drums, etc., break into pieces and fall down on the ground, and so on. He asked his retinue to be careful and addressed them saying. "One who is endowed with all the good signs and who has undergone many difficulties, comes of the Śākya family, and will subdue the members of the devil's kingdom. I have heard from the Heaven above that the Buddha, the Blessed One, has obtained Nirvāṇa. If these innumerable beings drink the nectar of his religion (*dhamma*) then I with my kingdom will perish for ever. Therefore you all these great hosts, muster strong and go there to conqueer that *Śramaṇa*. Oh, you four kinds of troops, be ready at once and march on. Oh, hosts, if you have love for me, you should not fly from the battle field. Though the world is full of *arahats*, victory will be ours our sorrows will come to an end, and we shall not be overcome by him If this man becomes victorious and becomes *Dharmarājā*, then there would be no end of his lineage." Then said *Māra's* son, "Oh, father, what hast thou done? Why does your face look dark? Your heart seems to be beating much and you are shivering so please tell me what you have seen or heard. I will serve you to the best of my ability." Then said *Māra*, "I have dreamt a dreadfull dream. If I am to narrate it before this gathering all of you will faint and fall on the ground." Then *Māra's* captain named Sārthavāha said to *Māra*, "If we get victory over him (Buddha) then there is little credit, but if the result be otherwise, our heads will be bent down in shame. Would it not be better if we refrain from fighting with him?" *Māra* replied the captain saying that he could not bow down at the feet of the Buddha and his followers. The brave should be known in fight. The captain rejoined him saying that it would be of no use for one, however great and powerful, to fight with a real hero. One proud and of gloomy nature cannot prosper. *Māra* turned a deaf ear to the captain's words. Four kinds of troops were ready by his order. With his troops, brave and dreadful to look at, having different faces wrapped up with many thousands of serpents, carrying swords, arrows, bows and various other terrible implements -- troops unforeseen and unheard of before by gods and men-*Māra* attacked the Blessed one. But the wise one who was powerful and quite unshakable like the hill Sumeru, cared nothing, saw and took *Māra's* threatnings and temptations bo be as evanescent as clouds of heaven. He sat in deep meditation. *Māra* saw him became terrified and turned mad. He said to his troops that the son of Śākya, whose shelter was religion who understood delusion and who had a mind as vast as the firmament, did not turn mad when he saw his (*Māra's*) army. Those sons of *Māra*, who had faith in the Buddha sat on the right side of *Māra* and those who did not believe in the Buddha sat on the left side of *Māra*. Then *Māra* discussed with his troops as to how he could conquer the Blessed One.

The captain, son of *Māra*, said, "I like to wake up the Nāga King, I like to wake up the king of elephants, I like to wake up the king of animals,I like to wake up the king of men to-day". Then spoke the devil named Durmati, "My eye- sight can render twain hearts of beings whom it will touch, and can divide the essence of the oldest tree in the world. No being on whom shall fall my sight, can survive. So if I fix my eyes on the Buddha, he will have no power to breathe again." Thus there arose disputes amongst the devils themselves. Afterwords there spoke another devil who was called Sārthavāha,, "Buddha is not ignorant. You do not know his powers; he controls the others side and by his merits all are defeated. Although sons of *Māra* are innumerable as the sands of the Ganges, they are poweless to shake even a hair of his person. It is useless to say that you will kill him. It is impossible you must not think of harming him but be humble and have faith in the Buddha, as he is the king of *Trilokas*. Better go back without fighting with him" Thus sons of *Māra* who were on the left side held a strong discussion about Buddha's power. Then another devil named Sena-Bhadra spoke to *Māra* thus. "If you and your followers bow down before the Buddha with folded palms, then Indra, Dharmapālas, hosts of Kinnaras, chief of Asuras, king of birds and others will bow before him without any question. The Buddha has seen your frightful and terrible troops but he does not get frightened. Surely he will conquer you all as a hero." Then from the right row a son of *Māra* named Pramayana said, "The sun, the moon the lion and the kings of the world need no help. The *Bodhisattva* surely needs no help." Thus many followers of *Māra* spoke and gave their reasons to refrain *Māra*, the emblem of evil, heard the arguments advanced by his followers. He grew jealous of the Buddha all the more. He saw a wonderful miracle. He saw that his troops had gone into the mouth of the Buddha rendering him (*Māra*) quite helpless, that he had to run away, from the spot, that he had mustered up courage and had turned up again with his vast army had attacked the Buddha with various sorts of weapons which were miraculously turned into garlands, canopies, bunches of flowers as if to decorate the Bodhi tree. This wonderful miracle strongly agitated *Māra* who asked the Buddha to leave the Bodhi tree and to go back to his kingdom to rule over it, and told him that he would not be able to attain *Nirvāṇa* with such a little knowledge. Buddha said to *Māra* in a soft and sweet tone, "Oh sinner you offered one sacrifice while I offered myriads and myriads of sacrifices". He then explained to *Māra* his sacrifices in detail. Then said *Māra* to the Buddha that he (the Buddha) had been defeated as he had seen only one offering. Buddha cited the earth, the abode of all animals, as his witness. He touched the earth and addressed her saying, "Oh, *Bhūmidevī*, be good enough to be my witness." The earth quaked for sometime in different ways. Them *Bhūmidevī* with her myriads and myriads of retinue appeared before the Buddha and said, "It is true what you have said, Oh, Thou Blessed One! You are the only one upon whom all the *devas* in the world can rely." So saying, disappeared *Bhūmidevī's* with her retinue. *Māra* heard *Bhūmidevī's* words and ran away quite helpless with his troops. He then called his daughters, sought their help and told them to go to the Bodhi tree to tempt the Blessed One by all lustful means to see whether the Buddha was mentally strong or degenerated. *Māra's* daughtes came to the Buddha and examined him very minutely. They found as radiant as the golden *caitya*. They found him unshakable like the hill Sumeru and a deep thinker. They then praised the Buddha danced before him and to arouse passion in him they sang charming songs which read as follows:-

"The season of lust is the spring when all flowers blosson. You have a beautifully shaped body. Your fame has brought us under your influence. We are born of all shapes and complexion. Beautiful as we are, we are for the enjoyment of gods and men. So turn away from the path of *Nirvāṇa* which is difficult to obtain. Better enjoy yourself with us who are ever young." Buddha did not yield to their temptations. He replied them in a very sweet and soft tone, "Desire is the root of all sorrows. It hinders *samādhi*, *riddhi*, etc.," He looked at their faces and bellies and explained various things. *Māra's* daughters, especially *Tṛṣṇā* (desire) *Rati* (passion) and *Prīti* (affection) disregarded Buddha's words and tempted him for the second time. The Buddha said, "Gods and men of the *Trilokas* worship me and my *Dhammacakra* will revolve in these *Triloka*. I will acquire *dasabala* (ten potentialities); many men, be they may disciples or not will gather around me and my heart will rejoice in a place where there are lovers of my religion"; but his words produced little effect. *Māra's* daughters whose number is legion, again tempted Buddha in various ways; but all their attempts were futile. At length they said to the Blessed one in eulogistic terms. "Oh Pure One, your person is as stainless as the lotus flower and radiates a dazzling light like a golden hill; your face is as lovely and beautiful and your purpose be fulfilled." So saying they went back to *Māra*, bowed down at his feet and addressed him thus, "Oh our only father! It is better that you should banish your wrath upon the Teacher of *Devas* and men who looked at us smilingly with his lotus eyes. The Blessed One is not a man of lust or temper. Hill Sumeru may shake, ocean may dry, the sun and the moon may be dislodged but the Blessed One who knows the sins of the *Trilokas* will by no means come under woman's power." *Māra* heard his daughters, grew enraged and rebuked them but they asked him again not to march against the Blessed One. Then there appeared eight jungle-*devīs* (Goddesses of forest) who after worshipping the Buddha and praising him said to *Māra* "Oh, sinner, Retire and restrain yourself; you are helpless like an elephant in the mire." *Māra* paid little attention to these words. He ordered his army to attack the Buddha for the last time with such a violent force as would not spare his life. *Māra's* army charged the Buddha with all sorts of weapons and implements and with various satanic means but all their hopes and attempts were frustrated. They were utterly defeated. Buddha said to *Māra*, "If the hill Sumeru shakes, if all the creatures die, if the countless stars fall down with the moon from the heaven above, then a man like myself subject to the *Bodhiraja* will never change his intention." *Māra* became very much distressed when he heard Buddha's reply and disappeared.

Then while the Buddha was being worshipped and honoured by Jyotiputradeva and *Brahmā* with flowers, etc., *Māra's* sons who were on the right side of *Māra*, brought an umbrella and a big canopy for the Buddha,and with folded hands they eulogised the Buddha in these terms, "Oh,Mighty One, We bow to your because you have defeated us. You have taken a firm seat, you do not rise up nor shake your person, nor do you speak, you are the only who exerts for the welfare of all the beings in the *Trilokas*. Myriads and myriads of devils could not interfere your action, nor could they shake you from your place under the Bodhi tree. Your charities are as countless as the sands of the *Ganges*." Then *Māra* came to the *Tathāgata* and told him that it was the time for his attainment of *Nirvāṇa*. He asked the Buddha to leave the world. Buddha said to *Māra*, "Oh, great sinner, my *bhikkhus* are quite firm in their faith; until I see them mild and pure, until I firmly establish in the world the name of Buddha, *Dhamma* and *Saṅgha*, I shall not pass away." When *Māra* heard these words, he bent down is head and stood in a corner, sad and demure. He thought that the *Tathāgata* had gone beyond his power. At this time came his three daughters, *Tṛṣṇā*, *Rati* and *Prīti* who promised him to bind the Blessed One by the force of their passion and to put him under their power *Māra* said, "The *arahata* who has attained perfect wisdom will not be overcome by passion. It grieves me much that he has advanced far beyond my powers." Then *Māra's* daughters without paying any heed to his words transformed themselves into youthful figures like the mother of one baby, appeared before the Blessed One, and exerted all their passionate powers to tempt him.. But the Blessed One took no notice of these temptations, and *Māra's* daughters became old women as the result of their evil *kamma*. They then came to *Māra* and appealed to him for regaining their former youth and beauty. *Māra* advised them to go to the *Tathāgata* to beseech him to have mercy on them and to give them back their former youth. *Māra's* dauthers acted up to their father's advice. Buddha forgave them and they got back their former adolescence. Thus ended all lustful activities of *Māra's* daughters. Complete defeat attended *Māra* and his army.

Māra tried to lead astray the *therīs* by painting the picture of the worldly enjoyments in brilliant colours, but here also all his attempts proved unsuccessful. *Māra* urged a *bhikkhunī*, thus, "Enjoy sensual pleasures; otherwise you will repent. Ālavikā replied, Kāma is like a spear. I do not find any pleasure in it. (*Saṁyutta Nikāya*Vol. I. p. 128). *Māra* went to Kisāgotamī, the great *therī*, and told her, "Why are you crying for a dead son? Go to the forest and select a suitable husband for yourself." She recognised *Māra* and told him. "I am sorrowful, I have no fear. I do not like to go after a man. I have destroyed all my attachments, the darkness of ignorance has been dispelled. I am now free from sins having conquered you and your army" (*Ibid* p. 130). On another occasion, *Māra* went to Vijayā *bhikkhunī* and told her, "You are young, I am also young, let us enjoy ourselves." Vijayā replied, "I do not find any delight in sensual pleasures. (*Ibid*. p. 131) *Māra* went to a *therī* named Cālā and told her, "What is it that you don't want?" She replied, "I do not want birth." He rejoined, "If you be born you can enjoy the pleasures of the senses." She replied, "If one is born, one is subject to death, one will have to suffer much. I wish to follow the *dhamma* preached by the Buddha for overcoming birth." (*Ibid*, p. 132). *Māra* went to another *therī* named Selā and addressed her thus, "By whom has this body been made? Who is the maker of it? What is it and how will it cease to exist?" Selā recognised *Māra* and replied, "I am not the maker of this body which has come into existence owing to some cause and it will pass away after the cause is destroyed." (*Saṁyutta Nikāya*, Vol. I. p. 134). Similar stories of temptations held out by *Māra* to many of the *therīs* are recorded in the *Therīgāthā*. Sukkā *therī* after having attained *arahatship* said thus, "Hold the *antimadeha* after defeating *Māra* and his army." (*Therīgāthā* Com., p. 61). Selā *therī* after having obtained *arathatship* went to *Andhavana* for spending the day. *Māra* in order to prevent her from meditating, said to her, "There is no salvation in this world. What good will you derive by meditation? Enjoy *Kāma*". The *therī* in reply told *Māra* that he was but a fool and that he was not aware that she had acquired *arahatship*. The *therī* further said, "*Kāma* is like a spear, why do you speak of sensual pleasures?" I do not find any delight in them. I am free from attachment.

You have been killed," (*Ibid* pp. 64-65). Somā *therī* attained *arahatship* and *Māra* tried to disturb her at *Andhavana*. *Māra* said to her, "What is difficult for a *ṛṣi* to get, how will you get being a little woman" She replied, "Although I am a woman, if my mind is stead fast, if I have wisdom, I shall see the *dhamma* perfectly. The state of a woman is no hindrance to my attainmet of *arahatship*. My attachment is destroyed, ignorance is dispelled and you have been defeated." (*Ibid* pp. 66-67).

Once Khemā *therī* sat under a tree to spend the day *Māra* in the guise of a youngman tried to induce her to enjoy wrldly pleasures and said, "You are young and beautiful, let us enjoy ourselves." The *therī* became aware that it was *Māra* who was trying to tempt her in that way and replied him thus, "This rotten body is much hated by me. I have destroyed *Kāmataṇhā*. I do not find delight in *kāma*, I am free from all sins. You have been destroyed."(*Therīgāthā* p. 136). *Māra* attempted to prevent Cālā *therī* from leading a holy life. Cālā told *Māra* thus, "I have received ordination after listening to the Buddha who has preached the four noble truths to me, I have received three *vijjās*. I am now beyond your dominion." (*Therīgāthā Commentary*, pp. 163- 164.)

Uppalavaṇṇā *therī* went to the sāl forest to spend the day. *Māra* addressed her thus. "If you, being alone, are oppressed by the wicked people, what will you do?" She replied, "If many wicked people come and oppress me, I an not afraid" "What will you do being alone? You will no be able to recognise me if I disappear from your presence and enter into your stomach or stand on your eye-brow?" I have acquired six *abhiññās*. I have mastered the *Buddhasāsana*. Therefore you cannot overcome me." (*Ibid* pp. 198-199.)

In the *Sutta Nipāta Commentary* we read that *Māra* tried to prevent Dhaniya and his wife from taking ordination from the Buddha by saying, "One having sons finds delight in them as cowherds find delight in cows. Attachment is the root of happiness." The Buddha refuted it (Vol. I. p. 44). From the *Jātakes* we learn that *Māra* cannot overcome the *bhikkhus* if they follow the subline eightfold path (*Jātaka*, Vol. III p. 532). *Māra* asked a householder not to offer charity. He also told him that if he did so he would suffer in a hell which he pointed out to him and which was full of burning charcoal and he acted according to his adive. (*Jātake,* Vol. I. p. 231) *Māra* also tried to dissuade a banker of Benares from making any gift to a *paccekabuddha* who came to him for charity. With this end in view *Māra* caused a shower of burning charcol to fall in front of the gate of the banker's house and there was such a heap of burning charcoal that it looked like the *Avīci* hell, thereby trying to prevent the *paccekabuddha* but at the interventiion of the *Bodhisattva, Māra's* attempt was baffled. (*Jātaka,* Vol. I. p. 232 foll). Buddha in course of his religius instruction to the *bhikkhus* told them thus "Don't walk in an improper place which is not the Buddha's property because *Māra* would find an opportunity of finding fault with you" (*Jātaka,* Vol. II. p. 60). A *thera* named Nandiya after obtaining saintship was once dwelling in a Deer-park Pācīnavaṁsa. In order to terrify him *Māra* went to him after having assumed a horrible appearance. Nandiya having recognised *Māra* told him. "You can't do any harm to a person who has gone beyond your kingdom. (*Therīgāthā Commentary,* Sinhalese Ed. p.82).

The Mahāyāna Buddhist texts contain some references to *Māra* and his activities. *Māra* tried to prevent a *Bodhisattva* named Sadāprarudita from acquiring merit. The *Bodhisattva* when he heard a divine voice that *Dharmodgata* would arise and take his seat in the midst of the town to preach the Law, he was elated with joy. The *Bodhisattva* then went to cleanse the spot and appointed a pulpit adoned with many gems. Then he desired to sprinkle water on the ground but he did not get it because all water had been hidden by *Māra,* the Evil One, in order to cause him to change his purpose and thereby to get the root of his merits disappeared. But the object of *Māra* was baffled because the *Bodhisattva* not finding any water drew out blood from his body for the purpose of cleaning the spot. (*Śikṣāsamuccaya,* translated by Bendall and Rouse pp. 42 foll.) The *Buddha-carita* Kāvya informs us that when Siddhārtha was sitting at the foot of the Bo-tree to obtain omniscience, *Māra* with his three sons, Vibhrama, Harṣa and Darpa and with his three daughters, *Rati, Prīti* and *Tṛṣṇā,* and himself armed with the flowery arrow, came to the Aśvattha tree to disturb him. *Māra* with his army tried to make him impatient but in vain. He then left the Buddha in despair. (Book 13., cf. *Saundarananda Kāvya,*

Canto III, Ślokas 7-8). After the Buddha had received *Sambodhi, Māra* came to him and told him. "Your object has been fulfilled. Obtain *nirvāṇa.*" The Buddha replied thus, "After having placed all people in *Dharma,* I shall obtain *nirvāṇa.*" At this *Māra* grew furious and returned home. The daughters of *Māra* made many fruitless attempts to tempt the Buddha. (*Ibid.,* pp. 11-36). *Māra* in the guise of Kauleśvara of the Śākya family came to the Buddha and requested him to return to Kapilavastu but the Buddha recognised him and asked him to return home. (*Buddha-carita Kāvya,* pp. 37-45). In the *Mahāvastu Avadāna,* we read that when the *Bodhisattva* came to the foot of the Bodhi tree, *Māra* became terrified and began to praise him saying, "You are unparalleled in beauty. You are possessed of seven gems. You are endowed with the thirty two signs of a great man. You enjoy women. The daughters of *Māra* are singing songs and throwing scented powder to cheer you up. Oh, prince, stay at home and enjoy yourself." The *bodhisattva* replied, "I have no desire for *kāma.* I am after salvation. *Kāma* is to be given up. Women are the cause of harm. The *Bodhisattva* is not attached to women. Don't speak of *Kama.*" *Māra's* son, Sārthavāha, said to his father thus, "Please listen to me. The *Bodhisattva* will remove that darkness of ignorance. He will be our savior. He will do good to the world. He will defeat all the army of *Māra.* You will not be able to move him by any means.'At this *Māra* grew angry with his son. The army of *Māra* attacked the *Bodhisattva* but he was not afraid. Māra and his army were thus defeated (Vol. II. p. 237 et. seq.)

The most detailed and elaborate account of the great struggle between Buddha and *Māra* is narrated in the *Lalitavistara.* When Prince Siddhārtha was about to attain *sambodhi, Māra* dreamt many inauspicious dreams, and came to know of the great effort that the Śākya prince was making for final emancipation. He at once roused his sons and assitants his general Iissimo Simhahanu by name all his friends and relatives, informed them of the activities of Siddhārtha and prepared a mighty host of all arms; his soldiers were fearful and terrible, of all queer and uncouth forms that the imagination of man can conceive of. His thousand sons were ranged in two battalions to his right and left. Those ranged on the right led by Sārthavāha urged him to submit to the *Bodhisattva* while those on the left argued to the contrary and were determined tonight to a finish. Then commenced the onset of *Māra* whose army began to strike at him with all sorts of weapons. Huge heaps of flowers and dreadful fire hurled at him formed an aureole round his body; dreadful and deadly weapons formed beds of sweet smelling flowers round about the Bodhi tree and many of them hanging from it in garlands added to its beauty. Then *Māra* appeared before him and urged him to rule over the earth but failing to tempt the Bodhisattva, he fled with his army. Then *Māra* urged his fascinating daughters to try all their arts and skill on the *Bodhisattva*. They tried at first the effect of the thirty-two womanly arts upon him but could not produce the least impression on him. Then they tried to tempt him with sweet *gāthās* to enjoy the pleasures of the senses in their company but the *Bodhisattva* discoursed to them on the futility of all desires. Then the daughters of *Māra*, trained and accomplished as they were in all the female arts and guiles, began to exercise on him the full strength of their powers but the *Bodhisattva* restrained them with soft and sweet words, unmoved alike by all that they said or did. Then they desisted and reported to their father of the futility of female charms against *Bodhisattva* but *Māra* would not still turn back. He then tries threats to frighten away the *Bodhisattva* but he was as unsuccessful as before. At last he made a final onset with all sorts of offensive weapons and the whole of his army, but he was utterly defeated. He was thus quite unable to turn away the Sākya prince from the great object he had placed before himself. He had then no alternative but retreat.

The *Divyāvadāna* describes a fight between *Māra* and the sage Upagupta who succeeded in binding the Satanic enemy and inflicted an insulting defeat on him. (p. 357 et.seq.).

In order to defeat *Māra*, Lord of the world of desire, one should accept the Law of the Buddha, which causes pain, sorrow and lamentation to *Māra*, the Evil one. (*Śiksāsamuccaya*, Tr. by Bendall and Rouse, p. 44).

Notes and References :

1. *Dhammapada Commentary* Vol. I.p. 202; *Saṁyutta Nikāya.* Vol. I. p. 124.
2. Windisch, *Māra and Buddha.*
3. Beal, Samuel, *The Romantic Legend of Śākya Buddha,* pp. 36. 199.
4. Kern, H. *Manual of Indian Buddhism,* pp. 16 ff. 20, 31, 42, 101
5. Rockhill, *The Life of the Buddha,* pp. 27, 31, 32, 39 and 119
6. Eliot, Sir Charles, *Hinduism and Buddhism* Vol. 1 pp. 143. 164, 175,; Vol. II, p. 160.; Vol III. pp. 69, 73, 350.
7. *Niddesa* (P.T.S.) p. 489.
8. *Jātaka* (Fausboll) Vol. IV, p. 123
9. *Dhammapada Commentary,* Vol III. pp. 403-404
10. *Saṁyutta Nikāya,* Vol. IV. p. 91.
11. *Aṅguttara Nikāya,* Vol. II. p. 17
12. *Saṁyutta Nikāya,* Vol. III. p. 73.
13. *Dhammapada, Yamakavagga, verse* 7 P.T..S. Ed.
14. *Ibid* p. 5
15. *Idem.*
16. *Ibid.* 6
17. *Ibid.* 7
18. *Ibid.* 8
19. *Ibid.* 40
20. *Ibid.* 50
21. Nettipakaraṇa pp. 8, 9
22. *Ibid,* p. 40
23. *Ibid* p. 85
24. *Ibid.* p. 39
25. *Samyutta Nikāya,* Vol. III. p. 124.
26. Vol.I. p. 73
27. *Visuddhimagga,* Vol. I. p. 79
28. In the Pāli account we find four *apāyas.*

CHAPTER-8

AN IMAGE OF WOMAN AS REFLECTED IN JĀTAKAS

—Dr. Harcharan Singh Sobti, M.A.; LL.B; Ph.D.

There are number of stories contained in the *Jātakaṭṭha-kathavaṇṇanā*, which are weaved in one single pattern, aimed at to denigrate woman, and thus painted licentious, in order to 'keep wide awake' the *Bhikkhus* as regard to woman. A very peculiar thing in the Buddhist tradition, in this context, is that at the same time it eulogizes women as *therīs*, whose life-sketches in the form of the *Therīgāthā* form an integral part of the Buddhist Canon. This means, that 'woman *is* capable' to attain *Nibbāna*. Two contrary views about woman, certainly, involve a contradiction. I propose to examine this very contradiction, in this paper.

The *Jātakas* in Pāli language form a very vast literature containing the teachings of the Buddha. They are in the form of 555 main stories of the previous births of the Buddha(but the number of *Jātakas* available so far is *547*) and a number of interlinking stories of the Bodhisatta striving for the fulfillment of ten perfections *(Pārmīs)*,[1] for the attainment of Buddhahood. The *Jātakas* in their original form were in verses (*gāthās*) and the number of verses contained in the available *547 Jātakas* is 2440. The theme of teaching has been interwoven through these verses. The details about them were surviving in oral tradition in the society. Since the Buddhist tradition was alive in India for centuries together, the people had no difficulty in understanding these verses and the ideas contained therein in the background of the introductory material already available in oral tradition. In course of time there was the chance of disappearance of the oral tradition.

Therefore, Buddhaghosa (5th century A.D.) an eminent commentator of the words of the Buddha, understood the psychological trends of the society and put all such materials into writing rightly adjusting them with the theme of the verses. Thus, each *Jātaka* appeared in the form of one complete story of the deeds of *Boddhisatta*. Of course, in many cases the story is further interwoven with a number of other stories connected with the theme. Every single *Jātaka* story consists of five component parts *viz.* (i) *Paccuppannavathu*, (ii) *Atitavathu*, (iii) *Gāthā*, (iv) *Veyyākaraṇa* and (v) *Samodhāna* or in other words it passes through these five successive stages. Right in the beginning, one is made familiar with the context (*paccuppaṇnavathu*) which prompts the Buddha to narrate a *Jātaka* story; then a story of the previous birth of the Buddha (*atitavathu*) when, actually he was *Boddhisatta*, is narrated; thereafter *gāthā* supported by *abhisambuddhagāthā* is recited followed by a word for word commentary of the *gāthā* (*veryyakarṇa*). The fifth and the last component part of the *Jātaka* story is *Samodhāna*. Here the characters of the 'story of the present', are identified with those of the 'story of the past' alongwith it the psychological effect of the discourse on the minds of the hearers is described.[2] Our main concern, at present, is with *atitavathu* and psychological effect on the minds of the hearers.

The *Jātaka* stories we have seclected for an appraisal, in the background of the Buddhist tradition, are contained in the *Itthivagga* of *Jātakaṭṭhakathāvaṇṇaṇā*. These stories depict woman as "lustful profligate, vile and degraded"[3] and are symbolized as "a sex composed of wickedess and guile, unknowable, uncertain as the path of fishes in the water",[4] "given opportunity all women work iniquity"[5] and last but not the least are compared to "highways, rivers, courtyards, hostelries or taverns, which to all alike extend universal hospitality".[6] The psychological effect of these stories on the minds of hearers is invariably that of renunciation of the household life in favor of entering into state of homelessness. Rati Lal N.Metha, while writing on 'Position of Woman' in his book *Pre-Buddhist India* (1939), based on *Jātaka* stories, is quite nearer to the truth when he opines that 'these utterances are from, and for the ascetics---those, who, perhaps, tired of their own weakness, and despaired of their failures want to run away from the world".[7] But, this tutored psychological effect involves wider issues connected with the Buddhist tradition and therefore, calls for an analysis as regard to the position of woman as contemplated in the said tradition.

2.

The Buddha was critical about women. This unhappy conclusion is readily derived, mainly from three Canonical evidences. These evidences are: (i) the Buddha's reluctance to admit women into *Saṅgha,* (ii) an institution of *aṭṭhagurūdhammā* exclusively meant for *Bhikkunis* and (iii) the Buddha's advice to Ānanda 'to keep wide awake' as regard to woman. It seems to be case of misreading of Canon. A misreading of Canon, whether intentional or otherwise, history of religions tell us, creates problems. At times, a misreading stems from an outlook not rooted in the soil of the land. It needs to look into an alleged hostility of the Buddha against woman, in the background of an indigenous cultural heritage.

The Buddha's reluctance, in the instant case, is rather revealing. Let us look into the circumstances in which the Buddha allowed an admission of woman into *Saṅgha*. While going through the text of Cullavagga,[8] (Which is second sub-part of the *Khanddhaka,* second book of *Vinaya Piṭaka),* we learn, that, when the Buddha was staying at Kapilavatthu, in the Nigrodha Park, Mahāpajapati the Gotami, Gotama's aunt and later on his foster-mother, visited the Buddha and asked for his permission thrice 'to enter the homeless state under the doctrine and discipline proclaimed by the *Tathāgata'*. But to her utter dismay the Buddha continued to remain adamant in not allowing women 'to enter the homeless state'.

If Gotama the Buddha was adamant Gotamī too was determined.

The story continues. But, now we find the Buddha staying in Mahāvana at Vesālī. Imagine for a while Gotamī alongwith number of ladies of Sākya clan, having her shaven head, wearing orange colored robes, with swollen feet and covered with dust, sad and sorrowful, weeping and in tears, arrives at Vesālī and is standing outside under the entrance porch of Mahāvana. The scene, so to say, is pathetic. Ānand requests the Buddha for admitting Mahāpajapati--the Gotamī and other ladies of Sākya clan into *Saṅgha*. Ānanda, repeats the request thrice, but, in vain. At the same time Ānanda, refuses to accept his defeat and changes his strategy. Now, Ānanda does not request but asks:

"Are women, Lord, capable when they have gone forth from the household life and entered discipline proclaimed by the Blessed One--are they capable of realizing the fruit of conversion, or of the second path, or of the third path, or of Arhantship?

"They are capable, Ānanda",[9] Buddha replies

Hence, at this juncture, Ānanda reminds the Buddha of Gotamī's great service rendered to him, when as aunt and nurse she nourished him and gave him milk, and on the death of his mother suckled the Blessed One at her own breast. Ānanda seems to have sentimentalized the whole situation. When Gotami, at one time, 'Suckled the Blessed One at her own breast', the Blessed One is not short of milk of human kindness. The Buddha's acceptance of 'capability' of women, and Gotamī's service rendered, prepared a ground for an admission of women into *Saṅgha*. The Buddha grants the permission, but, with condition, thus:

"If then Ānanda, Mahapajapati the Gotami take upon herself the Eight Chief Rules (*aṭṭhagurudhamma*), let that be reckoned to her as her initiation".[10]

Woman's 'capability' and the Buddha's reluctance to initiate woman *is* disturbing. Our primary concern, at the moment, of course, is to decode the meanings of the Buddha's reluctance.

Every human being is bisexual in the sense that it combines both the masculine and feminine characteristics irrespective of being man or woman. This psychological truth was discovered in India, long ago, and projected in the myth of *ardhanāriśvra* preserved in *Śivapurāṇ*.[11] The myth of *ardhanāriśvara* takes the form of masculinity and femininity, ingrained in human psyche. *Sakhisampradāya* of Swami Haridas that advocates the view that 'there is only one male and all others are females' has its roots in this very human psyche. The male adherents of this *sampradāya* dress themselves like woman and identify themselves with Rādhā and conduct themselves likewise. Those who are attracted towards this kind of devotion to God in the form of Krishna, certainly imbibe disproportionate quantity of feminine traits in their psychic beings. It is a case of projecting femininity rooted in the male biological organism.

The fact of human beings imbibing composite psychic nature, is also acknowledged by Gurū Nānak (1469-1539). The Founder- -Gurū of Sikhism, when he says, that;

> *"There is a woman in man*
>
> *and man in woman*
>
> *only the wise can discern it."*[12]

Bisexuality as a psychic phenomenon is a subject of study in modern psychology, too. "Every individual", discovered Sigmund Freud (1856-1939) "displays a mixture of the character-traits belonging to his own and the opposite sex; and he shows a combination of activity and passivity whether or not these last character-traits tally with his biological ones."[13] He identifies activity in woman as a masculine trait and passivity in man as feminine one. Therefore, psychologically speaking every individual is to be viewed in this background.

The Buddha on the one hand was reluctant to admit woman into *Saṅgha* and on the other hand he endorsed the query of Ānanda as regard to the capability of woman for realising 'the fruit of conversion' when 'entered the homeless state under the doctrine and discipline proclaimed by the Blessed One'. *'Womań is capable'*, here, woman is viewed as a psychological being that imbibes both the masculine and feminine character- traits. The capability of woman as a psychological being is directly linked up with 'the doctrine and discipline of the Buddha'. What is there in woman and doctrine and discipline, that goes well with each other? The basic thing in the doctrine of the Buddha is that it is meditative in nature. In order to draw any benefit from the doctrine of the Buddha it is imperative that it suits the temperament of the person concerned. In *Theravāda* Buddhism even an object of meditation needs to be selected, with the guidance of *Kalyān-mitta*, according to one's temperament.[14]

So it is a temperament of the person pursuing religious discipline that works as a deciding factor.

As already stated that the Buddhist discipline *is* meditative (and not devotional) in its approach. Now, whether it suits masculine or feminine temperament, it is yet to be seen. Masculinity in its contents is through and through assertive, active and hence egoistic. It is difficult for a person having a *overall* masculine temperament to accept 'the other'. It is prerogative of feminine temperament alone to accept 'the other' and melt *oneself* therein. There is 'no other' in *Theravāda* Buddhism conducive as an object of devotion that feeds the feminine-self. Therefore, we can safely conclude that the Way of the Buddha suits the person imbibing masculine temperament, alone.

The Buddha's acceptance of 'capability of woman' to become *arahata,* refers to the masculinity inherent in her being. Mrs. C.A.F. Rhys Davids in the introduction to *Psalms of the Sisters* (translation of *Therigāthā*) has made certain observations useful for our present discussion. While drawing a distinction between 'Indian Marys and their Christian sister's she states, that:

"But herein we note a sharp contrast between these Indian Mary's and their Christian sisters. Where, he the Central figure, intervenes, and gratitude is blent with adoration, the little poem (*Theri-gatha*) reveals no word of quasiamorous self-surrender to the person or image of the Beloved, such as characterizes not a little of that Christian literature for which the Song of Soloman--"I am my beloved's and my beloved is mine'-- was a sacred archetype".[15]

Again, Mrs. Rhys Davids comments that:

"The utmost length a *theri* presumes to go in relating herself to her Teacher, is to claim spiritual fatherhood in Him..."[16]

To add further, Mrs. Rhys Davids holds the view "that of the four notorious Magdalens who found peace and purity in the order of *Bhikkhunis*--Aḍḍhākasī, Vimlā, Abhay's mother and Ambapāli--not one expresses any deep 'feeling of personal attachment to the teacher".[17] The possibilities of imbibing feminine traits, such as, 'self-surrender', and deep personal attachment' by the *theris* numbering 101, whose, life-sketches and verses certifying the fact of having attained *arahathood*, we find in *Therīgāthā*, are ruled out. These *Therīs*, therefore, are exceptional woman being dominantly masculine in their mental disposition. This is also borne by the fact that "life under the Vinaya was one of both active and contemplative discipline".[18]

3.

Normally woman is more feminine and consequently less masculine. The feminitity inclines for love that needs a partner. This resulted in the involvement between the *Bhikkhus* and *Bhikkhunīs*. After allowing woman's admission to *Saṅgha* the Buddha told Ānanda, that:

"If, Ānanda, woman had not receive permission to go out from the household life and enter the homeless state, under the doctrine and discipline proclaimed by the (*Tathāgatā*), then would the pure religion, Ānanda, have last long, the good law would have stood fast for a thousand years. But, since Ānanda, women have now received that permission, the pure religion, Ānanda, will not now last so long, the good law will stand fast for only five hundred years".[19]

The Buddha anticipated the decline of 'good law' and 'pure religion' on account of expressive femininity of woman. The 'good' and 'pure' refers to the basic Buddhist doctrine and discipline that envisages meditation demanding fulls expression of masculinity inherent in human psyche. We know that the 'good' and 'pure' declined in due course of time because of intermixing'love' in it. Love made meditation 'bad' and 'impure'.

The Buddha's permission to woman was conditional demanding strictly observing *aṭṭhagurūdharmmā*. It is, in fact, the First Rule that caused much agitation in the minds of women for a just cause, in a way, and also for men only interested in painting the Buddha as anti-woman. The First Rule reads:

"A *Bhikkhuni*, even if of a hundred years standing, shall make salutation, to, shall rise up in the presence of, shall bow down before and shall perform all proper duties towards a *Bhikkhu*, if only just initiated..."[20]

It appears that the Rule commands subservience of *Bhikkhunis* to *Bhikkhus* irrespective of the former's seniority. But, the matter is not that simple. The Rule ought to be looked into in the background of indigenous cultural heritage. We know as Indians the value of reverence shown by man and woman for each other, in day to day living. When woman, in general, (except wife, of course) shows reverence for man, due to any reason, the latter, is handicapped to forge any sexual relation with that woman. Since, when a man gets reverence from a woman it feeds his ego. Inflow of sex leading to a relation costs man an ego and which he would rarely like to forego. The First Rule was simply to guard against an inflow of sexual feeling.[21] 'salutation', 'rising up' 'bowing down'--all these amount to show reverence for the *Bhikkhus*.

How ironic it seems to be that Ānanda who once pleaded the case of woman's admission into *Saṅgha* should ask the Buddha as to how to conduct themselves with regard to woman. The queries and its replies need to be examined in the background of Buddhist discipline. The dialogue between the Buddha and Ānanda dilating on the subject reads, thus:

> *"How are we to conduct ourselves*
>
> *Lord with regard to women-kind?"*
>
> *"As not seeing them, Ānanda"*
>
> *"But, if we should see them, what are we to do?"*
>
> *"No talking Ānanda"*
>
> *"But, if they should speak to us,*
>
> *Lord, what are we to do?*
>
> *"Keep wide awake, Ānanda"*[22]

The reference to womankind in this dialogue is generally construed to mean to denigrate woman. If we emphasize upon the expression 'seeing' and 'talking' the conclusion can not be otherwise. But, when viewed in the background of Buddhist doctrine and discipline, the emphasis should be on *"Sati Ānanda, upaṭṭhāpetabbaṁ"* or 'keep wide awake'. The *Bhikkhu* is 'to keep wide awake' at all times and in all circumstances. The reference to women is incidental.

Thus, we come across three dimensions of woman in Buddhist Canonical literature, such as, *therī*--who is exceptionally masculine and therefor has attained *Nibbāna; Bhikkhuni;* one who is on the path and an average woman who is painted licentious. The *Bhikkhu* is warned, if at all, as regard to licentious woman, one of the very popular theme in folk literature. He is also guarded against his own inflow of sexual feelings by not prejudiced against woman as such, rather, it presents a balanced view about woman.

Notes & References :

1. These ten *pārmīs* are: almsgiving *(dāna), goodness (sīla),* renunciation *(neśkamma),* wisdom *(Prajñā), energy (vīrya),* patience, *(khsānti),* truth *(Satta),* resolution *(Sankapo),* friendliness *(mettya)* and equanimity *(uppekhā).* These *pārmīs* are beautifully illustrated in *Jātaka* No. 35.
2. Mehta, Rati Lal N., *Pre-Buddhist India,* p. xix.
3. Cowell E.B. (Gen. Ed.) *Jātaka Stories,* (Vol. I+II), Vol. I, p.147.
4. *Ibid* p. 155.
5. *Ibid* p.151.
6. *Ibid* p.161.
7. Mehta, Rati Lal n., *op. cit.,* p. 289.
8. *Cullavagga* x. 1.2 to x. 1.4.
   Rhys Davids, T. W. and Oldenberg, Herman (Tr.) *Vinaya- Texts,* pp. 320-322.
9. *Ibid..*1.4. p. 322.
10. *Ibid.* x. 1.5. p. 324.
11. *Śiva-purāna: Śatarudrassaṁhitā* chapter III cf.
    Rao, Gopinath T.A., *Elements of Hindu Iconography,* Vol. II Part I, pp. 321-331. For statutes of *ardhanāriśara,* see plates No. 95-98.
12. Ā.G. p. 879.
13. Strachey, James (Gen. Ed.) *The Complete Psychological Works of Sigmund Freud,* Vol. III, p. 220
14. Nyanmoli, Bhikkhu (Tr.) *The Path of Purification*(translation of *Visuddhi magga*), pp. 102ff.

15. Rhys Davids, C.A.F., *Psalms of The Sisters-1* translation of *Therīgāthā), p. xxxii.*
16. *Idem.*
17. *Ibid*. p. xxxiii.
18. *Ibid*. p. xxxiv.
19. *Cullavagga* p. 256.
20. *Vinaya Texts, Cullavagga*, op. cit. x.1.4.
21. Rajneesh, *Essa Dhammo Sanantano*, Vol. I, p. 77.
22. *Dīgha Nikāya*, Part II, p. 141.

CHAPTER-9

SAṀSĀRA OR BUDDHIST PHILOSOPHY OF BIRTH AND DEATH

—*Rev. Narad*

That birth precedes death, and death, on the other hand, precedes birth, is one of the principal tenets of Buddhism. This constant succession of bitht and death in connection with each individual life-flux constitutes what is technically known as *Saṁsāra* (= wandering again and again).

What, then is the absolute beginning of *Saṁsāra*? Or to put it in other words, what is the ultimate origin of life? This is a question which perplexes the mind of every profound thinker. The expected answer has not yet been obtained despite the fact that it has received the attention of all thinking men, and it is not too much to say that in all probability if will never be.

The Intellectual Indian *Ṛṣis* have expended an enormous amount of labour and energy in order to comprehend this riddle of life. Deluded by the web of illusion, they have deduced all their so-called facts from the unwarranted hypothesis of an imaginary "self," and have concluded that life has for its origin the mystical *Paramātmā*.

Christianity, in attempting to give an explanation attributes everything to the fiat of an Almighty God.

With due deference to the teaching of Christ, suffices it merely to state in the words of Schopenhauer "the birth of an animal as an arising out of nothing, and accordingly, its death as an absolute annihilation, whilst man who has also originated out of nothing has yet an individual existence, is really something against which the healthy mind revolts, and which it must regard as absurd."

Unfettered by any religious belief, all dogmatic aassertions, but solely relying on *Comman sense*, modern science steps in and endeavours to tackle problem with her usual accurate investigation and ingenuity. In spite of her systematised knowledge she may fairly be compared to a child making its first observations in natural history. Nevertheless we gladly welcome her to our midst for she neither claims to be perfect, nor does she deem it a sacrilege if one has the audacity to contradict her views. To an age, or rather to people who strongly believe in the creation of an Omnipotent God, the scientific theories that life has had a beginning in the infinite past and that man is evolved from the ground ape, are indeed very valuable substitutes.

Buddhism interposes and pertinently says *"without beginning and end is Saṁsāra. A beginning of beings, en compassed by nescience,* who fettered by the thirst for life, pass on to ever new births, verily is not to be perceived." It seems further to address the enthusiastic seekers after truth and say: Young friends, worry not in vain, seeking for a beginning in a beginningless past. If life is an *identity* it must necessarily have an ultimate origin. Whether you are descended from an arboreal or ground ape, created by God or *Brahmā*, birth, death, and suffering to which all are subject in the long run, are inevitable. Seek therefore the cause of this 'faring on" that concerns all humanity, and utilise your valuable energy to transfer this life-stream to the sorrowless and peaceful state, the *Nibbāna*.

To a materialist who loves to speculate for the mere sake of argument, these words will of course be of no avail. Well, it makes no great difference to Buddhism. The word of Buddha is intended only for those sorrow-afflicted brethern to whom the *Dhamma* has become a necessity. "The *Dhamma* is like some painful cure which no rational person would undergo on its own account but because necessity compels."

In the search after the cause of birth and death Buddhism takes for its starting point the *being as he is*, here and now, and traces back the causes of his conditioned existence.

From the Buddhist point of view all men and animals are composed of inter-related mind and matter (*Nāma* and *Rūpa*) which constantly change with lightning rapidity, not remaining even for two consecutive moments the same. Though all are identical in as much as they posses the two common factors mind and matter, yet they are all so varied that, leaving animals aside, even amongst mankind no two persons are found to be alike in any respect - each person having his particular traits of character.

One might say the variation is due to heredity and environment. No doubt they are partly instrumental; but surely they cannot be solely responsible for the subtle distinctions between individuals. Otherwise we fail to understand why twins often physically alike, sharing equal privileges of up-bringing, are often temperamentally, intellectually, and morally totally different.

Tracing back the individual, therefore to the foetus in the womb to see where lies the cause, we again discover two common factors--the sperm cell and the ovum cell. Now a question might arise as to whether these two are the only materials for the production of the foetus. We must perforce answer the question in the negative. For we cannot comprehend why precisely *"he"* should spring from the particular sperm and ovum cell in question and not another, since one has equal claims as the other. Buddhism makes the matter clear by attributing this appropriation of cell-matter to the existence of a *third element* "By the conjunction of three things, O *Bhikkhus,*" runs a passage in the *Mahātaṇhā Saṅkhaya Suttanta* (No. 38) of the *Majjhima Nikāya* "does the formation of a germ of life come about. If mother and father come together but it is not the mother's proper period and the 'exciting impulse' (*Gandhabbo*) does not present itself a germ of life is not planted. If mother and father come together and it is the mother's proper period, and the 'exciting impulse' also presents itself, then a germ of life is there planted."

This newly discovered element is in the words of *Abhidhamma,* termed *Paṭisandhi Viññāṇa* (Linking consciousness).

We have now found the first term of the life's progression, but our limited knowledge does not help us to proceed further and determine the cause of this 'exciting impulse.' The Buddha however, developing a supernormal insight so as to penetrate into realms beyond the reach of normal sense, comprehended also the root of this third element. He tells us that the coming into being of the linking consciousness is dependent upon the passing away of another consciousness in a past birth, and that the process of coming-into-being and passing away is the result of an all-ruling powerful force known as *Kamma*. One might call for proofs. It must frankly be admitted that this proof cannot be furnished by an experiment upon the lecture table. Whether we believe in a past existence or not, it forms the only reasonable hypothesis which bridges certain gaps in human knowledge concerning facts of everyday life. Our reason tells us that this idea of past birth and *kamma* alone can explain the degrees of differences that exist between twins, how men like Shakespears with a very limited experience, are able to portray with marvellous exactitude the most diverse types of human character, scenes, and so forth, of which they could have no actual knowledge, why the work of the genius invariably transcends his experience, the existence of infant precocity, the vast diversity in mind and morals, in brain and physique, in conditions, circumstances, and environments, observable throughout the world, and so forth.

There is yet a further cause besides *Kamma* continues the Buddha. Not-knowing the four realities (*Saccas*), allured to life by the wholly illusory inclination to sensual pleasures, one does good and evil, which constitute what is known as *kamma*-energy that materialises in multifarious phenomena. Unknowingness (*Avijjā*) is, therefore, the cause of birth and death.; and its transmutation into knowingness or *Vijjā* is consequently their cessation.

The result of this Vibhajja method of analysis is summed up in the *Paṭicca-Samuppāda*. The *Paṭṭhāna* succinctly expresses the same in the following words: In virtue of unknowingness (Avijjā) Craving (*Taṇhā*), Activities (*Saṅkhārā*) Attachment (*Upādāna*), and Volition (*Cetanā*), arise Rebirth-Consciousness (*Paṭisandhi- Viññāna*), Mind and Matter (*Nāma-Rūpa*),Six Senses (*Salāyatana*), Contact (*Phassa*), and Sensation (*Vedanā*).

The first set of five causes produce the second set of effects which, in their trun, play the part of cause to bring about the former five. Thus the process of cause and effect continues *ad infinitum.* The beginning of the process cannot be determined as it is impossible to say since when this *life-flux was encompassed by nescience.* But when this nescience is turned into knowledge, and the *life-flux* diverted into *Nibbāna-Dhātu,* so to say, then the end of the life process or *Saṁsāra* comes about

Briefly expounding the cause of *Saṁsāra,* set forth in these enigmatic formulas of thought and dealing with the not less interesting problem of life's last episode, we find Buddhism assigning death to one of the following four causes:-

(1) The exhaustion of the force of Reproductive *Kamma* (*Janaka Kamma*) that gives rise to the birth in question (*Kammakkhaya*). The Buddisht belief is that, as a rule, the thought, volition, or desire, which is extremely strong during life-time, becomes predominant at the point of death and conditions the subsequent birth. In this last thought-moment is present a special potential force which may be either weak of strong. When the potential energy of this Reproductive *Kamma* is exhausted, the organic activities of the material form in which is corporealised the life-force, cease even before the approach of old age.

(2) The expiration of the life-term (*Āyukkhaya*). What are commonly understood to be natural deaths due to old age, may be classed under this category. There are various planes of existence according to Buddhism and to each place is assigned a definite age limit. Irrespective of the *kamma* force that has yet to run, one must, however, succumb to death when the maximum age limit is reached. It may also be said, if the force is extremely powerful the *Kamma* energy re-materialises itself in the same plane or ever in some higher realm as in the case of *Devas.*

(3) The simultaneous exhaustion of the Reproductive *Kamma*-energy and the expiration of the life-term (*Ubhayakkhaya*).

(4) The action of a stronger *Kamma* (*Upacchedaka*) that suddenly cuts off the Reproductive *Kamma* before the expiry of the life- term. A more powerful opposing force can check the path of the flying arrow and bring it down to the ground.

Just in the same way a very powerful *Kammic* force of the past is capable of nullifying the potential energy of the last thought moment and destroying the psychic life of the being. The death of Devadatta, the Judas of Buddhism, was due to an *Upacchedaka Kamma* which he committed during his current lifetime. The premeature death of the Crown Prince of Russia may also be instanced as an example of this class.

The first three types of death are collectively called *Kālamaraṇa* (timely death), and the last one is known as *Akālamaraṇa* (untimely death). An oil lamp, for instance, may get extinguished owing to any of the following four causes, namely: -- the exhaustion of the wick, consumption of oil, both exhaustion of the wick and consumption of oil, and some extraneous cause, such as wind. Death of an invidual may similarly be caused by any of the above mentioned four ways.

Explaining the cuases of death in the foregoing manner, Buddhism tells us that there are also four modes of birth, *viz,* egg-born creatures (*Aṇḍaja*) womb-born ceatures (*Jalābuja*), moisture born (*Saṁsedaja*), and creatures having spontaneous births (*Opapātika*). This broad classification embraces the entire rage of being that possess life.

Birds and snakes that are born of eggs belong to the first division

The womb-born creatures comprise all human beings, some devas inhabiting the earth, and those animals that take their concepition in a mother's womb. Those that take moisture as material for their growth, such as mosquitoes, are grouped in the third class.

Creatures having a spontaneous birth are generally invisible to the naked eye. They are said to be born with a form as if of fifteen or sixteen years of age appearing suddenly, independently of parents. Since they do not pass through the embryonic period which tends to obliterate the memories of the past, it is stated, they are capable of recollecting their past births. "Passing thence he was born as a Deva and glanced into the past to see what good act conditioned him to be born thus," is a passage which oft recurs in the Suttantas. Brahmās, Devas of heavenly realms, *Petas,* and the miserable ones who are subject to torments and sufferings in the wicked states (*Nirayas*) belong to this last division.

It must be mentioned here, before we come to deal with the actual process of re-birth, that Darwin's theory of evolution finds no place in Buddhism. Buddhists do not believe in a *succession of physical forms*. The new physical vehicle is not the successor of the past though it must be admitted that the coming into being of the present is conditioned by the passing away of the past. The multifarious forms are merely the manifestation of *Kamma*-force. "Unseen it passes whithersoever the conditions appropriate to its visible manifestation are present, here showing itself as a tiny gnat or worm, there makings its presence known in the dazzling magnificence of a Deva or an archangel's existence. When one mode of its manifestation ceases it merely passes on, and where suitable circumstances offer, reveals itself afresh in another name or form."

It is common to say after witnessing an outbreak of passion or sensuality in a person whom we deemed characterised by a high moral standard -"How could he have committed such an act., or followed such a course of conduct? It was not the least like him. It was not the least like what he appeared to others, and probably to himself." What did it denote? It denoted, Buddhists say part at any rate of what he really was, a hidden but true aspect of his actual self or in other words his *Kammic* tendencies.

Dormant but undestroyed, and with an ever present possibility of rising again there lie in us all-according to Buddhism-five natures, viz., divine (*Dibba*) human (*Mānusika*), brutal (*Tiracchīna*), ghostly (*peta*) and hellish (*Nerayika*). These natures - however civilised we may be may rise in disconcerting strength at unexpected moments so long as we are worldlings (*Puthujjana*). We live for one thought moment just as the wheel rests on the ground at one point, and are always in the present. The present is constantly slipping into the irrevocable past. Now we sow the seed of the future. Now, even now , we are creating the hells that we will be hurled into. Now even now, we are building the heavens that will comfortably accommodate us. *What we shall become is determined by this present thought moment*. In just the same way, according to Buddhist philosophy, the impending birth is determined by the immediately preceding thought which is the volition or desire that was extremely strong during our life-time. Therein, therefore, lies the possibility for the *Kamma* force that manifested in the form of a human being to re-manifest itself in the shape of the brute, ghost, *Deva* or a human being or, in other words, for a *Kammic descent in one bound* in the so called evolutionary scale of forms.

As there is the possibility for a *Kammic descent* so there is also the possibility for the contrary - a *Kammic ascent*. When the animal is about to die, for instance, it will experience a moral consciousness that will ripen into a human birth. This last thought-moment does not wholly depend on any action or thought of the animal, for generally it is dull and incapable of morality. It depends on some ancient good deed which it has done in the round of existence, and, which for a long time, has been prevented from producing its result. In its last moment the animal, therefore, cherishes ideas, desires or images which will cause a human birth.

Poussin, a French writer, illustrates this fact well by the law of heredity. "A man may be like his grandfather but not like his father. The germs of a disease have been introduced into the organism of an ancestor; for some generation they reman dormant; but suddenly they manifest themselves in actual diseases." "So intricate is the living complex, so mysterious the law of *Kamma*, so mysterious the effects of *Kamma*," a Buddhist would say.

And now to come to the most interesting and an extremely subtle point of our subject:-

Suppose a person is about to die. From the seventeenth thought- moment reckoned backward from the point of death no renewed physical functioning recures. Material qualities bor.- of *Kamma* (*Kammaja Rūpa*) arise no more, but those which come into being before the static phase of that thought moment persist till the time of the dying thought and then cease.

This critical stage may be compared to the flickering of a lamp just before it is extinguished.

To this dying man is presented a *Kamma, Kamma Nimitta*, or *Gati Nimitta*. By *Kamma* here is meant some action of his whether good or bad. It may be a weighty action (*Garuka Kamma*) such as *Samādhi* (established one pointedness of the mind) or parricide, and so forth. These are so powerful that they totally eclipse all others and appear very vividly before the mind's eye. If experience has afforded him nothing weighty he may take for his object of thought a *Kamma* done immediately before death (*Āsanna Kamma*) It would not be far from wrong to say that most of the soldiers who die fighting, would be having a death- proximate *Kamma*, such as the killing of their fellowmen. Consequently their rebirth cannot possibly be good. In the absence of an *Āsanna Kamma* a habitual meritorious or demeritorius act (*Āciṇṇa Kamma*) is presented, such as stealing in the case of a robber , or the curing of the sick in the case of a physician. Failing all these some casual act, that is one of the cumulative reserves of the endless past (*Kaṭattā Kamma*), becomes the object of thought.

By *Kamma Nimitta* is meant any sight, sound, taste, touch or idea which was obtained at the time of the commission of the *Kamma* , such as knives in the case of a butcher, patients in the case of a physician, and object of worship in the case of a devotee, etc.

Gati Nimitta is some sign of the place where he is to take birth a thing which invariably happens to dying individuals. When these indications of the future birth occur, and if they are bad they can be turned into good. This is done by influencing the thoughts of the dying man, so that his good thoughts may now act as the proximate *Kamma*, and counteract the influence of the reproductive *Kamma* which is about to effect in the next rebirth.

Taking for the object one of the above, a thought-process (*Citta- Vīthi*) then runs its course even if the death be an instantaneous one. It is said that the fly which is crushed by a harmmer on the anvil also experiences such a process of thought before it actually dies. *Abhidhamma* enumerates twenty types of rebirth processes, but as space does not permit of their description here, let us imagine for the sake of convenience that the dying person is to be re-born in the human kingdom and that the object is some good *Kamma*.

The process of decease-consciousness (*Cuti-citta-vīthi*) is as follows: - His *Bhavaṅga* consciousness is interrupted, vibrates for two thought moments and passes away, after which the mind door consciousness (*Manodvārā Viññāna*) rises and passes away.Then comes the psychologically important stage *Javana* process, which here runs only for five thought moments by reason of its weakness instead of normally seven. As such it lacks all reproductive power, its main function being the mere-regulation of the new existence. The object in the present case being desirable, the consciousness he experiences is probably moral one-automatic or volitional accompanied by pleasure, and connected with knowledge or not as the case may be. The *Tadālambana* consciousness which has for its function a registering or identifying for two moments of the object so perceived may or may not follow. After this occurs the death- consciousness (*Cuti-Citta*), the last thought moment to be experienced in this present life. There is a misconception among some that the subsequent birth is conditioned by this thought. What actually conditions re-birth, let it be said, is not this decease-thought,which in itself has no special function to perform but that which is experienced during *Javana* process.

With the ceasing of the consciousness of decease, death actually occurs. Then no more material qualities born of mind and food (*Cittaja* and *Āhāraja Rūpa*) are produced. Only a series of material qualities born of heat (*Utuja*) goes on till the corpse is reduced do dust.

By death is here meant, according to the *Abhidhamma*, *the ceasing of psychic life of one's individual existence,* or to express it in the words of a Western Philosopher, the *temporal end of a temporal phenomenon*. It is not the complete annihilation of the so-called being, for, although the organic life has ceased, the force which hitherto actuated it, is not destroyed. As the *Kammic* force remains entirely undisturbed by the disintegration of the fleeting body, the passing away of the present consciousness only conditions a fresh one in another birth. In the present case the thought experienced whilst dying being a moral one, the rebirth resultant takes of its material an appropriate sperm and ovum-cell of human parents. Simultaneous with its rising spring up the 'body-decad,' 'sex-decad,' and 'base-decad'- the seat of consciousness -(*Kāya-Bhāva- Vatthu-Desaka*) The re-birth consciousness then lapses into the sub-conscious state (*Bhavaṅga*).

"The new being which is the present manifestation of the stream of *Kamma*-energy is not the same as, and has no identity with, the previous one in its line; the aggregate that makes up its composition being different from, and having no identity with those that make up the being of its predecessor. And yet it is not an entirely different being, since it is the same stream of *Kamma*-energy, though modified perchance just by having shown itself in that last manifestation, which is now making its presence known in the sense perceptible world as the new being-" (*Na ca so na ca añño*--neither the same nor another).

The transition of the flux is also instantaneous and leaves no room whatever for any intervening stage (*Antara Bhava*). The continuity of the flux at death is unbroken in point of time. The time duration is equal to the time occupied by one thought moment i.e. less than the billionth part of the time occupied by a flash of lightining. The only difference between the passing of one thought moment to another, so to say, and of the dying thought moment to the re-birth consciousness, is that in the latter case a marked perceptible death is visible.

One might say here that a subject cannot exist without an object. What, then is the object of this sub-conscious state? The reply is : self-same object which was presented to the mind's eye immediately before death.

One might further ask:- Are the sperm and ovum-cells always ready waiting to take up this rebirth thought? As Dr. Dahlke puts it "this taking hold is not something that has law,that runs its appointed course according to definite laws, but it is law itself. A point on the ground is always ready to receive the falling stone."

We are as water-drops rushing ever onward to empty themselves inot the measureless ocean. Stealthily the days slip by; almost imperceptiby weeks gather into months. months into years; unexpectedly death finally steps in and puts an end to this brief span of life. Thus does this process of birth and death ever recur as long as the inexorable law of *Kamma* prevails.

CHAPTER-10

BUDDHIST VINAYA DISCIPLINE OR BUDDHIST COMMANDMENTS

—Dr. M. Nagai; D.Litt.

Everybody is aware of the existence of very rigid inhibitions in Buddhism, but not many persons seem to know for certain what their nature is, what significance and value they possess in Buddhism, how far they can be practised in the present age and if practised what value they possess. The object of this chapter is to throw some light on such questions.

Vinaya has been recognized from ancient times to be so important a component of Buddhist texts that in the first period of Buddhism it was given the same position as *Dhamma* (*Dhamma* and *Vinaya*), and in the next was included in the *Ti-piṭaka* (Three baskets) or the complete holy texts of Buddhism in the order of *Sutta, Vinaya* and *Abhidhamma*. In fact from very ancient times *Vinaya* has been given so great regard that at one time it was even put first in the order of the *Ti-piṭaka, Sutta* being placed next and *Abhidhamma* last, it being believed that Vinaya was āyu (life) or the very life of Buddhism and as long as it was observed the true religion would live, but if it were ignored the true religion would perish. Even at the present time this belief is very much alive among the so called Southern Buddhists of Ceylon and Siam. In China and Japan we have a sect known by the name of Risshū (lit. *Vinaya* Sect), which was founded on the teaching contained in the Shibun-ritsu (*Vinaya* of *Dhammaguttika).* It goes without saying that this sect makes the Vinaya-piṭaka the fountain head of its life.

What is *Vinaya* which has been given such importance? In a word, it is nothing but a series of prohibitions placed on conduct of *Bhikkhus* and *Bhikkhunīs* in their daily life, prescribing what they should not do. It is a code of negative morality consisting as it does of so many "don'ts." It is true that the Risshū (the *Vinaya* Sect) divides its text (the Shibun-ritsu) on which it stands, into two parts so as to make the first part (*Sutta-vibhaṅga* in Pāli) contain only negative commandments aimed at prevention of evil doings and the second (*Khandhaka* in Pāli) positive commandments aimed at encouragement of good deeds. But even the second part is in its essentials but an array of prohibitive or negative commandments, so that it is only right to regard it as an extension of the negative commandments making up the first part. A passage found in the preface to the commentary on a *Vinaya-piṭaka* in Chinese, which is to the effect that the fundamental character of *Vinaya* is restraint or prohibitive and negative one, well defines the basic motive with which it was instituted. In the *Zenken- ritsu-bibasha* or *Shan-chien Lip' a*-sa (lit the well looking *Vinaya-Vibhāṣā*)[1] in Chinese and also in the *Samantapāsādikā* in Pāli, which are commentaries on the *Vinayapiṭaka,* it is explained that *Vinaya* is the checking of various evil dees of body (*kāyakamma*), speech (*vacīkamma,* and thought' (*manokamma*). In such ways,*Vinaya* being mainly inhibitions concerning the daily life of priests and priestesses, we have to see why were and what made such prohibitions necessary. In other words, we have to investigate the condition of society or background existing at the time it appeared which made its institution imperative. It would be a great mistake, were one, without paying due attention to the causes time place and men, that necessitated the institution of it, to conclude that only because Buddha had instituted it,it should be strictly and literally observed. Such idea, it seems to me, is born of th narrow spirit of the socalled Hīnayāna school and will ultimately lead to the death of the spirit of Buddhism. On the contrary we should understand the fundamental motive with which *Vinaya* was instituted and adapt it to the needs of age, country and men, viz. society. This is realizing the true spirit of the so-called Mahāyāna school. That Buddhism continues to be a great living force in Japan is due to the fact that this spirit has never died among Japanese Buddhists.

Six Chinese translations of the *Vinaya-piṭaka* are existent, these being the so-called four *Vinaya-piṭakas* consisting of the *Jūju-ritsu* (*Vinaya* of old Sabbatthivādin), the *shibunritsu* (*Vinaya* of *Dhammaguttika*), the *Makasogi-ritsu (Vinaya* of *Mahāiṁsāsakā),* one called the *Konpon-setsu- issai-ubu-Vinaya (Vinaya* of new *Sabbatthivādin),* which was translated very much later than those four and one called simply Vinaya, which was translated earliest of all. Of the last mentioned only the first half of the *Vinaya-piṭaka,* which corresponds to *Suttavibhaṅga,* is existent. It is probably for this reason that it is not usually included in the list of the *Vinaya piṭaka* in Chinese, At any rate, these six *Vinaya- piṭakas* are existent, in addition to Pāli version.We have thus seven varieties of the *Vinaya-piṭak,* but looked from the points of the so-called Mahāyāna *Vinaya,* they belong to the so-called Hīnayāna *Vinaya* and are substaintially the same. As commentaries on the *Vinaya-piṭaka,* we have five treatises.These are the *Bini-mo-ron* (lit *Vinaya-mātā- vaṇṇanā,* the *Matoroga-ron* (lit, *mātikā* or *mātṛkā-vaṇṇan),* The *Zenken ron* (lit *pāsādikāvaṇṇanā*), the *Sabbata-ron* (lit *sabbatthi-vaṇṇanā*) and the *Myoryo-ron* (lit *pākaṭa vaṇṇakas* are called five ron (the classical Chinese for *vibhāṣā* or *vaṇṇanā* in this case). Of these the *Zenken-ron* or *Zenkern ritsu bibasha* was for a long time considered a commentary on the *Shibun-ritsu,* the *Vinaya* of *Dhammaguttika,* but this idea is wrong. It corresponds to the *Samantapāsādikā* which is a commentary on the Pāli version, and should not be taken as a commentary on any of the Chinese versions of the *Vinaya-piṭaka*. In order to know the contents of the *Vinaya,* any version will serve the purpose. As, however, the *Shibun-rtsu* was the foundation on which the *Risshū* (*Vinaya* Sect) was set up and has a close relation with Japanese and Chinese Buddhism I propose to discuss the subject of Buddhist inhibitions with this version as pivot.

Now in this version of *Vinaya* there are found 250 inhibitions (*sikkhāpada*) for *bhikkhus* (priests) and 341 for *bhikkhunīs* (priestesses). The 250 inhibitions for priests are classified as follows.

1. *Pārājika* 4
2. *saṅghāvaśeṣa (saṅghādisesa)* 13

3. *aniyata*	2
4. *niḥsargika-pātayantika (nissaggiya-pācittiya)*	30
5. *pātayantika (pācittiya)*	90
6. *pratideśanīya (paṭidesanīya)*	4
7. *śaikṣa (sakhiya)*	100
8. *adhikaraṇa-śamatha0 (samatha)*	7
total	250

It may be said of the above-mentioned inhibitions, the most important for Buddhist priests are the four pārājika. These are (1) Inhibition against any amourous relation with a woman, which is called inhibition against impurity or against lusts of the flesh. This inhibition has an additional one, which is an injunction against similar connection with a beast. (2) Inhibition against taking possession of anything not given, namely against stealing. This is called inhibition against taking possession of things not given or against stealing (3) Inhibition against homicide, including any act extolling the beauty of death,which might tempt a man to seek death. This is called inhibition against cutting off the life of a man or against homicide (4) Inhibition against speaking as if one has already mastered all that could be learned concerning the way of entering priesthoood before he has not, with the object of obtaining gifts from laity. This particular kind of lying set against ordinary lying was considered graver in wickedness and the inhibition against it is called inhibition against pretending enlightenment or against major lying.

A priest violating any of the above-mentioned four *pārājika* is excommunicated, that is to say, disqualified from re-entering into priesthood. These inhibitions are represented as four 'not to be done' (*cattāri akaraṇīyāni*) in the *Mahāvagga* of the *Vinaya- piṭaka* and the *Kammuvāca*, which came into being sometime late. According to these, a priest, who has committed an act of impurity is no longer a follower of Buddha and like a man, who cannot live on after having had his head cut off, has lost his life as priest. Such a priest is so utterly condemned that he is compared to a dead leaf torn off from a branch, which can never recover its green freshness, or a rock split into two, which cannot be joined together, or a *tāla*-tree or fan-palm which, having had its upper stem cut off, cannot grow and is doomed to death. It appears to me that of the above mentioned four *pārājika* the most difficult to keep for priest of the present time is the first namely the inhibition against impurity, the other three being comparatively easy to be confronted. As for the first inhibition, I propose to deal with it a little more fully later on.

The thirteen *saṅghāvaśeṣas* that come next are inhibitions of less gravity, it being prescribed that a priest who has violated any of the inhibitions in this group shall be condemned to isolated living that is to say, he shall be isolated from his *saṅgha* (church) to live alone for six days to undergo *mānatta* (penance) and be recalled when he has shown himself repentant. The act which are forbidden under this penalty are : (1) self-abuse, except involuntary pollution while asleep, (2) touching a woman with an immoral motive, (3) speaking loosely to a woman with an immoral motive, (4) insinuating a woman to offer her person after praising himself, (5) arranging a marriage or helping lovers to meet, (6) exceeding prescribed measures in building unaided by donors a small house on his own account without bearing the opinion of his *saṅgha* (church), (7) exceeding prescribed measures in building aided by donors a large house without hearing the opinion of his *saṅgha,* (8) attempting in an excess of anger to charge without ground another priest with an offence of *pārājika,* (9) persecuting another priest by interpreting as an offence of *pārājika* a blunder committed by him which bears resemblance to it, (10) plotting rupture of his *saṅgha* refusing to listen to adviceto stop it, (11) abetting the above mentioned act, (12) breaking into another man's house and acting violently without listening to remonstra ıce, and (13) being obstinate, refusing to follow advice of other priests. All these acts were no doubt of great importance to the *saṅgha* at that time the inhibition was laid down and established against them. Even now such an act as plotting rupture of one's *saṅgha* (church) is highly objectionable and one must refrain from committing any of the act above enumerated towards women. In fact, the above-mentioned inhibitions contain much which priests and laymen of to day alike must faithfully observe.

Next in order come two *Aniya-dhammas,* the term meaning indefinite rules. It was so called because a priest, who was found to be sitting with a woman in a secluded or exposed place, and was suspected of his act was judged on the strength of evidence given by a trustworthy *upāsikā* (believing woman) whether he was guilty of violation of *pārājika, saṅghāvaseṣa (saṅghādidesa)* or *(pātayantika-pācittiya).* Seen from the standpoint of to-day, the acts prescribed are not of much importance.

The fourth class of inhibitions is thirty *niḥsargika pātayantika (nissaggiy-pācittiya).* These are mostly inhibitions concerning clothes and contain two concerning bowls. Briefly all these may be said to be commandments requiring a priest to hold a spirit of unselfishness by getting rid of avarice and be content with only a little in regard to these things. It must not be forgotten that the inhibitions grouped in this class were instituted more than 2,000 years ago and had as their background life in a warm country like India. To try to obey the inhibitions literally without regard to time, place and society is in my opinion next to madness. There is, however, one inhibition which holds good for al times, places and men. It is to the effect that a priest shall not try to make his own anything that has been given to be made the common property of a body to which he belongs.

Next come ninety *pātayantka (pācittiya).* A priest committing any of the sins prescribed against in this class of inhibitions was pardoned on repentance being shown. Ninety items are mentioned in the *Shibun-ritsu-biku-kaihon (Bhikṣu-Pātimokṣa-Sūtra* of the *Dhammaguttika)* but the *Bhikku-Pātimokkha* of Pāli version contains ninety two.

Many of the inhibitions in this group appear to us to be nonsensical. For instance, a priest is forbidden to dig the ground by himself or cause somebody to do so. He is also prohibited from travelling together or taking the same boat with a priestess or a laywoman by appointment. At the time these inhibitions were instituted, there was no doubt good reason, but were we to try to obey them to-day formally without considering the motive underlying them, we would be compelled to keep ourselves away from a railway train, a steamer or a tram-car. There is one inhibition, which is particularly anachronic. It is to the effect that a priest shall not take meal after midday. Such an inhibition cannot be observed at the present time unless by a man in certain special conditions. These are also inhibitions against witnessing a military review or a battle after spending a few nights with troops. But the ninety *Pātayantika* include some commandments, which hold true for all time, places and men, these being inhibitions against lying, using abusive language, being double-tongued and drinking.

We now come to four ways of repentance and one hundred *Śaiṣa*. The latte consist chiefly of detailed injunctions concerning the etiquette and manners of a priest, the way of wearing clothes and the table manner. In this case, too, we should remember the conditions of the church and society of the time which necessitated the institution of these injunctions and appreciate the fundamental motive with which they were established, which was, after all, to enjoin dignty and politeness in the daily life of a priest. For instance, there is no reason why a priest, when taking meal, should follow the table manner, which was prescribed on the basis of the Indian custom of eating with hand, instead of using chopsticks or a knife and a fork. As for the seven *Adhikaraṇa-śamatha* (settlement of cases) that constitute the last class of inhibitions, any full discussion may be dispensed with, as they are simply rules showing how to settle disputes that may arise in the church.

The inhibitions so far dealt with are those that may be called fundamental inhibitions and looked from the standpoint of the Mahāyana school of Buddhism are what are made light of as of the Hīnayāna school. And as time went on, the 250 inhibitions (as specified in the *Shibun-ritsu*) were found to be insufficient and some were supplemented thereto, these new additions being minor inhibitions found at intervals among the so-called positive commandments, which are included in the *Khandhaka* of Pāli version. In the Pāli version or others, it is mentioned that priests can eat fish and meat which are pure to them in three cases; if they do not see slaughter, if they do not hear of it, if they do not suspect it to have been done for them. Such fish and meat are pure ones. In the *Shibun-ritsu* it is mentioned that eating of the meat of an elephant, a horse, a dog or a dragon is *dukkaṭa-offence* and that of human meat *thullaccaya* offence. Eating of garlic (*lasuna*) is also mentioned as *dukkaṭa*-offence, but this offence being one later added is not found included in the fundamental inhibitions. It is noteworthy that these supplementary inhibitions are given the name of *thullaccaya* or *dukkaṭa* and are not mentioned under the old classification such as *pārājika* and *saṅghāvaśeṣa*.

According to the *Vinaya-piṭkaka*, the fundamental inhibitions were as a matter of course, but all the supplementary minor ones were instituted by Buddha from time to time as the occasion demanded. This allegation was most probably made for the purpose of making the commandments authoritative. In fact, I can hardly believe that even the foundametal inhibitions were all established by Buddha, for it is impossible to think that He was so lacking in personal authority and influence that in order to maintain discipline in His *saṅgha* or chuch He was obliged to draw up a code very much akin in character to a penal law. No doubt He had occasions to reprove some of his disciples for misdemeanours and it is most likely that words spoken by Him on such occasions were remembered and later compiled a sort of law. In all likelihood it was in such a way that the fundametal inhibitions were set up. In other words, as it was found that after the demise of Buddha, His influence gradaully waned, while the *saṅgha,* He had founded, gained in extension but lost in discipline, the institution of such strict inhibitions was, as I take it, made imperative in order to be kept intact. Thus undue importance began to be given to the commandments, until they were made into a sort of sacred and inviolable rules and in regard to their application their underlying spirit was sacrificed for formality. For instance, it was considered that in an act of stealing there must be five conditions in order to interpret it as an offence of *pārājika;* first the thing stolen must be the property owned by another person; secondly the man stealing it must be conscious that it belongs to another person; thirdly it must be a valuable thing worth more than five *māsaka* (penny); fourthly than stealing it must have an intention to do so; fifthly, it must be removed from the postion which it occupies. Suppose a man goes in search for a treasure with the intention to steal it. In India valuables are kept buired under the ground. Accordingly on such an expedition he carries with him a hoe and a basket (*piṭaka*). He reaches a spot, where he thinks some treasure lies buried under, and after removing grass and vines growing over it, digs the ground and finds as he expects, a pot containing treasures. In case he moves it, he is considered guilty of *thullaccaya,* but he is guilty of *pārājika* only in case he removes it even by an inch. With regard to the inhibition against drinking too, wine is defined in respect to colour, smell and taste and one is said to have committed *dukkaṭa-offence* when he drinks what he takes for wine but which is not really wine, while one is said to be guilty of *pācittiya* in case he drinks wine without being aware that it is wine. All such restrictions place importance on results only at the expense of motives and are incompatible with the fundamental spirit of Buddhism, which regards will (*mano*) as of supreme importance. Were this sort of things carried to the extreme, the spirit of Buddhism would be destroyed by formality.

There are also commandments to *Bodhisattva,* which were drawn up after the example of the above-mentioned commandments to *bhikkhus.* These inhibitions include four *pārājika,* which are (1) to abuse other persons by speaking highly of one's virtues with some selfish aim, (2) to be chary of one's property and not to pity the poor and give them alms and to refuse to teach the *Dhamma* to those who desire to learn of it, (3) to utter abusive language against some person and not content with it, to strike him with hand or stick or stone and to refuse to listen to remonstrances, and (4) to speak ill of the *Piṭaka* of *Bodhisattva* and preach a similar *dhamma* and endeavour to establish it, but after wards to repent and follow the adive of other persons. The commandments to *Bodhisattva* also contain about forty inhibitions under the name of many *dukkaṭa* offences.' As for the four *pārājika* included in the commandments to *Bodhisattva,* they are altogether different in character from those included in the commandments to *bhikkhus.* In short the former is found to be much more altruistic than the latter. In a chapter entitled the *Bosatsu-shin-ji-Kaihon* (*Bodhisattva citta- bhuūmi-sikkhāpada*) of the *Bonmo-kyo* (the *Brahmajālasutta*),[2] ten *pārājika* offences are mentioned. These are (1) homicide, (2) stealing, (3) indulging in licentiousnes, (4) criticising other persons' sins and shortcomings, (7) denouncing other persons by praising oneself, (8) refusing to give alms by being miserly (9) abusing another person in anger and striking him with hand, sword or stick, and (10 disparaging "three sacred treasures" -

namely, Buddha *Dhamma* and *Saṅgha*. These are offences, against which major inhibitions are provided. Next to them forty-eight minor offences (*dukkaṭa*) are described. Among the inhibitions of this group there are one against taking up a wine cup with the object of urging a man to drink, it being said that one who commits this offence will be reborn five hundred times without hands, one against eating all kinds of meat and five things of hot taste (such as garlic and onion) and one against killing nd eating all living creatures, it being taught that as all men are one's father and all women one's mother, while all creatures transmigrating the six stages or existence are one's parents, one who kills and eats any of them is guilty of patricide and also of eating one's own flesh in a former existence. As compared with the inhibitions for *bhikkhus* (priests), these inhibitions for *Bodhisattva* display a spirit of altruism. The following comparison will classify the points just mentioned:

Pārājika for Bhikkhus.

1. Obscenities
2. Stealing
3. Homicide.
4. Major lying

Pārājika for Bodhisattva.

1. Obscenities.
2. Stealing.
3. Homicide.
4. Lying.
5. Selling intoxicants.
6. Criticising shortcomings. of four classes of people (*bhikkhu, bhikkhumī, sāmanera, sāmanerī*).
7. Denouncing other persons and praising one self.
8. To be miserly and to inflict injuries on other persons.
9. To be in anger and reject advice.
10. To slander Three Sacred Treasures (Buddha, *Dhamma, Saṅgha*).

Looked from the standpoint of the Mahāyāna school these inhibitions for *bhikkhus* are nagative commandments and are no more than so-called *Setsu-ritsugi-kai* (controlling one's acts). The commandments laid down by the Mahāyāna school, however, are more positive and lay stress on *Setsu Zenbo-kai* (holding of good deeds) and *Setsu-Shujo-kai* (benevolence towards all creatures). While *Vinaya* is negative in nature as already explained, *Sīla* comprises all Buddhist moral rules both positive and negative. In this essay, I confine myself to the discussion of *Vinaya*.

There are five commandments for devout laymen (*upāsaka*) and devout laywomen (*upāsikā*), these being not to kill, not to steal, not to commit adultery with others' wives, not to tell a lie, and not to drink, while for novices (*sāmanera*) the following ten commandments are laid down: "not to kill not to steal, not to commit obscenities, not to speak falsehood, not to drink not to see plays and dancing, not to apply perfumed oil to the body, not to sit high, not to eat at an unusual time, and not to accept money." As the result of my study of this subject, I have arrived at a theory that for devout laymen (*upāsaka*) the Three Refuges (Buddha, *Dhamma* and *Saṅgha*) only were established, but in view of the fact that before them *bhikkhus* were given 250 inhibitions (227 in Pāli version) and novices ten commandments it was concluded that they should have at least five commandments and the first five were chosen for them from the ten commandments for novices, amending the third commandment not to commit obscenities (*abrahmacariyā veramaṇi*), not to commit an illegitimate act of lewdness (*kāmesu micchācārā veramaṇī*). As a matter of fact although killling, stealing, visiting a woman who is not one's lawful wife, telling a lie and drinking wine are mentioned in the *Dhammapada* as five evil and in the Chinese versions of the *Vinaya-piṭaka* the five commandments to be strictly observed by devout laymen (*upāsaka*) are mentioned, yet in the *Vinaya piṭaka* and *Nikāya* of Pāli version devout laymen are described to have taken refuge in Three Treasures only, it seems that the Chinese versions were brought into being after the five commandments for laymen were established. I cannot believe by all means that during the time Buddha walked on earth, anything like penal code was in force requiring even priests and priestesses to observe "such and such commandments under such and such penalties," though he no doubt warned them against misconduct from time to time. Much less can I believe that such formal commandment as the ten for novices or the five devout layment were established in this time. It may be supposed that those, who followed Buddha, during his lifetime, did not need any formal commandment as they lived and behaved themeselves under influence and inspiration of the perfect personal character of their great teacher. As Buddha taught during a long period of forty five years even if inhibitions were given in order to maintain order and discipline in the church, they no doubt came into being as already said, with place, time and actor as background. In view of this there is no need for Buddhist priests and believers of the present day, who live in different time place and environment, to observe those commandments literally, though of course they must respect the spirit with which the inhibitions were established and live in conformity with it.

With regard to the problem of inhibition of priests, one that will remain perplexing for a long time to come is the inhibition concerning sexual relations.To me it appears that the problem of inhibitions for the Buddhist priests of the presnet day (except those belonging to the *Shinshū* sect) depends upon the manenr of interpretation of this particular inhibition. If it is interpreted as one requiring all Buddhist priests to observe celibacy, I fear that very few priests will be found living in Japan, who are really worthy of the name *bhikkhu*. With regard to the five commandments for laymen, the one, that will be found extremely difficult to keep by ordinary devout layment is the commandment not to kill (even a worm). For fishermen and hunters and people like Mongolians who make pork their staple food, the commandments is one that is impossible to obey. If the five commandments must be strictly obeyed a man like myself has no qualification even of an *upākasa*. I would rathr be a simple *upāsaka* taking refuge in the Three Sacred Treasures. In one of his messages to his believers, Saint Shinran, the founder of the *Shinshū Sect*, wrote; "I should think it very wicked to believe to be right for a man to act as he pleases, namely to allow himself to do what he should not do to say what he should not say and to think what he should not think." The idea underlying the passage quoted of the great exponent of the doctrine of salvation by faith seems to sum up the proper attitude of mind the present day followers of Buddha should take. In other words, we should always bear in mind the spirit of the commandments, which requires us to abstain as much as possible from doing all evils of body, speech and mind, and endeavour to elevate our character. We should look within ourselves, find out whatever shortcomings we may posses and then institute inhibitions for ourselves in whatever number. In my opinion, in order to become true followers of Budhha we need not literally follow the five commandments, or the ten commandments or the two hundred and fifty commandments.

Notes and References :

1. See Takakusu's A Pali Chrestomeathy' pp. lxxii - lxxix
2. Quite different from *Brahmajāla Sutta* in the *Dīgha-Nikāya*.

CHAPTER-11

THE MIDDLE-WAY BETWEEN WAR AND PEACE

—Dr. Harcharan Singh Sobti, M.A; LL.B; Ph.D.

The Buddha's Way is the Middleway. And, Middleway means balancing between two extremes. War and peace-these are two extremes. Dilating on peace, one may allege, is to move from one extreme to another. Rather, it may be defied as deviation from the Way of the Buddha. Viewed in this perspective, can (or should) the Buddhist view adhere to and preach the practice of the Middleway between war and peace?

This is the dilemma, I propose to examine in this paper.

What are precisely the nuances of the Buddha's Middleway? The Middleway discovered by the Buddha, if one cares to appreciate, impels one in no other way than to enter upon to enquire into the anatomy of the functioning of the human mind. Mind, according to Buddhism, is the main motivating force that governs the entire gamut of man's *Saṁsāric* living. In the opening verse of the *Dhammapada*, mind is introduced as "fore- runner of all conditions. Mind is chief: and the *cetasikas* or the mental concomitants are mind-made".[1] The *modus- operandi* of mind, therefore, is to move. The mind can only move between the extremes of past and future. Movement of mind is not possible in the present. In the present there is no space, at all, required for the mind to move. Furthermore, thinking, an activity of mind exists only, when the mind can function. When the mind is brought in the middle i.e. in the present, through meditation or with an aid of any other device, the mind simply disappears, or, in other words one acquires a state of no mind. Not only the mind thus disappears, its contents such as thoughts and ego, very subtle material entities, disappear, as well. Motivations are dropped. One is neither an indulgent nor an ascetic. In the middle, one truly becomes spiritual. This is being balanced, being *Samyak*.[2]

Shakespear's play *King Lear* depicts, in some form, both an extreme and middle positions taken up by three daughters of King Lear. The king decides to divide his kingdom into three as as 'to shake all cares and business from his age, conferring them on younger strengths.' And addresses his daughters thus:

"Tell me, my daughters

... ...

which of you shall we say doth love us most?

... ...[3]

Goneril, the eldest-born speaks first:

"Sir, I love you more than my words
can wield the matter.
Dearer than eye-sight, space and liberty;
... ...
As much as child e'er loved, or father found,
... ..."[4]

The text of the play, after this, reads as:

"Cordelia (aside) What shall Cordelia do /
Love, and be silent."[5]

Next to speak is Regan:

... ...

"In my true heart
I find she names my very deed of love;
Only she comes too short: That I profess
Myself an enemy of all other joys
Which the most precious square of sense possesses.
And find I am alone felicitate
In your dear highness' love"[6]

Now is the turn of Cordelia, 'So young and true.'

At her father's command, she expresses:

"Cordelia: Nothing my Lord.

Lear : Nothing?

Cordelia : Nothing.

Lear : Nothing will come of nothing: Speak again.

Cordelia;... ....

I love your majesty

According to my bond, no more no less.

(Cordelia continues) ... .

Why have my sisters husbands, if they say

They love you all? Happily when I shall wed.

That lord whose hand must take my plight shall carry

Half my love with him, half my cares and duty

Sure I shall never marry like my sisters,

To love my father all."[7]

King Lear expects love from his daughters in terms of 'most'. Goneril and Regan, with an aid of clever use of the words, satisfy King Lear's ego. Later on, both of them, after manipulating their equal share of kingdom, divided into two, take the extreme positions, in conduct, in reverse order. Cordelia too, loves her father and prefers to remain silent and say 'nothing,' which, in a way, speaks of her being in the middle. Cordelia's position, when she is made to express herself, and she does, in terms of 'no more no less' is no other than of middle way. She is'no more and no less' in the given situation, than being *Samyak*, being balanced. King Lear at a later stage, adores Cordelia, when she is no more, with these words:

"Her voice was ever soft,

Gentle and low, an excellent thing in women."[8]

These are some of the noble qualities of a person, rooted in the Middleway.

Pāli Canon is full of such references, which, fully substantiate the view that the Buddha's way is the Middleway. The very fact that the Buddha, in his very First Sermon, identified as *Dhammacakkapavattana Sutta,* should name his way as *Majjhima paṭipadā* or the Middleway, hardly leaves any scope for conjectures, with regard to the identity of the Way. The Buddha spelled out his Way, as below:

"These two extremes, brethren should not be followed by one who has gone forth as a wanderer;

Devotion to the pleasures of senses-a low and pagan practice, unworthy, unprofitable, the way of the world (on the one hand) and on the other hand devotion to self-mortification. which is painful, unworthy, unprofitable

By avoiding these two extremes he who hath won the Truth (the Buddha) has gained knowledge of that Middlepath..."[9]

Initially, of course, the Buddha, as the instant *Sutta* suggests, devised the Middleway only for those who had already entered the state of homelessness; but it would be erroneous to construe that the Way is meant, exclusively, for the *Bhikkhus* to practise. The Buddha, here, referred to the specific kind of extremes of self-indulgence and self-mortification to transcend, otherwise there would be hindrances in the way of spiritual progress. The realization, as such, was not the result of a rationalistic grasp of the situation,rather was based on his experiments and experiences. But, the middle between any set of extremes, if once achieved is decidedly to transform the entire outlook. The Middleway, then, never remains an isolated phenomenon, it becomes a pattern--a universal principle--and encompasses all pairs of extremes within its range of operation.

There is a beautiful illustrative reference highlighting the significance of the practising of the Middleway. Under the caption *Soṇassa pabbajja*, in the fifth chapter of *Mahāvagga*, the first sub-part of the book *Khandhaka*, it is recorded that Soṇa after his ordination at the hands of the Buddha, went to *Sitavana* to practise meditation. The manner he adopted was, "walking up and down all the while; so much so that his feet began to bleed profusely".[10] The Buddha came to know of it and went to him. The Buddha could very well see that Soṇa had failed to practise meditation, successfully. The Buddha, during the discourse, reminded Soṇa, of those days, prior to becoming *Bhikkhu*, when the latter could play upon *Vinā*, skillfully. Thus, the Buddha helped Soṇa in restoring the balance of his psyche, while making use of the analogy of *Viṇā*. The Buddha, ultimately, made him realize that when the strings of *Viṇā* are "neither too much stretched nor loose, but fixed in even proportion", i.e. in the middle, only then it is in a "fit state to be played upon".[11] The same principle, whenever, followed must prove fruitful.

The position taken up by the Buddha with regard to metaphysical questions, demanding answers in terms of either/or, is not different and corroborates the view that the Buddha's Way is the Middleway. There is a list of ten questions that T.W. Rhys Davids calls 'indeterminates' that the Buddha refused to entertain and answered through noble silence.[12] For instance, to the question put forth by a wandering ascetic Vacchagotta, whether 'I' is existent or not existent the Buddha kept silent.[13] The Buddha refused to take either position for the simple reason that such attempts would not help, being not conducive in solving the self- evident problem of human Suffering. This indicates not only the Buddha's attitude of indifference towards futile doctrinal exercises, but, also, lays stress upon his foremost preference for contemplating on the practical side of human predicament. Besides, the Buddha's silence in the instant case is prompted by his awareness of the import of the Middleway.

The Buddha, of course, observed silence and did not take sides when metaphysical issues were involved. But, to presume that he always remained and preached indifference to whatever the situation might be, is to misconceive the Buddha's Middleway. In *Kuṇāla Jātaka* (No. 536) the Buddha appears in the battle-field as a peacemaker. The Skāiya and Koliya, both the tribes used to avail the water of *Rohiṇi*-river for cultivating agricultural land. Then at one time, quarrel arose over the distribution of the river-water. The mighty kings of both the tribes, alongwith their armed forces had arrived at the battle-field. Both the sides were ready to attack each other, when, the Buddha reached there, on the spot.

Buddhaghosa's Jātakaṭṭhakathā records these crucial moments, *as:*

The Buddha asked, "Why are ye come here, mighty kings?"

"Holy Sir" they answered, "We are come, neither to see this river, nor to disport ourselves, but to get up a fight."

"What is the quarrel about, Sirs?"

"About the water."

"What is the water worth?"

"Very little, Holy Sir."

"What is the earth worth?"

"It is of priceless value."

"What are, worriors chief worth?"

"They too are of priceless value."

"Why on account of some worthless water are you destroying chiefs of high worth.?"[14]

The Buddha's pursuasion worked and both the mighty kings were dissuaded with success, from waging war and to settle their dispute, peacefully. Both the mighty kings after taking refuge in the Buddha, confessed, that:

"Had not the Master come, we should have slain one another and set flowing rivers of blood. It is owing to the Master that we are alive."[15]

The peaceful settlement arrived at between the two mighty kings not only timely saved the kingdoms from turning into 'the river of blood', but it also initiated the principle of peaceful co- existence to prove mutually beneficial in future too, if followed without reservations.

The Super Powers, today, are ready to wage war, presumably against each other, armed with nuclear weapons. As referred to, earlier, that in the middle when ego disappears, one truly becomes spiritual. True and enduring Compassion (not of political nature) springs up only when and where there is a spiritual balance. The Super Powers intend to cause a diversion and thus propagate that they are manufacturing nuclear weapons for the beneficial use and/or for their respective survival, whereas the truth is that they are in competition with each other. Their prestige is involved; their ego is at stake. In short: they are caught in their own net-the spider's web.

The Buddha's main thrust, as it is amply clear from his Sermons, was to eliminate Suffering and for which he succeeded in discovering the Middleway further elaborated into eight steps reckoned as *ariyo aṭṭhaṅgiko maggo* or

Noble-Eight-fold Path. The significant thing is not the number of steps but the term *sammā* preflexed to each step.[16] In *Pāli English Dictonary* the term *sammā,* and its variations are described as: 'calm, in the right way, as it ought to be, perfectly and in harmony.[17] To sum up: *sammā,* further conforms to the principle and practice of the Middlewayed-ness.

The need of the hour, today, is to set the turbulent world-our ancestral home-in order and to contribute to reshape it as to make it conducive for the spiritual health of mankind. Using Keats's phrase 'What ails thee oh World?" It is extremism, manifesting in multiple forms that is causing grave anguish. The world, today, stands sharply divided into hostile ideological camps. At times, we pursue our national policies, deliberately, ignoring international interests, as if both the spheres are mutually exclusive. Zangwill seems to set the record straight when he writes that. "It takes two men to make one brother. Internationalism, far from being the antitheses of nationalism, actually requires nations to inter relate"[18] The *others* too have every right to prosper the way they Will. To subscribe to this view is to uphold the Doctrine of the Middleway. A.J. Bahm is not far from truth, when discussing the Buddha's Middlway, he observes that, "The Middleway avoids extremes yet it does not extremely avoid extremes"[19] So, the situation plays its role. The world situation, today, is such that the Middleway is the only way out from potential threats of nuclear war and must not be only advocated, but ought to be practised, even if, it is denigrated as cowardice. The precept of peaceful co-existence is the Middleway between war and peace. If practised without reservation, can go a long way to scatter dark clouds of nuclear war destined to destroy *us* and the *others.*

Notes and References :

1. *Manopubbaṅgamā dhammā manoseṭṭhā manomayā.* Narad, Mahāthera, *The Dhammapada,* pp. 3,319,320.

2. Rajnesh, Bhagwan, *The Hidden Harmony:Discourses on the Fragments of Heraclitus,* pp. 43-44, 84,88.

3-7. Shakespere, William, *King Lear,* Act I, Scene I.

8. Ibid., Act V, Scene 3.
9. Mv. i. 10. (*Dhammacakkapvattana Sutta*). *Dve me bhikkhave antā pabbajitena na sevītabbā. Katame dve? Yo cāyaṁ kāmesukāmāsukhallikānuyogo hīno gammo pothujjoniko anariyo anathasaṁhito, yo cāyaṁ atthakilamatanu yogo dukkho anariyo anathasaṁhito. Aito kho, bhkkhave ubhoante anupagamma, majjhimāpaṭipadā tathāgatena...*
   Woodward, F.L., *Some Sayings of the Buddha*, p. 7.
10. Mv. i. 181ff. cf. *Theragāthā*, verses: 632-644; Guttila Jātaka No. 243.
    Rhys Davids, T.W. and Oldenberg, H. , *Vinaya Texts*.
11. Ibid., p.9.
12. Rhys Davids, T.W., *Early Buddhism*,p. 69, cf. S. iv. 373ff.
13. S.iv. 400. Grimm, George, *The Doctrine of the Buddha*, p.140.
    Also see, Chapter, *Dukkha*, p.215.
14. (i) Fausboll. V. The *Jātakas*, Vol. V, p.144.
    (ii) Cowell, E. B. The *Jātakas*, Vol. v, p.220.
    cf. The Ceylonese Chronicle: *Mahāvaṁsa, 1.12ff*.
15. Ibid. (i) p.414.
    Ibid. (ii) p. 221.
16. Mv.i. 10: *ayaṁ eva ariyo aṭṭhangiko maggo. sammā diṭṭhi ...sammā samādhi*.
17. Rhys Davids, T. W. and Stede, William, *The Pali-English Dictionary*, p. 695.
18. Quoted in, Narla, V. R., *Traditional Indian Culture and other Essays*, p. 124.
19. Bahm, A.J., *Philosophy of the Buddha, p.* 75.

CHAPTER-12

SĪLA

—*Professor Mahesh Tiwary M.A; Ph.D.*

As soon as we proceed for presenting a descriptive analysis of the Buddhist Ethics, we find *Sīla*, as the nearest concept to convey almost all its aspects and add something more, which is special contribution of the tradition. It is rather a psycho- ethical discipline entirly devoted to highlighting the moral and immoral states, exhibiting their inseparable link with the actions, resultants and thereby appearance of beings in various forms in different states of existence. It has found a beautiful exposition in the sermons of the Buddha independently as well as in the process of explaining his path of purification. In the present context, there is an attempt to briefly append a descriptive analysis of the concept in above two senses.

Sīla is the first step of the path of the Buddha. In general sense, it is rendered as 'nature, character, habit, custom, practice, conduct, etc. In popular sense, it is expressed as morality, virtue, moral deeds, moral principles and so on. The traditional sense further goes to describe it as basic foundation of moral life or the pivotal point of the holy life.[1] In highly technical sense, it is the moral volition (*kusala-cetanā*).

A fourfold exposition is again seen in the commentarial literature. It is in the form of indicating its characteristics, functions, manifestation and proximate cause. Its basic characteristics, (*lakkhaṇa*) is to become the ground of all the moral states. It provides them a base and grants support for their sustenance (*upadhāraṇa*) Its function (*rasa*) is in the way of putting a stop of the physcial and vocal misdeeds (*dussilya-viddhasantā*) and helps in developing of a quality of faultlessness (*anavajja-guṇa*) Its manifestation (*paccupaṭṭhāna*) is marked with the emergence of piety (*soceyya*), generally understood through each of the activity of one, who is in its possession. The proximate cause or the back- ground (*padaṭṭhāna*) includes the two factors 'individual shame (*hiri*) and social shame (*otappa*).[2]

Literally, the word *Sīla* is interprated in three ways,[3] namely; as a foundation-stone (*sīlana-attena*), calming down (*sītala atthena*) and acting as fore-runner (*sira-atthena*). *Sīla* in the first sense (*sīlāna*) is an ethically symoblical expression. As a foundation stone, it symbolizes the massiveness of the building to be developed thereupon, so also it symbolically expresses the sense of sound and un-shakable nature of virtuous life to be developed establishing in it. It preserves the sense of the foot of that mountain of massive stone which does not shake even after the strongest push of the storm:---

"*Selo yathā ekaghano, vātena na samīrati*"

The second sense as, 'calming down' (*sītala*) refers to the intrinsic nature of *Sīla* in process of its functioning. The three kinds of blazing fire, which burn a man internally, are the fire of attachment (*rāga-aggi*), fire of antipathy (*dosa-aggi*) and the fire of ignorance (*moha-aggi*). All the undesirable and ignoble activities which find association with a man, are generated by the piercing heat caused by them. *Sīla* minimises and calms down such heat like the Ganges-water does to the external buring sensation.

Thirdly, it functions as the fore-runner (*sira*) or the supreme force. Whenever, there is a desire to lead a virtuous life, *Sīla* comes the first. It prepares the mind in generating a congenial atmosphere for inculcation of the moral principles. It is just like cultivationg, weeding-out and making all the requirements available by the farmer for sprouting up of the seeds. As without having such condition, the sprouting up is not possible, so also without *Sīla*, the virtuous life cannot proceed and be firmly established. In the sequence, it is emphatically remarked---"*Sāsane kulaputtānaṃ patiṭṭhā natthi yaṃ vinā.*"[4]

It is in this way *Sīla* finds expression with niceties of senses in various contexts of the Pali cononical, non-canonical and commentarial literature. Now putting an expressional restraint here, I like to consider only three questions:---

1. What is Sīla?
2. How does it function? and
3. What are its benefits?

(1) The first question is about the definition of *Sīla*. A number of synonyms togther with the shades of meanings have been given just in previous pages. In the background, it seems a logical necessity to indicate the exact connotation of the term *Sīla*. Really speaking, it is a very difficult task to convey into English the exact sense of the concept expressed through a Pāli or Sanskrit term. A concept appearing through a word, has a long history of its development as well as its being crystalized as such. However, we have now no other means to communicate the ideas except the words. In the situation, a sincere attempt is made to reach the nearer one as far as possible. Thus *Sīla* may scriptually be defined in three ways. As a discipline, it is the physio-vocal culture. As a psycho-ethical analytic process, it is the name of a moral volition (*kusala-centanā*). As in popular monastic-cum household religiosity, it refers to the moral precept. The third one is the most popular and lively surviving expression in our country and the countries nearby where Buddhism a living faith, in one form or the other.

The first one covers a very wide range, involving itself in a number of evaluating processes of analysis and giving determinate expression of an action as moral and immoral. The basic determinative bases are roots, technically known as *Hetu*. They are both the moral and immoral. Greed (*lobha*), Hatred (*dosa*) and ignorance (*moha*) are the three immoral roots. Sacrifice (*alobha*). Friendliness (*adosa*). and Right Understanding (*amoha*) are the moral roots. A consicousness rooted in any one of the immoral roots is an immoral consiousness (*akusala-citta*). An action inspired and generated by such consicouness is an immoral action (*akusala- kamma*). Similarly, a consciousness rooted in moral roots is a moral consciousness (*kusala-citta*) and the action generated by its inspiration, is moral action (*kusala-kamma*). Besides, these immoral and moral roots, there are also their associates which find association according to the intensity or the nature of cosciousness and the presence of other conditions related to internal and external situations.[5]

An action does not end with its cessation. Immediately after it ceases to exist, it leaves its impression on the functional surface of mind which gradually is stored in its lower surface known as *Bhavaṅga*. It is called *vipāka* or the Resultant Consciousness. It is also regulated with the force of roots associated with the consciousness and emerging actions. It means that a moral action yeilds moral resultant and the immoral one produces the immoral resultant. They further serve as the atomic generating-force (*kamma-bīja*) for similar action.[6] It is in this way, it covers the entire activities done from the moment of entering into the womb of mother (*paṭsandhi*) till the moment of death (*cuti*).

Sīla as moral volition refers to the right psychic efforts of indulging in moral deeds or refraining from the immoral ones---"*cārittavāritta-vasena.*" It manifests through three doors, namely; mind-door, physic-door, and speech-door. First of all, there arises a determinative attitude of mind to do such and such act. When it remains harbouring on the functional surface of mind, it is called mental action or '*mano-kamma*'. On its manifestation through body-door, it is called phyical action or '*kāya-kamma*'. When the same appears through the speech-door, it receives its name as vocal action or '*vaci-kamma.*'[7] The volition remains as underlying force in all these activities. It finds further manifestation in the form of twenty one types of moral consciousness in their four spheres.[8]

Sīla, as moral precepts, is enormously large, both horizentally and vertically. The Buddha, as a successful teacher, has given numerous moral instructions in forty five years of his continuous way-faring in full consideration of the temperament, latent factors and the belief of the persons concerned. Even a brief note on these instructions will cover a big range of deliberation and will not find adjustment in this limited scope of the paper. Therefore, with a view to add an introduction to it a brief exposition under nine heads of moral precepts are given below. They are the *Pañca-sīla, Aṭṭha- sīla, Dasa-sīla, Maṅgala-sīla, Disā-pūjana-sīla, Indriya-samvara-sīla, santosa-sīla, Ājiva pārisuddhi-sīla, and Pātimokkha-Samvara- sīla*.

Pañca-Sīla

Pañca-Sīla or five moral precepts are the basic norms for both the housholders as well as for the renunciates.[9] Only in case of the third precepts, there is some difference. A householder is required to refrain from sexual misdeeds where as a monk has not at all to indulge in any kind of sex. These precepts are to create an initial ethical harmony in three-fold activities of the man who observes them. They are the :---

1. Refraining from killing (*Pāṇātipātā virati*),

2. Refraining from stealing (*Adinnādānā virati*),

3. Refraining from sexual misdeeds (*kāmesu micchācārā virati*).

4. Refraining from telling lie (*musāvādā virati*)

5. Refraining from taking intoxicants (*surāmeraya-majjappamādaṭṭhānā virati*).

It may be seen here that the first three are connected with curtailment of physical misdeeds. The fourth one is to put a restraint on the vocal ones where as the fifth one has to exercise overall restrainment over the mind body and speech in general and the mind alone particular. The first prepares an intitial psychic leaning for sprouting up of the feeling of universal friendliness. The second one is to generate the feeling of non-covetousness. The third one has a vital role for developing the family-feeling in the society and the fourth one is to inculcate the sense of reacting truely amidst the situation projecting even unfavourable from all sides. An attempt to maintain a balanced state of mind has been intiated in the fifth one. Thus the five precepts proceed from the gross to subtle, encircling the vitally recting physio-psychic points of a being. They are symoblical as regards the number as *Five* and their appearances in five ways.

In this context, a specimen of their functioning with underlying moral stream derserves consideration. The first precept is "Refraining from killing." What is killing; to whom it is related to; what is that which when destroyed, we name it killing; and how it has bearing with sinfullness; are a number of questions which naturally arise as soon as this issue is taken up. What we say killing is generally known as *Pāṇa-badh, 'Pāṇa- ghāta'* etc. *'Pāṇa'* here refers to a being, a man. The man is a conventional expression given to the five aggregates for our paractical purpose. There is no soul or any eternal principle in him. He is mere a complete whole of these pure *Dhammas*. These five aggregates are united together as a complex whole forming the personality of a man due to one force known as *jivitindriya* or the life factor. It is the life of the being and therefore, the destruction of *'jivitindriya'*is killing in true sense of the term. This killing is the name of volition of killing---*'vadhakacetanā'*. The *'jivitindriya'* is available in the vast range of beings prossesing life. In the present context we generally limit ourselves to the man. How, it is materialized? It is materialized under the presence of five conditions, namely; a being, consicousness of there being living one, volition of killing (intension), effort for the same, and lastly the subsequent destruction of life. There are six means to carry out the act. They are the---one's own hands, instigation, misslies, permanent devices, occult power and skillful plots.

Killing, in general, is an immoral deed. Its sinfulness and degree vary with reference to the beings with whom the action takes place. There are two main basis for such evalutive detemination;---virtue and the tenure of application of volition of killing. If it is performed in the connection with a man of great virtue, it entails a great misdeed or sin in comparision to a person who is less virtuous. In his case it entails a small misdeed. The reason of variation of sinfulneess is based on the degree of virtue possessed by the man. When physciai virtues are equal, the sin is smaller or greater according as the volition and efforts are weaker or stronger. Among the animals deviod of virtue, it is a small misdeed in case of a smaller creature and a great misdeed in that of a large one. It is due to the temporal duration of the volition of killing. It will be naturally in case of an animal of big size, than that of small size. In case of killing of the animals of similar size, the variation in degree of sin may be marked as great and small in respect of the intensity of efforts of killing. Thus the tradition examines the various types of morally unwhole-some deeds on the basis of the volition of ill will etc. The other immoral activities like stealing etc., may be understood in the same line.[7]

(b) *Aṭṭha-Sīla*

Both the householders and the renuciates have the equal right of leading virtuous life, of course, the householders have some difficulties due to variegated reponsibilities. Sometimes, a house-holder finding himself well established in five moral precepts, steps further and accepts three precepts in addition to those five. In such case, he follows eight precepts.[8]

The additional three precepts are as below---

1. Refraining from un-timely meal (*vikāla-bhojanā-virati*),

2. Refraining from dance, music and vulgar show (*nacca-gīta-vādita-visūka-dassanā virati*) and

3. Refraining from the use of garland, perfumes and other cosmetics (*māla-gandha- vilepana...vidbūsanaṭṭhānā virati*).

The three precepts are connected with minimization of the desire of three senses---tongue, eye and nose and to inculcate and develop the attitude of 'mere act only' and not indulging in or taking delight in the object etc.

(c) *Dasa-sīla*

Dasa-Sīla or the ten precepts are also called *Dasa-Sikkhāpada*. They are meant for those who just abandon the domestic life and take up the life of a recluse. They are the new entrants, tenchnically called *Sāmaṇera* (novice). They, living in the monastic order, strictly follow the ten moral precepts. They add two more to the eight ones already stated.[9] They are the:---

1. Refraining from the high and lofty beds (*uccāsayana-mahāsayanā virati*),

2. Refraining from receiving silver and gold (*Jātarūpa-rajata-paṭgahaṇā virati*).

Here, it may be seen that the first one is an effort to reduce the desire for bodily comforts related to touch. The second one generates virtuous efforts for not receiving the gold and silver which one has already left for taking up the life of a recluse.

(c-a)*Another ten precepts)*

In course of enumeration of moral actions, a list of such ten types of actions is available which is regarded as the ten moral precepts for the housholders. They, by their nature, are of mixed expression of socio-moral deeds.[10] The enumeration proceeds as--- *Dāna, Sīla, Bhāvanā, Apacāyana, Veyyāvacca, Patti-dāna, Pattānu-modans, Dhamma- savana, Dhamma-desanā and Diṭṭhi-uju-karaṇa.*

1. *Dāna* means offering, parting with the possession that one belongs to. In traditional sense, it is an act of regular offering of a portion of his earning to a needy and deserving person. There is the sciptural sanction of offering to the extent of one fourth of one's earning (*catudhā vibhajate loke*). More emphasis is seen in respect of *Sangha* which is devoted for the benefit and happiness of all. This offering is of three types as like a slave, like a friend and like a lord. Offering of a little portion of his belongings with a very weak consciousness is the slave-like offering as there remains dominance of the wealth at the moment of parting with. Offering of a sizeable portion with friendly consciousness is the friend-like-offering. And the offering of all of his belongings to a deserving person for the benefit of all, is the lord-like offering.

2. *Sīla* refers to the following of the moral precepts. Here the emphasis is on un-wavering confidence and unshakable belief inspired by right understanding. Taking any one of the precept and following the same with above state of mind is desired here.

3. *Bhāvanā* means practicing meditation. It may be one-pointed attention on any of the fourfold mindfulness or on any object prescribed for the purpose.

4. *Apacāyana* is the name of a respectful gesture in honour of the elderly peple. Standing and receiving the teachers, partents and other elderly people with honour may be included in it.

5. *Veyyāvacca* means serving the above types of people together with the needy one's with friendlines and compassion.

6. *Patti-dāna*: *Patti* means the fruit of the meritorious deeds. One does moral action and accumulates the fruit of such action. It goes on accumulating with virtuous being.

He, for the removal of the suffering of others, makes an offering of such fruits. it is called *Patti-dana*.

7. *Pattānumodana*: It is an act of receiving the offering of merit (*patti*) given by some-one with clear heart, pure consciousness and shoothing stream of honour from within.

8. *Dhamma-savana*: Hearing the discourse on virtue, human values, sublime ideals etc.

9. *Dhamma-desanā*: It means giving discourse connected with moral teachings for purfication of beings.

10. *Diṭṭhi-ujukaraṇa*: The term *Diṭṭhi* is the synonym of wrong view. It covers the nature of reality and makes the man illusioned, bewildered and blind with ignorance. This act is the removal of such wrong view and making the mind awakened in the process of right thinking.

(d) *Maṅgala-Sīla*

The term *Maṅgala* stands for noble deeds, which are socially and ethically sound. A list of such deeds have been given in the *Maṅgala-Sutta*. It includes the activities like keeping the company of virtuous men, becoming grateful, speaking sweet and true words, serving the parents, developing forbearance, referaining from taking intoxicants, nourshing true spirit for good life, understanding four noble truths and relizing the state of eternal Bliss.[11]

(e) *Disā-pujā*

The Buddha as a successful teacher has given the instructions on *Sīla* in various ways with full consideration of the receiving capacity of the person concerned. He has taken the help of similes, parables, illustrations etc to make them understandable. A beautiful example is seen in the *Sigālovāda-sutta* wherein the moral precepts have been given with the simile of six directions. The six directions- --east, west, south, north, upper and lower have been advised to be worshipped in a symbolical way. The parents are the eastern clime. The teachers symbolize the southern one. The sons and wife are the western clime where as the northern clime refers to the friends and relatives. The lower clime stands for the slave and workers and the upper clime for the recluses and *Bāhmaṇas*.[12] A set of duties towards each other has been enumerated here and performing the same rightly is the worshiping of these six directions. The duties enumerated in this context are to help the foster growth of social and moral harmony in the society.

(f) *Indriya-samvara-sīla*

Here the word *Indriya* refers to the six senses operating in the process of day-to day life with reference of their respective objects. They are the eye, ear, nose, tongue, body and mind. There are six respective objects as visible object, audible object, odorous object, sapid object, tangible object and ideational object. It is a naturel phenomenon that an object comes in the range of a sense-organ and there is the successive receiving by that. The misdeed lies in the fact of being indulging and taking delight there in. Such indulgence and delightfully relishing, develop attachment and give rise to suffering. Thus putting restraints over the senses is to receive the object as receiving only and not indulging there in. In the case of appearance of a visible object, the seeing should be mere seeing and no furtherence of delightful leanings. Similar attitude should also be developed in respect of functioning of other sense organs.[13]

(g) *Santosa-sīla*

The term *santosa* has been used here in the sense of inculcation of the mental attitude of little desire. "The greater is the degree of dis-satifaction and desire, the greater is the amount of suffering; of minimization of such desire is the minimization of the amount of suffering" has been emphatically stated by the Buddha. Such minimization has been suggested to the extent to remain satisfied with the simple food to maintain the body and the simple cloth to cover it by total curtailment of sense of beautifying, adorning or making an attractive show of himself. It should emerge from within with saturation with the flavour of sublime ideals of the virtuous way-faring of life.[14]

(h) *Ājiva-pārisuddhi-sīla*

Ājiva means the way of earning livelihood. *Pārisuddhi* refers to purity. The moral precepts connected with the purity of livelihood are called *Ājiva- pārisuddhi-sīla*. The tradition maintains the norms of properly reacting in process of earning livelihood. The best way is that of a bee. As a bee moves to the different flowers and without causing any harm either to the shape or colour of flowers, collects sustenance and amintains its living; similarly, one should earn one's livelihood without causing any injury to any one.[15] One should prepare one's mind to develop the way of smooth living with limited resources at his disposal.

For a householder, trading in human beings, weapons, meat, intoxicants and poisons has strictly been forbidden by the Buddha.[16] Further a number of wrong ways of earning livelihood have been enumeruted from which both the hous-holders and the renunciates are required to keep themselves aloof. Only a few are given here for understanding the nature.[17]

1. *Kuhanā*: It is a wrong way of earning by making deceitful appearance and attracting the people thereby. Making an appearance of a saint by matted hair, putting ash on the body, and developing an attractive posture sitting on a cross road, is a type of it.

2. *Lapanā*: It is a way of earning livelihood by using attrative words in mysterious way and thereby entrapping the passerby.

3. *Nemittikata*: Marking a sign in the body of a man and giving interpretation in a very charming and convincing way is *Nemittikatā*. It is highlighting a sign with highly resounding mystic expressions.

4. *Nippesikatā*: It is the name of means of attracting the people by using the expression of criticism, rebuking, anger, charge for an imaginary fault etc.

5. *Lābhenalābha-nijiginsanatā*: This describes a way of earning by giving up the small gains in the hope of some more profitable achievement.

6. *Tulākūṭa*: It is way of deceiving people by means of balance and having some gain thereby.

7. *Kaṅsakūṭa*: The word *Kaṅsa* means a measure made of bronze for use of sale and purchase of grains. It is wrongly used in a deceitful manner by taking more at the time of purchase and giving less at the time of selling.

8. *Māna-Kūṭa*: It is another way of cheating the customers by using a wrong weight. It is used with a weighty magnet

in the bottom at the time of purchase and by removal of the iron bit from the bottom hole at the time of selling.

Further, the *Brahmajāla-Sutta* presents a very long list of wrong means which a recluse must avoid. They are also not to be adopted by the house-holders as well.

(i) *Pātimokkha-samvara-sīla*

The *Pātimokkha* is the name of a book in the *Vinaya*. It is rather the code of conduct for the monks and nuns leading the monastic life. It has two parts, *Bhikkhu-Pātimokkha and Bhikkhuni-Pātimokkha*. The former contains two hundred and twenty-seven rules for the monks, divided in eight sections according to seriousness of the offences. The sections are like *Pārājika, Saṅghādisesa, Aniyata, Nissaggiya, Pācittiya, Paṭidesaniya, Sekhiya and Adhikaraṇa-samatha*. The *Pārājika* means defeat. It contains four such acts, which entails a monk defeat in leading the holy life. They are the killing, stealing, indulging in social misdeeds and claiming some supernormal power which one does not really posses. Doing any one of them, one is expelled from the order permanently.

The latter is the *Bhikkhuni-Pātimokkha* which contains three hundred and eleven rules to regulate the life of a nun in monastic order. It is divided into seven sections as above,except the *Aniyata-Dhamma*. They have been arranged according to the serious nature of the offences. Some of them, in both the parts, form the mere instructions to be followed in their monastery or entering into village for alms-round.

The *Pātimokkha* is regarded as the back-bone of the moanstic life. Both the monks and nuns strictly follow them. They, on the days of *Uposatha*, both on the fourteenth and full- moon-days, make a confession of their transgressions before the congregation of monks and nuns and gladly receive punishment or make expiation of their faults. Following it, the rules are recited in the purely orthodoxical way and accepted with un- wavering faith by them. A monk or a nun, while leading the monastic life is always mindful in following these rules. He avoids even the slightest transgression, and maintains the strictness with true spirit. Such restrainment in following the rules is called the *Pātimokkha-Samvara-Sīla*.[18]

(ii). How does *Sīla* function, is the second question. It has been pointed out that *Sīla* is volition (*cetanā*) and as such funtioning with reference to the objects, is its intrinsic nature. In the back-ground, it seems desirable to state here only the three things.---the means of its functioning, process of its functioning, and its keeping association with the other *Dhammas* in this process.

As regards the first, *Sīla* has three means through which it finds manifestation. They are the mind, body and speech. It basically initiates from mind, creates a moral stir on it and passes through the body and speech according to the situation. When it functions at the surface of mind, it projects as sacrifice (*anabhijjhā*), Friendliness (*abyāpada*) and Right vision (*sammādiṭṭhi*). Appearing through the body, it is seen in three forms of abstinances. They are the refraining from killing, stealing and committing sexual misdeeds. Similarly, its appearance through speech has fourfold expressions and they are the refraining from telling lie, harsh speech, slandering and ignoble gossips. Such manifestation through either of the three doors is a natural moral projection radiating through each organ and their movements. The story of *Assāji* may be cited here to show the radiation of *Sīla* through each atom of the body.[19]

Its process of functioning is also threefold. First of all it exhibits the viability of the man. "The man alone is the lord of himself. No one, except him, is responsible for his bondage or freedom.[20] Even the Buddha is only a guide, the work is to be done by him.[21] One can pollute him by his own immoral deeds. Both the purity and impurity, freedom and bondage are the fruits of his own actions. There is none who can purify others."[22]--are the basic instructions appearing as functions of *Sīla*. A crystal clear stream of such thinking may be marked in the following verses---

"Attanā hi kataṃ pāpaṃ, Attanā sankillissati,
Attanā akataṃ pāpaṃ, attanā va visujjhati,
Suddhi asuddhi paccattaṃ, nāññaṃ visodhaye."

× × ×

"Na santi puttā tāṇāya, na pitā nāpi bāndhavā,
Antakenākenādhipannassa, natthi ñātisu taṇatā."

× × ×

"Etamattha vasaṃ ñatva, paṇḍito silasamvuto,

Nibbānagamanaṃ maggaṃ khippameva visodhaye."

Here the freedom of work with complete harmony with the law of *karma* may rightly be observed in the light of the middle way of the Buddha.

The second function of *Sīla* is to precribe criteria to determine an action as moral or immoral. For this, firstly, it exhibits the basic, immoral roots---*Lobha* (greed), Dosa (ill will) and *Moha* (ignorance) together with their sprouting up and developing as four *Āsava* (intocicants), four *Ogha* (flood), four *Gantha* (ties), four *Yoga* (yoking factor), five *Nivaraṇa* (hindrances), ten *Kilesa* (pollutions), ten *Sanyojana* (fetters) etc. A clear indication of the ten types of immoral consciousness and the actions generated by them is also seen here.

Again it points out their counter parts, the moral roots, moral consciousness and moral actions generated by them. *Alobha* (sacrifice) *Adosa* (frindliness), *Amoha* (right understanding) are the three moral roots. Their off-springs like-four *Sattipaṭṭhāna* (mindfulness), four *Samappadhāna* (right efforts), seven *Bojjhaṅga* (factors of enlightenment), eight *maggaṅga* (constitutents of path), Twenty two *Indriya* (facuties) also form the part of display in this context. The manifestations as twenty one types of moral consciousness together with twenty five types of psychic factors as well as the ten types of moral actions are exhibited here too.[23]

Thirdly it proceeds in generating faith in the merit of righteousness and enquisitiveness for gradual receptibility and pliancy. A number of references show how the Buddha gradually gave the discourses on the merit of offering, observing the moral precepts, pleasure of the divine kingdoms, peril of the sensuous pleaure etc. With these, he used to make the mind more and more pliable for receiving the higher teachings related to more subtle ideals.

Sīla does not function alone. It has a number of associates which function together and form the properties of *Sīla*. The description of all is not possible in this limited frame-work. However, a brief description of only five of them is appended here. They are the---*Saddhā, Sati, Viriya, Hiri and Otappa*.

(1) *Saddhā:* It literally means faith. Technically, it is the faith balanced with right understanding, un-wavering in the nature. It is an initial leaning towards within from without. Secondly *Saddhā* has the characteristics of cleaning, washing away the dirt of mind. As the muddy water becomes pure, tranquil and drinkable by putting a peice of water-purifying gem in it, similarly, it removes the dirt of consciousness like that of a fine ornament by the goldsmith. Thirdly, it generates efforts for higher and higher realization. As looking a man crossed the flooded and unfathomed river with strong determination, the other men, standing on the shore, also cross the river,; similarly, marking the attaining of the state of *Sotāpanna or Sakadāgāmi* etc., it inspires for attainment of the stages of *Anāgāmi* and *Arahata*. In this way, *Saddhā*,as a psychic factor, performs three-fold activities in generating faith, dirt- cleaning and inspiration for spiritual gain.[24]

(2) *Sati*: It means mindfulness. It is a psychic state, the function of which is to generate awareness to the man with whom it remains. It is just like the door keeper at mind-door. As on being alert of the door-keeper, no undesirable persons dare to enter into the house, similarly, on the appearance of Sati, no immoral states dare to arise and function in mind.

Secondly, it makes the man aware of his inner strength, having possession of psychic powers like---*Saddha-bala, Sati-bala, Viriyabala, Samādhi-bala, Paññā-bala* and inspires for fearless wayfaring. It functions like the minister of home-affairs to the king, advising him to remain mindful of his being so. It is its *'apilāpana-lakkaṇa.'*

Thirdly, it inspires for having un-interrupted possession of the psychic wealth like friendless, compassion, joy, equanimity etc., and the light of these sublime states for the benefit of all. Here it excercises its function of *'upagahaṇa.''*[25]

(3) *Viriya*: It is the third associate of *Sīla*. It is rendered as energy in its literal sense. Technically, it stands for the moral support on the occasions of psychic depression due to onslought of immoral forces. As finding wooden pillar as support, the falling thatch does not come down, similarly, receiving the support of *Viriya* the moral states do not suffer destruction. On other occasions, it serves as a flowing stream of strength through the physio-psychic organism.[26]

(4) *Hiri*: The term *Hiri* is generally translated as 'shame' or individual shame. Really speaking, it is a moral psychic state, which funcions in arousing the sense of greatness of man as a rational being and makes him feeling ashamed to do any thing immoral. On the moment of doing any thing immoral, it spontaneously springs up from within and refrains him from doing so by acclerating the sense of his being the most rare creation on the earth with the faculty of right understanding (*Paññindriya*). It is just like a maiden of a noble family (*kula-kumāri*) whose each moving step has an unshakable link surcharged with the sublime tradition developed through the pious deeds of the family members, which go on reminding within and refraining her from doing any thing wrong to it.[27]

(5) *Otappa*: It is another name of social shame in generic expression. It, as a moral psychic factor, helps the generation of the sense of honour for the society. There are occasions, when one finds himself on the point of doing some thing socially immoral. Particularly on such occasion, there emerges from within a psychic life for strengthening the flow of the greatness towards the social order and refrains him from doing so. It cuts down the immoral leaning, puts a restraint over the mind and vigorous stop in further proceeding. It is due to this factor, one does not do anything unsocial. The more it is developed in men, a more sound and harmonious social order develops.[28]

3. The third question is about the benefit of *Sīla*. The charateristics, manifestations etc., of *Sīla* have already ben presented in fore-going pages. In the background, one may assess the benefits deeping down through them. In the texts much light has been thrown on it. It has been stated to be the basic quality of a man. The name *"Manussa"* (man) is justified only when there is the possession of *Sīla* with him. Further after rightly observing the moral precepts, there remains no chance to become remorseful. His all moments are utilized in moral deeds just like putting the flowers in the form of beautiful garlands. The things like moral, immoral, moral resultant, immoral resultant, state of awe, and the state of bliss, are all crystal clear before him. He is in possesion of the capacity to mould himself as he likes by directing his activities in the right direction etc. In this way the texts

present it in so many ways. Hence a set of five benefits is being appended which has been repeatdly told by the Buddha. 'Five, O householders, are the benefits of the virtuous, in perfecting the virtue. "Where ever he goes in the assembly of any type, he reamins fearless. His demonic fear (*bhyab-herava*) disappears for ever. He, because of his virtue and diligence, makes the earning of both the earthly and spiritual wealth. His fair name spreads in all the directions, He is loved by men, animals and gods, alike because of his infinite range of sublime friendliness. He never loses awareness and even in the moment of his death, he is mindful of the reality. In the end, he achieves a good state of existence due to the acccumulation of the fruition of his moral actions after expiry of the tenure of the present state of the life force.[29] In the end it is rightly remarked that---

> *"Sobhantevaṃ na rājāno, muttāmaṇivibhusitā,*
> *Yathā sobhanti yatino, sīla-bhūsanabhūsitā.*
> *Attānuvādāādibhayaṃ viddhansayati sabbaso,*
> *Janeti kittihāsaṃ ca, sīlaṃ sīlasamaṃ kuto,*
> *Dvāraṃ va pana Nibbāna-nagarassa pavesane."*[30]

Notes and References :

1. S. 1.14,164
2. Vm.pp.5-6
3. Ibid.p.5
4. Ibid.p.6
5. D.S.p.229
6. D.S.p.230
7. A.S.pp.67-72
8. D.S.pp.3-91
9. A.S.pp.80-84
10. K.1.p.4
11. K.1.p.5
12. A.S.p.5
13. K.1.pp.5-6
14. D.3.pp.139-142

15. D. 1.pp.62-63
16. A.2.454
17. D.1.3-10
18. Vm.pp,11-13
19. A.S.pp.63-66
20. K.133
21. K.142

    "Tumhehi kiccaṃātappaṃ, akkhātāro tathāgatā,
    Paṭipannā pamokkhanti, jhāyino mārabandhanā."
22. K.1.33
23. D.S.pp.22-294
24. Mp. pp.26-27
25. Ibid.pp.28-29
26. Vm.324
27. A.S.pp.99-100
28. Ibid.324
29. D.2.61-69

    "Idha, gahapatayo sīlavā sīlasampanno appamadādhikaraṇaṃ mahantaṃ bhogakkhandhaṁ adhigacchati, puna ca paraṃ sīlavato kalyāṇo kittisaddo abbhugacchati. Puna ca paraṃ sīlavā yaññadeva parisaṃ upasankamati visārado upasamkamati amankubhūto. Puna ca paraṃ sīlavā asammūlho kālaṃ karoti. Puna ca paraṃ sīlvā kāyassabhedā paraṃ maraṇā suggatiṃ saggaṃ lokaṃ upapapajjati."
30. Vm.pp.6-7.

CHAPTER-13

NIBBĀNA

—Dr. Harcharan Singh Sobti, M.A; LL.B; Ph.D.

Nibbāna is the only out for Suffering humanity. This idea operates as unifying principle and provides coherence to the Buddhist scriptures, otherwise amorphous in appearance. The Buddha has described the unifying feature of his doctrine and discipline, making use of a simile of an ocean and its taste--- the taste of salt,as: "And even, monks, as the great ocean his one taste, the taste of salt, even so, monks, does this *dhamma* and discipline have one taste, the taste of freedom."[1] Again, *Nibbāna* as an underlying idea of the Sermons of the Buddha is expressed through the simile of flowing of Ganga into ocean, thus: "Even as the river Ganges streams and flows to the ocean, as its bourne and finds repose only in the ocean, so does Gotama's whole congregation, laity as well pilgrims, stream and flow to *Nirvāṇa* as its bourne, finding repose only in *Nirvāṇa*"[2]. So, in the Buddhist scheme of thought, the disciple is instructed to guard himself against even the slightest deviation from the Path culminating in *Nibbāna*. There is a beautiful illustration, in the Pāli Canon, to that effect. It is recorded in the *Saṁyutta Nikāya*, that once the Buddha was staying at Kosambi in *Siṁsapā* forest. The Buddha took up few *Siṁsapā* leaves scattered on the ground in his hand enquired from the *Bhikkhus,* surrounding him, whether few leaves in his hand were more or other leaves in *siṁsapā* wood above. The anwer could not be other than this that leaves in his hand were small in number and much were in the *Siṁsapā* forest above. "Just so, monks much more in number are those things I have found out, but not revealed; very few are the things I have revealed. And why, monks have not revealed them? Because they are not concerned with profit, they are not rudiments of the holy life, they conduce not to revulsion, to dispassion, to cessation, to tranquillity, to full comprehension, to the perfect wisdom, to *Nibbāna*. That is why I have not revealed them."[3]

The disadvantage contemplated in the above Sermon points to the distraction of the mind from the Path. The questions leading to the disgression from the Path, the Buddha answered through silence. There is a list of ten questions, that Rhys Davids[4] calls 'Indeterminates', the Buddha refused to entertain, for the simple reason that such attempts would not help the Buddhist disciple in any way. For instance, the answer to the question whether the world is eternal or not is hardly conducive in solving the self-evident problem of human Suffering. In the *Majjhima Nikāya*, the Buddha tells Māluṅkyāputta that:

"The living of the Brahma-faring'. Māluṅkyāputta, could not be said to depend on the view that the world is eternal. Nor could the living of the Brahma-faring, Māluṅkāputta be said to depend on the view that the world is not eternal. Whether there is the view that the world is eternal or whether there is the view that the world is not eternal, there is birth, there is ageing, there is dying, there are griefs, sorrow, Suffering lamentation and despair, the suppression of which I lay down here and now."[5]

These questions do mean a lot for the scholars. The Buddha was practical man whose main concern was to show the Path, he had discovered, to the mankind, leading to the annihilation of Suffering i.e. *Nibbāna*. The Buddha thus, does not belong to the community of scribes and scholars, whose intellectual activities end only in a blind alley of views.

2.

In *Puggalapaññatti*[6] the book of the *Abhidhamma Piṭaka*, there is a description of four classes of saints coinciding with the same number of stages of *Nibbāna*. The four stages are:

(1) *The Stage of Sotāpanna*: The Pali expression *Sotāpanna (Sanskrit: Srotapanna)* consists of two component words i.e. *Sota and apanna*. *Sotā* means stream and *apanna* means one who has entered. Thus, in Theravāda tradition, *Sotāpanna*

stands for one who has entered the stream---that is destined to merge, finally, in the ocean of *Nibbāna*. The image of stream, though indirectly, hints at its banks inhabited by the multitudes of people and these are 'ignorant worlding' people. The *Sotāpanna* alienates himself from the 'way of the world' and puts himself on the first stage of the Path. The *conversion* is not instantaneous; it is part of the process. Sometimes, it is confined not to a lifetime process, but, extends to a long succession of lives. He must have opened up himself to *Dhamma*, first, and then faithfully adhered to its precepts. At this stage, the *Sotāpanna* gains threefold freedom, in successive order, which is celebrated in the *Dhammapada* as follows.

"Better than sovereignty over the earth, better than going to heaven, better than lordship over all worlds is the reward of *Sotapatti*, the first stage of the Path in holiness.[7]

The threefold-freedom is:

(a) *Freedom from the delusion of self*: The delusion (*Sakkayadiṭṭhi*) thought of, in this context, has direct bearing on the doctrine of *anattā*. The Buddha in his second *Sermon*, the *Anattālākkhaṇa Sutta*[8] addressed to the *Pañcavaggivā Bhikkhu*, has spelled out the basic postulates of this doctrine. It may be fruitfufl to point out that the doctrine of *anattā* was certainly not the consequence of an attempt to achieve theoretical ends. It was, in the ultimates analysis, an outcome of the Buddha's contemplative response to the existential situation, preserved in the legend of Four Sights.

Etymologically the word *anattā* consists of the negative prefix *an* and *attā* underlying an idea of no-self or no-soul. And, again, the Buddha put forth his doctrine of *anattā* by way of refuting different theories of soul[9] or *attā (Sanskrit:ātma)*, deemed to be quite popular with his contempories with the sole purpose of liberating them from the delusion of self. In *Anattālakkhaṇa Sutta*, the *Pañcakkhandha*, constituting human personality are analysed, one after the other, and concluded thus: "This does not belong to me; this is not what I am; this is *not my self*."[10] The conversation between Venerable Nāgasena and King Milinda on the subject of personality, also echoes identical views, of course, in metaphorical language, thus:

Even as the word of "chariot" means
That members join to frame a whole;
So when the Groups appear in view.
We use the phrase, "A living being!.[11]

Besides following the mode of analysis of *Pañcakkhandha*, the ethical implications have also been looked into. Firstly, it is argued in *Anattālakkhaṇa Sutta,* in case, there happens to be some immortal entity call it soul or self, it cannot be subject to Suffering. Secondly, when all the *khandhas* are subject to Suffering, this inevitably implies that they are plagued with impermanence. Now, finally, all the *khandhas* being subject to impermanence and hence root cause of Suffering, their true nature stands revealed. In the light of this discovery one develops aversion and gradually moves towards divesting oneself of passion. One who has entered the stream on his own, does not follow the course of repressing passion, he simply does not co-operate and is steadily watchful.

So, the human personality that consists of *pañcakkhandhas,* has to be kept under constant vigilance, in order to not to identify self with any one of these separately or collectively (or anything existing beyond the frontiers of personality and subject to flux.) Failure shall inevitably lead to fall into the trap of delusion of self. It is precisely to guard oneself against this malady, the Buddha armed us with the doctrine of *anattā*. The entire thrust of this doctrine is on *what one is not*.

(b) *Freedom form doubt*: The blind faith can hardly be exalted as a positive counter part of doubt (*vicikicchā*) But, at the same time, it is not possible to move a head on the Path, in case, the doubt continues to subsist with all its credibility. Lakshmi Narasu's observations in this matter, are quite reveailing. "Buddhism does not underestimate the value of doubt.", he writes, "during the period of investigation". Its doubt "is of that sort whose aim is to conquer itself by high aspiration and incessant toil, not of the sort which, born of flippancy and ignorance, tries to perpetuate itself as an excuse for idleness and indifference."[12] The kind of doubt, the *Sotāpanna* casts away, concerns the truth, difficult to own, revealed through the doctrine of *anattā*. As a result, he believes in it, and, clings no more to the personality-factors i.e.*Pañcakkhandhas.*

(c) *Freedom from rituals*: Buddhism is religion wherein the efficacy lies only in an individual's efforts. The Buddha never allows to be complascently disposed to the epitome of his teachings; and he exhorts the Brethern, saying "work out your salvation with diligence".[13] The emphasis on individual's effort was aimed at to dedivinize the human consciousness. The idea of God has no place in Buddhism, because it cannot be allowed to contradict the causal nexus operating throughout the phenomenal existence. Furthermore, belief in God helps man to shift responsibilities of his action on other/others, and also leaves him on the mercy of God, a direct reflection of his incapacity he experiences in day to day living. This way, he turns towards God, who is not there, and makes attempts to please him through the performance of religious rites and ceremonies, as if effcacious in nature. The *Sotāpanna* redeems himself form such a set of beliefs and reposes his faith in his own efforts, alone. And, practice of meditation takes the place of offering of prayers and performance of rituals etc.

Sotāpanna freed from three fetters (*Saññojana*) is compared to the sun in the background of natural setting, during autumn, as follows:

"Just so, monks, in the autumn season when the sky is clear and the clouds have fled, the sun leaping up into the firmament drives away all darkness from the heavens and shines and burns and flashes forth,---even so in the Ariyan disciple arises the flawless, tainless eye of wisdom, and along with this arising three fetters are abandoned, to wit: The views of the person-pack, doubt-and wavering and wrong handling of rite and ritual."[14]

And, he is in position to claim that:

"Hell is destroyed for me, and rebirth as an animal, or a ghost, or in any place of woe. I am converted, I am no longer liable to be reborn in a state of Suffering, and am assured of final salvation."[15]

But, the *Sotāpanna* has to take birth for seven times[16] more among men and gods, before he finally escapes the cycle of *Saṁsāra*.

(ii) *The Stage of Sakadāgāmin*: At this stage, the disciple only learns to weaken the dark passion e.g. the sensual lust (*kāma*) and anger (*paṭigha*). When, in the course of satisfying sensual desires, an obstacle crops up, the mind flares up with anger. The very fact that the disciple is required, only to weaken the passion, and a distinct stage is devised for the purpose, only shows the extent of invincible nature of these passions. After freeing oneself from these two fetters along with the three already destroyed, one becomes *Sakadagāmin*---Once-retuner. He has only conquered the gross desires, like desire for power and status etc. but, still clings to certain subtle desires, e.g. desire to become *arahata*. The subtle desires lurking the mind bring him back to the world for once. The result achieved at the second stage of *Sakadāgāmin* are described in *Aṅgutara Nikāya*, in the following words:

"Now, Monks, in this matter a monk keeps the law of mortality in full, he is moderately given to mental concentration, moderately given to striving for insight.....Such an one, by destroying three fetters is a stream-winner, one not doomed to the down fall, one assured, one bound for enlightenment."[17]

(iii) *The Stage of Anagāmin:* After having successfully outgrown the first two stages, the disciple qualifies himself to enter the third stage of *Anagāmin*. Here, he redeems himself completely from the remaining foot-prints of various fetters. A small amount of clinging to body that remains with him also disappears at the time of death. He no more returns to the human world but returns to the world of pure-form. It is stated of *Anagāmin*, thus:

"Moreover, a monk keeps the laws of morality in full, he practices concentration in full, but he is moderately given to striving for insight......Such an one by the destruction of the five fetters bind to the lower worlds, takes birth spontaneously (in the Pure Abodes), there to pass away, destined never to return thence."[18]

(iv) *The Stage of Arahata:* The term *arahata* is derived from *ari*. *Ari* means enemy and *arahata* is one who has conquered his enemies. On the path to *arahatship*, the disciple has to conquer the rest of five enemies or generally called fetters which are identified as follows:

6. *Rūparāga:* When attached to this desire one seeks rebirth in the world of forms that include sixteen divine kingdoms known as *Brahma-loka*. The disciple must cross the stream of existence of whatever form it may be.

7. *Arūparāga*: Across the world of forms, their exist formless worlds, four in number. The man, no more, has material forms but still he exists. The existence, by all means constitutes an integral part of *Saṁsāra,* and the Buddhist disciple must escape from this cycle of Saṁsāra, to attain the goal of *Nībbāna*.

8. *Spiritual Pride (Māno)* and 9. *Self-righteousness*. As a a result of having freed oneself from several factors, it is quite normal to assume an air of pride and acclaim self-righteousness. The disciple must see to it that these fetters, no more, create problems for him.

10. *Ignorance (avijjā)* Ignorance may be last in the list, but it is all pervasive. It is ignorance that generates the twelve fold *Nidānas.* Actually, the disciple undergoes a discipline for the gradual elimination of ignorance, the root-cause of Suffering. The stage of *arahata* is culmination of both the complete annihilation of ignorance and the attainment of *Nibbāna*.

3.

Nibbāna is a state of mind to be realized and not to be merely believed or intellectually grasped. All the hindrances on the way to such realization, the Buddha analysed and removed for the benefit of those alone who resolve to attain *Nibbāna*. The Buddha's first attack was on the mythological character, he found as an integral part of the contemporary religious culture. He compared his *Dhamma* with a Sāl tree, free from leaves and twigs etc. thus: 'It is like a giant *Sāl tree* on the outskirts of a village or township which, by the course of change, loses its leaves and foliage, sheds its bark and rotten stuff and poorer wood, so that in time, when all that is gone, it stands in the clean strength of its choice timber alone...even so, in many a figure, has Gotama, made his Doctrine clear."[19] Mythologising, the Buddha considered and condemned to be an attempt at befogging what could be clearly *seen*.

Theorising is still a greater hindrance, more subtle and hence more successful in misleading the disciple from following the right Path. And the Buddha's contempt for such a mode of thinking can be well measured from the piece of advice he rendered to Bhaddiya in the *Aṅguttara Nikāya*. "Come now, Bhaddiya! Be not misled by report or tradition or hearsay.Be not misled by proficiency in the Collection, nor by mere logic or inference, nor after considering reason, nor after reflection on and approval of some theory nor because it fits becoming"[20] The Buddha's instruction of detachment from oneself, and directed towards the disciple, also include the Buddha's own person and thus he adds: "Nor by the thought: The recluse is revered by us."[21] The Buddha demands from his disciple to posses a discriminating mind and further tells: "But, Bhaddiya, when you know for yourselves: These things are unprofitable, these things, are blame-worthy, these things are censured by the intelligent, these things, when performed and undertaken, conduce to loss and sorrow,---then indeed, Bhaddiya, do you reject them."[22] So, the Buddha's entire thrust is 'to gain the insight' and discard all the hindrances that come on the way.

It is the insight that paves the way for the realization of *Nibbāna*. *Nibbāna is to be experienced 'by the wise in his own interior.' The Buddha* tells a *Brāhmaṇa* that: "*Brāhmaṇa*, one who is ablazed with lust...depraved with malice....bewildered with delusion.....if lust be abandoned no longer plans thus, no....longer suffers thus. To that extent, *Brahmaṇa*, Nibbāna, is seen in this life...it is to be realized for themselves by the wise."[23] *Nibbāna* is to be experienced. The use of congnitive verb denoting visual perceptions is quite common. In the *Ther.gāthā*, we find an expression: "*I saw Nibbāna*."[24] Similarly in the *Aṅguttara Nikāya*[25] the expression, we have already referred to, used for an experiential state of *Nibbāna* are: "visible here" and "inviting to come and see." A frequent use of acquisitive verbs at the time of describing *Nibbāna*, also supports our contention. Such expressions, "in order to attain *Nibbāna*,"[26] "acquired *Nibbāna*."[27] *and "may he gain Nibbāna*,"[28] sufficiently substantiate our claim that it is imperative for the Buddhist *Bhikkhus* to explore his potentials in order to 'see' or 'attain' or 'gain' *Nibbāna.*

Now, the question is: how to attain *Nibbāna*? In India, there may be two ways: One that of the *Brāhmaṇa,* another that of the *Śramaṇa.* The path of the *Brāhmaṇa* recommends seeking for the Grace of God, which in turn, nullifies efficacy of man's effort, altogether. So, the prayer to God for evoking His Grace is the only way. The path of the *Śramaṇa* is diametrically opposed to the path of the *Brahmaṇa.* The word *Śramaṇa* is derived from *Śrama* which means effort. The Buddha's Path is the path of the *Śramaṇa.* As, there is no place of God in the Buddhist scheme of thought, the attainment of *Nibbāna* has nothing to do with the Grce of God. The Buddhist disciple has to look towards the Buddha as *margādātā* and not as *muktidātā.* For the various stages of attainments, while treading on his Path, the disciple has to rely, exclusively on the grace of his own. The Buddha replaced prayer by meditation. There is no need of belief in God as a prerequisite for practising meditation. Meditation in Buddhism, is the method for exploring the purity of mind, already existing in latent form and described as synonymous with *Nibbāna.*

4.

When Sāriputta, in the *Aṅguttara Nikāya*[29] describes *Nibbāna* as bliss, Udāyan questions the validity of this expression on the ground, that, how the state absolutely devoid of sensation can be characterized as blissful. Udāyan's suggestion, here, seems to be that bliss is nothing but a kind of pleasant sensation that accompanies our perceptions and thus belongs to the realm of consciousness. Sāriputta, reiterates, thus: *Nibbāna* is bliss bereft of sensation. The dilemma calls for an analysis.

Man is a Willing being. Naturally, he prefers exercising his Will for achieving pleasant results. The Will operates through the sense-organs. To accomplish the desired ends man confines the operation of his Will to the pleasant objects, alone. Such attempts, if and when successful, result in originating pleasant consciousness. The consciousness thus produced is certainly transitive in nature. Because the instruments originating consciousness themselves i.e.sense-organs, suffer from an ailment of transtoriness. The desired ends are ultimately, reversed. Man's search for an enduring happiness, thus, acquires a new dimension.

One can safely infer from the foregoing analysis that Will is the root-cause of *man's Suffering.*[30] Now, the fundamental problem is to determine the relation between man and his Will; whether man is Will or man *has* Will. If we subscribe to the former view, then there is no escape form Suffering and man has only to learn to live with it. Buddhism holds the view that man *has* Will and hence it is possible for man to escape form Suffering.[31] To illustrate; the clouds that appear in the sky have nothing in common with the sky. Similarly, Willing that arises in man has nothing in common with man's 'true' self. So, the man's Willing is akin to appearing of the cloud in the sky. What ensues, for us, is transitory nature of man's Will. It is, precisely, for this very nature of man's Will that old Willing can be replaced by the new one. The new Willing, in order to alienate itself from Suffering, must be rooted in the insight into the transitory nature of phenomenal existence. The Will rooted, thus, in such an insight is adorned as the *holy will*. The *holy will* is acclaimed to be the killer of the possibilities of arising of a Will that originates man's Suffering.[32] The Will that operates as the nucleus of man's Suffering, is appropriately marked out, in the Buddhist scheme of thought, as *thirsting will*. Now,as we are aware of this distinction, we are in position to appreciate the spirit of an expression we come across in the *Saṁyutta Nikāya* as: 'For the sake of abandoning desire to Will (*chandapahānatha*), *brāhmaṇa*, the holy life is lived under the Exalted one.[33] *Chanden'eva chandaṁ pajahati*, Will is denied only through Will: Only when through Will holiness is gained, and which is nothing less than will-lessness, then the Will is said to be satisfied.

The state, acquired as a result of denying the *thirsting will* with an aid of *holy will*, is defined as a state of *Nibbāna*. Negatively speaking, such a state of mind is described as absolutely devoid of Suffering. Whereas, *khema* or tranquillity[34] *Sāntī* or peace,[35] *sukhaṁ or* happiness[36] are some of the expressions denoting positive chartertistics of the state of *Nibbāna*.

5.

Buddhism recognizes two kinds of followers, namely, recluse and laity. The Path,primarily devised for recluse, ensures, if followed diligently, to attain *Nibbāna*. Whether the laity can also attain *Nibbāna*, this question has been answered in two different ways. There are Buddhist scholars who do not subscribe to the view that laity can also attain *Nibbāna*. Their basic contention seems to be, that, if laity can also attain *Nibbāna*,then, what is the use of becoming recluse? The argument is not altogether unfounded. Let us look into its nuances. Poussin is one such scholar, who categorically denies a right to laymen to attain *Nibbāna*. "Laymen, however faithful, generous, and virtuous they may be, even if they practice the fortnightly abstinence and continence of the *upavāsa*" writes Poussin in his book, *Way to Nirvāṇa* "Cannot reach *nirvāṇa*[37] Copleston also holds the similar view and advocates his stand from the point of view of distinction between a recluse and a laity, pointed out in the *Sutta Nipāta*, in the following words:

"As the crested bird with the blue neck (the peacock) never attains the swiftness of the swan, even so a householder does not equal a *Bhikkhu*, a secluded *Muni* meditating in the wood."[38]

The distinction between a recluse and a laity becomes all the more significant when we find it extending to cover the range of their respective attainments. The Buddha was once asked whether any laity had ever, after the dissolution of his mortal frame, gained the end of Suffering? He, emphatically replied negatively. But, he admitted that hundreds of laities secured entry into heaven after death.[39] This shows that laity can achieve any height of religious significance, except the highest i.e. *Nibbāna*. Thus, the possibility of attaining *Nibbāna* straightway from the position of laity is ruled out. The good laity may, if he continues to be good in the Buddhist sense, in due course of time, attain *Nibbāna*.

We have looked into the views unfavorable to the laity. There are Buddhist scholars who consider laity an equally competent to attain *Nibbāna*, and they also quote scriptures in support of their views. The laity after having attained

Nibbāna is identified as *layman-arahat*, and we find in the *Aṅguttara* Nikāya, reference to twenty-one such *lay-arahatas.*[40] T.W.Rhys Davids in his introductory remarks to the *Sāmaññaphala-Sutta* has also exalted them as *laymen arahatas*[41] *Kathāvatthu* also mentions that Kulaputta Yasa, Uttiya and Setu attained *Nibbāna* and thus became *arahatas* while pursuing their course of life as laities.[42] There is no dearth of such references in Pāli Canon, but, the very fact that this problem finds a place as one of the dilemmas in the *Milindapañha*, only shows that it kept the followers and the schoars both, occupied. Nāgsena, satisfying the questioning mind of King Milinda clarifies the issue at hand, that irrespective of the fact that whether one is a recluse or laity can attain *arahatship* provided he gains insight into the supreme conduct of life.[43] Here, at this point, it is quite pertinent to point out, that Nāgsena is of the view that after a layman has attained *Nibbāna* either he should enter the *Saṅgha* or he dies, "for beyond that day he cannot last" and there is no third course open to him.[44]

So, we find references in the Buddhist scriptures, substantiating both the views, opposing each other, that laity can and cannot attain *Nibbāna*. Then, where lies the solution? The solution always lies in putting question in correct form. Here, the problem lies in the use of expression laity or laymen. Who is a laity? How to identify him? This question is answered via negative. Any one who is not recluse is laity. This answer is handicapped by two factors. Firstly, it is an over simplified version of laity and secondly, it reduces laity to the level of a static concept. In other words, the change in the course of life of a laity is altogether overlooked. The laity in the present birth enjoying all that is possible to enjoy through the doors of senses may attain *Nibbāna*, for the sample reason that he had accomplished his training and purified his conduct in the course of his previous births.[45] When scholars like the Poussion and Copleston disqualify the laity from attaining *Nibbāna* they have, somehow, a static concept of laity in their minds; and either they depend upon those references which refer to the laity adhering to mere morality or they fail to see the gradual growth in the life of laity extending to several former births.

To conclude: the laity, under favorable circumstances, may attain *Nibbāna* in order to keep it, he must renounce the world.

6

Heraclitus (540-480 B.C.) ancient Greek philosopher, while summing up his doctrine of universal flux by using the river analogy, stated that "upon those who step into the same rivers different and again different waters flow".[46] And, "Plato (429- 347 B.C.) according to Aristotle (384-322 B.C.) "accepts the Heraclitean doctrine (of Universal Flux) so far as sensible things are concerned, but points out that there are non-sensible things not subject to flux"[47] Taking clue from Plato we can appreciate more the state of *Nibbāba* described in Buddhism, wherein every thing is said to be subject to flux except *Nibbāna*. *Nibbāna*, already described, has nothing to do with human personality that operates as a sense-apparatus, which is subject to change, eternally. The state of *Nibbāna,* contrary to every thingelse that forms the part of phenomernal existence, therefore is unchanging or eternal.

To describe *Nibbāna* as eternal implies that it is ONE. Now, let us see what the Buddhist scriptures have to tell about it. In *Udāna* we read, thus: "just as monks, whatsoever streams flow into the mighty ocean whatsoever floods fall from the sky, there is no shrinkage nor overflow seen thereby in the mighty ocean---even so, monks, though many monks pass finally away in that condition of *Nibbāna* which has no remainder, yet is there no shrinkage nor overflow in that condition of *Nibbāba* seen thereby".[48] This means that all those who experience, experience the same Nibbāna is described as One, this One not oridnal, it is rather spatial. The ordinal One suggests temporal order, whereas, *Nibbāna* is ONE in the sense of being eternal.

7.

Nibbāna is ONE. The pluralistic description of ONE, only indicates several standpoints. The most common is negative description. Even the term *Nibbāna* is negatively worded. But, what is substantially negated when *Nibbāna is* realized? In the *Saṁyutta Nikāya* the Buddha tells Rādha, "the destruction of craving is *Nibbāna*."[49]

Negative expressions such as 'cessation of *saṁsāra*','of consciousness',freedom form *dukkha*' from fear, from ignorance, hate and illusion etc. are by no means other than the byproduct of the 'destruction of desire'. These negative descriptions prompted some Buddhist scholars of repute, like Oldenberg, Bigandet Burnouf and Paul Dahlke to infer that the Buddha when determines *Nibbāna* as goal of life advocates nothing but nihilism. Poussin[50] also joins with these scholars when he shares identical views and expression with Olernberg[51] and states that "*Nibbāna* is annihilation". For Burnouf, *Nibbāna* is 'absolute nothing.'[52] Dalkhe, of all these scholars seems to be most enthusiastic to establish *Nibbāna* 'purely a negative thing' when he writes, that:

"Only in Buddhism does the conception "freedom form pain"remain purely a negative thing and not a positive in disguise---heavenly bliss."[53]

Bishop Bigandet too identifies the state of *Nibbāna* as "the bottomless gulf of a total annihilation".[54] Only those scholars, in our opinion, have charged the Buddha advocating nihilism, who are crawling on this side of Ocean of Existence. Consequently, they failed to discern that the teachings of the Buddha lead to the annihilation of desire, which is the root cause of Suffering. They also could not follow that after the extinction of desire, the *arahata* enters into *Nibbāna-nagara orCity of Nibbāna.*[55]

In the *Saṁyutta Nikāya*[56] destruction of desire is explained by making use of parable of sand-castles that the children build-up on the sea-shore. Children play with sand-castles so long as they desire to paly with, without carrying any impression whatsoever.

Negative descirptions of *Nibbāna* are intelligible, when viewed from the stand-point of one who has experienced it. He describes the state of *Nibbāna* negatively with reference to the state of affairs existing prior to the realization of *Nibbāna*. This is also, in a way, to inspire others, indirectly, to switch over to the Path. Moreover, *via negativa* is very much in accord with the Buddha's method of enquiry, who begins acknowledging Suffering as an existential reality and finally succeeds in finding the way out for Suffering humanity.

Negative descriptions of *Nibbāna*, when viewed in isolation, inevitably, result in the distortion of the true picture of *Nibbāna*. The true picture as described in the *Saṁyutta Nikāya* and quoted by S.Radhakrishnan, by way of approval, is that "*Nibbāna* is not a lapse into a void, but only a negation of the flux and a positive return of the Self to itself."[57] The simultaneity of negative and positive aspects of *Nibbāna* is also referred to in the *Saṁyutta Nikāya*, thus: "The mortal who delights in *nibbāna* is freed from all *dukkha*".[58] It may be stated further that the *āsavas* eliminated as a result of realization of *Nibbāna* are described to give way to their contraries, such as, '*kāma* giving place to '*santi* (peace)"[59] *bhava to dhuvaṁ*' (constant).[60]

In the *Mahāvagga*, the Buddha after having attained *sambodhi* while sitting under the Mucalinda tree, it is described how the dark passions gave way to the noble passions and thus highlighted the positive aspect of *Nibbāna*, as under:

"Happy the solitude of him who is full of joy who has learnt the Truth, who has seen Truth. Happy is he who in this world has no ill- will, self-restrained to all beings that have life. Happy is freedom from lusts, the getting right away from them. The highest bliss is freedom from the pride of the thought "I am."[61]

8

The state of *Nibbāna* is also described as indescribable As already discussed, *Nibbāna* is a state of mind to be realized; it is a felt experience and dicursive thinking can hardly comprehend and communicate it to others. Even the things and experiences of mundane nature are had to describe, exhaustively. We describe thing and experiences viewing from the outside. Can we ever describe the smile of Monalisa, to our heartful satisfaction? The answer is invariably in the negative. To unravel the mysterious nature of even mundane experiences we must view them from within. This means, that description cannot take the place of experience. But those who experienced the state of *Nibbāna* have also described it. All the means of communication, available through the use of language suffer from the inherent limitations since these means belongs to the mudane order of reality. Moreover, experience denotes togetherness and mode of thinking can only analyse it and thus reduce it to as many conceptual terms as possible. Only way left open to them could be to communicate their experience through analogies and similies. The simile of fire finds special mention in the Buddhist scriptures and it is used to convey more than one aspect of *Nibbāna*. *Nibbāna* itself symbolizes extinction of fire of *lobh, dosa and moha*. To describe the *Nibbānic* state of mind, the simile of fire too, is deemed to be inadequate. When the fire is exitnguished, this point is made out in the *Majjhima Nikāya,* it is not possible to describe as to what happened to it and to trace out its locale. Similarly, it is inferred that the state of mind of *arahata,* who has attained *Nibbāna,* is beyond the reach of human imagination.[62] To the question whether an *arahata* does not exist or does he exist eternally, the Buddha answered, avoiding both the expected versions, and simply described the delivered one as beyond "all kinds of such disputes".[63] The only reason for describing it as indecrilable is, that the expressions, 'does not exist', or 'does exist', which ask for explanation, belong to the spatio-temporal order of reality, different in kind, and hence, inapplicable to *Nibbāna*. Furthermore, the Buddha, while explaining the state of *arahata,* after he has been delivered from the Five Aggregates, tells Vaccha, that to presume that he is reborn would be far from truth. And, to presume that he is not reborn would be also far from truth. Also to presume that he is neither reborn nor not reborn would be also far from truth.[64] This state of affair, identified as an ineffable has been described by Buddhaghosa in the following words:

"For there is Suffering, but none who suffers. Doing exists althoguh there is no doer: Extinction *(Nibbāna)* is but no extinguished person;

"Although there is a path, there is no goer."[65]

The notion of incomprehensibility has also been described using an analogy of a bird flying in the air, in the following manner:

"Men...who have perceived void and uncoditioned freedom (*Nibbāna*), their path is difficult to understand like that of bird in the air."[66]

Dilating on the different aspects of *Nibbāna*, Nāgasena conveincingly tells King Milinda, that, as regard to the time and place, *Nibbāna* must remain a mystery.[67] This, only, further extends the range of nature of *Nibbāna* as indescribable.

But, it would be wrong to conclude that even the Buddha could not trace out an *arahata* after the latter's death or an *arahata* failed to recognize other *arahatas* when the latter were alive. In the *Dīgha Nikāya*.[68] Ānanda informed the Buddha that some people and died in Nādika. The Buddha could tell Ānanda that among the dead one was *arahata*. Similarly, in the *Saṁyutta Nikāya*[69] it is recorded that Mahā Moggallāna while in the company of five hundred *arahatas* could, or in a way, certify that their mind (*citta*) was freed and deviod of any basis leading to rebirth. This means firstly, that indescribability does not amount to unknowability and secondly, it is relative term and refers to those who have not yet attained *Nibbāna* and,thus, become *arahata*.

9.

Asaṅkhanta Saṁyutta[70] provides biggest collection of attributes, we may uncritically term these as synonyms for *Nibbāna*. Here, we find as many as 32 synonyms for *Nibbāna* and the list includes its both the negative and positive aspects. In whom the fire of *lobha, dosa and moha* has been exitinguished, their state of mind is described using such synonyms positive in nature and also subjectively considered, as:'peace or calm', *santam*,'happiness,*sivam*,'stable', *dhuvaṁ*, 'health',*anītika*, 'purity', *suddhi*, 'the end or goal', *anatam*, and the 'island', *dīpa etc.* When *Nibbāna* is viewed form within, only then, one can paint *Nibbāna* as a positive state of mind. Some of the positive attributes, enlisted above, therefore, stem form the soil of experience of *Nibbāna*.

Dhammapada[71] is full of references, expressing peace and happiness as attributes of *Nibbānic* state of mind, and we quote:

23: "These wise people, meditative, steady, always possessed of strong powers, attain to *Nibbana*, the highest happiness."

96: "His thought is quite, quite are his words and deed, when he has obtained freedom by true knowledge, when he has thus become a quiet man."

98: "In a hamlet or in a forest, on sea or on dry land, wherever venerable persons (*Arahanta)* dwell, that place is delightful."

99. "Forests are delightful; where the world finds no delight, there the passionless will find delight, for they look not for pleasures."

204: "Health is the greatest of gifts, contentedness, the best riches; trust is the best relationship, *Nirvāna* the highest happiness."

The word 'happiness', or *sukha*, is frequently used as a synonym for *Nibbāna* and it also denotes pleasure of mundane nature. The two-fold use of the world *sukha* does create problem while communciating the ture impot of the term *sukha*, describing an attribute of *Nibbāna*. This problem crops up when Sāriputta in the *Aṅguttara Nikāya*[72] describes *Nibbāna* as: "Friend, this *Nibbāna* is happiness. The use of the word *sukha* or happiness causes confusion in the mind of one of the monks present, Udāyin by the name, and he puts quite a penetrating question: "Friend, Sāriputta, what is then here the happiness tht is not felt in this (*Nibbāna*)"? Sāriputta, then after enumerating, states these five types of sense pleasures is called the happiness of the sense pleasures. The happiness that the *Bhikkhus* relish, explains Sāriputta, is cut off from the sense pleasures. This is way *Nibbāna* is not categorized as *Vedanā* that operates as a great hindrance in the way to realize *Nibbāna*.

After one has realized *Nibbāna* one's *citta* or consciousness becomes purified and purified *citta* is said to be 'stable', *dhuvaṁ* and 'called', *vūpasanta*[73]. To the question[74] whether an *arahata* is aware of the fact that his obessions are destroyed, Ānanda replies in affirmation, and, also emphatically points out that whether he is walking or standing or asleep or awake the obsessions are no more there and he is also conscious of the transformation of his total personality. In the *Therigātha,*[75] Vimalā, the *Theri,* has, reflected and expressed, thus:

> *"Now all the evil bonds that fetter gods*
> *And men are wholly rent and cut away.*
> *Purg'd are the Āsavas that drugg'd my heart*
> *Calm and content I know Nibbāna's Peace.*

This verse expresses the affirmation of her having become *Aññā,* a subjective synonym for *Arahatship.*

We also find *Nibbāna* described in terms of health. Freedom from disease or *abyādhi*[76] and health or *anītika,*[77] both the words are used as synonyms for *Nibbāna.* To have healthy mind means not to identify oneself with any of the Five *khandhas* and to be able to see the true nature of things and beings plagued with impermanence.[78]

In the *Majjhima Nikāya,* the Buddha, in quite an unimbiguous language descibes in the manner the delivered one achieves an End of life or Goal, and that reads, thus:

"---And to him thus Delivered comes knowledge of his Deliverance in the conviction: Rebirth is no more; I have lived the highest life; my task is done; there is now no more of what I have been."[79]

The Buddha, as usual,has also made use of simile to identify the nature of *Nibbāna* e.g.*dīpa,* the island. In *Dhammapada* it is taught that by "rousing himself,by earnestness, by restraint and control, the wiseman may make for himself an island which no flood can overwhelm"[80]. Similarly, in the *Sutta Nipāta,*[81] feeling of having attained *Nibbāna* is expressed by making use of a simile "cool like the waters of a lake." The Buddha, also at one place expressed identical feeling thus: "I have become cool and have attained *Nibbāna*"[82].

But, it is the negative terminology describing *Nibbāna,* that has drawn more attention of the Buddhist scholars, perhaps, they could intune themselves much more, only, when viewed from outside. Rune Johansson, in his book, *The Psychology of Nirvāṇa,* has classified negative attributes of *Nibbāna* into several groups, referring to social world, personal conditions, general conditions and phychological attributes.[83] The negative descriptions of *Nibbāna* such, as *sambāha,* 'uncrowded' *akhalita*, 'undisturbed', *nirupatāpa*, 'untroubled', and *abhaya*, 'free from fear', suggests Rune Johanassons, refer to the social world which has, obviously, the characteristics contrary to the state of *Nibbāna*. Similarly, when we come across descriptions, e.g., *ajāta*, 'freedom from birth', *abhuta*, 'freedom from becoming' *akata*, 'freedom form creation', *asankhata* 'freedom from compounding', *abyadhi*, 'without illness', *ajara*', 'freedom' from old age', and *amata* 'deathless' etc., these negative expressions only stand to negate general conditions of life inflicted with dukkha. Again, it is a matter of common experience that the world is full of hostility, aggression and impurities. The *Nibbānic* state presents a contrast when described as : *asapatta* 'without hostility', *avya-appaja*, 'harmless', and *asasankilliṭṭha*. The negative descriptions, directly concerning our consciousness e.g., *anāsava*, 'without obsession', *nippañca*, 'without illusion', *asoka*., 'free form sorrow,' and *viraga*, 'without desire', describe state of mind after the attainment of *Nibbāna* and with reference to the state of mind that it has negated. We have referred to the state of *Nibbāna* identified as freedom. Besides the expressions quoted above, we find *mukti* or release and *anālaya* or freedom used as aynonyms for *Nibbāna*. "Release means *Nibbāna*" this is categorically stated in the *Saṁyutta Nikāya*.[84] Again, we read: "Nibbāna, said the Master, is the deliverance from every tie".[85] Here, we should not forget that the Buddha while defining *Nibbāna* as freedom means freedom gained at the level of *citta*, that ultimately leads to the cessation of *saṁsara*.

Earlier, we have referred to the negative expressions, describing the nature of *Nibbāna*, and indirectly, referring to the general conditions of life. A passage in Udāna, presents a conclusive argument on the subject, that reads:

"Monks, there is a *[atthi] not born (ajatam)*, not become (*abhutaṁ*), not-made (*akataṁ*) not compounded (*assaṁ-khataṁ*). If that unborn, not-become, not-made, not-compounded were not, there would be apparent no escape form this here that is born, become, made, compounded. But since, monks, there is an un-become, un-made, uncompounded, therefore is apparent the ascape form this here that is born, become, made compounded."[86]

The *escape* described is not only logical construction; it is rather practical. After the *escape*, from conditioned reality, an *arahata* enters into *Nibbāna-nagar* or City of *Nibbāna* which is "spotless, and stainless, pure and white, ageless and deathless, where is security and calm and bliss."[87]

Nibbāna, when described objectively is identified in *Therīgāthā*[88] as : (i) Truth, (ii) the Highest Good, (iii) Supreme opportunity, (iv) regulated life (v) communion with the Best, and (vi) bringing congenial work etc.

10.

Nibbāna as described in *Itivuttaka*[88] is tow-fold viz. *Sa-upādiseasa-nibbāna* and *An-upadi-seasa- nibbāna*. The key-expression, in both the word-formations, is *upādi*, which as an entity comes into existence as a result of formation enjoined by the five groups of grasping, we name personality. *Sa-upādi-sea-nibbāna*, therefore, means *Nibbāna* attained in this life, or in other words, exitinction of defilements or *upādi* still remaining intact. Whereas *an-upādi-sesa nibbāna* means extinction not only of all defilements, but along with these the five aggregates (or *upādi*) are also, rendered extinct which, of course, happens when the *arahata* dies.

Sa-upādi-sesa-nibbāna i.e. Nibbāna attained during the course of living, naturally, evokes curiosity in the mind of those who have not tasted *Nibbāna*, and thus fail to grasp the manner in which the *Nibbānic* state of mind continues to operate, until the death occurs. An attempt has been made to satisfy the curious mind by making use of a simile of the potter's wheel.[90] As the potter's wheel continues to move even after the potter has removed his operating hand, likewise, *kamma* continues to carry on the bodily existence of the *arahata*, although, the extinction of *taṇhā* or thirst that operates as a cause for coming into exitence, has taken place. Besides the simile of the potter's wheel, there are concrete references too, that go a long way in explaining the kind of *Sa-upādi-sesa- nibbāna*. we shall refer to, when and where required.

After preliminary remarks, let us probe into the problem, extracting detailed results. Our first concern pertains to *Sa-upādi-sesa-nibbāna*. What is after all, the mode of living of *arahata?* How does he conduct himself in day to day living? The anwers to these questions can only be given after analysing the psycho-phycial frame-work of a living *arahata*. The description of *arahata* contained in the *Itivuttaka*, reads thus:

"Herein, monks, a monk is *arahant*, one who has destroyed the cankers, who has lived the life, done what was to be done, laid down the burden, won the goal, worn out the fetter of becoming, one released by perfect knowledge. In him the five sense-faculties still remain, through which , as they have not yet departed, he experiences sensations pleasent and unpleasant, undergoes pleasure-and pain. In him the end of lust, malice and delusion, monks, is the condition of *Nibbāna* with the basis still remaining."[91]

The story of *Aṅgulimāla*, a living *arahata*, explains the nature of *sa-upādi-sesā-nibbāna* i.e. 'Nibbāna with the substrate left'. In the *Majjhima Nikāya*[92] we read about Aṅgulimāla, "a ruffian whose hands were red with blood, who was always killing and wounding and showed no mercy to any living creature," who was converted by the Buddha, later on attained *Nibbāna* and thus became *arahata*. One day, the story continues, while he was on his way, begging for food, he was given severe beating with sotnes and sticks and returned to the Buddha streaming with blood. Besides that, the story explains the 'hidden chain of Suffering', it also reveals the state of an *arahata* who, no doubt, has attained *Nibbāna*, during the course of present life, called *sa- upādi-sesā-nibbāna*, but, has to undergo Suffering on account of five aggregates or *upādi*, still remaining intact. The Buddha's ailment during the last few months of his life, also supports the view expressed above.

Through the insight, an *arahata* has gained, he perceives the five aggreates as being *anattā* or No-self and thus develops aversion for each one of them. The aversion, ultimately, results in detachment. Now, the entire outlook is transformed and the normal course of functioning of the five aggregates is totally changed. The influx of impurities is, now, no more possible. As students of Buddhism, we know the all pervasive character of causality, that operates in the phenomenal existence. Causality retains its operation even in the life-process of an *arahata* with a difference. The causal pattern reveals itself, but now through entirely different causal factors. This change is described in the following manner:

"The elimination of ego-consciousness produces revulsion (*nibbāda*) with regard to things earlier were grasped as being substantial. Revulsion produces detechment (*viraga*) Detachment produces freedom (*vimutti*), and therefore one attains stability *(thitata)* of mind so that one does not tremble or is not agitated as a result of gain (*labha*) or loss (*alabha*), good repute (*yasa*) or disrepute (*ayasa*), praise (*pasaṁsā*), a blame (*nidā*), happiness (*sukha*) or Suffering (*dukkha*)."[93]

These are the eight factors called *aṭṭhalokadhamma,* that usually affect the course of life of one who has not yet attained the *Nibbānic* state of mind.

An *arahata's* attitude towards *maraṇa* or death, also undergoes a radical change. Because of the result of an attainment of *Nibbāna taṇhā* or thirst for Becoming is extinguished, he is no more attached to present life nor concerned with the life after death. He has, in a way, conquered death and is no more afraid of it. This attitude, with regard to death, in the words of Sāriputta, is recorded in *Theragāthā,* in the manner as follows:

"Not fain am I to die nor yet to live.

I shall lay down this mortal frame anon with mind alert,

with consciousness controlled.

With thought of death I dally not, nor yet

Delight in living. I wait the hour

Like any hireling who hath done his task."[94]

What is precisely the state of an *arahata* freed from *dukkha,* is a query that remains to be enquired into. For the purpose of unraveling the mystery of the state of an *arahata,* the Buddhist scholars have invariably focused their attention in analysing the four passages in the *Udāna*. These passages relate to *Nibbāna*. Before we discuss and draw conclusions, let us reproduce the text of the four passage and which is as follows:

(i)"Monks, there exists that condition wherein neither earth nor a water nor fire nor air: wherein neither the sphere of infinite space nor of infinite consciousness nor of nothingness nor of neither-consciousness-nor-unconsciousness; where there is neither this world nor a world beyond nor both together not moon-and-sun. Thence, monks, I declare is no coming to birth, neither is going (from life); there in is no duration: thence is no falling; there is no arising. It is not something fixed, it moves not on, it is not based on anything. That indeed is the end of Ill."

(ii) "Hard is the infinite to see; truth is no easy thing to see; craving is pierced by him who knows; for him who seeth naught remains."

(iii) Monks there is not-born, a not-become, not made, a not- compounded. Monks, if that unborn, not become, not-compounded were not, there would be apparent no escape form this here that is born, become made, compounded."

(iv) "For him who clings there is wavering; for him who clings not there is no wavering. Wavering not being, there is calm; calm being, there is no bending. Bending not being, there is no coming-and going (to birth); coming-and going not being, there is no decease-and rebirth. Decease-and rebirth not being, there is no "here" or "yonder" nor anything between the two. This indeed is the end of Ill."[95]

These four passage describe three stages viz. *saṁsāra, Nibbāna* and the transit between them. The passage no. (iii) refers to 'escape from the born, become, made, compound' and these are the characteristic features of *Saṁsāric* existence. An indirect reference to earth, water, fire, moon and sun etc. in the passage no. (i) further adds into the picture of *saṁsāra*. Also, reference to 'craving' in passage no. (ii) and wavering in passage no. (iv) hardly refers to anything else, but the psychological impact of *saṁsāric* mode of living.

In the passage no. (i) we read: 'Thence monks, I declare is no coming to birth, thither is no going (from life)....no falling, no arising'. These expressions signifying cessation, of course, of rebirth, unambiguously underline the state of *Nibbāna*. The concluding words: 'this indeed is the end of ill' further supports our contention. When the monk escapes form *saṁsāra* he enters into *Nibbāna nagar* described in passage no. (iii) as, 'not-born, not become, not- made, not-compounded. The passage no.(ii) while referring to 'Truth', attempts to add into the positive attribute of *Nibbāna*.

The transit form *saṁsāra* to *Nibbāna* is primarily worked out in passage no. (iv). The traformation is effected through renewed pattern of Causality. The non-attachment leads to no-wavering or steadiness of mind which brings forth calmness. "When there is calm', it is stated, 'there is no bending'. The absence of bending results in 'no- coming and going', and which means cessation of rebirth. This cessation is deified as *Nibbāna,* which, in the ultimate analysis, is gained through the exinction of *tāṇhā* or thirst. But, as pointed out earlier,[96] 'he retains his senses', which only wait to be destroyed, finally,by the death, he does experience pleasant and unpleasant sensations. When it is stated that there is neither earth, water, fire, air, moon and sun, nor coming and going, this simply means that an *arahata* is immune to these things or nothing that belongs to this world causes him anxiety any more.

Nibbāna means cessation of *taṇhā* or thirst. There is no *taṇhā* when there is cessation of perception and feeling, because according to the doctrine of dependent origination, 'depending on feeling arises taṇhā."[97] Of course, there is striking similarity i.e. absence of *taṇhā,* in both the states of mind. But, these two states are not identical in nature. There is a difference and it lies in their different nature of consciousness. When we find an *arahata* exposed to pleasant and unpleasant sensation, this only mens that nature of his consciousness is not devoid of differentiation. Whereas, in the case of cessation of perception and feeling, the working of sense-apparatus is altogether (although temporarily) suspended. Thus, one who has attained the state of cessation of perception and feeling in the *Saṁyutta Nikāya,* such a state of being is compared and contrasted with a dead person, that reads as follows:

"In a dead man, housefather, in one who has made an end, the activity of body has ceased, become calmed. So also have the activities of speech and mind,---they have ceased, become calmed. Life has run out, vital heat has ceased, the faculties are scattered. In him, housefather, who has attained the ceasing of perception and feeling, the activity of body also has ceased, become calmed. So also have the activities of speech and mind. But his life has not run out, vital-heat has not ceased, the faculties have become clarified. That is the difference between a dead man, one who has made an end, and one has attained the ceasing of perception and feeling."[98]

There are several instances, referred to in the Buddhist scriptures, which fairly illustrate the point under discussion. In the *Majjhima Nikāya*[99] it is stated, that reverend Sanjaya was competent enough to attain the state of cessation of perception and feeling without any hardship and he could do so while sitting any where under the foot of a tree or some solitary place. Once when he was absorbed in the said state of mind, some cow-herds, goat-herds, and wayfarers took him to be dead and these country folk gathered some grass and sticks and then offered him to the fire. After a long time Sanjaya arose form his absorption, next morning, shook his garments, got ready and went to the near by village as usual, for alms of food. It was astonishing, indeed, for those, to see him alive, who took him as dead and gave him to the fire. Thus, one who has attained the state of cessation of perception and feeling, hardly needs to exercise an effort to nullify say, the attacks of *Māra* on his sense-apparatus. On the other hand, an *arahata* remains in alive contact with the phenomenal existence. But, since, an *arahata* has gained full control over his psyche, successfully prevents the process of attachment to take place. This is why, in the description of the state of *sā-upādi- sesa-nibbāna*, reference to the cessation of perception and feeling is conspicuously absent.

Our next problem is to know about an *arahata*, when he has relinquished his psycho-physical frame-work, technically termed as *an-upādi-sesa-nibbāna*. Regarding this state of an *arahata*, we read in Itivuttaka, thus:

"Herein a monk is *arahant*...released by perfect knowledge, but in him this very life all things that are sensed have no delight for him, they have become cool. This is called "the condition of *Nibbāna* without basis."[100]

The description of dead *arahata*, only, refers to the cooling of his feelings, which he did not relish during his life time. It is silent on the question of his survival after death. The fundamental problem, regarding *an-upādi-sesa-nibbāna*, that the Buddhist scholars have been trying to solve, is whether an *arahata* exists or does not exist after his death. Frequent reference is made to *Aggivacchagotta Sutta*, wherein, Vacchagotta, a *brāhmaṇa*, once put this question to the Buddha, which latter replied using an analogy of fire. When, Vacchagotta asserted, that after the fire is extinguished for lack of fuel to sustain it, it is not possible to locate fire, then at this juncture of time, the Buddha explains the position of an *arahata* after he is dead, thus:

"Just in the same way, Vaccha, all things material---all feelings- all perception-all plastic forces-all consciousness-every-thing by which the truth-finder might be denoted has passed away for him,---grubbed and stubbed, leaving only the bare cleared site where once a palm-tree towered,---a thing that once has been and can be no more. Profound, measureless, unfathomable, is the truth finder even as the mighty ocean, reborn does not apply to him nor not-reborn nor any combination of such terms; everything by which the truth-finder might be denoted, has passed away for him, utterly and for ever."[101]

The fact that five aggregates become extinct at the time of death of an *arahata*, neither it means that he exists in some other identifiable form, nor does it imply that he is totally annihilated. The Buddha in order to avoid both the extreme positions maintained by the eternalists and annihilationists preferred to remain either silent or replied in paradoxical language.[102] But, once to the question, 'Has he (only) disappeared, or does not exist (any longer), or is he for ever free from sickness',[103] the Buddha answered thus:

"For him who has disappeared there is no form. O Upasiva---that by which they say he is, exists for him no longer when all things (*dhamma*) have been cut off, all (kinds of) disputes are cut off."[104]

The term (*dhamma*) in this context, is used in the sense of corporeality and which is quite intune with the description of an *an-upādi-sesa nibbāna* i.e., *nibbāna* 'without substrate left.' The very fact that a dead *arahata* is compared with deep ocean only means to suggest there is no conceptual channel to comphrehend his state of 'existence. So, the very question, that whether an *arahata* after death exists or does not exist needs to be modified, if at all possible, to avoid an error involved in the use of expression,'exist', that belongs to the arena of phenomenal reality. 'Like can be known only by like', is a proverbial saying and in this background it may only be said:

> *"Just as the borun of a blazing spark of fire*
> *Struck form the anvil, gradually fading,*
> *Cannot be known,---so in the case of those*
> *who've rightly won release and crossed the flood*
> *Of lusts that bind, and reached the bliss unshaken,*
> *The bourn they've won cannot be pointed to."*[105]

Notes and References :

1. *Culla vagga* 238. Horner, I.B., *The Book of the Discipline,* Vol.V,p.335.
2. M.73 (*Mahā-vacchogotta Sutta*): M ii 493, Chalmers, Vol.I.p.347.
3. S.V.347. Woodward, Vol.V.p.370.
4. D.9.(*Potthapāda Sutta*): D.i.186. Rhys Davids, T.W., *Early Buddhism.* p.69.
5. M.63. (*Cūla-Mālunkya Sutta*): M.ii.430 ii.430; Horner, I.B., Vol.II.p.100.
6. Law, B.C., *Designation of Human Types,* (47-50) pp.26-27; cf. Grimm, George, *The Doctrine of the Buddha, pp.307ff.*
7. Dhp. 178. Maxmuller.
8. MV.(Vin).i.13-14.
9. D-1 (*Brahmajāla Sutta*): D.i.31,34
10. Mv. (Vin) i.13-14.
11. Warren Henry, Clark, *Buddhism in Translation, p. 133.*
12. Narasu, P.Lakshmi, *The Essence of Buddhism,* p.107.
13. D.16 (*Mahā-Parinibbānā-Sutta*): D.ii.162.
14. A.i.241 Woodword, Vol.1,p.221.
15. D.16 (*Mahā-Parinibbāna-Sutta*): D.ii.93; S.B.E., Vol.XI.p.26.
16. S.ii.134. cf., *Points of Controversy,*book XII, Sec,5,9.

17. A.i.231-232. Woodword, Vol.1.pp.211-212.
18. A.i.232: Woodward, Vol.1.p.212.
19. M.72 (*Aggi.Vacchagotta Sutta*): M.i.488-489. Chalmers, Vol.1,p.344.
20. A.ii.190, Woodward, Vol.II.p.200
21. Idem.
22. Idem.
23. A.i.158 Woodward, Vol.1.p.141.
24. Ti.97: "addasaṁ, nibbānaṁ."
25. A.i, 158: "sandiṭṭhika; ehipassika".
26. Sn.454: "nibbānapattiyā"
27. Ti.432: "nibbānañ ca labhassu".
28. Ta 637: "nibbābaṁ abhiharye".
29. A.IV, 414.
30. S.IV. 328: "Sabbaṁ taṁ chandamūlakaṁ chandanidānaṁ. chando hi mūlaṁ dukkhassa."
31. Grimm, George, op.cit., pp. 235,262.
32. Ibid.pp.262,264.
33. S.V.272: Woodward, Part V,p. 243.

    'Kimthiyaṁ nu kho,bho Ānanda, Samane Gotame brahmacariyaṁ Vussti" ti?
    Chandapphanathāṁ kho brāhmaṇa, bhagvati brahmacarijaṁ vussti."ti?
    "Attthi paṇa bho Ānanda, maggo attith paṭipadā aitassa chandhassa phānāyā" ti?
    "Katmo pana, bho Ānanda, maggo katama paṭipada aitassa chandhassa phānāyā" ti?
    Also see: Grimm, George, *op. cit;* p. 264
34. It 27: "ātāpi....nibbānāya bhabbo anuttarassa yogakkhemassa adhigamāyā."
35. Sn. 933: Sānti ti nibbuṭiṁ ñatvā.
36. Dhp.203: *Nibbāṇaṁ paramaṁ sukkhaṁ.*
37. Poussin, *Way to Nirvāṇa*, pp.150,151.
38. (i) Sn.220: S.B.E., Vol.X, part II.p.35.

    (ii) Copleston, *Buddhism Primitive and Present, p.205.*

39. M.71. (*Tevijja-vacchagotta Sutta*): M.i.483: See Chalmers, Vol.1,341.

40. A.iii.451.

41. Rys Davids, T.W., *The Dialogues of the Buddha,* (S.B.B) Vol. II, Part-1, p.63.

42. *Kathāvatthu,* (P.T.S.) p.268.

43. *The Question of King Milinda,* S.B.E.Vol.XX *na tena nibbānadhātuyātinattaṁ vā purattaṁ vā psññāyati* VI, Part-II, pp.56-57.

44. Ibid. Part-II, pp.96,97.

45. Ibid. part-II, 253.

46. Heraclitus, *The Cosmic Fragments, Fragment*12, p.367.

47. Ross, Sir David, *Plato's Theory of Ideas,* p.19.

48. Udāna 55: *evaṁ eva kho bhikkhave bahū ce pi bhikkhā anupādisesāya nịbbānadhātuyā parinibbāyanti,* Woodward. *The Minor Anthologies of the Pāli Canon,* pp.66-67.

49. S.iii. 190: "Taṇhakkhayo hi, Rādha, nibbānaṁ: ti. Wooward, Part III,p.157; cf.S.iv, 368-372.

50. Poussin, *Way to Nirvāṇa,* p.150.

51. Oldenberg, H., *Buddha, His Life His Doctrine His Order,* p.273.

52. Maxmuller, *Studies in Buddhism,* p.57.

53. Dalkhe Paul, *Buddhist Essays,pp.47-48.*

54. Maxmuller, *Studies in Buddhism,* p.51.

55. Horner, I.B. (trs). *Milinda's Question, Vol.II pp.98, 175, 214.*

56. S.iii, 190: Woodward, Part III p. 156.

57. S.iii.25, Radhakrishan, Dr., Indian Philosophy, Vol.I, p.386.

58. S.i.38: "nibbānabhirato macco sabbadukkhā pamuccatī ti.

59. M.i.504.

60. S.iv.370.

61. Mv. (vin) i.2. *Rhys Davids, T.W.Early Buddhism, p.39.*

62. M.72 (*Aggi-Vacchagotta Sutta*): M.i.487.

63. Sn. 1075: "na pammāṇamatthi" cf. *Brahmajāla Sutta;* S.B.B., Vol-II p.54.
64. M.72 (Aggi-Vacchagotta Sutta): M.i.486.
65. Vm.XVI.90. (Nyāṇamoli).
66. Dhp. 92. (Maxmuller).
67. Mp.See: Dilemma 81 and 82.
68. D.16 (*Mahā-Parinibbāna Sutta*): D.ii.91f.
69. S.i., 194: *"Tesaṁ sudaṁ ayasmā Mahā- Moggallāno cetasā cittaṁ samanesati vippamuttaṁ nirupadhiṁ.*
70. S.iv. 368-372.
71. Dhp.23,96,98,99,204, (Maxmuller).
72. *A.iv.414f."Sukhaṁ idaṁ,āvuso nibbānaṁ", ti...kiṁ panettha āvuso Sāriputta sukhaṁ, yad ettha natthi vedayitaṁti? Pañcime'...kāmāguṇā...idaṁ vuccatavuso, kāmasukhaṁ vivicc eva kāmehi...Hare, E.M., Vol.IV. IV.p.279-80.*
73. D.i.71.
74. M.76, (Sandka-Sutta): M.i.523...*tasa carato c'eva tiṭṭahto ca suttassa ca jāgarassa ca satatṁ samitaṁ....'Khīnā me āsavā. ti api ca kho pannaṁ paccavekkhamāno janā ti: khiṇā me āsavā ti....,*
75. Ti, 76: Rhys Davids, C.A.F., *Psalms of Early Buddhists,* Part-I, p.53.
76. M. 75 (*Māgandiya Sutta*), M. 26 (*Ariya- Pariyesana-Sutta*):M.i.173.
77. M.75 (*Māgāndiya Sutta*) M.i. 511 (*ārogya*: 'health').
78. S. iii, 46.
79. M. 7.(*Vatthūma-Sutta*) M.i. 38.
80. Dhp. 25, (Maxmuller)
81. Sn. 467 :*parinibbuto udakarahado va sīto.*
82. M.i, 171: *Sītibhuto' and nibbuto.*
83. Johansson, Rune E. A., *The Psyohology of Nirvāṇa*, pp. 45-46.
84. S. iii. 110: *Vimutti...nibbānathtthā.*
85. S.i.210: *Nibbānaṁ Bhagava āhu sahhaganthappamocanaṁ* Rhys, Davids C. A. F., Part-I, p. 270.
86. U. 81.

87. *The Questions of king Milinda* S.B.E., vol. XXXVI, p. 213.

88. Rhys, Davids, C.A.F., *Psalms of the Early Buddhists*, p. xxxviii (Introduction).

89. It. 38: *'Saupādisesā ca nibbānadhātu anupādi-sesā ca nibbānadhātu'*.

90. Silva Lynn A de, *The Problem of the Self in Buddhism and Christanity*, p. 67.

91. It. 38: *'.......tassa titthanteva pañe- indriyāni-yesaṁ avihātattā manāpāmanāpāṁ paccanubhati, sukhadukkhaṁ patisamvedi- yati: tassa yo rāgakkhayo dosakkhayo mohakkhayo, ayaṁ vuccati.... Saupādisesa nibbānadhātu.* Woodward, *Minor Anthologies of the Pāli Canon*. Part- II, p. 143.

92. M.86: (*Aṅgulimāla-Sutta*): Chalmers, Vol. II, p. 153.

93. Kalupahana, David j, *Buddhist Philosophy*, p. 73 cf. D. iii 260 Aṭṭha loka-dhammā lābho ca alābho ca yaso ca ayaso ca nindā ca passṁsā ca sukhañ ca dukkhañ ca.

94. Ta: 1002-1003: Rhys Davids, C.A.F., : *Psalms of the Early Buddhists*, Part-II, p. 346.

95. U. 80-81:

(i) *'Atthi bhikkhave tad āyatanaṁ, yattha n'eva pathavi nā āpo na tejo na vāyo na ākāsānañcāyatanaṁ na viññānāñcāya tanaṁ na nevasaññānāsañāyatanaṁ nāyaṁ loko na paralokko ubho candi-masūriyā tad ahaṃ bhikkhave n'eva āgatiṁ vadāmi na gatiṁ na thitiṁ na cutiṁ na upapattiṁ appatitthaṁ appavattaṁ anārammaṅaṁ evataṁ, es'ev' anto dukkhassā' ti.*

(ii) *'Duddasaṁ anattaṁ nāma, na hi saccaṁ sudassanaṁ; paṭividdhā taṇhā jānato, passato n'atthi kiñcanan ti.*

(iii) *'Atthi bhikkhavetajataṁ abhūtaṁ akātaṁ asankhataṁ na ce taṁ bhikkhave abhavissa ajātaṁ abhūtaṁ akataṁ asankhataṁ, na yidha jātassa bhūtassa katassa sankhatass nissaraṇaṁ paññāyetha. Yasmā na kho bhikkhave atthi ajātaṁ abhūtaṁ akātaṁ asankhataṁ, tasmā jotossa bhūtassa katassa sankhatassa nissaraṇaṁ paññāyati'*

(iv) *' Nissitassa ca calitaṁ, anissitassa calitaṁ n'atthi, caliteasati passaddhi, passadhiyā sati rati na hoti, ratiyā asati āgatigati na hoti, agāti-gatiyā asati cutūpapāto na hoti, catupayāte asatin ev'dha na huraṁ na ubhayamantare, es' ev' anto dukkhassā'ti.* Woodward, *Minor Anthologies*, p. 97-99.

96. It. 38.
97. *'Vedanā paccayā taṇhā'*.
98. S. iv. 294: Woodward, Part IV, p. 202.
99. M. 50, (*Māra-Tajjaniya Suta*). Also see D. 16. *Mahāaprinibbāna-Sutta* Wherein the states of cessation of perception and feeling of Alara Kalam and the Buddha are mentioned. Chalmers, Vol. I, p. 240.
100. It. 38: *'tassā idheva..... sabbavedayatāni anabhinanatidāni sītabhavissanti*: Woodward. *The Minor Anthologics*, part-II, p. 143.
101. M. 72: (*Aggi-vacchagotta-Sutta*) : M. i. 486f.
     Chalmers, Vol. 1, p. 344.
102. See Ref. 95.
103. Sn. 1074; *'Atthaṅgato so uda vā so n'atthi udāhu ve sassatiyā arogo'*.
     Fousboll, S.B.E., Vol.X, Part-II, p. 198-199.
104. Sn. 1075, Ibid., p.199.
105. U. 93.
     Woodward, *The Minor Anthologies*, Part II, p. 114.

CHAPTER-14

THE HOME OF PĀLI

—Dr. A.B. Keith, M.A; D.C.L; D.Litt.

If we follow the guidance of a great pioneer the study of Pāli[1] we must belive that the Buddha's mother tongue was Kosalan, the vernacular of a powerful kingdom of the 7th and 6th centuries B.C The Pāli Canon as the *Vinaya* and the four *Nikāyas,* with the possible exception of the supplements, falls within a century of the Buddha's death, and the rest belongs to the following century. The language of these texts is based on this standard Kosalan. It is true that in Ceylon the tradition attested by Buddhaghosa held that the language of the Canon was Māgadhi, but this must not mislead us. It is clear that the reference is not to the Māgadhi of the Prākrit grammarians, since these wrote centuries later, nor to the contemporary dialect of Magadha. What is meant is that the language was that used by Aśoka, the king of Magadha, seeing that the Canon was brought by his son Mahinda, by oral tradition, not in writing. Now the edicts of Aśoka reveal the existence of a standard language, and this Māgadhiā is devoid of the peculiarities which are normally associated with the idea of that dialect, being in fact a younger form of the standard Kosalan *lingua franca* already montioned. The fact that Kosaln should have thus retained its supremacy despite the fact that the king of Magadha became king of Kosala may be explained by a peaceful succession of the former to the Kosalan throne. There is a parallel available in the case of the Scottish dynasty ascending the English throne; the dialects remained apart, but spread at the expense of the Scottish. Thus we may conceive of Kosalan as spreading over an area from Delhi in the west, to Patna in the east and from Sāvatthiā in the north to Avanti in the south. Pāli may thus be held to be a literary dialect, based on the spoken language of Kosala, probably in the form which it assumed at Avanti.

Windisch[2] and Geiger[3] also agree in defending the authenticity of the traditional view of Pāli as Māgadhī. The speech of the Buddha, which is assumed to be reproduced in the Canon, was doubtless the educated *lingua franca* which had been devised for the needs of the intercourse of learned men in India. Such a speech naturally would not be marked by strong dialectical characteristics, but it would vary from place to place, for it would assume a local tinge. The Buddha was not a Magadhan, but his activities there would result in his preaching assuming a definite tinge of Māgadhī, which would therefore naturally be regarded as his form of speech. But this Māgadhī would be without the extreme characteristics of that speech, and would rather be the Ardha-Māgadhi or Ārṣa and the Buddha preached in a similar form of language. Nor can it be admitted, on this theory, that the Canon was redacted in any speech other than that of the Buddha himself. Geiger adduces in proof of the fidelity with which it was sought to preserve the speech of the Master the account in the *Cullavagga*, v.33.1, of the instruction given by the Buddha, when it was represented to him that it might be desirable that his teaching should be handed down *chandaso*, that is doubtless in the literary Brahmanical language. The Buddha replied: *anujānāmi, bhikkhave sakāya niruttiyā buddhavacanaṁ pariyāpuṃtuṁ* meaning thereby according to Buddhaghosa, to command the monks to learn the precepts of the Buddha in his own speech, that is Māgadhī. Despite, however, the stress laid on this interpretation by Geiger, it is impossible in the context to accept his rendering. Doubtless, if the phrase cited stood alone it is capable of bearing the sense given, but it follows on the express statement that the monks, as of different families and origin, were corrupting the sayings of the Buddha in repeating them *sakāya niruttiyā*, which in that context can only mean "each in his own speech." The passage, therefore, is decisive; even in the early school there was a definite tradition ascribing to the Master himself the grant of authority to depart from the tradition of his speech. That Pāli is

Māgadhī or Ardha-Māgadhi in any sense, therefore, is not favoured by the *Cullavagga*.

It has, however, been suggested by Max Walleser[4] that the name Pāli itself goes back to Pātalī, and that to Pātaliputra,while Pātali, of course, is present in Pātaliputra, the name of the Magadhan capital. That term again must be deemed as equivalent to Pātalipura, the change being due to contamination with Vajjiputta. The theory is not without difficulties, for so far as the evidence goes it seems dubious whether Pāli was really used as the name of a language, but the decision of the issue is of no great importance from the present point of view. If indeed the term was found in the *Pitakas*, the sense would be important, but it does not appear there but in the commentaries, and carries us little further than the tradition in Buddhaghosa that the speech of the Canon was Māgadhi.

The views of Rhys Davids and Geiger alike see in the Canon something approaching the actual language used by the Buddha, and to those who hold on other grounds that the Canon is of much later origin than even the first century after his death, this view naturally has little plausibility. But, of course, even if we admit that the texts were composed as eartly as is suggested by these scholars, the question arises whether we can place any faith in the view that the language has not changed substantially. In all probability we must assume that the texts in the course of oral transmission, which doubtless long preceded written form, suffered steadily from change to adapt them more closely to the current vernacular of the monastic circles. We are, therefore, at liberty to examine the nature of the language of the older texts without any assumption that we are bound by tradition or probability to find in them a basis of Māgadhī.

Both Rhys Davids and Geiger are careful to recognise that the language of the Buddha was essentially a *lingua franca*, and that, therefore, it must have shown dialectic mixture. This is abundantly proved by the extreme irregularity of Pāli phonetics.The equivalents for-ry-in Sanskrit are varied;the simple-yy-is found by assimilation in *kayya* and *ayya* for *kārya* and *ārya;* but in lieu we have epenthesis in *kariya* and *ariya;* yet again we find *kayirā* for *kuryāt*, and *ayira*, which can be explained by metathesis from the preceding form,or by epenthesis after metathesis of y and r. Yet again the y passes before the r by metathesis, and then merges with the preceding vowel: thus for Sanskrit āscarya and *aisvarya* we find *acchera* and *issera*. For Sanskrit-ks-we have variant treatments; *ikka (rkṣa)* beside *pakkha (pakṣa); akkhi* and *acchi* for *akṣi; culla* and *chuddha* for *kṣulla* and *kṣudra*. Or again *hrasva* gives *rassa*, but *hradas rahada; rātri* gives *ratti*, but *Śatru satthu;* we have *addhā* for *addhvā* but-*vhe* for-*dhve; rasmi* for *raṣmi* but *amhi* for *asmi; leyya* for *lehya* but *mayhaṁ* for *mahyaṁ; jabbhara* for *gahvara* but *jivhā* for *jihvā* and so on. For -*r*-we have extreme variations, *accha* and *ikka (ṛkṣa).uja (ṛju), brahant (bṛhant),* and *iruveda (ṛgveda)*. Very significant is the fact that in no small number of cases we find two different forms with specific senses; thus *vaḍḍḍhi*, success, but *vuddhi*, growth; *maga*, wild beast, *miga*, gazelle, *khaṇa*, moment, *chaṇa*, festival; *khamā*, mercy, *chamā*, earth[5]; *attha*, thing, *aṭṭta*, lawsuit; *vattati*, he becomes, *vaṭṭati*, it is proper; *vatta*, duty, and *vaṭṭa*, round. For the common *prthiví*, we have *pathavī*, *paṭhavií, puthaví,* and *puṭhavī*, and it is easy to multiply cases of variation. No doubt these need not all be explained by dialectical mixture. It is true that Pischel's[6] proposal to distinguish between-*kkh*-and-*cch*-as representing Aryan-*kṣ*-and-*śṣṣ*-respectively has been by no means successful,[7] but allowance must be made for the operation of analogy and for the fact that sound changes do not set in suddenly affecting every word, but operate gradually, so that we may come upon a stage of language in which the operation of the change is still incomplete. But it is not possible to ignore that there must be dialect mixture to explain so much irregularity, just as in the case of Latin the necessity of admitting the existence of loan words is now freely conceded, as the only means of explaining the presence therein of abnormal forms.[8] Moreover, we must, as also in the case of Latin, remember that dialectical distinctions need not be local only; in a society with sharp divisions as in ancient India, the speech of the educated classes may well have progressed far more rapidly than among the superior classes, whose speech was deeply affected by education, and by the influence of Sanskrit. It is in this way that we can explain the occurrence of the Greek form Palibothra for Pāṭaliputra, or Peṭenika as a derivative from Pratiṣṭhāna or Kusināra for

Kuśinagara, at a time when normally phonetic change had not proceeded so far in cultivated speech; as Walleser points out Stuttgart locally has lost its-*tt*-, and London preserves its-*d*- only in careful diction.

Accepting, however, the fact of dialect mixture, the view of Rhys Davids, Windisch and Geiger demands that the basis should be Māgadhī which they contemplate is something much more primitive than the Ardha-Māgadhī which has been handed down in the Jaina Canon, which was redacted late and in which the language has unquestionably undergone much change. That we must recognise a considerable influence of Old Ardha-Māgadhī is asserted by Lüders,[9] whose view, however, differs essentially from that of the scholars just mentioned. He holds that Pāli is essentially as preserved in the Canon a dialect based on a western speech, not a Koine based on Ardha- Māgadhī, and that the Magadhisms found in it are due to retention of these forms when the Canon was being rendered from Ardha-Māgadhī into Pāli. The discussion of the issue is difficult, because we have to reconstruct what we may believe Old Ardha-Māgadhī[10] to have been from the Pillar inscriptions of Asoka, and the evidence later given by the fragments of the dramas of Asvaghoṣa. The Māgadhī of the grammarians definitely represents a different dialect than that of the Pillar inscriptions, and has an analogue in the language of the Yogiímārā cave on the Rāmagarh hill.

When we pass over phenomena shared by Ardha-Māgadhí with other dialects, the number of Ardhamāgadhisms in the early Pāli texts is not imposing. The characteristics-for - as or-ar in Sanskrit appears in some adverbs, *pure, sve* or *save;* in the formal address to the disciples, *bhikkhave,* and the curious *bhante;* in the nominative singular masculine, as in *purisakāre,* and rarely the neuter, as in *dukkhe* while vocatives such as *Bhesike* are best explained as nominavives transferred to vocative use. The Vedic *dharmāsas* gives *dhammāse.* The form *se* for *tad* has parallels in Māgadhí *se* and Ardha-Māgadhī *se,* and it is significant that it is stereotyped in *seyyathā, tad yathā.* So again we find *ye* for Sanskrit *yad.* The *l* found in some cases in Pāli may well be traced to Ardha-Māgadhi influence. A number of more or less distinctive forms may be noted; *sakkhiṁ* (*sākṣam*) has a parallel in Ardha-Māgadhī *sakkhaṁ;* both have *tharu* for *tsaru, velu for veṇu, and naṅgala* for *lāṅgala;* both lingualise the *d* in *dam's* and *dah;* both have *khiīla* for *kīla; phusita* and *phusiya* stand for *pṛṣata, chāpa* and *chāva* for *śāva; cheppā* and *cheppa* for *śepas; hata* and *hada* for *hṛta,* and for *trayastriṁśat* they have *tāvattiṁsa* and *tāvattīsa* respectively. Again after vowels and nasalised vowels the Ardha-Māgadhiā of Asoka and Aśvaghoṣa uses *yeva* for the normal Pāli *eva,* and this variant is found here and there in Pāli. Very interesting is the argument of Lüders based on meter. In Pāli verses we find here and there accusatives plural masculine and rarely nominatives in-*āni* in lieu of the normal-e, where that would ruin the metre simply substituted for the Ardha-Māgadhī of the Jain Canon despite the fact that it has been influenced by western dialects. As Magadhan Müller[11] reckons the gerunds *abhihaṭṭhuṁ* and *daṭṭhu.*

It is clear that these examples do not go far to prove that Ardha- Māgadhī was the basis of Pāli, and there are excellent reasons for refusing to accept such a basis. Lüders' researches suggest that Ardha-Māgadhī had as characteristic signs, in addition to the use of *yeva* above mentioned, the regular appearance of-*e* where Sanskrit has-*as;* the use of *l* to the exclusion of r; the use of a dental nasal only to the exclusion of the palatal or lingual between vowels; and the lengthening of the vowel before the suffix-*ka.* None of these nor of certain other minor phenomena can be found regularly observed in Pāli, and it seems unreasonable to admit that Ardha-Māgadhi can be held to form the base.

Lëvi[12] again has carried out important researches which negative the view that the language of the Canon, as we have it in Pāli,is approximately that of the Buddha. But, while the Old Ardha-Māgadhī reconstructed by Lüders is a dialect which neither softens hard consonants between vowels nor sacrifices medial consonants, the dialect of which Lëvi discovers traces is one far further advanced in phonetic change. The Buddha and Mahāvīra alike, he holds, used a Magadhan dialect in which degradation of consonants had proceeded a long way; when, however, the scriptures came to be redacted, there was aparting of the ways. The Jains rigorously carried out the reduction of intervocalic consonants to the *ya śruti,* but the Buddhists acted in an opposite sense under the influence of the western elemennts who had gained control of the Saṅgha. The language consecrates the triumph of the Pāṭheyakasa of the west as against the Pācīnakas, the heroes of the council of Vaiśālī. But this prevalence of Sanskrit influence was not accomplished by the time of Aśoka or even of the later Mauryas, as the evidence of the inscriptions shows.

The evidence adduced for Lëvi's theme rests on a number of curious forms found in Pāli and in Buddhist Sanskrit, and supported by terms used in the inscriptions. It certainly is striking that in the Bhabra inscription we should find *Lāghulovāda* for *Rāhulavāda* and *adhigicya* for *adhikṛtya* of Sanskrit, where the softening of the K is rare in Pāli and the retention of cy is alien to it. At Bhārhut we have Anādhapedika for Anāthapiṇḍika, Maghādeviya Jātaka for Makhādeva Jātaka, and very remarkably *avayesi* for *avādesi*. Pāli and the Jain Canon have Māgandiya for Sanskrit Mākandika while Kauśika is represented by Kosiya. Pāli represents by Kajaṅgala the village which Sanskrit calls Kacaṅgala. Buddhist Sanskrit has the form Ṛṣivadana where Pāli has Isipatana compelling us to assume the existence of an older dialectical form obliterated by Pāli. Pāli has preserved Ālavī as a place name but has restored *aṭavi* forest. By misunderstanding it has replaced Ajīravatī as a river name by *Aciravatī* and *Pokkharasāti* really stands for *Pauṣkarasādin* of Sanskrit. Similarly we may explain *uposatha* as opposed to Buddhist Sanskrit *poṣadha* and *opapātika* is a replacement of thr original derivative from what is Sanskrit appears as *aupapāduka*. Very significant are three certainly obscure terms in the *Pātimokkha*, *Pārājika*, *Saṅghādisesa*, and *Pācittiya*, which are to be regarded as derivatives of Sanskrit Pāracika, *saṅghātiśeśa*, and *prākcittika* respectively. So *ekudi* is really the *ekoti* of the *Śatapatha Brāhmaṇa*, and the crux *jalogi pātuṃ* of the record of Vaiśālī is explained by *jalauka*. The inscriptions of Aśoka offer additional evidence of the weakening of intervocalic consonants; thus Delhi has *libi* for *lipi*, *Jaugaḍa laheyu* and hidaloga, Dhauli *lahevu* and *ajala* (Jaugaḍa *acala*), while Palibothra and Kusināra are only explicable by weakening.

Geiger[13] objects to the arguments of Levi as insufficient to prove the existence of this pre-Canonic language, but his contentions are not wholly adequate. It is true that not all of Levi's etymologies are sound, but many comparisons are satisfactory. It is also true that the weakening is found not merely in technical terms which may naturally be deemed to be taken over, but in more common words. But this contention may be met by interpreting the facts as pointing to a more considerable influence of pre-Canonic speech on Pāli than Levi contended for. Moreover, the fact that hardening is also found in Pāli in some degree at least explained most naturally as by Levi to be due to the errors of the redactors who in restoring the original form now and then went too far and created false forms. After making all allowances, it seems clear that Levi has proved that Pāli as we have it has been influenced by a dialect of Magadha in which weakening of consonants had gone to considerable lengths. But such a dialect cannot possible be trusted as lying at the base of Pāli any more than the Old Ardha-Māgadhī whence borrowings are traced by Lüders. Both these dialects, it seems clear, have influenced Pāli,a view which accords well with the opinion of those who hold that the Pāli canon is comparatively late and post Aśokan, representing the presentation in a western dialect of traditions current in more than one Magadhan dialect.

It is significant that the evidence that Pāli is far from purely Magadhan has induced Sir George Grierson[14] to modify essentially the theory of Windisch that Māgadhī is at the basis of Pāli. His view is that "Literary Pāli is the literary form of the Māgadhī language, the then Koine of India,as it was spoken and as it was used as a medium of literary instruction in the Takṣaśilā University." The point of the change of view is that it enables Sir G. Grierson to explain satisfactorily the coincidences between Pāli and Paiśācī Prākrit insisted on by Konow,[15] who on the strenght of them claimed Pāli as a dialect of the Vindhyas and perhaps of the regions to the south and east. It must, however, be pointed out that it is difficult to accept the view that the Pāli Canon was redacted at Takṣaśila, and the antiquity and importance of the study of the Pāli Canon at that university certainly cannot be established satisfactorily on the strength of the evidence of the Jātaka book. But the more important fact is that there is little cogency in the comparisons of Paiśācī and Pāli drawn by Konow and Grierson. (1) The hardening of sonant mutes is ascribed to both. In fact, however, the process is purely sporadic in Pāli; in the principal Paiśācī it is compulsory only for *d* and the weak cases of *rājan*, and even in Cūlikā Paiśacī only one variety demands the hardening of all sonant medials. Infact the phenomenon is sporadic throughout Prākrit and no identification is possible between Pāli and Paiśācī on the strength of it. (2) The retention of intervocalic consonants is common to all three types of Prākrit found in Aśvaghoṣa and is a sign of early date, not of special connection between Pāli and Paiśācī. (3) The use of epenthesis in *bhāriya, sināna,* and *kasaṭa* is an ordinary Prākrit feature as regards the first two terms, while, if *kasaṭa* is not a metathesis of *sakaṭ* as often held, Konow justly adduces comparison with Māgadhī *kasṭa.* (4) The change of jñ, ṇy, and ny to ññ is shared by Māgadhī, and probably is characteristic of all early Prākrits as indicated by those of Aśvaghośa. (5) The preservation of Y in lieu of change to J is found in Māgadhi, and is probably common to all early Prākrits. (6) The termination-o in nominal basesis not merely found in Paiśācī but also in western dialects and is Sanskritic in origin. (7) The inflexional system of Pāli is generally similar not merely to that of Paiśaācī but also to those of other western dialects. (8) The use of *r* in Pāli can as easily be traced to the western dialects and to Sanskrit as to Paiśācī, and in fact only standard Paiśācī retains *r*. These arguments for the close association in space of Pāli and Paiśācī thus do not prove what is claimed and it becomes therefore a matter of no importance in this connection whether Grierson[16] is right in claiming Paiśācī for the northwest or know in asserting the claims of the *Vindhya*. The latter view has the support of what is the more probable view[17] of the dialect and place of origin of the Bṛhatkathā of Guṇādhya, though the points involved are far from being certain. But it is noteworthy in this connection that Grierson admits that Piśācas may have advanced into Rājputānā and the Konakan. One point also, it may be noted, tells against the view of Grierson, namely the fact that Paiśacas has only the sibilant s, which would be strange if it were really a dialect of the north west.

Grierson's view, however, coming as it does, from a believer in the Māgadhī basis of Pāli, is a significant admission of the strength of western influences, and, as has been pointed out, while it is not proved that Paiśācī is essentially involved, there is evidence for western affinities in some of the points and all of them are consistent with such affinities. This brings us back to the suggestion early made by Westergaard[19] and adopted by E. Kuhn[20], which sees in Pāli the dialect of Ujjayinī, arguing partly from the fact that Pāli has closest affinity with the Girnār form of the Aśokan language, and partly from the legend that this was the mother tongue of Mahinda, who brought Buddhism to Ceylon. It is now possible to support this connection of broader lines, and to argue that at the base of Pāli there unquestionably lies a western dialect as opposed to an eastern. Lüders[21] stresses inter alia the striking similarity between the *girnār* dialect and Pāli in the formation of the locative singular of-a-stems, and in the accusative plural masculine in-e. In his work on Pāli and Sanskrit R. Otto Franke establishes a long list of points in which Pāli differs from the eastern Prākrit of Aśoka, and the equally demonstrates that it departs in important matters from the north-western Prākrit. He shows at the same time that in the north-western and the western dialects there are important coincidences with Pāli. Thus we find parallels for the assimilation of ly to ll; for the retention of in *brāhmaṇa;* u represents ṛ in the declension of nouns of relationship in place of i in the eastern dialect; *ahaṁ* serves as nominative masculine and feminine of the demonstrative. In other cases the parallels are confined to the Prākrits of Madhyadeśa and the south-west. Thus we have in the equivalents of Sanskrit kṛta; laṭhi for yaṣṭi; masculine and neuter of-a stems; -ā for the dative of such stems; oblique cases of-u and -ū stems in- uyā in the instrumental singular of-ṛ stems; and cha for ṣaṭ. A more precise location for Pāli is deduced from the fact that to its dhīā(duhitṛ) base forms, there are parallels from Mathurā, Sāñnchī and Bhārhut, while south of Nāsik, which has both *dihitu* and *duhitu*, forms in *duhu*-or *dhu*-prevail. But a location south of Mathurā, Sāñchī and Bhārhut is indicated by such facts as the frequent use of ri for ṛ in Mathurā; by the appearance there of kṣaṇa for kṣuṇa; ;by-ye forms from feminines in -ā, -ī, -u and -ū; and by-are in the instrumental of-ṛ stems. Special connection with the south is indicated by the occurrence there of forms with Pāli parallels such as *paṇuvisa* at Junnar; sattari at Nāsik; r for d in the equivalent of daśa, and ch in cikīcha in girnār, where also are found the potentials asa and asu; feminine plurals in-āyo; and third plural Ātmanepada endings in r. The parallelism with the south, however, is not invariable. Thus we have seen that south of Nasik forms in *duhu*-or *dhu*-prevail; in Nasik we find varisa in place of vassa; p or pp, in Girnār[22] tp(pt), are found in the equivalents of *ātman*, where Pāli has tt; bi-and be represent Sanskrit dvi-and dve, while Pāli had dvi-, di-,or du-, though it shares with these dialects bā-for dvā-in dvādaśa. Girnār again represents the abstract suffix-tva by-tpa(-pta), and it omits frequently the aspiration in the equivalents of Sanskrit sth and ṣṭh.

From these and similar observations Franke deduces a location for the dialect at the basis of Pāli south or south-east of the Kharoṣṭī country, the home of the north-western Prākrit; south of Mathurā, and perhaps also of Sāñchī and Bhārhut or at least not in the vicinity of these places; west or south-west of the region of the north-eastern Prākrit; north of Nāsik and east of Girnār. This suggests the area between the west and the middle Vindhya as the probable location, and Franke conjectures that Ujjayinā might be deemed the headquarters of the language, since Aśoka was governor there before he became Emperor, his wife, the mother of Mahinda, was a native of Cetiyagiril, near Sāñchī. and Mahinda himself lived there in his boyhood before he carried Pāli literature to Ceylon. To these latter details we need not attach much value. It may be noted that, if Konow's location of Paiśācī in the Viñdhya region is correct, the parallels between Paiṣśeī and Pāli agree with the results of Franke, and this agreement strengthens the value of Konow's suggestion; though in fact our knowledge of Paiśāci rests on too unsatisfactory a basis to render discussion of this issue of much real value. From the point of view of the history of the development of the Buddhist Canon Przyluski[23] has suggested that the claim of Kauśāmbī as we have it the dialect of that place played a part. It would in fact be unwise to seek to define closely the area of the base dialect of Pāli on the strength of the miserably inadequate and unreliable information presented by the scanty inscriptions. What we can reasonably say is that the basis was a western, not an eastern dialect, and that neither Māgadhī nor Ardha- Māgadhī should be deemed to furnish the foundation. On the other hand, there is every reason to admit that both earlier and later Magadhan dialects have left traces of their forms, probably as the result of the retention of forms from the Buddhist texts current in

Magadhan dialects. The results of Levi are specially important, for they render it extremely difficult to believe in the theory of the existence of an early Buddhist canon in a Magadhan of the type envisaged in the theories of Rhys Davids and Geiger, and they confirm the doubts on this score which have been adduced on grounds wholly independent of language.[24]

Pāli as resting on a western dialect should naturally be found to be strongly under Sanskritic influence and closely related to the early forms of Śaurasenī Prākrit. It is, therefore, very significant that the conclusions of Lüders[25] as to the character of Old Śaurasenī, based on the fragments of Aśvaghoṣa, show that that dialect had many affinities with Pāli as recorded. Thus there is no elision in Old Śaurasenī of consonants, and on instance only of softening of t to d; normaly, intervocalic n remains unaltered; an initial y is never altered to j; as in Pāli dy in udyāna gives yy, not as later jj; jñ and ny result in ññ, not as later ṇṇ; dāni and idāni occur as in Pāli; in adaṇḍāraho we have a as the epenthetic vowel, not i as later; duguṇa shows du-for dvi-, later di-alone is allowed, while Pāli has both forms; Aśvaghoṣa again uses tuvaṁ, as in Pāli for the later tumaṁ, and has tava for tuha; he has also karotha, common in Pāli, in later Prākrit unknown, and for gerund kariya, found in Pāli. Moreover we find pekkh-(Sanskrit prekṣ) as sakkiti, dakkhiti.

As against this evidence no stress can now be laid on the argument of Oldenberg[26] who did not accept as historical the mission of Mahinda, and held instead that Pāli came to Ceylon from Kalinga, a view accepted also by E.Müller,[27] who pointed out that the oldest settlements in Ceylon were founded from the mainland opposite and not-as the Magadhan theory of Pāli suggested-from Bengal. Oldenberg supported his view by comparing Pāli with the dialect of the Khandagiri inscription. But the comparison yields nothing decisive, and there is now a substantial body of evidence which points to western India as the prime source of the Aryan element in Ceylon.[28] Lāṭa, Gujarat, is associated with the legend of Vijaya, and, however slight is the value of that legend in other respects, there is no reason to dispute the importance of the place name, when it is found that the affinities of Sinhalese lie with the western dialects.

We must, therefore, conclude that the basis of Pāli is a western dialect; but in its literary form, in which alone we have it, it is a very mixed language of the literary type, far removed from a vernacular, and under a strong *Sanskritic* influence. The date of the development of this literary speech and the evolution of the Pāli Canon, doubtless on the base of older tradition larlgely in Magadhan dialects, canont be ascertained with any certainty; probability points to a date posterior to Aśoka, the silence of whose inscriptions on the existence of the Pāli Canon is most naturally explained by the assumption that it did not then exist. The asoription of a comparatively late date is greatly supported by the fact which must be stressed as against Rhys Davids,[29] that the forms of Pāli are not historically the oldest of those Prākrit forms known to us.[30] These are to be found in the north-western dialect of the Aśoka inscriptions where the maintenance in some measure of the three sibilants, the transformation of r into ir or ur, the maintenance of r in conjunction with other consonants, and the retention of tm are, among other points, indications of a state of affairs linguisticlly older than the facts of Pāli. Even in the case of the *Girnār* dialect of the Aśokan inscriptions,it would be impossible to establish the priority of Pāli. Girnār[31] manifests such phenomena as the retention of long vowels before double consonants, and traces of the retention of r in certain consonantal combinations, as well as the use of sṭ which Pāli assimilates. Moreover, it appears that it preserved for a time the distinction between the palatal and the lingual sibilants. There is accordingly nothing in the linguistic facts to throw doubt on the view that the dialect on which Pāli is based was one current some time after the Aśokan period.

To sum up the conclusions suggested by our deplorably scanty evidence, we may say(1) that the Buddha's language cannot be definitely ascertained from the records, and it is only by conjecture that we can assert that it was of Kosalan rather than Magadhan type. Similarly it is purely a matter of speculation how far the Kosalan or Old Ardha-Māgadhī(if for convenience we so style it) and the Magadhan or Māgadhī corresponded with the Ardha-Māgadhī of the Jain texts as we have them and the Māgadhī of the grammarians. In the former case certainly, and in the latter probably, we should allow for much dialect mixture in the later forms. (2) The teachings, or the supposed teachings, of the Buddha were handed down in various dialects, and in one at least of these the process of phonetic change had advanced further than is normal in our Pāli texts. (3) The Pāli texts represent the doctrines accepted by a special school which used as the language of their Canon the dialect of the educated classes of some western area, whether Kauśāmbi or Ujjayinī or some other place cannot be determined with any certainty. (4) the date of this Pāli canon cannot be defined with any exactitude. The one source of tradition on which we have to rely insists that a Council under Aśoka determined the Canon including as an essential element the Kathāvatthu. The Aśokan inscriptions ignore entirely the Council, and, when Aśoka in his Bhabra edict, mentions passages of special importance in the teaching of the Buddha, grave difficulties[32] arise when supporters of the existence of the Pāli Canon in Aśoka's time seek to identify the passages, suggesting the obvious conclusion that Aśoka knew nothing of the Canon. Further, it is certain that the language of the texts known to Aśoka was not the Pāli of the Canon. Again, it is significant that even those who are inclined to greater faith in the tradition than it is easy to feel have much difficulty in believing that the Kathāvatthu is of Asokan date,[33] but what is clear is that this is an essential element in the tradition of the Council, and that if it is not accepted as true, it becomes extremely difficult to attach any value to the legend of the Council. We may well believe that the views embodied in the Pāli Canon were current in circles in Aśoka's time-it is clear that they were not the points which appealed to Asoka himself whose Dhamma is far more popular-, and we can, if we like, suppose that in Aśoka's reign some steps were taken towards formulating these views in definite form and commencing the preparation of the Canon in the language we now know as Pāli. But there is no reason to accept the alleged patronage of Aśoka, and we cannot be absolutely certain that even so much respect should be paid to the traditions current in Ceylon.

Notes & References :

1. *Buddhist India* pp. 153ff. *Cambridge History of India* i. 187 *Pāli Dictionary*, p. V
2. *Actes du xiv congres international des orientalistes* (Paris, 1906), i. 252 ff.
3. Geiger, *Pāli Literatur und Sprache* (1916) pp. 3, 4
4. *Sprache and Heinat des Pāli Canons* (1924); *Was bedeutet "Pāli"*? (1926)
5. This derivation is not unquestioned.
6. *Grammatik der Prākrit-Sprachen*, pp. 219ff.
7. Geiger, op cit, p. 50 Michelson, JAOS. xxx 88,n. 3
8. Meillet, *Histoire de la latine*, ch. V; *Ernout, Les elements disalectaux du vocabulaire latin* (1909)
9. *Bruchstücke budddhistischer Dramen* pp. 40f. Sitz Berl. Akad, 1913 p. 1003
10. Strictly speaking we cannot prove that this old Ardha-Māgadhī is historically continued by Ardha- Māgadhi, which we must assume to have been subjected to storng influence from other dialects.
11. *Grammar of the Pāli Language*, p. 128
12. *Journal Asialique*, ser 10 xx 495 ff. cf. L de la Vallee Poussin, *Indo-Europans, et Indo-Iraniens*, pp. 201ff.
13. Geiger, Op cit, p. 4
14. Bhandarkar Commemoration Volume, pp. 117-..
15. ZDMG lxiv. 95ff JBAS. 1921. pp. 244f. 424f.
16. ZDMG ixivi 49ff
17. Keith, *Sanskrit Literature*, pp. 267ff.
18. *Reichelt Stand and Aufgaben der Sprachwissenschaft*, p. 245
19. *Ueber den ultesien Zeitraum der indischen Ueschichte*, p. 47
20. *Beurge tur Pāli-Grammatik*, p. 9
21. *Sita, Berl Akad*, 1913 pp. 990 1006
22. On this combination see Franke op cit p. 118; Michelson, JAOS xxxi, 235 f
23. *Legende de l' Empereur Asoka*, pp. 71, 89
24. Keith, *Buddhist Philosophy* Ch. I

25. *Bruchetieke Buddhistischer Dramen* pp. 47ff.
26. *Vinaya Piṭaka,* i,. pp. L ff.
27. Pāli Grammar, p. iii
28. Chatterji, Suniti Kumar *Bengali Language,* i. 15, 72 73; Geiger, *Literature and Sprache der singhalesen* pp. 90f.
29. *Buddhist India* pp. 153f.
30. *Reichelt Stand and Aufgaben der Sprachwissenschaft,* pp. 243, 247, The more archaic character of the north western dialect is now easily seen from the grammar given by Konow, *Kharoshṭhī Inscriptions* pp. xcv-cxv. Cf. Michelson JAOS xxx, 87 88
31. Michelson, JAOS xxxi 243ff.
32. L de la Valle Poussin, *D Inde aux temps des Mauryas* (1930) pp. 126ff. For a revolutionary view see M. Walleser, *Das Edikt von Bhabra* (1923); *Nochmals das Edikt von Bhabra* (1925)
33. Poussin, op. cit p. 139.

Bibliography

Andersen, Dines; and Smith, Helmer(Ed); *Suttanipāta*. P.T.S. (1913), reprint 1965

Aung, S.Z.; and Rhys Davids, Mrs; *Compendium of Philosophy*. Trans. of *Abhidhammattha Saṅgaha*. P.T.S, (1910), reprint 1979.

.....................*Points of Controversy*. Trans. of *Kathāvatthu*. P.T.S. (1915), reprint 1979

Ādi Granth, Sri Damadmi Biṛ; various editions. standard pagination, 1430pp.

Bahm, A.J; *Philosophy of the Buddha*. Vikas Publishing House; Delhi, 1982

Barua, Benimadhab; *A History of Pre-Buddhistic Indian Philosophy*. Moti Lal Banarsi Das; Delhi, (London, 1951), reprint 1981.

.....................*Prolegomena to a History of Buddhist Philosophy*. Munshi Ram Manohar Lal; Delhi, 1974.

.....................*The Ājīvikas*
University of Calcutta Journal, Calcutta, 1920.

Basham, A.L; *History and Doctrines of the Ājīvikās*. Moti Lal Banarsi Das; Delhi, (London, 1951) reprint 1981.

Ballantyne, J.R(Trs), *Sāṁkhyasūtra of Kapila*. Asiatic Society, Calcutta

Beal, Samuel; *Life of Buddha*. S.B.E.;XIX.1883

...................*Si-yu-ki or the Buddhist Records of the Western World* (2 vols) Trans. from Chinese original of Hiuen-Tsang. (1885) London, 1906.

..................*Romantic Legends of Sākya Buddha.* Moti Lal Banarsi Das, Delhi, 1985.

Bhandarkar Commemoration Volume. Bhandarkar Research Institute, Poona, 1917.

Bhandarkar, R.G. *Research Papers* (vol. I) Bhandarkar Research Institute, Poona, 1933.

Bohtlingk, Otto. *Indische Spruche* (3 vols) St. Peterburg. 1870-73.

Buddhadatta, A.P. (Ed); *Abhidhammāvatāra* P.T.S., Vol. I (1915), Reprint 1980.

Buhler G and Kielhon F (Ed); *Pañcatantra* Bombay Sanskrit Series, Bombay, 1886, 1891.

Carpenter, J. E (Ed); *Dīgha Nikāya* P.T.S.; Vol. III. (1910), reprint 1976

Chalmers, R. (Ed); *Majjhima Nikāya* P.T.S; Vol.II 1896-98; Vol. III, 1899-1902.

ChatterJi, Suniti Kumar; *Origin and Development of Bengali Language.* Rupa and Co; New Delhi, (1926), reprint 1993.

Childers, R.C; *A Dictionary of the Pali Language.* London, 1875.

Copleston, R.S; *Buddhism: Primitive and Present.* Longman; London, 1946

Cowell, E.B, (Gen. Ed); *Jātaka Stories* (7vols). Trans. of *Jātakaṭṭhakathāvaṇṇaṇa* P.T.S., (6 vols, 1895-1907; Index 1913, reprint in 3 Vols 1981.

.................and Neill, R.A. *Divyāvadāna* Cambridge University Press, Cambridge; 1886

Dalal, C.D; and Shastry, R.A. (Ed); *Kāvya-mimanisā (of Raja Sekhra).* Oriental Institute; Baroda, 1934.

Dalkhe, Paul; *Buddhist Essays.* Trans. From German original by Bhikkhu Silacara. Indological Book House; Delhi, 1978.

Dutt, Manmathanath, *The Rāmāyāna* (7 vols) Translation to English prose. G.C.Chakravarty, Calcutta; 1891-94.

Edwardes, S.M, *The Jaina Gazette* Bombay, 1925, 1927.

Eliot, Sir Charles; *Hinduism and Buddhism* (3 vols). London, 1954.

Feer, L. (Ed); *Saṁyutta Nikāya* (5 vols). P.T.S; Vol. I, 1884; II, 1888; III, 1890; IV, 1893; V, 1898.

Fousboll, V, (Ed); Jātaka *(Jātaṭṭhakathāvaṇṇaṇa) (7 vols). P.T.S; Vol. I, 1877; II 1879; III 1883; IV 1887; V, 1891; VI 1896; VII Indexes (Ed. Andersen, Dines), 1897*

Geiger; W; (Ed); *Mahāvaṁsa* P.T.S; 1905

..................*The Great Chronicles of Ceylon*. Trans. of *Mahāvaṁsa*.P.T.S; 1908

.................*Pali Literature and Sparche*. Strassburg; 1916

Gough, A.E, (Trs) *Vaiśeṣika-sūtrās* of Kaṇāda, Banaras.

Grimm, George; *The Doctrine of the Buddha*. Moti Lal Banarsi Das; Delhi, (Berlin, 1958), reprint 1973

Hardy, E (Ed); *Petavatthu Commentary (Param-atthadipanī IV). P.T.S; 1894*

..............(Ed); *Vimānavatthu Commentary (Paramartha dīpanī III). P.T.S; 1901*

..............(Ed); *Aṅguttara Nikāya* (5 vol). P.T.S. Vol. III, (1895), reprint 1976; IV (1899), reprint 1979; V (1900) reprint 1979.

..............(Ed); *Npttipakaraṇa*, P.T.S. (1902), reprint 1962

Hastings, J. (Ed); *Encylopaedia of Religion and Ethics* (13 vols) T and T Clark; Edinburgh, 1914.

Horner, I.B; *Clarifier of the Sweet Meaning*. Trans. of *Madhuratthavilāsinī*, Commentary on *Buddhavaṁsa*. P.T.S; 1978

..............;*The Book of Discipline* (Vol. IV). Trans. of *Mahāvagga*. P.T.S; (1951), Reprint 1982

..............;*The Middle Length Sayings (3 vols) Type? of Majjhima Nikāya*. P.T.S; Vol. I, (1954), reprint 1976; II, (1957), reprint 1975; III (1959), reprint 1977.

...............;*Milinda's Question*. Trans. of *Milinda pañha*. P.T.S; Vol.I, (1963), reprint 1969; II (1964), reprint 1969.

................;(Ed); *Madhuraṭṭhavilāsinī* (Commentary on *Buddhavaṁsa)* P.T.S.; (1946), reprint 1979

Jacobi, Hermann; *Jain Sūtras* (2 vols). S.B.E, vol. XXII, XLV. 1892-95

Jain Itihās Series Part I Agra; 1902

Jain, K.P. *The Ādipurāṇa and Bṛhatkathā,* Indian Historical Quarterly vol. V, 1929.

Jain, R.C; *Confluence of Opposites.* Jain Library; London, 1922

Jaini, J.L. *Tattvartha-sūtram* (A Trestise on the Essentials of Jainism) of Umāsvāmi, Delhi; 1956 (22nd Edition).

Jaini, Manak Chand. *Life of Mahāvīra,* Allahbad; 1908

John Ston, E.H. *The Saundarānanda or Nanda the Fair*. Trans. of *Saundarānanda Kāvya* Oxford, 1932.

Jones, J.J. (Ed); *Mahāvastu* (3 vols). S.B.B. Vol. 16, (1949); 18, (1952); 19 (1956).

Kakazu, Okakura; *The Ideals of the East* Calcutta, 1973

Kalupahana, David, J; *Buddhist Philosophy*. The University Press of Hawaii; Honolulu, 1976.

Keith, A.B; *Buddhist Philosophy* Oxford, 1922.

.............*History of Sanskrit Literature*. Moti Lal Banarsi Das, Delhi, 1973.

Kern, H; *Manual of Indian Buddhism*. Strassburg, 1896.

Lakshmi, Narasu. P; *The Essence of Buddhism*. Thacker and Co; Bombay, (1907), reprint 1948.

Law, B.C; *Historical Geography of Ancient India*. Societe Asiatique Deparis; Paris; France, 1954

..............; *Some Kśatriya Tribes of Ancient India*. D.K. Publishers; Delhi, 1975.

..............;*Designation of Human Types*. Trans. of *Puggala paññatti* P.T.S; 1922

.... *Heaven and Hell in Buddhist Perspective*. Thacker Spink, Calcutta; 1925.

.... *Historical Gleanings*. Thacker Spink, Calcutta; 1982.

Legge, J. *Fa-Hien's Record of Buddhist Kingdoms*. Oxford, 1886.

Maxmuller, F; *The Dhammapada*. Trans. of *Dhammapada*. S.B.E; vol. X

..............; *Studies in Buddhism*. Indological Book House Varanasi, 1978.

Mehta, Rati Lal, N; *Pre-Buddhist India. Anmol Publications, Delhi*, reprint 1985

Morris, R. (Ed); *Cariya Pṭkaka* P.T.S; 1882

...............(Ed); *Buddhavaṁsa* P.T.S.;1882

...............(Ed); *Aṅguttara Nikāya* P.T.S; Vol. I 1885; II, 1888

...............(Ed); *Dhammasaṅganī* P.T.S, (1885), reprint 1978

...............(Ed); *Aṭṭhasālinī* P.T.S, (1897), revised reprint 1979.

Muller, E; *Simplified Grammar of Pali Language*. London, 1884.

Narla, V.R; *Traditional Indian Culture and Other Essays*. Vijay Books; Vijayvāda, 1969.

Nemicandra; *Dravya-saṁgraha*. The Central Jaina Publishing House; Arrah.

Norman, H.C. (Ed); *Dhammapada Commentary* (6 vols). P.T.S; Vol. I (1906, 1909), reprint 1970; II (1911), reprint 1970; III (1912), reprint 1970; IV(1914), reprint 1970; bound with vol. V. Indexes by L.S. Tailong (1915), reprint 1970

Norman, K.R; *The Elder's Verses* prose Trans. of *Theragāthā* Vol. I, 1969; *Therīgāthā II 1971, P.T.S.*

Ñyaṇmoli, Bhikkhu; *The Path of Purification*. Trans. of Buddhagosha's *Visuddhimagga*. Buddhist Publication Society; Sri Lanka, 1975

Oldenberg, Hermann (Ed); *Vinayapiṭaka* (5 vols). P.T.S.; Vol. I (1879), reprint 1964; II, (1880), reprint 1977; III, (1881), reprint 1964; IV, (1882) reprint 1964; V (1883), reprint 1982.

.............;*Vinay Texts*. Trans. of *Vinaya Piṭaka* S.B.E. Part III, vol. XX.

.............; *Dīpavaṁsa*. Trans. Edinburgh, 1979.

.............; *Buddha, His Life, His Doctrine, His order*. William and Norgate, 1882.

.............and Pischel, R. (Ed); *Thera-therī gāthā* P.T.S., 1883

Peterson, P. *Nyāya-bindu* Asiatic Society of Bengal; Calcutta; 1889.

Poussin, L. De la Vallee; *The Way to Nirvāṇa* (Hibbert Lectures, 1916) The University Press, Combridge, 1917.

..............and Thomas, E.J; (Ed); *Niddesa, Mahā*. P.T.S., Vol. I, (1916); II (1917); reprint 1978

Radhakrishan, S; *Indian Philosophy* (2 vols). George Allen and Unwin, London, 1962 (7th impression)

Rajagopalacari, C; *Mahābhārat*. Bhartiya Vidya Bhavan, Bombay, 1958.

..............;*Ramāyana*, Bhartiya Vidya Bhavan, Bombay, 1957.

Rajneesh, Bhagwan; *Essa Dhammo Sanantano*. Rajneesh Foundation; Pune, 1976

..............;*The Hidden Harmony: Discourses on the Fragments of Heraclitus*. Rajneesh Foundation; Pune, 1976.

Rao, Gopinath, T.A. *Elements of Hindu Icnography*. Indological Book House; Delhi, 1971.

Rapson, E.J. (Ed); *Combridge History of India:Ancient India* Vol. I (1922) S.Chand and Co. Delhi, 1967

Rhys Davids, Mrs; *The Book of Kindered Sayings*. Trans. of *Saṁyutta Nikāya* P.T.S; Vol, I (1917), reprint 1979; II, (1922), reprint 1982.

...............; (ed); *Vibhaṅga*. P.T.S, (1904), reprint 1978

...............;*Psalms of the Early Buddhists* : Trans. of *Therīgātha*. as (i) *Psalms of The Sisters* 1902 and (ii) *Psalms of the Brethern* as trans. of *Theragāthā* (1937), reprint 1980

..............; *Dialogues of the Buddha*. Trans. of *Dīgha Nikāya* P.T.S, Vol. III (1921), reprint 1977

...............(Ed); *Visuddhimagga*. P.T.S; Vol. I and III (1920, 1921), reprint 1975

...............; *Buddhism : Its Birth and Dispersal* AMS Press; 1934

Rhys Davids, *T.W.* (Ed); *Abhidhammattha-saṅgaha*. P.T.S, (Journal), 1884

.................; *Early Buddhism*. Indological Book House, Dalhi (1877), reprint 1973

................; *Dialogues of the Buddha*. Trans. of *Dīgha Nikāya* P.T.S; Vol. I (1899), reprint 1977

................*Buddhist India*. Moti Lal Banarsi Das; Delhi, 1971

..................; *Buddhist Suttas*. Trans. S.B.E. Vol. XI, 1896.

..................; *Buddhism : Its History and Literature*. London; 1896.

...................and Rhys Davids, Mrs; *Dialogues of the Buddha* Trans. of *Dīgha Nikāya* P.T.S; Vol. II, (1916), reprint 1977

..................and Carpenter; J.E (Ed); *Dīgha Nikāya* P.T.S. Vol.I (1889), reprint 1975; II, (1903), reprint 1982; III (1910), reprint 1976

.................and Carpenter, J.E. (Ed); *Sumaṅgala vilāsinī* P.T.S. Vol. I (1886), reprint 1968

....................and Stede, William; *The Pāli English Dictionary*. P.T.S. 1921-25

Rockhill, W.W; *Life of the Buddha*. London, 1884

Ross, Sir David; *Plato's Theory of Ideas*. Clarenden Press; Oxford, 1851.

Saunders, K.J. *Gotama Buddha. AMS, New York.*

Sānti Deva; *Sikśa-Samuccya* Trans. by Cecil Bendle from Sanskrit original. London. (1912). Moti Lal Banarsi Das; Delhi; reprint 1981.

Shakespeare, William; *Complete Works of Shakespeare*. Abbey Library; London.

Sharma, R.S. *Material Culture and Social Fromations in India*. Macmillan Ltd; Delhi, 1983

Shastri, H. Ed; *Saundarānanda Kāvya*. Asiatic Society of Bengal; Calcutta, 1910

Silva, Lynn A De. *The Problems of Self in Buddhism and Christianity*. Macmillan, 1979.

Smith, Helmer. (Ed); *Khuddakapāṭha* (with Commetary, *Paramattha Jotika I*) P.T.S; (1915), reprint 1978

..................(Ed); *Suttanipāta* with Commentary *Paramattha Jotika* II). P.T.S, Vol. I, (1916); reprint 1966; II, (1917), reprint 1966

Smith, V.A; *Early History of India*. Oxford University Press, 1962

Sobti, Harcharan Singh; *Nibbāna in Early Buddhism*. Eastern Book Linkers; Delhi, 1985.

Speyer, J.S, *Jātakamāla* Trans. of Aryasura's *Jātakamāla*. Moti Lal Banarsi Das, Delhi; 1982.

Stede, William (Ed); *Sumaṅgalavilāsinī* P.T.S; Vol. II (1931), reprint 1971; III (1932), reprint 1971.

Stevenson, Sinclair Mrs. *The Heart of Jainism*. Oxford, 1915.

Strachey, James. (Gen. Ed); *The Complete Psychological Works of Singmund Freud*. The Hogarth Press; London, (1953), reprint 1965

Subba Rau, S (Trs) *Srimad Bhāgavatam* (2vols) Sri Vyasa Press, Tripupati, 1928

Subhuti, W. (Ed); *Abhidhānappadipikā* Colombo, 1883.

Sumaṅgala, Suriya goda (Ed.) *Dhammapada* P.T.S, 1914

Suzuki, M, 'The First Buddhist Council' in Monist Vol. xiv, 1904

Takakusu, J and Nagi, M. (Ed); *Samantapāsādika* (8 vols). P.T.S; vol.I, (1924), reprint 1975; II (1927), reprint 1969; III (1930), reprint 1968; IV (1934), reprint 1967; V, (1938), reprint 1966;

VI, (1947); VII, (1947), reprint 1981; VIII(Indexes) By Kopp, H. (1977)

Taylor, A.C. (Ed); *Kathāvatthu*. P.T.S, Vol. I, (1894); II, (1897), reprint 1979

Tin, Daw Mya; *The Dhammapada : Verses and Stories*. Translation of *Dhammapada* with its Commentary. Central Institute of Higher Tibetan Studies, Sarnath; Varanasi, 1990

Tin, Pe Maung; *The Path of Purity*. Trans. of Buddhaghosha's *Visuddhimagga*. P.T.S, Vol. I,II,III (1922, 1928, 1931), reprint 1975

Tiwary, Mahesh. (Ed); *Abhidhammāvatāra* (of Buddhadatta). Pali Privena, Delhi, 1987.

Trencker, V. (Ed); *Milindapañha*. P.T.S, (1880), reprint 1962

..............(Ed); *Majjhima Nikāya* P.T.S, (1888), reprint 1979

Vaidya, P.L. (Ed); *Lalitavistara*. The Mithila Institute; Darbanga, 1958.

Vidyabhushana, S.C, (Trs) *The Nyāya Sūtras* of *Gotama*. Panini Office, Allahbad.

Warren, Henry Clarke. *Buddhism in Translation* (Harvard Oriental Series, 1896), Asian Publication Services; New Delhi, 1980.

Watters, T. (Ed). *On Yuan Chwang's Travels in India* (2 vols). London, 1904-5.

Windisch, E. *Māra and Buddha*, S. Hirzel. S, Leipzig; 1895

Woodward, F.L. *The Book of Kindered Sayings* Trans. of *Saṁyutta Nikāya* P.T.S, Vol. III (1924), reprint 1975; IV (1927), reprint 1980; V, (1930), reprint 1979.

...............; *The Book of Gradual Sayings*. Trans, of *Aṅguttara Nikāya* P.T.S, Vol. I, (1932), reprint 1979; II (1933), reprint 1982; V, (1936), reprint 1972

..............; *The Minor Anthologies*. Trans. of *Udāna* and *Itivuttaka* (Vol. II) P.T.S; (1935) reprint 1948.

Index

D

E

F

G